First World War
and Army of Occupation
War Diary
France, Belgium and Germany

4 DIVISION
Headquarters, Branches and Services
General Staff
1 August 1917 - 31 December 1917

WO95/1447

The Naval & Military Press Ltd
www.nmarchive.com
Published in association with The National Archives

Published by

The Naval & Military Press Ltd

Unit 10 Ridgewood Industrial Park,

Uckfield, East Sussex,

TN22 5QE England

Tel: +44 (0) 1825 749494

www.naval-military-press.com

www.nmarchive.com

This diary has been reprinted in facsimile from the original. Any imperfections are inevitably reproduced and the quality may fall short of modern type and cartographic standards.

© Crown Copyright
Images reproduced by permission of The National Archives, London, England, 2015.

Contents

Document type	Place/Title	Date From	Date To
Heading	4th Division General Staff August 1917		
War Diary	G 16 b 77	01/08/1917	06/08/1917
Miscellaneous	War Diary General Staff 4th Division	01/08/1917	01/08/1917
War Diary	G 16 b 77	07/08/1917	31/08/1917
Heading	Operation Order 52 App. 1		
Operation(al) Order(s)	Reference Table "A" attached to 4th Division Operation Order No 52 dated 5th August 1917, Serial No: 1 will be amended to read:-	05/08/1917	05/08/1917
Miscellaneous	Reference 4th Division Operation Order No. 52 of 3rd August and G.S.70/13/a of 5th August	05/08/1917	05/08/1917
Operation(al) Order(s)	Reference 4th Division Operation Order No. 52	05/08/1917	05/08/1917
Miscellaneous	Programme of Artillery Bombardment		
Miscellaneous	Action Of 4th Division Machine Guns on 8th August		
Operation(al) Order(s)	4th Division Operation Order No. 52	03/08/1917	03/08/1917
Operation(al) Order(s)	4th Division Order No. 53	12/08/1917	12/08/1917
Operation(al) Order(s)	4th Division G.S. 79/15	13/08/1917	13/08/1917
Operation(al) Order(s)	4th Division Operation Order No. 54	13/08/1917	13/08/1917
Operation(al) Order(s)	4th Division Operation Order No. 55	14/08/1917	14/08/1917
Operation(al) Order(s)	Reference Divisional Operation Order No. 55 Dated 14th August 1917	14/08/1917	14/08/1917
Miscellaneous	11th Inf. Bde. BM. 68/321	17/08/1917	17/08/1917
Operation(al) Order(s)	Reference Divisional Operation Order No. 55	14/08/1917	14/08/1917
Operation(al) Order(s)	Addendum No. 2 to 4th Division Order No. 56	18/08/1917	18/08/1917
Operation(al) Order(s)	Addendum No. 1 to Division Order No. 56		
Operation(al) Order(s)	4th Division Order No. 56	15/08/1917	15/08/1917
Operation(al) Order(s)	4th Division Operation Order No. 57	27/08/1917	27/08/1917
Miscellaneous	Warning Order	28/08/1917	28/08/1917
Miscellaneous	Headquarters XVII Corps	09/08/1917	09/08/1917
Miscellaneous	Action Of 4th Division Machine Guns on 9th August	09/08/1917	09/08/1917
Miscellaneous	General Condition Of Trenches		
Miscellaneous	Amended Copy of 4 Division Defence Scheme		
Miscellaneous	Herewith amended copy of 4th Division Defence Scheme	29/08/1917	29/08/1917
Miscellaneous	4th Division Defence Scheme		
Miscellaneous	Light Railways, Water Service and Roads Used as Lines of Supply Appendix 1		
Miscellaneous	Appendix 2		
Map	Map "A"		
Map	Map "B"		
Heading	4th Division War Diaries General Staff September 1917		
War Diary	G 16 b 77	01/09/1917	07/09/1917
War Diary	G 16 b 77 Basseux	08/09/1917	08/09/1917
War Diary	Basseux	09/09/1917	19/09/1917
War Diary	Basseux Proven (Central Camp)	20/09/1917	20/09/1917
War Diary	Proven	21/09/1917	28/09/1917
War Diary	Proven Welsh Fm	29/09/1917	29/09/1917
War Diary	Welsh Fm	30/09/1917	30/09/1917
Miscellaneous	War Diary General Staff 4th Division 1st 30th Sept 1917	01/09/1917	01/09/1917
Operation(al) Order(s)	4 Division Operation Order No. 58	02/09/1917	02/09/1917

Miscellaneous	Movement Table Issued 4th Division Operation Order No. 58		
Miscellaneous	4th Division No. G.B. 9/51	04/09/1917	04/09/1917
Miscellaneous	Battalion Attack Two Companies Each On Two Platoon Front.		
Miscellaneous	Battalion Attack Four Companies Each on one Platoon Front		
Miscellaneous	Programme of Training 4th Division 9th to 15th September	09/09/1917	09/09/1917
Miscellaneous	Special Order	15/09/1917	15/09/1917
Miscellaneous	Warning Order	14/09/1917	14/09/1917
Operation(al) Order(s)	4th Division Order No. 59	15/09/1917	15/09/1917
Operation(al) Order(s)	Addendum No. 1 to 4th Division Order No. 59	17/09/1917	17/09/1917
Operation(al) Order(s)	Addendum No. 2 to 4th Division Order No. 59	18/09/1917	18/09/1917
Miscellaneous	Warning Order	14/09/1917	14/09/1917
Operation(al) Order(s)	Addendum No. 2 to 4th Division Order No. 60	26/09/1917	26/09/1917
Operation(al) Order(s)	4th Division Order No. 60	24/09/1917	24/09/1917
Miscellaneous	Table 'A' To Accompany 4th Division Order No. 60		
Miscellaneous			
Operation(al) Order(s)	4th Division Order No. 67	27/09/1917	27/09/1917
Map	Broembeek		
Operation(al) Order(s)	Instructions No. 1 to 4th Division Order No. 6	27/09/1917	27/09/1917
Miscellaneous	Addendum No. 1 to Instructions No. 1	28/09/1917	28/09/1917
Operation(al) Order(s)	Instructions No. 2 to 4th Division Order No. 6	27/09/1917	27/09/1917
Map	M.I.		
Miscellaneous	Message Pad		
Miscellaneous	Addendum No. 1 to Instructions No. 2	28/09/1917	28/09/1917
Operation(al) Order(s)	Instructions No. 3 to 4th Division Order No. 61	27/09/1917	27/09/1917
Miscellaneous	Addendum No. 1 Instructions No. 3	30/09/1917	30/09/1917
Operation(al) Order(s)	Instructions No. 4 to 4th Division Order No. 61	29/09/1917	29/09/1917
Operation(al) Order(s)	Instructions No. 5 To 4th Division Order No. 61	27/09/1917	27/09/1917
Operation(al) Order(s)	Instructions No. 6 To 4th Division Order No. 61	27/09/1917	27/09/1917
Operation(al) Order(s)	Addendum No. 1 4th Division Order No. 61	28/09/1917	28/09/1917
Operation(al) Order(s)	Instructions No. 7 to 4th Division Order No. 61	30/09/1917	30/09/1917
Map	To Accompany Instructions No. 7 To 4th Div. Order No. 61		
Map	Part of Broembeek		
Miscellaneous	Distribution of Troops (Reference 4th Division Order No. 61)		
Operation(al) Order(s)	Reference Addendum to 4th Division Order No. 60	25/09/1917	25/09/1917
Operation(al) Order(s)	4th Division Order No. 62	28/09/1917	28/09/1917
Operation(al) Order(s)	Appendix 'A' to 4th Division Order No. 62	02/10/1917	02/10/1917
Operation(al) Order(s)	Amendment to Appendix "A"-4th Division Order No. 62	02/10/1917	02/10/1917
Miscellaneous	4th Division Position Of Units-29th September 1917	29/09/1917	29/09/1917
Miscellaneous	4th Division Billeting List to take effect from 21st instant.		
Miscellaneous	Preliminary Orders For Machine Gun Barrage	27/09/1917	27/09/1917
Map	Broembeek		
Miscellaneous	Defence of Monchy. Appendix 7		
Miscellaneous	Reference 4th Division Defence Scheme Dated 29/9/17	05/09/1917	05/09/1917
Miscellaneous	Defence of Monchy Appendix 7		
Miscellaneous	Reference 4th Division Defence Scheme Dated 29/8/17	07/09/1917	07/09/1917
Miscellaneous	4th Divn. No. G.A. 4/20	30/09/1917	30/09/1917
Miscellaneous	4th Division Defence Scheme (Provisional)		
Heading	4th Division War Diary General Staff October 1917		

Heading	4th Div G.S. October 1917		
War Diary	Elverdinghe (Welsh Fm)	01/10/1917	08/10/1917
War Diary	Canal Bank C19a00	09/10/1917	14/10/1917
War Diary	Proven	14/10/1917	15/10/1917
War Diary	Poperinghe	15/10/1917	16/10/1917
War Diary	Duisans	17/10/1917	24/10/1917
War Diary	Arras	25/10/1917	31/10/1917
Miscellaneous	War Diary, General Staff, 4th Division 1st-31st October 1917	01/10/1917	01/10/1917
Miscellaneous	Account Of Operations By The 4th Division N.E. Of Ypres Between The 4th And 12th October 1917	12/10/1917	12/10/1917
Miscellaneous	Account Of Operations 12th October Appendix 22A.		
Map	Broembeek		
Operation(al) Order(s)	4th Division Order No. 63	04/10/1917	04/10/1917
Operation(al) Order(s)	4th Division Order No. 64	04/10/1917	04/10/1917
Operation(al) Order(s)	4th Division Order No. 65	05/10/1917	05/10/1917
Operation(al) Order(s)	4th Division Order No. 66	06/10/1917	06/10/1917
Operation(al) Order(s)	Instructions No. 1 to 4th Division Order No. 66	06/10/1917	06/10/1917
Operation(al) Order(s)	Instructions No. 2 to 4th Division Order No. 66	07/10/1917	07/10/1917
Operation(al) Order(s)	Addendum No. 3 to 4th Division Order No. 6	07/10/1917	07/10/1917
Operation(al) Order(s)	Instructions No. 3 to 4th Division Order No. 66	07/10/1917	07/10/1917
Operation(al) Order(s)	Amendment No. 1 to 4th Division Order No. 66	06/10/1917	06/10/1917
Operation(al) Order(s)	Reference Amendment No. 1 to 4th Division Order No. 66	08/10/1917	08/10/1917
Operation(al) Order(s)	Addendum No. 2 to 54th Division Order No. 66	06/10/1917	06/10/1917
Operation(al) Order(s)	Addendum No. 4 to 4th Division Order No. 66	07/10/1917	07/10/1917
Miscellaneous	Distribution of Troops (Reference 4th Division Order No. 66)		
Heading	Account Of Operation 9th October		
Miscellaneous	4th Division No. G.A. 3/163/1	11/10/1917	11/10/1917
Operation(al) Order(s)	4th Division Order No. 67	09/10/1917	09/10/1917
Miscellaneous	Table 'A' to Accompany 4th Division Order No. 67		
Operation(al) Order(s)	Reference 4th Division Order No. 67 Dated 9th October 1917	09/10/1917	09/10/1917
Miscellaneous	Table 'A' To Accompany 4th Division Order No. 67 Dated 9th October 1917	09/10/1917	09/10/1917
Miscellaneous	4th Division No. G.A. 3/163/1	11/10/1917	11/10/1917
Miscellaneous	Amendments To Table "A" Accompanying 4th Division Order No. 67 Dated 9th October 1917	09/10/1917	09/10/1917
Miscellaneous	C Form Messages And Signals		
Operation(al) Order(s)	4th Division Order No. 68	09/10/1917	09/10/1917
Operation(al) Order(s)	Addendum No. 1 to 4th Division Order No. 68	10/10/1917	10/10/1917
Map	Schaap-Balie		
Heading	4th Dr Oct 17		
Map	Broembeek		
Map	Schaap-Balie		
Map	Spriet		
Diagram etc	Identification Trace for use with Artillery Maps		
Operation(al) Order(s)	4th Division Order No. 69	13/10/1917	13/10/1917
Miscellaneous	March Table Issued With 4th Division Order No. 69 Dated 13th October	13/10/1917	13/10/1917
Miscellaneous	4th Division Warning Order	15/10/1917	15/10/1917
Operation(al) Order(s)	4th Division Order No. 70	15/10/1917	15/10/1917
Operation(al) Order(s)	Reference 4th Division Order No. 70	15/10/1917	15/10/1917
Operation(al) Order(s)	4th Division Order No. 71	19/10/1917	19/10/1917
Miscellaneous	Table "A"		

Heading	Moves And Dispositions Of Brigades On 5th And 6th October Appendix 13		
Miscellaneous	4th Div. G.A. 22/17	02/09/1917	02/09/1917
Miscellaneous	Reference 4th Divn. G.A. 22/17	02/10/1917	02/10/1917
Heading	Battle 4th October 1917 App 14		
Miscellaneous	Telephone Conversations		
Map	Schaap-Balie		
Miscellaneous	Contents		
Heading	Out Messages Battle 4th October 1917 App 16		
Miscellaneous	Contents		
Heading	Telephone Conversations 9th October 1917 App 17		
Miscellaneous	Telephone Conversations		
Heading	In Messages Battle 9th October App 18		
Miscellaneous	Contents		
Heading	Out Messages Battle 9th October App 19		
Miscellaneous	Contents		
Heading	In Messages Battle 12th October 1917 App 20		
Miscellaneous	Contents		
Heading	Out Messages Battle 12th October 1917 App 21		
Miscellaneous	Contents		
Heading	Telephone Conversations Battle 12th October 1917 App 22		
Miscellaneous	Special Order	13/10/1917	13/10/1917
Miscellaneous	4th Division Summary Of Operations 12th October, 1917	12/10/1917	12/10/1917
Operation(al) Order(s)	Addendum No. 1 to 4th Division Order No. 66	06/10/1917	06/10/1917
Miscellaneous	Telephone Conversations.		
Heading	Attachment of American Officers Appendix 23		
Miscellaneous	4th Division No. G.D. 156	31/10/1917	31/10/1917
Miscellaneous	XVIII Corps	29/10/1917	29/10/1917
Miscellaneous	4th Division	29/10/1917	29/10/1917
Miscellaneous	4th Division	25/10/1917	25/10/1917
Heading	List of Position Calls Appendix 27		
Miscellaneous	4th Division No. G.A. 12/35	22/10/1917	22/10/1917
Miscellaneous	Positions Calls Right Divisional Sector		
Heading	Congratulatory Messages Appendix 28		
Miscellaneous	4th Division No. G.S.81	18/10/1917	18/10/1917
Miscellaneous	To All Ranks Of The 4th Division	13/10/1917	13/10/1917
Miscellaneous	G.O.C. R.X. Right Artillery	13/10/1917	13/10/1917
Operation(al) Order(s)	4th Division Summary Of Operations	04/10/1917	04/10/1917
Map	Maps		
Miscellaneous	4th Division Summary Of Operations	04/10/1917	04/10/1917
Map	Maps		
Miscellaneous	Summary Of Operations On 4th Divisional Front	09/10/1917	09/10/1917
Map	Broembeek		
Miscellaneous	Summary Of Operations Of 4th Division	09/10/1917	09/10/1917
Map	Broembeek		
Heading	4th Division War Diaries General Staff November 1917		
War Diary	Arras	01/11/1917	07/11/1917
War Diary	Arras	01/11/1917	30/11/1917
Miscellaneous	War Diary General Staff 4th Division	01/11/1917	01/11/1917
Operation(al) Order(s)	4th Division Order No. 74	03/11/1917	03/11/1917
Operation(al) Order(s)	4th Division Order No. 75	05/11/1917	05/11/1917
Operation(al) Order(s)	4th Division Order No. 76	06/11/1917	06/11/1917
Operation(al) Order(s)	Amendment No. 1 to 4th Division Order No. 76	03/11/1917	03/11/1917
Operation(al) Order(s)	Instructions No. 1 to 4th Division Order No. 76	12/11/1917	12/11/1917

Operation(al) Order(s)	Addendum No. 1 to Instructions No. 1 to 4th Division Order No. 76	23/11/1917	23/11/1917
Operation(al) Order(s)	Instructions No. 2 to 4th Division Order No. 76	18/11/1917	18/11/1917
Operation(al) Order(s)	Instructions No. 3 to 4th Division Order No. 76	18/11/1917	18/11/1917
Operation(al) Order(s)	Instructions No. 4 to 4th Division Order No. 76	20/11/1917	20/11/1917
Miscellaneous	4th Division No. G.A. 3/205	01/12/1917	01/12/1917
Map	Approximate British Front Line		
Map	Hamblain-Les-Pres Ed.5		
Operation(al) Order(s)	4th Division Order No. 77	07/11/1917	07/11/1917
Miscellaneous	Legend		
Map	Trenches Not Drawn Accurately		
Operation(al) Order(s)	Reference 4th Division Order No. 77	19/11/1917	19/11/1917
Operation(al) Order(s)	Instructions No. 1 to 4th Division Order No. 77	13/11/1917	13/11/1917
Map	Legend		
Map	Maps		
Operation(al) Order(s)	Instructions No. 2 to 4th Division Order No. 77	12/11/1917	12/11/1917
Map	Trenches Corrected		
Operation(al) Order(s)	Instructions No. 3 to 4th Division Order No. 77	13/11/1917	13/11/1917
Map	Legend		
Map	Trenches not Drawn Accurately		
Operation(al) Order(s)	Amendment No. 1 to Instructions No. 3 to 4th Division Order No. 77	19/11/1917	19/11/1917
Operation(al) Order(s)	Reference Instructions No. 3 to 4th Division Order No. 7	16/11/1917	16/11/1917
Operation(al) Order(s)	Instructions No. 4 to 4th Division Order No. 77	07/11/1917	07/11/1917
Miscellaneous	4th Division No. G.A. 79/22	18/11/1917	18/11/1917
Operation(al) Order(s)	Instructions No. 5 to 4th Division Order No. 77	13/11/1917	13/11/1917
Operation(al) Order(s)	Reference Instructions No. 5 to 4th Division Order No. 77	14/11/1917	14/11/1917
Miscellaneous	Instructions For Discharged of Smoke	19/11/1917	19/11/1917
Miscellaneous	4th Div. G.A. 79/23	26/10/1917	26/10/1917
Operation(al) Order(s)	4th Division Order No. 78	17/11/1917	17/11/1917
Miscellaneous	To Accompany 4th Division Order No. 78 Table Of Tasks For Monchy Sector Bombardment		
Miscellaneous	Machine Gun Table Of Tasks For Monchy Sector Bombardment In Co-Operation With Artillery	17/11/1917	17/11/1917
Miscellaneous	4th Division No. G.D.79/22	26/10/1917	26/10/1917
Operation(al) Order(s)	4th Division Order No. 79	19/11/1917	19/11/1917
Miscellaneous	4th Division No. G.D. 79/22/1	21/11/1917	21/11/1917
Miscellaneous	Distribution of Units after relief of 12 Bde by 11 Bde App 8		
Miscellaneous	4th Division Disposition And Movement Report	25/11/1917	25/11/1917
Operation(al) Order(s)	4th Divisional Order No. 80	27/11/1917	27/11/1917
Operation(al) Order(s)	4th Division Order No. 81	27/11/1917	27/11/1917
Operation(al) Order(s)	Addendum No. 1 to 4th Division Order No. 81	27/11/1917	27/11/1917
Map			
Operation(al) Order(s)	4th Division Order No. 82	28/11/1917	28/11/1917
Map	Trenches Not Drawn Accurately		
Operation(al) Order(s)	Addendum No. 1 to 4th Division Order No. 82	30/11/1917	30/11/1917
Operation(al) Order(s)	4th Division Order No. 83	28/11/1917	28/11/1917
Miscellaneous	4th Division Disposition And Movement Report	29/11/1917	29/11/1917
Heading	4th Division War Diaries General Staff December 1917		
War Diary			
War Diary	Arras	07/12/1917	31/12/1917
Miscellaneous	Minor Operation Attempted Enemy Raid On 4 Div. On 21 Dec 1917	21/12/1917	21/12/1917

Type	Description	Date	Date
Miscellaneous	Third Army No. G.12/180 XVII Corps No. G.25/14 4th Division No. G.D. 79/34	23/12/1917	23/12/1917
Heading	War Diary, General Staff, 4th Division		
Miscellaneous	4th Division Dispositions And Movement Report	03/12/1917	03/12/1917
Operation(al) Order(s)	4th Division Order No. 84	08/12/1917	08/12/1917
Operation(al) Order(s)	4th Division Order No. 85	09/12/1917	09/12/1917
Operation(al) Order(s)	4th Division Order No. 86	10/12/1917	10/12/1917
Operation(al) Order(s)	4th Division Order No. 87	11/12/1917	11/12/1917
Miscellaneous	4th Division Disposition And Movement Report	11/12/1917	11/12/1917
Operation(al) Order(s)	4th Division Order No. 88	16/12/1917	16/12/1917
Operation(al) Order(s)	4th Division Order No. 89	17/12/1917	17/12/1917
Miscellaneous	4th Division Disposition And Movement Report	18/12/1917	18/12/1917
Miscellaneous	4th Division No. G.D. 79/34	23/12/1917	23/12/1917
Operation(al) Order(s)	4th Division Order No. 90	23/12/1917	23/12/1917
Miscellaneous	Report On Enemy Raid On 'Y' Sap Held By 1st R. Warwicks. Regt. 231217	23/12/1917	23/12/1917
Miscellaneous	4th Division Dispositions And Movement Report	27/12/1917	27/12/1917
Operation(al) Order(s)	4th Division Order No. 1	31/12/1917	31/12/1917
Miscellaneous	4th Division Defence Order	06/12/1917	06/12/1917
Miscellaneous	Amendment No. 1 to 4th Division Defence Orders	11/12/1917	11/12/1917
Miscellaneous	4th Division Defence Scheme Appendix 'B'.	17/12/1917	17/12/1917
Miscellaneous	4th Division Scheme		
Map	Defence Lines		
Map			
Map	Approximate British Front Line		
Map	J. Corps. T.S. No 94 (c)		
Map	Broken Mill Trench Map		
Map	Pelves Trench Map		
Diagram etc			
Miscellaneous	4th Division Defence Scheme Artillery. Appendix 'C'.	18/12/1917	18/12/1917
Miscellaneous	4th Division Defence Scheme Trench Mortars Appendix 'D'	18/12/1917	18/12/1917
Miscellaneous	Amendment No. 1 to Appendix 'D' 4th Division Defence Scheme Dated 18th Decr, 1917	18/12/1917	18/12/1917
Map			
Map	Barrage Map		
Map	Arras		
Map			
Miscellaneous			
Map	Schaap-Balie		
Map	Broembeek		
Miscellaneous			

4th Division
War Diaries
General Staff

August 1917

WAR DIARY or INTELLIGENCE SUMMARY

Army Form C. 2118.

HQ G.S.(I) 951 387

Place	Date	Hour	Summary of Events and Information	Remarks and references to Appendices
G16697	1/8/17		During the afternoon a corporal crawled out from Sap A (I 25 d 15,30) to the enemy's wire & there found a German bomb. He threw it into the enemy's trench where it exploded. No return by the enemy followed. Hostile Artillery was inactive.	
	2/8/17		1st R. Irish Fus. leave 4th Division, after having been in the division for 6 years. Massed bands played them to the station, where they were bade Farewell by the Corps Commander, GOC 4th Div'n etc. In the ROEUX Sector enemy trench mortars were active. 2/10 Middlesex Regt were posted to 10th Infantry Brigade.	
	3/8/17		12 Bow Trench was shelled & blown in at 4 points. CEYLON was also shelled. A daylight patrol crawled to near the enemy's wire; they fired at a man walking down the trench. Our 4.5 How. fired on a working party near I 27 b 63, obtaining direct hits with the first two shells. OP O.Rd. 5.2 rained (?)	Appp.
	4/8/17		A deserter from the 76th R.I.R. gave himself up. More enemy movement has been noticed near our lines, in most cases they were successfully engaged by artillery, M.G. or rifle fire.	
	5/8/17		Lan Fus relieve Kings Own in left subsector of PELVES Sector. At 10.30 p.m. our artillery directed intense harassing fire on enemy positions in PELVES Sector; the enemy replied by shelling our front line.	
	6/8/17		Essex Regt relieve Dukes in right subsector. Enemy Aircraft active. Oerposten in ROEUX sector report enemy's wire is now continuous; also hear enemy's trench officer to be duck boarded. In PELVES Sector our sniper crawled out at 11 a.m. They observed two enemy sniper also in NO MAN'S LAND; they accounted for one of these.	

WAR DIARY, GENERAL STAFF, 4th DIVISION.

1st - 31st August, 1917.

APPENDICES.
----

1. Operation Order 52.
2. Division Order 53.
3. Operation Order 54.
4.   "   " 55.
5. Division Order 56.
6. Operation Order 57.
7. Warning Order (G.A.6/11).
8. Report on Raid carried out by the 12th Brigade 9/
9. Work Report for month of AUGUST.
10. Amended copy of 4th Division DEFENCE SCHEME.

Army Form C. 2118.

WAR DIARY
or
INTELLIGENCE SUMMARY.
(Erase heading not required.)

Instructions regarding War Diaries and Intelligence Summaries are contained in F. S. Regs., Part II. and the Staff Manual respectively. Title pages will be prepared in manuscript.

Place	Date	Hour	Summary of Events and Information	Remarks and references to Appendices
Gibb 77	7/8/17		R. War R relieve Sea. Hrs in Sector North of river. Our patrols again engaged enemy wire near BIT LANE. 4 Dwl shots were held & proved a great success.	
	8/8/17		Our artillery opened at 3·30 a.m. in reply SOS signal by 17th Dvn. Enemy wire near BIT LANE reported cut. Increased enemy activity in reply to our shell fire in PEEVES Sector.	
	9/8/17		A raid was carried out against DEVILS Trench near BIT LANE at 7·45 p.m. Hostile barrage fell on our front & support Trenches 3 minutes after zero. Our MGuns in RO63x coord killed 7 enemy near APE trench (N.E of FINGER). Our Trenches have been renamed.	
	10/8/17		1st R. Bde move to TILLOY (G.25 d.92) for work under A.D.S. Quiet Day.	
	11/8/17		About 8 a.m. 3 E.A. were engaged by 5" of our machines. One E.A. appeared to crash, another was driven down.	
	12/8/17		A daylight patrol observed enemy working in front trench. Enemy shelled front line I25/2 – I25/3 also C Ro MP track. Movement again observed near VICTORIA Copse; our artillery shelled this area. A.A. Rds fired 53 rounds (b)	See App. 2
	13/8/17		11th M.G. Coy @ T M B relieve 12 M.G. Coy @ T M B in PEEVES area. 2 Prisoners were captured in a Post about 150 yds East of our Nº 1 post (N of Canal) by Major H. O'Neill 3/10 Middlesex, assisted by 1 Sgt & 2 men. The remainder of the garrison of the post happened to be away. Time of capture about 5 a.m. 14/8/17 op Order 54 issued (b)	(a) See App. 3

WAR DIARY
or
INTELLIGENCE SUMMARY.
(Erase heading not required.)

Army Form C. 2118.

Place	Date	Hour	Summary of Events and Information	Remarks and references to Appendices
G.16 b 77	14/8/17		Hampshires relieve Kings Own in Support (HIMALAYA). 1st R.Berks relieve 1/LAN FUS in left subsector (PELVES Sector). 11"TMB completes relief of 12"TMB. ARCHIE Trench & shelters nearby were bombarded by our heavy T/Mortar. Those enemy who were located were followed by shrapnel & MG Fire. One enemy was driven to our wire from where he was brought in by a patrol at night. Op ordered 55 rounds (a)	(a) See app. 4
	15/8/17		Hampshires relieve 2nd Essex in Right subsector (PELVES Sector). 11"E.LAN.R move to WILDERNESS Camp, & also G&H Posts. SLI to HIMALAYA. Enemy Artillery was more active, notably at HIMALAYA in the afternoon & on the front line in PELVES Sector at night. OP ordered 56 rounds (a)	(a) see app. 5
	16/8/17		HIMALAYA Trench was heavily shelled with 10.5 cm and 15 cm between 8.15am & 10.15 am. — EA were very active over our lines between 4 hm & 6 hm. Two E.A. of a new type were reported flying at a low altitude over our front line at 4.30 pm.	
	17/8/17		A daylight patrol with a Lewis Gun, went out from I.20.c.85.80 at 4.30 am. with the intention of bombing the enemy out of any shell holes he might be holding. None were put up. — Quiet day.	

Army Form C. 2118.

WAR DIARY
or
INTELLIGENCE SUMMARY.
(Erase heading not required.)

Instructions regarding War Diaries and Intelligence Summaries are contained in F. S. Regs., Part II. and the Staff Manual respectively. Title pages will be prepared in manuscript.

Place	Date	Hour	Summary of Events and Information	Remarks and references to Appendices
G.16.b.7.7.	18-8-17		The Right of the 4th Division was extended to the North edge of NORTHERN TWIN COPSE - (O.2.a.10.7) in relief of the 12th Division. The Right of the Left Brigade was extended to SCABBARD ALLEY (inclusive) (I.31.b.4.8) in relief of the Right Brigade. A Corporal of the 8th Coy - 2nd Bn - 76th R.I.R - 17th Res. Division (normal identification) was killed behind our post at I.25.b.5.9 early in the morning. No further Germans were discovered in the vicinity.	
g.16.b.7.7	19.8.17		Our Patrol did not gain contact with any parties of the enemy. A hostile patrol near I.31.d.99 was dispersed with Lewis gun fire.	
	20th		Hostile artillery which was quiet by day became more active by night. A patrol which was inspecting enemy wire opposite I.20.c.88 met a party of enemy. Capt Jk McConnel, 20th Hussars, took over duties of GSO III from Capt P&S Taylor, Sherwood Foresters.	
	21st		During afternoon enemy dugouts along BIT LANE were shelled. Late enemy shell holes on I.32.e were fired on with Gas shell.	
	22nd		At 10.5 p.m Dugouts behind DELBAR RIDGE were fired on with Gas shell.	
	23rd		Between 5 p.m & 7 p.m CARTRIDGE Trench shelled.	

WAR DIARY
or
INTELLIGENCE SUMMARY.
(Erase heading not required.)

Army Form C. 2118.

Place	Date	Hour	Summary of Events and Information	Remarks and references to Appendices
G.16.b.77	24th		Enemy artillery active against MONCHY.	
	25th		Enemy bombarded our posts east of ROEUX with T. Mortars & rifle grenades. Under cover of this he attempted a raid by stealth on our No 2 post (I 20 a 8 2). His party were caught with Lewis gun fire & was found to have withdrawn after about 10 minutes.	
	26th		Hostile activity below normal.	
	27th		Another quiet day. Enemy were noticed working near a telegraph about I 31 b 77 by a daylight patrol of two officers. They returned & collect rifle grenades which they fired at the spot. Op. Order 57 issued. (B)	(a) App 6
	28th		Enemy was found in ARROW trench. Two white rockets sent up from ARROW trench was the signal for our front line to be shelled with T.M. shells warning & orders issued for wind & 4"Stokes & Lethum & 3"Stokes. (a)	(a) App 7.
	29th		Enemy T mortars were active especially on ROEUX Sector. Enemy used Very lights & signal to his T Mortars. ARROW was again occupied.	
	30th		A Quiet day	
	31st		In PELVES Sector our support line was shelled intermittently during day. A continued shoot by Heavy T Mortars & M Guns was carried out on APE & ARCHIE.	

A5834 Wt.W4973/M687 750,000 8/16 D.D. & L. Ltd. Forms/C.2118/13

App. 1

Operation Order 58

app 1

- S E C R E T -   4th Division No. G.S. 79/13/A

12ᵗʰ BRIGADE.

Reference Table "A" attached to 4th Division Operation Order No: 52 dated 5th August 1917, Serial No: 1 will be amended to read :-

| Time | | Trench Mortars. | 4.5" Hows. | 6" Hows. | Heavy Hows & Super Heavy Hows. | 60 pdr Guns and 18 pdr Guns. |
From	To					
6.15 a.m.	8.15 a.m.	Front system of trenches vide Map.	Front system of trenches (GREEN on Map)	Trenches etc. (BROWN on Map)	No change	Stand by for opportunity targets.

P.F.C.Williams
Lieut:Colonel,
General Staff., 4th Division.

Copies to :-
    10th Brigade.
    C.R.A, 4th Divn.
    D.M.G.O, 4th Divn.
    12th Division.
    17th Division.
    XVIIth Corps.
    War Diary (2)
    File.

SECRET.

4th Div. G.S. 79/13/B.

12th Brigade.

Reference 4th Division Operation Order No.52 of 3rd August and G.S.79/13/A of 5th August.

1. Phase 3 of the Artillery bombardment will continue for 1½ hours from ZERO onwards.

2. *Attached map shows :-

    (a) The forming up line from which the Infantry will advance at ZERO hour.

    (b) Localities selected for Artillery bombardment and Artillery barrages; for details see Table (C).

3. The raid will be carried out in accordance with 12th Inf.Brig. Operation Orders Nos.59 and 59/1 dated 4th and 5th August respectively.

4. A General Staff Officer will be at 12th Inf.Brig. H.Q. at 6 p.m. on 7th August and at 11 a.m. 8th August to synchronise watches.

5. ACKNOWLEDGE.

* To 12th Bde.only.

6th August, 1917.

A.F.C.Williams
~~Lieut~~.Colonel,
General Staff, 4th Divn.

Copies to 10th Brigade.
         C.R.A. 4th Div.
         12th Division.
         17th Division.
         XVII Corps.
         War Diary (2).
         File.

SECRET.

12th Brigade.
REFERENCE 4th DIVISION OPERATION ORDER NO. 52.

Issued to 12th Bde. only.

1. The Artillery bombardment will last 13 hours and will commence at 8.15 a.m. It will be divided into three phases.

Attached maps and Table (A) set forth the details of the bombardment during the first two phases.

Orders for phase 3 accompanied by the barrage map will be issued later.

2. During phase 1 all trenches will be cleared within 300 yards of the enemy front trench.

During phase 2 the 12th Division will vacate 150 yards of the Eastern portion of TWIN Trench.

Arrangements for clearing trenches for registration purposes prior to 8th August will be made direct between G.O.C. Corps H.A. and B.G.C. 12th Inf.Brig.

3. Table (B) gives details of Machine Gun action on the 8th instant.

4. ZERO Hour will be 7.45 p.m.

Rehearsals of the Artillery procedure at ZERO Hour will be carried out at 11 a.m. and 2 p.m. on 8th August.

5. ACKNOWLEDGE.

A.F.C.Williams.
Lieut.Colonel,
General Staff, 4th Divn.

5th August, 1917.

Copies to 10th Brigade.
        C.R.A. 4th Div.
        D.M.G.O. 4th Div.
        12th Division.
        17th Division.
        XVII Corps.
        War Diary (2).
        File.

Table A

PROGRAMME OF ARTILLERY BOMBARDMENT.

Serial No.	Time From	Time To	Trench Mortars.	4.5" Hows.	6" Hows.	Heavy Hows.	Super Heavy Hows.	60 pr. guns and 18 prs.
Phase 1.								
1.	6.15 am	8.15 am			C.B. work on selected hostile batteries.	C.B. work on selected hostile batteries.	C.B. (ANF targets).	—
	7 am	8.15 am	Registering front system of trenches.	Registering front system of trenches.				
2.	8.15 am	11 am	2" Trench mortars front system of trenches (Yellow on map). 9.45" trench mortars (Blue on map).	Front system of trenches (Green on map)	Trenches, etc. (Brown on map)	C.B.	—	Stand by for opportunity targets.
3.	11 a.m.	11.5 am	Rehearsal of "Z" procedure.			C.B.	C.B.	
4.	11.5 am	2 pm	→ Continues tasks as for Serial No. 2. →					
5.	2 pm	2.5 pm	Rehearsal of "Z" procedure.			C.B.	C.B.	
6.	2.5 pm	6.15 pm	→ Continue tasks as for Serial No. 2. →					
Phase 11.								
7.	6.15 pm	7.40 pm	Gradually take up the bombardment of front trenches when 6" Hows lift (Yellow and Blue on map).	Gradually take up the bombardment of front trenches when 6" hows lift (Green on map)	Gradually lift to objectives 300 yds. from forming up line (Brown on map).	C.B.	C.B.	18 prs as shown on map and as necessary will assist 2" T.Ms. and 4.5" Hows. when 6" Hows. lift. Remainder "stand by" for opportunity targets.
8.	7.40pm	7.45pm	All natures of ordnance will gradually work into their places for ZERO hour.					

Table B

ACTION OF 4th DIVISION MACHINE GUNS on 8th AUGUST.

1. **10th M.G.Company.**   **TARGET.**

    2 guns ROEUX Wood   Enfilade GUN Trench from
                                     I.32.a.35.55. to BIT Trench.

    4 guns   JUNCTION COPSE and DELBAR Wood.

12th M.G.Company.

    2 guns in G Post)   CARTRDIGE Trench I.32.b.25.15.
    2 guns in H Post)   to I.32.d.4.7.

    2 guns HALBERD Trench   To sweep "No Man's Land" and the
                                     embankment in I.32.a. The fire
                                     of these guns must not be South
                                   of the embankment. FIRE AT ZERO.

    2 guns about BOMB Trench.   DEVIL'S Trench from I.32.c.85.10.
                                     to junction with CIGAR Wood.
                                   Lift at ZERO to SACK Wood.

234th M.G.Company.

    2 guns M Post   Enfilade PELVES Lane from
                                   I.26.a.6.3.

    4 guns LANCER Lane   Tracks in I.26.b.

    2 guns K Post   ANGEL Trench.

    2 guns K Post   SHELL Trench.

2.   The 12th Division will co-operate by enfilade fire on BIT Lane.

3.   All guns, except those in HALBERD Trench will fire bursts of 30 rounds at irregular intervals from ZERO minus 11½ hours to ZERO.

    At ZERO all guns increase to 200 rounds a minute.

    Fire will cease on the return of the raiders.

SECRET.   Copy No. 9

4th DIVISION OPERATION ORDER NO. 52.

Reference 1/10,000 Trench Map.   3rd August, 1917.

1.   The 12th Division will bombard the enemy's trench line and batteries opposite their front for a period of 13½ hours on August 8th.

The Northern limit of the bombardment will be an East and West line drawn through the point where ARROW Trench cuts BIT LANE.

One and a half hour's before the termination of the bombardment the 12th Division will send Infantry Patrols into the hostile front system with a view to obtaining identifications and of killing or capturing any survivors from the bombardment; the advance of these patrols will be covered by an 18 pdr. barrage and their operations and eventual withdrawal will be covered by a screen of Lewis Guns which will be pushed out well in front of them.

2.   The 12th Inf.Brig. will co-operate in this operation by carrying out a Raid on DEVILS Trench in I.32.c N. and S. of BIT LANE.

3.   ZERO hour will be in the late afternoon about 1½ hours before the termination of the 12th Division bombardment. Exact hour will be notified later.

4.   12th Inf.Brig. will submit proposals for the composition of parties and method of attack.

5.   Special instructions as to Artillery and Machine Gun action will be issued separately.

6.   Watches will be synchronised from Divisional H.Q. to 12th Division, C.R.A. 4th Division and to 12th Brigade at 11 a.m. on 8th August.

7.   ACKNOWLEDGE.

                                          A.F.C.Williams, Lieut.Colonel,
Issued at 6 p.m.   General Staff, 4th Division.

Copy No. 1 to 10th Brigade.   Copy No. 6 to 17th Division.
        2 to 12th Brigade.   7) to XVII Corps.
        3 to C.R.A. 4th Div.   8)
        4 D.H.G.O. 4th Div.   9) to War Diary.
        5 to 12th Division.   10)
                                             11 to File.

- S E C R E T -
****

app 2

Copy No: 15

4th DIVISION ORDER NO: 53
****

12th August 1917.

1. The 11th Infantry Brigade will relieve the 12th Infantry Brigade in the PELVES Sector, by battalions, on the nights 14th/15th, and 15th/16th August.

2. The relief of Machine Guns and Light Trench Mortars will take place 24 hours before the Infantry reliefs.

3. All details of relief will be arranged between the Brigade Commanders concerned.

4. Command of the PELVES Sector will pass to B.G.C, 11th Infantry Brigade on completion of all reliefs.

5. To ensure continuity of work, details regarding the relief of all working parties, supplied by the Reserve Brigade, will be arranged direct between Brigade Commanders concerned.

Working party, Serial Y (300 men for work nightly under instructions from A.D. Signals, XVIIth Corps) will NOT be required on the night of 14th/15th August.

This party will be supplied on the night 15th/16th August, until further orders, by a Battalion of the 12th Infantry Brigade, which will be accommodated in the Camp near TILLOY-LES-MAFFLAINES, vacated by a Battalion of the 11th Infantry Brigade.

6. Completion of all reliefs will be reported to Divisional Headquarters.

7. A C K N O W L E D G E.

Lieut:Colonel,
General Staff., 4th Division.

Issued at 7 h.m.

Copies to :-
10th Inf. Brigade.
11th Inf. Brigade.
12th Inf. Brigade.
C.R.A, 4th Divn.
C.R.E, 4th Divn.
A.D.M.S, 4th Divn.
A.P.M, 4th Divn.
Signals, 4th Divn.

D.M.G.O, 4th Divn.
234th M.G.Coy.
XVIIth Corps. (2)
12th Division.
A.D.Signals, XVIIth Corps.
War Diary (2)
File.
4th Division "Q" (3)

app.3

4th Division G.S.79/15.

S E C R E T.

To all recipients of 4th Division Operation Order No. 54.

Reference 4th Division Operation Order No. 54.

The Raid is postponed until further orders.

Please ACKNOWLEDGE.

[signature]

Lieut.Colonel,

13/8/17.   General Staff, 4th Division.

SECRET.	Copy No. 14

4th DIVISION OPERATION ORDER No. 54

13th August, 1917.

Reference 1/10,000 Trench Map.

1. The 10th Infantry Brigade will carry out a raid on the enemy's trench system and dug-outs to an average depth of 150 yards, between I.20.b.0.5 and I.14.c.8.1. on the night of 16th/17th August, on the lines already approved by the Divisional Commander.

2. Zero hour will be notified later.

3. Details of artillery support will be arranged direct by B.G.C. 10th Infantry Brigade with C.R.A.

4. Instructions for machine gun co-operation by No. 234 Machine Gun Company will be issued by D.M.G.O.

5. B.G.C. 10th Infantry Brigade will apply direct to C.R.E. for any R.E. detachments which may be required for clearing dug-outs.

6. Any additional measures to those at present in force for clearing wounded will be arranged by A.D.M.S.

7. Prisoners will be sent to ATHIES LOCK where they will be taken over by the A.P.M.

8. ACKNOWLEDGE.

Issued at 8.30 a.m.

A.F. Williams.
Lt-Colonel,
General Staff, 4th Division.

Copies to :-
```
         No. 1. to 10th Inf. Bde.    No. 8. 12th Division.
          "  2.  " 11th Inf. Bde.     "  9. 17th Division.
          "  3.  " 12th Inf. Bde.     " 10. XVII Corps.
          "  4.  " C.R.A., 4th Div.   " 11. A.P.M. 4th Div.
          "  5.  " C.R.E., 4th Div.   " 12)
          "  6.  " A.D.M.S.           " 13) War Diary.
          "  7.  " D.M.G.O.           " 14)
                                      " 15  File.
```

SECRET. Copy No.

App. 4

4th DIVISION OPERATION ORDER NO 55.

14th August, 1917.

Reference 1/10,000 Trench Map, PLOUVAIN Sheet.
1/10,000 Corps Plex Trench Maps T.S. No M.24(b) & (c) dated 28/7/17.

1. On night of 18th/19th August, the right of the 4th Division will be extended up to, and inclusive of, O.2/6 Trench in relief of 12th Division.

2. The new boundaries will then be :-

   (a) Southern Divisional Boundary.

   O.2/6 Trench, North edge of Northern TWIN COPSE - Southern Corner of ARROWHEAD COPSE - Junction of ORCHARD Reserve and BRIDOON LANE, thence along ORCHARD Reserve, to the present boundary line.
   ORCHARD Reserve and ORANGE AVENUE will be inclusive to 12th Division but 4th Division will have a right of way through them.

   (b) Brigade boundary.

   I.25/1 - SCABBARD ALLEY - Bn H. Qrs (H.30.d.1.3) - railway crossing at H.23.b.65.35 (all incl. to left Brigade).
   LANCER and JOHNSON AVENUES will be common to both Brigades.

3. (a) The 11th Infantry Brigade will extend its front to hold the additional line, to O.2/6 (incl.) in relief of 36th Brigade.

   O.C. 11th M.G.Company will relieve 2 guns of 36th M.G. Company in BRIDOON LANE by 6 p.m. on 18th August.

   11th and 12th Infantry Brigades will continue to hold the Southern Sector from O.2/6 (incl.) to I.25/1 (excl.) relieving each other as heretofore.

   These Brigades will continue to find, in turn, all garrisons of LANCER AVENUE and Strong Points in the old PELVES Sector.

   Right Bn H.Q. will be established in MUSKET RESERVE.

   (b) 10th Infantry Brigade will take over from I.25/1 (incl.) to River SCARPE. The Northern Sector will then be held as follows :-

(1)

(i) <u>From I.25/1 (incl.) to River SCARPE</u>.

    1 Coy in front line and support, H.Q. SCABBARD SUPPORT.

    1 Coy in Reserve, H.Q. WELFORD RESERVE.

    2 Coys H.23.

    Bn H.Q. H.30.d.1.3.

(ii) <u>From River SCARPE to Northern Divisional boundary</u>.

    1 Bn, front system of trenches, H.Q. CRETE TRENCH.

    The remaining 2 battalions of this Brigade will be at STIRLING and MIDDLESEX Camps.

4. Details of relief will be arranged between B.G's.C. concerned.

5. Brigades will be responsible for all work East, and exclusive, of the Reserve line, but troops in actual occupation of the latter, will arrange for its maintenance.

6. C.R.A will arrange to cover the new portion of the line taken over and to readjust the artillery barrage line at the new point of junction of the two Divisions from 8 a.m. on 19th August.

7. Command of the additional front taken over from 12th Division will pass to G.O.C. 4th Division on completion of reliefs, which will be reported to Divisional Headquarters.

8. ACKNOWLEDGE.

R.F.C. Williams.
Lt-Colonel,
General Staff, 4th Division.

Issued at 7 p.m.

Copies to:-

    No. 1. 10th Infantry Brigade.   No. 9. 4th Divn. Signals.
        2. 11th Infantry Brigade.   10. A.P.M., 4th Divn.
        3. 12th Infantry Brigade.   11. 4th Divn. "Q" (3)
        4. C.R.A., 4th Divn.   12. XVII Corps. (2).
        5. C.R.E., 4th Divn.   13. 12th Division.
        6. A.D.M.S., 4th Divn.   14. 17th Division.
        7. D.M.G.O., 4th Divn.   15. War Diary (3)
        8. 234th M.G. Company.   16. File.

SECRET.   4th Division No. G.S. 6/9.

Reference Divisional Operation Order
No. 55 Dated 14th August, 1917.

1.   Two guns of the 234th M.G.Company will relieve the guns of the 11th M.G.COMPANY in ELBOW Alley and SCABBARD Alley.

        Relief to be complete by 6 p.m. 18th August.

                                                  Lt-Colonel,
16th August, 1917.   General Staff, 4th Division.

Copies to :-

    D.M.G.O.   C.R.A.
    10th Inf. Bde.   C.R.E.
    11th Inf. Bde.   4th Divn. "Q"
    12th Inf. Bde.
    234th M.G.Company.

S E C R E T

11th Inf. Bde. BM 68/321.

....

Headquarters Right Front Line Battalion will be established at I.31.c.35.10. junction of CURB SWITCH South and ORANGE AVENUE.

[signature]
Captain.
Brigade Major,
11th Infantry Brigade.

17/8/17.

SECRET.   4th Div. G.S. 3/92.

<u>Reference Divisional Operation Order No.55,
dated 14th August, 1917.</u>

1.   The Post in Northern TWIN COPSE at present held by 35th Inf.Brig.(12th Division) will be handed over to 11th Inf.Brig. (4th Division) tonight 22nd/23rd August.

       Details to be arranged between Brigadiers concerned.

       Completion of relief to be reported to Divisional H.Q.

2.   The Divisional boundary between 4th and 12th Divisions will then run from O.2/6 Trench (O.2.b oo.70) - South edge of Northern TWIN COPSE - Southern corner of ARROWHEAD COPSE - then present boundary line.

3.   ACKNOWLEDGE.

                                                    A.F.C.Williams.

                                                    Lieut.Colonel,

22nd August, 1917.   General Staff, 4th Division.

Copies to all recipients of
Operation Order No. 55.

App. 5

SECRET.

ADDENDUM No. 2, to 4th DIVISION ORDER NO. 56.

Reference Map 1/100,000 LENS and AMIENS.

1. In continuation of 4th Division Order No. 56 dated 15th August, 1917.

   Reference para 2.

   The 23rd Army Brigade R.F.A. (less C/23rd and 107th Batteries) will be transferred to 50th Division VI Corps moving to MERCATEL on the 20th August.

   Route ARRAS - BAPAUME Road.

   Move to be completed by midnight 20/21st.

   Details to be arranged direct between C's.R.A. 4th and 50th Divisions.

2. ACKNOWLEDGE.

A. F. C. Williams.
Lt-Colonel,
General Staff, 4th Division.

18th August, 1917.

Copies to all recipients
    of 4th Division Order No. 56.
        and 50th Division.

S E C R E T.

ADDENDUM NO.1, to 4th DIVISION ORDER No. 56

Reference Map 1/100,000 LENS and AMIENS.

1.   In continuation of 4th Division Order No. 56 dated 15th August 1917.

Reference para. 2.

(a)   The two 18-pdr. batteries (C/23 and 107) of the 23rd Army Brigade R.F.A. will be temporarily transferred to III Corps and will move by road as under to III Corps area.

Date.	To	Route	Billets from	Remarks
Aug.18th	BAPAUME	ARRAS - BAPAUME	Town Major BAPAUME.	To arrive 6 p.m.
Aug.19th	PERONNE	Most Suitable.	Town Major PERONNE	To arrive 1 p.m.
Aug.20th	34th Div. Area	Under orders of III Corps.		

(b)   Not less than 10 18-pdr. guns fit for offensive operations will accompany these two batteries.

(c)   No proportion of Brigade Ammunition Column will be transferred.

(d)   No ammunition will be taken.

(e)   Rations taken to and for 20th instant, afterwards by 34th Division.

2.   ACKNOWLEDGE.

A.F.C.Williams
Lieut.Colonel,

Issued at 3 p.m.   General Staff, 4th Division.

Copies to all recipients
     of 4th Division Order No. 56.

SECRET. Copy No. 20

4th DIVISION ORDER NO. 56.

15th August, 1917.

1. Para 6 of 4th Division Operation Order No. 55 is cancelled.

2. The 23rd Army Field Artillery Brigade will be transferred to VI Corps.
Two 18 pounder Batteries will be withdrawn from action on the night 17/18th August, prior to marching away. Further orders will be issued regarding this march and the moves of the remainder of the Brigade.

3. Consequent on above, the present front of the 4th Division and the additional line to be taken over from the 12th Division on the night 18/19th August, will be covered from 12 noon on the 18th August by the 29th & 32nd R.F.A. Brigades, reinforced by one 18 pounder battery and one section 18 pounder of the 48th Brigade R.F.A. (12th Division).

4. The necessary re-adjustment of battery positions between 4th and 12th Divisions will be completed by 5 a.m. 18th August and of barrage lines by 12 noon on the same date.

5. Details to be arranged between C's.R.A. concerned.

6. Telephone communications will be left intact in all battery positions and observing stations.
Observing stations covering the extended portion of the 4th Division front will be taken over from 12th Division.

7. ACKNOWLEDGE.

A.F.C.Williams.
Lt-Colonel,
General Staff, 4th Division.

Issued at 9.30 p.m.

Copy No. 1. 10th Inf. Bde.
2. 11th Inf. Bde.
3. 12th Inf. Bde.
4. Div. Arty.
5. Div. Engrs.
6. A.D.M.S., 4th Div.
7. D.M.G.O., 4th Div.
8. 234th M.G.Company.
9. DivN Signals.
10. A.P.M., 4th Div.
11)
12) "Q" 4th Divn.
13)
14) XVII Corps.
15)   -do-
16. 12th Division.
17. 17th Division.
18)
19) War Diary.
20)
21. File.

SECRET.　　　　　　　　　　　　　　　　　　Copy No. 17

app. 6

4th DIVISION OPERATION ORDER NO. 57.

Reference Sheet 51 B　　　　　　　　　　　　27th August, 1917.
1/40,000.

1. The 12th Inf.Brig. will relieve the 11th Inf.Brig. in the PELVES Sector, by Battalions, on the nights 30th/31st August and 31st Aug./1st Sept.

2. All details of relief will be arranged between Brigade Commanders concerned.

3. Command of the PELVES Sector will pass to B.G.C. 12th Inf.Brig. on completion of relief.

4. Details regarding the relief of all working parties, supplied by the Reserve Brigade, will be arranged direct between B.Gs.C. 11th and 12th Inf.Brigs.

5. The two Lewis Gun detachments of the 12th Inf.Brig. at present providing for the Anti-aircraft defence of St. POL Station will not be relieved by the 11th Inf.Brig., but will remain at St.POL until relieved by the 21st Division on 1st September.

6. Completion of all reliefs will be reported to Divisional Headquarters by wire.

7. ACKNOWLEDGE.

A.F.C. Williams.

Lieut.Colonel,
Issued at 12 noon.　　　　　　　General Staff, 4th Division.

Copy No. 1 to 10th Brigade.
　　　　2 to 11th Brigade.
　　　　3 to 12th Brigade.
　　　　4 to C.R.A. 4th Div.
　　　　5 to C.R.E. 4th Div.
　　　　6 to A.D.M.S. 4th Div.
　　　　7 to A.P.M. 4th Div.
　　　　8 to Signals 4th Div.
　　　　9 to D.M.G.O. 4th Div.
　　　10)
　　　11) to 4th Div. Q.
　　　12)
　　　13 to 12th Division.
　　　14)
　　　15) to XVII Corps.
　　　16)
　　　17) to War Diary.
　　　18 to File.

SECRET.   4th Div. G.A. 6/11.

10th Brigade.
11th Brigade.
12th Brigade.

WARNING ORDER.

Reference 1/10000 PLOUVAIN, FAMPOUX and ARRAS Sheets.

Reference 4th Div. G.S. 6/11 of 27th August.

1. The 4th Division (less Artillery) will be relieved by the 15th Division (less Artillery) on the front between the Northern TWIN COPSE (inclusive) in O.2.a and a point on the front line I.14.c 6.2.

2. On relief the Division (less Artillery) will move to VI Corps (ADINFER) area.

3. (a) 11th Inf.Brig. will march direct from their camps at G.18.a and G.24.b to the new area on 5th September.

    (b) Brigades in the line will be relieved as under :-

        10th Inf.Brig. night 6/7th September.
        'th Inf.Brig. night 7/8th September.

    Whole relief to be completed by 10 a.m. 8th September.

4. Detailed orders will be issued later.

5. ACKNOWLEDGE.

                                    _____. Lieut.Colonel,
28th August, 1917.   General Staff, 4th Division.

Copies to C.R.A.
         C.R.E.
         4th Div.Q.
         A.D.M.S.
         A.P.M.
         Signals.
         12th Division.
         17th Division.
         XVII Corps.
         War Diary.
         File.

CONFIDENTIAL.

4th Division No. G.S. 79/13.

app. 8

Headquarters,
XVII Corps.

REPORT ON RAID CARRIED OUT BY THE 12th INFANTRY BRIGADE ON 9th AUGUST 1917.

Reference attached map.

1. On August 9th, after a bombardment of the enemy trenches and battery positions East and North East of MONCHY lasting 11½ hours, the 12th Infantry Brigade carried out a raid on DEVILS TRENCH, North and South of its junction with BIT LANE, in co-operation with raids by the 12th Division on their right.
Zero hour was 7.45 p.m.

2. The object of the raid was to :-

   (a) Capture or kill any of the enemy encountered,

   (b) Obtain identifications,

   (c) Destroy the enemy's trenches and dug-outs.

3. The raiding force consisted of :-

   (a) <u>Southern Party.</u> 3 officers and 100 men of 2nd Essex Regt, 2 officers and 30 men of 2nd Bn West Riding Regt, with two detachments of 9th Field Coy R.E.

   (b) <u>Northern Party.</u> 4 officers and 80 men of 2nd Bn Essex Regt, with two detachments of 9th Field Coy R.E.

4. At Zero - 4 minutes, parties moved from their trenches and lined up in front of them, parallel to the enemy's trench, and at Zero + 2 minutes, moved forward behind our artillery barrage.

   (a) <u>Southern party.</u>

   The detachments of 2nd West Riding Regt moved forward slightly in advance of the 100 men of 2nd Essex Regt, with the object of taking and holding ARROW TRENCH. They reached ARROW TRENCH, which they found to be unoccupied, and held it till the conclusion of operations.

   The 100 men of 2nd Essex Regt almost immediately came under heavy machine gun and rifle fire, first, from the high ground in rear of DEVILS TRENCH, and then from both flanks. This party was unable to advance beyond the line of ARROW TRENCH.

   The enemy came out of his trenches, towards our raiding party, and fired rifle grenades and stick bombs at our men, but was compelled to retire by the rifle and Lewis gun fire of the raiding party.

The enemy's wire although difficult to see, is reported by the Southern party, to have been fairly satisfactorily cut.

(b) **Northern party.**

The 80 men of the Essex Regt, under cover of the ridge, were able to advance about 150 yards before they were held up by heavy machine gun and rifle fire from front and both flanks. The enemy advanced from his trenches, covered by a rifle, grenade and bomb, barrage, to shell holes in front of DEVILS TRENCH.

Our rifle and Lewis Gun fire forced the enemy to withdraw to DEVILS TRENCH, inflicting severe casualties on him, but the party was unable to occupy the trench, though some men reached the wire which was found to be cut only in a few places.

3. The artillery preparation does not appear to have sufficiently damaged the enemy's trench, nor to have extended far enough beyond our left flank, with the result that the enemy was able to guess accurately the front of attack.

The enemy's barrage which came down at Zero + 4 minutes, was placed on our support and reserve lines, and was not heavy, being chiefly on the Northern sector about SCABBARD and ELBOW TRENCHES.

The enemy's S.O.S. Signal, North of BIT LANE, appeared to be 1 Green and 1 Red light. South of BIT LANE, it was an orange light.

4. From Zero to about Zero + 15 minutes, our aeroplanes, about 30 in all, co-operated very successfully with the raiding parties, by driving off hostile machines and firing into the German trenches. From Zero + 15 minutes to about Zero + 30 minutes, our machines were flying either very high or behind our own lines, thus enabling two or three enemy machines to fly very low over the area being attacked, firing at our men and signalling with lights to their own troops. At about Zero + 30 minutes, our fighting machines returned again, and drove off the enemy machines. Several aerial combats then followed, but none appeared to be decisive.
This large concentration of aeroplanes just before the Zero hour appears to have given the enemy warning as to our time of attack.

5. During the operations, our machine guns, from the support and Reserve trenches, rendered valuable aid to the raiding parties, engaging the enemy when he left his trenches with good results, (vide "ACTION OF 4th DIVISION MACHINE GUNS" attached).
During the day, the 24 machine guns fired 59,000 rounds.

6/. I attribute the failure of the raid to the following :-

(a) That the Heavy Artillery bombardment on the Left flank was not sufficiently heavy to destroy the enemy's trenches and dug-outs.

(b) To the thinness of the artillery barrage.

(c) To the fire of the enemy's machine guns from front and flank, which was very severe.

(d) To the fact that the enemy seems to have concentrated some of his best and steadiest troops in the vicinity of BIT LANE, as much stronger resistance was experienced here, and on the left flank of the 12th Division, than on the other parts of the line raided.

It is probable that in or round BIT LANE, dug-outs or shelters of an extensive nature exist, as in all operations in this locality, resistance has always been most obstinate.

7. Our casualties were as follows :-

2nd Essex Regt.	Captain S.R.E.O'HALLORAN.	Killed.
	Lieut: S.G.SHOWERS.	"
	2/Lieut: A.J.BENNETT.	"
	Lieut: L.W.LAKE.	Wounded.
	2/Lieut: B.ABBEY.	"
	2/Lieut: D.F.NORMAN.	"
	2/Lieut: CUTLER.	Missing.

	Other Ranks	Killed 16
		Wounded 39
		Missing 15

| 2nd W.Riding Rgt. | 2/Lieut: WOOD. | Killed. |

	Other ranks.	Killed 3
		Wounded 3
		Missing 2

9th Field Coy R.E. Other Ranks.		Killed 1
		Wounded 1
		Missing 1

Total 8 Officers and 81 Other ranks, out of a total of 9 Officers and 222 Other ranks.

Sd/ W.LAMBTON. Major General,

12th August 1917. Commanding 4th Division.

TABLE "B"

ACTION OF 4th DIVISION MACHINE GUNS ON 9th AUGUST

1. 10th M.G.Coy   Target

    2 Guns, ROEUX WOOD.   Enfilade GUN TRENCH from
                                            I.32.a.35.55 to BIT TRENCH.

    4 Guns.   JUNCTION COPSE and DELBAR WOOD.

    12th M.G.Coy.

    2 Guns in 'G' Post.)   CARTRIDGE TRENCH
)   I.32.b.25.15 to
    2 Guns in 'H' Post)   I.32.d.4.7.

    2 Guns HALBERD TRENCH.   To sweep "NO MAN'S LAND" and the
                                            embankment in I.32.a. The fire
                                            of those guns must not be South
                                            of the embankment. FIRE at ZERO.

    2 Guns about BOMB TRENCH.   DEVILS TRENCH from I.32.c.85.10
                                            to junction with CIGAR WOOD. Lift
                                            at ZERO to SACK WOOD.

    234th M.G.Coy.

    2 Guns "M" Post.   Enfilade PELVES LANE from
                                            I.25.a.6.3.

    4 Guns LANCER LANE.   Tracks in I.26.b.

    2 Guns "K" Post.   ANGEL TRENCH.

    2 Guns "K" Post.   SHELL TRENCH.

2. The 12th Division will co-operate by enfilade fire on BIT LANE.

3. All guns, except those in HALBERD TRENCH will fire bursts of 30 rounds at irregular intervals frpm ZERO minus 11½ hours to ZERO.

    At ZERO, all guns increase to 200 rounds a minute.

    Fire will cease on the return of the raiders.

@@*@*@*@*@*@*

4th Div. G.S.

app 9

XVII Corps.

GENERAL CONDITION OF TRENCHES.

FRONT LINE.

(a) South of the River SCARPE the condition of the front line is on the whole good. With the exception of O 2/6, O 2/7 and parts of the line in I.25.d the trenchboards are practically continuous. There are sufficient fire steps, though some need repair. Rifle racks and waterproof recesses for S.A.A. and bombs have been installed.

The post near I.25.b 5.9 has been trench-boarded and revetted.

(b) North of the River SCARPE the conditions are as follows :-

The post near I.20.c 8.8 is trench-boarded and in good condition.

At the Eastern exit of ROEUX our trenches have at times been considerably damaged by shells and trench mortars; taking this into account they are in good condition and trench boarded in swampy places.

The new front line, which has been dug in I.20.a, is sufficiently deep to give cover from view but requires widening. At the occupied posts there are fire steps and a few trench boards; timbered cubby-holes are being constructed.

SUPPORT LINE.

(a) South of the SCARPE

No Support line exists behind the front line Eastwards from BIT LANE. BRIDOON ALLEY will act as a switch or support in case of attack.

This line is continuous to BIT LANE. Firesteps are being re made in many places.

Trench boards exist in the Southern half of SCABBARD SUPPORT, RIFLE SUPPORT, CHAIN SUPPORT. The Northern half of SCABBARD is being treated with trench frames owing to poor nature of soil and constant shelling.

(b) North of the SCARPE.

From I.19.d 20.70 to I.19.d 40.75 the trench is not trench-boarded or sufficiently firestepped.

The proposed extension is shown in green.

The support line is continuous from the junction of CORONA and CABBAGE to sunken road I.19.d 40.75; this trench is trench-boarded throughout.

Sufficient fire steps exist.

RESERVE LINE.
(a) South of the SCARPE.
MUSKET RESERVE is a well traversed and firestepped trench with trench boards throughout.

WELLFORD RESERVE Trench is in the process of being dug out and improved. In the vicinity of JOHNSON AVENUE the trench is in good condition, and is trench-boarded where occupied; fire steps are good and sufficient.

(b) North of the SCARPE.

From CAMP Trench to CEYLON AVENUE this trench is in good condition; it is trench-boarded where the nature of the soil makes it necessary, i.e. in front of MOUNT PLEASANT WOOD. There are a sufficient number of good firesteps.

From CEYLON AVENUE to CORFU AVENUE this trench requires trenchboarding and the addition of some firesteps.

SWITCHES.

BRIDOON ALLEY. This trench is sited for the most part in very wet ground, and requires careful treatment with trench frames. The Southern half has been so treated and the work is being proceeded with.

3.

The trench is continuous and fire-stepped facing East; trench boards exist throughout.

CURB SWITCH SOUTH. This trench is continuous, fire-stepped and trench-boarded.

CURB SWITCH NORTH. The Southern half of this trench has been recently dug out, fire-stepped and trench-boarded. The Northern half is being similarly dealt with.

INTERMEDIATE LINE consists of :-

(a) 5 strong points G. H. K. L. and M.

(b) and 2 portions of LANCER LANE as shown on attached map.

Reference (a) These strong points are provided with a dug-out, and fire-stepped and trench-boarded.

(b) The whole of LANCER LANE is trench-boarded, the fire positions in this communication trench are fire-stepped.

COMMUNICATION TRENCHES.

CEYLON AVENUE except for 300 yards at its Eastern end)
JOHNSON AVENUE) Are trenchboarded
LONE AVENUE) throughout.
BRIDOON AVENUE)
LANCER LANE)

(B) The state of of the entanglement is shown in detail on the attached Map B.

(C) Amount of accommodation in deep dug-outs (completed).

	Officers	Men
SUPPORT LINE	20	300
RESERVE LINE	14	130
INTERMEDIATE LINE	10	200
OTHER PLACES	26	575
	70	1205.

(D) **Amount of accommodation in deep dug-outs** (in process of construction).

	Officers	Men
SUPPORT LINE	6	100
RESERVE LINE	1	30
INTERMEDIATE LINE	–	–
OTHER PLACES	2	75
	9	205

(E) **Numbers and nature of Machine Gun emplacements.**

Position.	Dugout.	Nature of emplacement.	Number of alternative emplacements.

PELVES SECTOR.

Position.	Dugout.	Nature of emplacement.	Number of alternative emplacements.
O.1.b 45.45.	Yes	Open	–
O.1.b 5.5.	Yes	Open	–
O.1.a 55.85.	Yes	Open	2
I.31.d 7.2.	Yes	Open	1
I.31.d 65.60.	Yes	Open	1
H.36.d 30.45.	Yes	Open	1
H.36.c 95.85.	Yes	Open	1
H.36.b 90.20.	Yes	Open	–
I.31.b 45.05.	Yes	Open	–
I.31.b 25.00.	No.	Open	# 1
I.31.a 50.95.	Yes	Open	1
I.25.d 10.00.	No.	Open	–
I.25.d 10.75.	Yes	Open	1
H.30.c 70.20.	Yes	Open	–
H.30.c 05.60.	Yes	Open	1
H.29.b 55.50.	Yes	Open	1
H.23.d 75.60.	Yes	Open	1
I.35.b 35.35.	Yes	Open	1

ROEUX SECTOR.

Position.	Dugout.	Nature of emplacement.	Number of alternative emplacements.
I.19.d 0.2.	Yes	Open	2
I.19.d 10.25.	Yes	Open	2
I.19.d 85.30.	No.	Open	–
I.19.b 85.50.	Yes	Open	1
I.19.b 50.60.	Yes	Open	2
I.19.a 65.05.	No.	Open	2
I.20.a 45.45.	Yes	Open	–
I.19.c 70.50.	Yes	Open	1
I.19.c 10.60	No.	Anti-aircraft.	
H.23.b 80.45.	Yes	Open	2

(F). **MISCELLANEOUS.**

TRENCH TRAMWAYS – is in process of completion (75%); delay has been due to lack of material.

WATER SUPPLY. The reserve at the water point at H.36.a 1.6 has been raised to 850 gallons storage.

ROAD REPAIR. 350 loads of brick and stone have been dumped alongside CHINSTRAP LANE for its repair.

(G). DIVISIONAL ARTILLERY.

23rd A.F.A. Bde.

Communication trenches near Battery positions have been extended. Work has been done on gun pits and dug-outs. Some of the latter having been made 5.9" proof. In 'C' Battery position a telephone pit was under construction.

29th Bde. R.F.A.

Gun pits have been floored with bricks and those of 125th Battery modified so as to increase the arc of fire. Several dug outs have been strengthened with concrete. The water level of the lake in 128th Battery position has been lowered and duck boards have been laid.

Ammunition dumps have been rendered waterproof.

32nd Bde. R.F.A.

Gun pits have been bricked or timbered and recesses for ammunition have been enlarged. Some new pits have been constructed by 135th Battery.

Considerable work has been done on dug-outs throughout this Brigade, accommodation for officers, telephonists and men having been improved.

Some of the O.P's have been rendered weather-proof.

The camouflage of 135th Battery has been repaired and blast-marks have been concealed.

26th August, 1917.

Major General,
Commanding 4th Division.

App. 10

Amended copy of 4 Division
DEFENCE SCHEME.

app 10

SECRET.   Copy No. 16

Herewith amended copy of 4th DIVISION DEFENCE SCHEME.

Please acknowlodge receipt.

* The original copy issued to you on 8th July, 1917, should be destroyed.

                                                           A.E.C. Williams,
                                                          Lieut-Colonel,

29th August, 1917.   General Staff, 4th Division.

Copy No. 1 to 10th Brigade.
        2 to 11th Brigade.
        3 to 12th Brigade.
        4 to C.R.A., 4th Divn.
        5 to C.R.E., 4th Divn.
     * 6 to D.L.G.O.
     * 7 to 234th M.G.Coy.
        8 to Signals, 4th Divn.
        9 to A.D.M.S.
      10 to 4th Divn. "Q".
      11 to XVIIth Corps.
      12 to 12th Division.
      13 to 17th Division.
      14 to File.
      15) to War Diary.
      16)

    * Not issued.

4th DIVISION - DEFENCE SCHEME.

INDEX.

1. General.
2. Boundaries.
3. General description of country and main tactical features.
4. Detail of defences.
5. Organisation and development of trenches.
6. Communication trenches.
7. Dispositions.
8. Machine Gun defence.
9. Anti-Aircraft Machine guns and Lewis guns.
10. Action in case of attack.
11. Communications.
12. Signal Communications.
13. Artillery defence and Liaison with Infantry.
14. Medical arrangements.
15. Administration of areas.

MAPS.

Map A. Boundaries and Lines of defence.

Map B. Machine gun defence.

Plan C. Signal Communications. ***

APPENDICES.

1. Light railways, Water Service and Roads used as lines of supply.
2. List of Camps.
3. Distribution of Ammunition and Grenades.
4. System of Salvage.
5. Strong Points.
6. Inland Water Transport - River SCARPE.

*** NOT attached as the original Plan C issued on 8th July, 1917, does not require to be amended.

4th DIVISION DEFENCE SCHEME.

1. GENERAL.

The XVII Corps front is divided into a Right, a Centre and a Left Sector, each of which is held by one Division.

The Centre Sector is held by the 4th Division, on a frontage of approximately 4000 yards, astride the River SCARPE.

The front of the 4th Division is sub-divided into two Sectors, viz.-

　　PELVES Sector on the right and
　　ROEUX Sector on the left.

2. BOUNDARIES.

(a) Between VI Corps and XVII Corps.

　　GORDON AVENUE inclusive to XVII Corps from its junction with the front line about O.14.a 7.6, to N.18.a 0.7, thence the grid line between Squares N.17 and N.11 produced Westwards.

(b) Between XVII Corps and XIII Corps.

　　I.1.b 0.8 - road junction at H.4.b 8.5 - GAVRELLE-St.NICHOLAS road (inclusive to XIII Corps) as far as POINT DU JOUR - thence due West along grid line to the St.CATHERINE-LES TILLEULS road.

(c) Between the Right and Centre Divisions.

　　O.2.b 0.6 - Southern edge of Northern TWIN COPSE - Southern corner of ARROW HEAD COPSE - Junction of BRIDOON ALLEY and ORCHARD RESERVE - thence along ORCHARD RESERVE, ORANGE AVENUE and APPLE AVENUE (all inclusive to the Right Division) - thence along Southern grid line of H Square to its junction with the ARRAS-CAMBRAI road - thence along the road (inclusive to Right Division).

(d) Between the Centre and Left Divisions.

　　I.14.c 6.2 - Trench junction I.13.d 95.25 (to 4th Division) - junction of CUSP TRENCH and CORFU ALLEY (to 17th Division) - CORFU ALLEY (to 17th Division) to junction with CRUMP Trench - Railway bridge over River SCARPE in H.24.a (to 4th Division) - thence the River SCARPE (to 4th Division).

　　N.B. The River SCARPE will be a common waterway to both Divisions.

(e) Between the Right and Left Brigades.

　　I.31.b 35.85 - SCABBARD ALLEY - Battn. H.Q. (H.30.d 1.3) - Railway crossing at H.23.b 65.35 (all inclusive to the Left Brigade).

3. GENERAL DESCRIPTION OF COUNTRY AND MAIN TACTICAL FEATURES.

(a) Enemy's position.

The main physical feature on the immediate front of the Division is the Spur, running from what is known as GREENLAND HILL on the North of the Railway to HAUSA and DELBAR WOODS, which screens from view all the ground immediately East of it and gives the enemy excellent observation. From Hausa Wood the ground falls steeply to the River SCARPE. In front of the ROEUX Sector there is a slight rise before the ground falls into a depression running N.E. from the Eastern end of ROEUX. This depression which would otherwise be dead ground, can be observed from our positions at the Eastern end of ROEUX. Beyond this depression the ground rises to HAUSA and DELBAR Woods, which dominate our positions North of the SCARPE. The enemy also has excellent observation from the main spur running from MONCHY LE PREUX towards BIACHE ST.VAAST and from the high ground about JIG SAW and HATCHET Woods, from which points the whole of the area North of the SCARPE between GREENLAND HILL and the FAMPOUX line is under observation.

(b) Our own position.

The GAVRELLE-FAMPOUX line North of the River (in the Left Division area) and ORANGE HILL South of the River give good observation as far as the GREENLAND HILL - DELBAR Wood Ridge. From MONCHY LE PREUX a good view can be obtained of the slopes running South and East from DELBAR Wood down to the River SCARPE, and of the enemy's lines South of the River.

(c) Tactical points in our lines.

(i) North of the SCARPE.

The CHEMICAL WORKS and STATION Buildings (Left Division area) form the most likely objective for a local attack. The Eastern end of ROEUX might also be attacked with a view to denying to us observation up the Valley in front of DELBAR Wood mentioned in (a).

(ii) South of the SCARPE.

MONCHY LE PREUX (Right Division area) forms the most probable objective for any attack on the XVII Corps front and it is unlikely that an attack in force would be made on the 4th Division front except in connection with the above.

4. DETAIL OF DEFENCES.

Defences within the Divisional area consist of :-

(a) Front System - consisting of firing line, support and reserve line.

(b) Intermediate Line.

(c) Corps Line.

The above are shown on attached Map 'A'.

5. ORGANISATION AND DEVELOPMENT OF TRENCHES.

(a) Front Line. South of the SCARPE, from Trench O 2/6 to Trench I 25/3, there is a continuous fire trench.

The field of fire is generally restricted but the greater part of the front South of the River can be flanked by fire from near RIFLE Farm (I.31.d 8.6) and from the vicinity of ARROW HEAD COPSE.

The lower ground in the SCARPE Valley does not admit of digging and the line is held, both South and North of the River, by means of detached posts.

North of the SCARPE from the Eastern end of ROEUX Village the front line is again continuous.

(b) Support Line. The Support Line from Right to Left runs along CHAIN SUPPORT, RIFLE SUPPORT and SCABBARD SUPPORT to the Lagoon in I.25.a. North of the SCARPE the Support Line runs along CORONA SUPPORT from I.19.d 4.7 to I.14.c 0.2.

(c) Switches.

(i) BRIDOON ALLEY forms a switch line between CHAIN SUPPORT (at its junction with BIT LANE) and ORCHARD RESERVE, in the event of the Front Line East of MONCHY being lost.

(ii) CURB SWITCH NORTH forms a flank defence between RIFLE SUPPORT and MUSKET RESERVE in the event of CHAIN SUPPORT and BRIDOON ALLEY being lost.

4.

  (iii) CURB SWITCH SOUTH joins MUSKET RESERVE to ORCHARD RESERVE and forms part of the RESERVE LINE, facing South East.

  (iv) CORONA SWITCH, North of the River, when completed, will form a flank defence between CORONA SUPPORT and CORDITE RESERVE facing South, in the event of the Eastern end of ROEUX being lost.

  (v) COLOMBO SWITCH connects the front line with the Support Line and forms a defence facing N.E. in the event of the front line in I.14 being lost.

 (d) <u>Reserve Line</u>. South of the River, runs along CURB SWITCH SOUTH, MUSKET RESERVE and WELFORD RESERVE; and North of the River along CORDITE RESERVE.

 (e) <u>Intermediate Line</u>. South of the River SCARPE runs along LANCER AVENUE and includes Strong Points G.H.K.L. and M.

  North of the River SCARPE (Left Division area) the Intermediate Line is being dug and wired in H.17.b and H.11.c. FAMPOUX and the low ground between it and the Railway are defended by cross machine-gun fire; a gun being maintained by the 234th M.G.Coy. near the Railway Bridge (H.24.a 45.75) to cross with machine guns of the Left Division in the Intermediate Line.

 (f) <u>Corps Line.</u> The general line is shown (in yellow) on Map 'A'.

6. <u>COMMUNICATION TRENCHES.</u>

 <u>PELVES SECTOR.</u>

  (i) APPLE AVENUE - ORANGE AVENUE together with ORCHARD RESERVE - BRIDOON ALLEY form a communication trench to the extreme right of the Divisional Front.

  (ii) LIME ALLEY when completed will form a communication trench between ORANGE AVENUE (H.36.d 4.4) and LANCER AVENUE via the HAPPY VALLEY in H.36.a.

  (iii) LONE AVENUE, connects LANCER AVENUE with RIFLE SUPPORT. MUSKET RESERVE together with CURB SWITCH NORTH or SOUTH also form a communication trench to the right of the Divisional Front.

ROEUX SECTOR.

(i) JOHNSON AVENUE (South of the River).

(ii) CEYLON AVENUE (North of the River).

(iii) CORDITE RESERVE — CORONA SWITCH, when completed, will form an alternative means of communication.

7. DISPOSITIONS.

(a) The PELVES sector is held by one Brigade with two Battalions in the front line, finding their own supports, and reserves, and two Battalions, (less two Companies) in Reserve in WILDERNESS CAMP.

One Company of each of the Battalions in Reserve is in the Intermediate Line; they provide garrisons for Strong Points G.H.K.L. and M. (vide Appendix 5.)

The garrison of each of these Strong Points will also include one M.G. detachment (vide Appendix 5.)

A small garrison will always be kept in CURB SWITCH NORTH and SOUTH.

(b) The ROEUX sector is held by one Brigade with two Battalions in the front line, one North and the other South of the River SCARPE, finding their own supports and reserves.

Two Battalions are in Reserve; one in STIRLING CAMP and one in MIDDLESEX CAMP.

(c) Divisional Reserve. One Brigade is in Divisional Reserve, distributed between BAROSSA, BALMORAL, BLANGY PARK, RIFLE, FIFE and DINGWALL CAMPS. Brigade H.Q. is in LOGAN CAMP.

8. MACHINE GUN DEFENCE.

Map 'B' shows Machine Gun Battle Positions and the allocation of M.G. Companies to positions. The 234th Machine Gun Company will earmark 8 machine gun detachments to man the positions in the Corps Line shown on Map 'B'. The officers and N.C.Os. concerned will be thoroughly acquainted with the quickest way to the positions which their guns are detailed to occupy.

9. **MACHINE AND LEWIS GUNS FOR ANTI-AIRCRAFT DEFENCE.**

Brigades holding the line are responsible for Anti-aircraft Machine and Lewis Gun defence in their respective areas.

One A.A. gun of the 234th M.G.Company is in position at I.19.a 1.6.

10. **ACTION IN CASE OF ATTACK.**

(a) The front and support lines will be the main lines of resistance and will be defended to the last. Any local successes will be neutralized by immediate counter-attacks made by the local supports and reserve.

Plans for action in case of attack will be drawn up by the G.O.C. each Brigade sector, and by battalion and Company Commanders in the line.

All battalions are at the disposal of Brigade Commander with the exception that the garrisons of the Strong Points G.H.K.L, and M. will not be ordered to leave them.

(b) The Brigade in Divisional Reserve, under Divisional orders will be closed up to the front and occupy the Corps line South of the River with two battalions. Assembly areas, and the routes to them, for the remainder of the Brigade will be reconnoitred.

(c) <u>Action of working parties.</u>

Working parties in the front system will assemble and report to the Battalion Headquarters of the Sector in which they are working, those West of the front system will assemble and report to the Headquarters of their own unit.

11. **COMMUNICATIONS.** (See Appendix 1.)

12. **SIGNAL COMMUNICATIONS.**

(a) <u>Telephones and Telegraph.</u>

From Divisional Headquarters to the forward exchange in the Railway Embankment H.14.a 1.7, there are 3 distinct routes, all of which are buried 6 ft. over part of the distance

From the forward exchange to the Brigades in the line there are 2 routes. One is a 6 ft. bury up to the Right

Brigade Headquarters. Here the bury branches at a test box in 3 different directions. One comes back to the Left Brigade Headquarters. The second continues to the report centre of the Right Brigade at the Gun Pits, H.35.b 9.0; from this, buried lines are taken off, pinned into the sides of the trenches and led into the 2 Battalion Headquarters in the line of the Right Brigade, and to the right battalion of the Left Brigade, which are close by the route, and thence on to the front line. The third branch goes forward to the left battalion in the line of the Left Brigade and thence in trenches to the front line.

From the Divisional exchange in the Railway Embankment H.14.a there is an alternative line which is buried 6 ft. for about 500 yards, it then runs along the Railway Embankment as far as the SCARPE, whence it is pegged into the bank of the SCARPE up to the wooden bridge, East of ATHIES LOCK, thence overland in to the bury at the Left Brigade Headquarters and on to the Right Brigade Headquarters.

The two Brigade Headquarters are connected laterally by a 6 ft. buried route.

From Divisional Headquarters to each Brigade Headquarters in the line, there is one direct line, on which speaking and telegraph work is done simultaneously. It is connected through permanently at the exchange in the Railway Embankment H.14.a. There are several lines from Divisional Headquarters to this exchange, and spare lines from it to Brigades, which can be plugged through as required.

The Reserve Brigade has a direct telephone line with telegraph superimposed.

All lines are metallic pairs, Fullerphones being worked on those forward of the Brigades.

(b) <u>Wireless</u>.

At the LONE COPSE Battalion Headquarters, H.30.d 1.3, there is a wireless station which is in communication with a Corps wireless station at ARRAS. Messages received in ARRAS through this set are transmitted by wire to any unit on the

telephone or telegraph system.   There is also at the LONE COPSE
station an Amplifier which receives from three Power Buzzers on
the South of the SCARPE.   One Power Buzzer is allotted to each
battalion and is in position at one of the Company Headquarters in
the line.

At Pt.H.24.b 6.4 in CRUMP Trench there is an Amplifier
station which receives from a Power Buzzer at one of the Companies
in the line of the Battalion North of the SCARPE.   This Amplifier
station is in telephonic communication with the Battalion Headquarters in CRETE Trench.

(c) Visual.

Visual is established from each of the two Battalions of
the Right Brigade to a station close to Right Brigade Headquarters.

The two battalions of the Left Brigade are in visual
communication with one another and the left battalion is in
communication with the Left Brigade.

(d) Artillery Communications.

A forward office has been opened at H.13.d 8.6 in the
Railway Embankment.

From this office telephonic communication is established
to all brigades of Artillery under the command of the C.R.A. 4th
Division, to Corps Artillery Brigades, and to the 2 Inf.Brigs.
in the line.

13. ARTILLERY DEFENCE.

    (a) ZONES.

        (i) The front is covered by two Field Artillery Groups.

            Right Group. 32nd Bde.R.F.A. and 1 18 pdr. Bty. 48th
                              A.F.A.Bde. cover Right Inf.Brig.

            Left Group. 29th Bde.R.F.A. and 1 18 pdr. Seetn.
                              48th A.F.A.Bde. cover Left Inf.Brig.

        (ii) The senior Brigade Commander commands the Group.

    (b) LIAISON.

        (i) Group Commanders keep in close touch with Inf.Brig.
             Commanders and maintain a direct wire to them.

        (ii) A Field Artillery Liaison Officer remains at each
             Battalion H.Q. in the line and maintains a direct
             line to his respective Artillery Brigade.

(c) S.O.S.

    (i) S.O.S. 18 pdr. barrage is put down 200 yards in front of our front line trench or posts; 4.5" Hows. fire on selected points, Heavy and Siege Artillery on areas and points beyond Field Artillery barrages.

    (ii) S.O.S. barrage is fired on demand by telephone or firing of S.O.S. Signal from the Central Station in each Group.

14. MEDICAL ARRANGEMENTS.

(a) The Medical Aid Posts are as follows :-

1. H.24.b 2.8 (for battalion North of the SCARPE).
2. H.30.d 4.9.
3. H.36.a 2.2 (shared by the two battalions of Right Brigade).

(b) Relay Posts.

1. I.31.c 3.8.
2. TRIPLE ARCH (shared with Division on left for loading pontoons).
3. H.24.c 5.7.
4. H.29.c 5.5.
5. ARRAS Basin (for unloading pontoons).

(c) Advanced Dressing Stations.

1. FAMPOUX Lock.
2. FEUCHY.

(d) Main Dressing Station.

Deaf and Dumb Institute, ARRAS.

(e) Evacuation.

North of the SCARPE. By hand carriage to TRIPLE ARCH H.24.a 5.6; thence by pontoon to FAMPOUX.

South of the SCARPE. (a) From Right Battalion of Left Brigade by hand carriage and wheeled stretcher to FAMPOUX along CHINSTRAP LANE.
(b) From forward Battalions of Right Brigade by hand carriage and wheeled stretcher to FEUCHY by cross country tracks.

    The right battalions of Left Brigade and two battalions of Right Brigade are only cleared by night, on account of enemy observation of lines of evacuation. If it is necessary to get rid of walking cases from these battalions during the daytime, they can be directed to FAMPOUX via LANCER LANE.
    From FAMPOUX cases are evacuated by barge to ARRAS Basin and thence by motor ambulance to M.D.Stns.
    From FEUCHY cases are evacuated to the M.D.Stn. either by motor ambulances or by railway to G.22.a 3.8 and thence by motor ambulance to the M.D.Stn. ARRAS.
    From ARRAS by motor ambulances to C.S.Stns.

15. ADMINISTRATION OF AREAS.

(a) Administrative Areas.

The Divisional Area is sub-divided into three areas for the purpose of accommodation, sanitation and general administration as follows :-

    (i) ATHIES BLANGY AREA, Headquarters G.17.d 3.5; all that portion of 17th Division area North of River SCARPE to 4th German System (excl.) in which troops of 4th Division are quartered.

    (ii) FEUCHY AREA, Headquarters H.19.central; the Divisional area South of the River SCARPE, and North of Railway up to HIMALAYA Trench (excl.)

    (iii) ORANGE HILL AREA, Headquarters H.31.b; the Divisional area South of the Railway to HIMALAYA Trench (incl.)

(b) Camps.

A list of Camps is given in Appendix 2.

(c) R.E. Dumps.

Main Divisional Dump.   BLANGY G.23.b 5.3.
Advanced Divisional Dumps. ATHIES LOCK and H.34.d 9.4.
Forward Emergency Dump.   CRUMP WHARF H.24.central.

Stores are moved by lorry or Decauville Railway to Advanced Divisional Dumps and thence principally by water transport or tramway to the nearest point where the stores are required.

(d) Water Supply.

Water tanks have been installed at H.36.a 2.8; they are filled by pipe line from a Reservoir at H.29.c 5.6, which is supplied from the Corps main.

Some water tanks, which have been placed at H.24.a 4.7, are filled by pipe line from a well near FAMPOUX LOCK.

The following wells exist in ROEUX at I.19.b 3.6, I.19.b 4.3, I.19.d 6.6. As regards the first mentioned it can be reached by a communication trench; it has a pump and two tanks; it gives good water.

There are the usual village wells in ATHIES and FAMPOUX; a sufficient number are kept in working order to meet requirements.

11.

Water points for filling carts and water bottles exist at the following places :-

<u>Carts and bottles.</u> G.24.b 7.5, H.20.b 6.1, H.31.a 6.5, H.32.d 8.0.

<u>Bottles only.</u> H.28.a 4.2, H.28.a 5.8, H.28.c 5.8.

(e) <u>Ammunition.</u>

The positions of dumps are as follows :-

(i) Main Divisional Dump.   CHESTER CAVE G.29.c 1.9
(ii) Advanced Divisional Dumps. ATHIES LOCK (H.21.a 3.7).
    FEUCHY DUMP (H.21.d 8.1).
    H.34.b 5.0.
(iii) Right Brigade Dump.   H.36.c 1.8.
(iv) Left Brigade Dump.   H.23.b 7.4.
    (H.24.d 9.8 Emergency Dump).
(v) A reserve S.A.A. dump for use in the Corps Line has been placed beside the Decauville Railway near H.34.a 8.6.

The distribution of S.A.A., grenades and bombs is given in Appendix 3.

(f) <u>Salvage.</u>

The location of Salvage Dumps and the general system of salvage is given in Appendix 4.

APPENDIX 1.

LIGHT RAILWAYS, WATER SERVICE and ROADS
USED AS LINES OF SUPPLY.

The following lines of supply are available in the Divisional area for all stores and working parties.

A. Light Railways.

The main station on this line is at 'Q' Dump, ARRAS.
There are two main branches, one to the North and one to the South of the River SCARPE.
The Northern branch calls at BLANGY LOCK, RAILWAY EMBANKMENT (H.13.d 7.3) and railhead at FAMPOUX LOCK.
The Southern branch calls at IVORY DUMP (G.23.d 1.3), Point G.24.d 1.6, Railway Triangle and railhead at H.22.d 7.3.
A further branch runs South from H.20.d up BATTERY VALLEY to behind ORANGE HILL.

R.E. Stores.

Indents for R.E.Stores (showing destinations to be carried by this railway should be submitted to the Adjutant, R.E., by 10 a.m. each day. Loading of stores at the main R.E.Dump and off-loading at the advanced R.E.Dump at H.34.d 9.4 will be arranged by C.R.E.; at all other points off-loading parties must be arranged by units concerned, and one man should accompany each consignment.
In the case of the advanced R.E.Dump at H.34.d 9.4, all stores must be removed by transport or carrying parties the same night that they arrive.

Rations, etc.

Application for truck accommodation should be sent direct to the O.C. 31st Light Railway Operating Company, R.E., 'Q' Dump, by Quartermasters for the conveyance of rations, etc.
Arrangements for loading and off-loading must be made by units concerned.

Ammunition, etc.

The same procedure should be adopted by 'Q' for the conveyance of ammunition, etc.

B. Pontoon Service.

This service is arranged by the I.W.T., to whom indents are sent at ARRAS Basin.
Barges run from ARRAS Basin to FAMPOUX; they are available for transport of personnel, including casualties, R.E. material, also ammunition up to 18 pdr. and 4.5" How. shells.
A time table is given in Appendix 6.

C. Roads.

The following roads are open to wheeled transport :-

(i) St.NICHOLAS - St.LAURENT BLANGY - ATHIES - FAMPOUX - FAMPOUX LOCK ROAD.

(ii) BLANGY - FEUCHY (South of River SCARPE).

(iii) ATHIES - ATHIES LOCK - FEUCHY - FAMPOUX LOCK ROAD.

(iv) FAMPOUX LOCK - LEVEL CROSSING (H.23.b 7.3) - PELVES ROAD as far as H.30.b 7.2.
Care must be taken in using this road in dry weather and when the wind is in the West, to prevent the noise of the traffic reaching the enemy.

(v) ARRAS - St.SAUVEUR - TILLOY ROAD up to FEUCHY CHAPEL, thence due North along CHAPEL ROAD for half a mile - thence due East by track to H.36.c 1.9.
The track from CHAPEL ROAD to H.36.c 1.9 is liable to be cut up in wet weather.

D. Overland Tracks.

Arrangements have been made for overland tracks from H.36.a 3.3 along LONE LANE up to its junction with RIFLE TRENCH, and along MUSKET TRENCH AND MONCHY TRENCH up to its junction with CHAIN TRENCH. An Artillery track, which runs roughly parallel to JOHNSON AVENUE, leads into the RAVINE in I.25.d; a branch track connects with CHINSTRAP LANE.

E. Lateral communication across the SCARPE.

(i) The St.LAURENT BLANGY - BLANGY main road.
(ii) The ATHIES - FEUCHY road.
(iii) From FAMPOUX via FAMPOUX LOCK to junction of roads at H.23.b 2.4.

In addition to the above, there are the following bridges across the River SCARPE :-

(iv) At G.16.d 3.3 - wooden bridge to take Infantry in fours and field guns.
(v) At H.13.c 25.35 - wooden foot bridge.
(vi) At H.13.d 9.3 - wooden foot bridge.
(vii) At H.22.a 75.20 - wooden bridge to take light vehicles.
(VIII) At H.24.a 45.75 - wooden bridge to take Infantry and pack animals.
(ix) H.24.a 6.4 - wooden - Infantry in file.
(x) H.24.central - Infantry in file.
(xi) H.24.d 65.70 - Infantry in file.

APPENDIX 2.

The following is a list of Camps in the Divisional Area (and part of 17th Division Area), showing the estimated accommodation in each available for Divisional troops. The whole of the Embankment and Camps at H.13.d from the road to the River will be known as STIRLING CAMP, and that part North of the road as LANCASTER CAMP.

CAMP.	Map Reference.	Marquees.	Boll Tents.	Shelters.	Bivouacs.	Accommodation Officers.	Accommodation Other ranks	Remarks.
LOGAN	G.16.b 4.7.	—	—	15	1	Brig.Headquarters.		4 Nissen Huts.
FIFE	G.16.b 7.7.	—	23	6	2	15	360	
BALMORAL	G.18.a 2.7.	1	11	12	8	15	500	
BAROSSA	G.18.a 5.5.	—	—	Tin Shelters.	—	25	800	
DINGWALL	G.18.c 4.9.	—	29	8	7	15	480	
STIRLING	H.13.d 6.6.	—	18	53	128	25	1000	Will be 1700 when finished
RIFLE	G.24.b 7.4.	1	113	—	—	20	1200	
BLANGY PARK	G.24.b 3.6.	1	37	—	—	8	400	
TRIANGLE	H.19.central.	—	—	Tin Shelters.	Dug-outs.	40	900	
MIDDLESEX	G.18.c 2.9.	—	33	—	—	8	300	
BLANGY village	G.24.a 8.6.	—	—	Cellars	—	6	200	
WILDERNESS	H.25.d 9.2.	—	—	69	Dug-outs.	20	800	
SCOTS VALLEY	H.25.c	—	40	20	—	25	500	

APPENDIX 3.

DISTRIBUTION OF GRENADES AND BOMBS.

ECHELON	WHERE STORED	STOKES	No.24	GRENADES MILLS	No.23	VERY Lights
Sectors ..... In front line system ..... 2 Battns. ...	20% fire trench) 30% support ") 50% Reserve Co.)	400	500	2000	1000	5000
Support Bn.	In reserve line) of front line) system.)	-	-	2000	-	5000
Reserve Bn.	In camp.	-	-	2000	-	-
Bde.Reserve.	--------	1000	500	5000	1000	-
Total per Bde.Sector.	--------	1400	1000	11000	2000	10000
Div.Reserve.	--------	2000	1500	15000	2000	15000

MOBILE RESERVE.

Div.Amm.Col.	--------			5520		
Inf.Units.	--------			9984		

COLOURED LIGHTS (VERY) AND GROUND FLARES ISSUED ACCORDING TO THE ALLOTMENT MADE BY THE CORPS.

DISTRIBUTION OF S.A.A. FOR A BRIGADE SECTOR.

ECHELONS.	NUMBER OF GUNS.	TOTAL NUMBER OF ROUNDS
2 Bns. in front line (each 50000)	-	100000
Lewis Guns in front line system at 2000 rounds per gun.	32	64000
Support Battalion.	16	82000
Reserve Battalion.	16	82000
M.G.Coy. (at 4500 per gun).	16	72000
Brigade Reserve.	-	200000
		600000

DIVISIONAL RESERVE - 400000 rounds.

APPENDIX 4.

SALVAGE.

1. Salvage operations are carried out generally under the supervision of the Divisional Salvage Officer who resides at Divisional Headquarters.

The system is as follows :-

(a) Operations in the area forward of the YELLOW Line, N. and S. through H.29.a 0.0 are conducted by the salvage sections of the Brigades in the line.

(b) Operations behind this line are conducted under the direction of the Divisional Salvage Officer, who has at his disposal the salvage section of the Brigade not actually in the line, and about 25 O.R. of the Divisional Employment Company.

2. An Emergency Salvage Dump is established at FAMPOUX LOCK.

The main Divisional Salvage Dump is situated at ATHIES LOCK.

3. The method of assembling salvage at main dump is briefly as follows :-

Salved material is collected and is handed into any of the dumps.

The material collected under Brigade arrangements is, whenever possible, sent direct to the main Divisional Dump or to the Divisional shed at the XVII Corps dump by returning supply wagons.

Material handed in at FAMPOUX is conveyed by pontoons or light railway to ATHIES, thence by light railway to the XVII Corps Dump G.29.c 1.3.

Material collected at ATHIES by Light Railway to the XVII Corps Dump G.29.c 1.3.

4. On arrival at the Corps Dump the material is taken into the Divisional shed where it is checked and sorted under the direction of the Divisional representative, who then hands over the material to the Corps Salvage Officer.

APPENDIX 5.

STRONG POINTS.

1. A series of Strong Points have been constructed in the Intermediate Line with a view to breaking up an attack should the enemy succeed in penetrating our front line system. They will be defended to the last.

2. These Strong Points, which are 5 in number, are lettered G. H. K. L. and M.
   The map location and permanent garrison of each is as follows :-

POST.	LOCATION.	PERMANENT GARRISON.
G. Post.	H.36.d 3.4.	1 officer, 20 o.r. and a M.G. Detachment.
H. Post.	H.36.c 9.9.	-- do --
K. Post.	H.30.c 0.6.	1 N.C.O. 10 men and a M.G. Detachment.
L. Post.	H.29.b 55.50.	-- do --
M. Post.	H.23.d 75.55.	-- do --

Note. The M.G. Detachments for G. and H. Posts will be provided by the M.G.Coy. of the Brigade holding the PELVES Sector; those for K. L. and M. Posts by the 234th M.G.Coy. The Battalion furnishing the garrisons for K. L. and M. Posts will detail an officer to supervise the three posts.

3. The garrisons will not leave their posts except for work within a distance of 200 yards, without orders from Brigade H.Q.
   In the event of an enemy attack, the Machine Guns and Lewis Guns may be taken forward to suitable positions to obtain a better field of fire.

4. The garrison is responsible for the maintenance of their post and the wire around it. A programme showing work in hand will be posted up and handed over to relieving garrisons.

5. The following S.A.A., stores, etc. will be maintained in each post. They will be handed over on relief, and a receipt obtained for them :-

    100 rounds S.A.A. per man.
    5000 rounds S.A.A. per Machine Gun.
    100 sandbags.
    6 boxes of bombs.
    20 shovels.
    10 picks.
  * 1 day's reserve rations per man.
  * 12 petrol tins.

  * 'G' and 'H' Posts only.

APPENDIX 6.

INLAND WATER TRANSPORT - RIVER SCARPE.

LAUNCH TIME TABLE ISSUED.

UP.

	a.m.	a.m.	p.m.	p.m.	p.m.
ARRAS dep	5.0	9.0	1.0	5.0	9.0
BLANGY arr.	5.40	9.40	1.40	5.40	9.40
ATHIES arr.	6.10	10.10	2.10	6.10	10.10
FAMPOUX arr	6.50	10.50	2.50	6.50	10.50

DOWN.

	a.m.	a.m.	p.m.	p.m.
FAMPOUX dep	7.0	11.0	3.0	7.0
ATHIES arr.	7.25	11.25	3.25	7.25
BLANGY arr.	8.0	12.0	4.0	8.0
ARRAS arr.	8.30	12.30	4.30	8.30

1. There is a service of motor launches and barges on the river SCARPE in charge of the INLAND WATER TRANSPORT.

2. In addition to the regular service an extra service will be run whenever required to meet special demands.

3. For the present the maximum load that can be **transported** on each trip is - Personnel 100, material 10 Tons.

4. On all journeys from FAMPOUX to ARRAS preference will be given for the carriage of sick and wounded.

5. A launch will always be at the disposal of the Medical Authorities, FAMPOUX, for the carriage of urgent cases.

6. Application for either regular or special services will be made to the D.O.I.W.T. No. 2. Quay, ARRAS.

7. When carriage for explosives or inflamable material is demanded it should be stated on the indent. Under no circumstances is any explosive to be put on board the **barges** without previously informing the N.C.O. i/c of the Convoy.

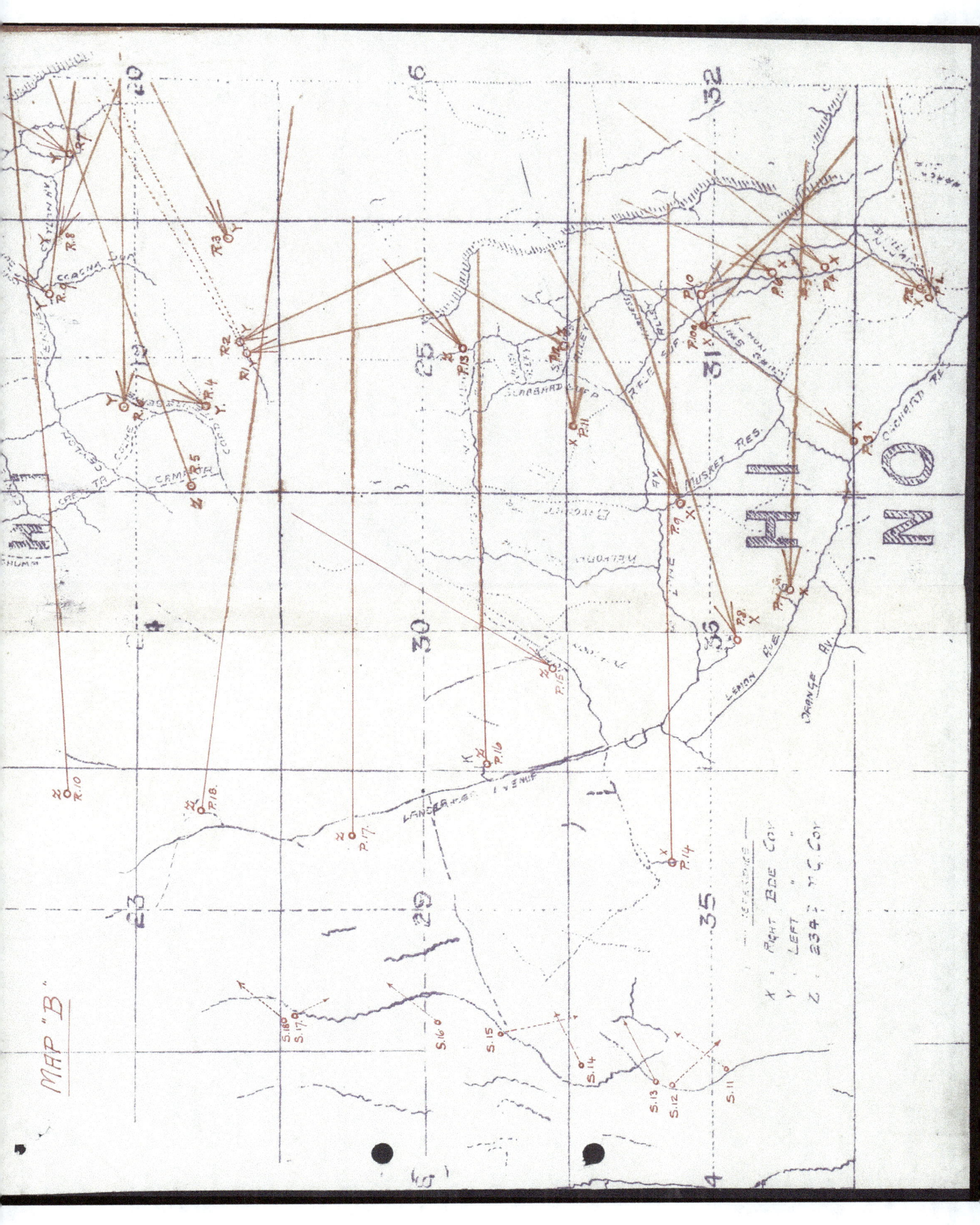

4th Division
War Diaries
General Staff

September 1917.

WAR DIARY or INTELLIGENCE SUMMARY.

Army Form C. 2118.

Place	Date	Hour	Summary of Events and Information	Remarks and references to Appendices
G.16 b 7.7.	1st	F	Increased hostile artillery activity	
"	2nd		Our Artillery carried out harassing fire on FUZE & CARTRIDGE trenches. New work in I.27.a & tracks in I.32.b. O.O. No 58 (a) for relief of 4th Divn by 15th Divn was published.	(a) see appendix 1
"	3rd		Quiet day. Reliefs from right to left: DUKES by ESSEX. KINGS OWN by LAN: FUS. WARWICKS by SEAFORTHS. MIDDLESEX by HOUSEHOLD Bn.	
"	4th		FEUCHY shelled with 15 c.m. shells. Normal harassing fire by our Artillery & MGuns	
"	5th		Patrols report enemy 2nd row of wire near I.20.a & b has been thickened. Considerable amount of fresh tracks noticed notably to west of PICCADILLY trench right of to SCARPE river, also between CYPRUS and CANDY on forward slope of DELBAR RIDGE. During the recent bad weather Div Observers have frequently reported movement in these areas & spotted the latter trench. 11th Brigade Group move to POMMIER area (Move of 16th Brigade to BAILLEUL to BAILLEULMONT (Support & reserve Battalions))	
"	6th		Junction of CEYLON & CABBAGE again damaged by Heavy T. Mortars. Move of 16th Bde group to BAILLEULMONT area completed.	
"	7th		Command of ROEUX Section passed to BGC 45th K/ Bde. area completed	

WAR DIARY
or
INTELLIGENCE SUMMARY.
(Erase heading not required.)

Army Form C. 2118.

Place	Date	Hour	Summary of Events and Information	Remarks and references to Appendices
G.16.b.77.9 BASSEUX	8th		Command of PELVES Sector handed to B.G.C. 46th Inf. Bde. 12th Bde Group went to HENDECOURT area. at 10 am Command of Centre Divl Front passed to G.O.C. 15th Divn. & HQ 4th Divn. opened at BASSEUX.	
BASSEUX	9th to 17th		Training was carried out on the lines detailed in 4th Divn G.B. 9/51 (b) Throughout this period the weather was excellent. The range accommodation, both for the shorter ranges & for Field Firing was good. The instruction in Formation for the attack was based on the latest notes from the Fifth Army as in attached Diagrams A & B (c) A programme of Training is attached (d)	(b) see appendix 2 (c) see appendix 3 (d) see appendix 4
	12th		Major General Lambton CVO. CB. CMG. DSO met with a severe accident while riding round the training areas; his horse came down while crossing a concealed shell hole.	
"	13th		29th F.A. Bde, 22nd F.A Bde & DAC move to XIVth Corps.	
"	14th		Major General T.G. Matheson appointed G.O.C. 4th Divn. Farewell message (e) from General Lambton. Yukon Pack competition under Divl arrangement - Seaforth Hyhrs 1st; 10th M.G.Coy 2nd.	(e) see appendix 5
"	14th		Warning Orders issued (f) & Divn (Arty) will be released to entrain on 18th & Wright on transfer to 5th Army.	(f) see appendix 6
"	15		Divnl Order 39 issued (g) re move of Division to 5th Army.	(g) see appendix 7.

Army Form C. 2118.

WAR DIARY
or
INTELLIGENCE SUMMARY.
(Erase heading not required.)

Instructions regarding War Diaries and Intelligence Summaries are contained in F. S. Regs., Part II. and the Staff Manual respectively. Title pages will be prepared in manuscript.

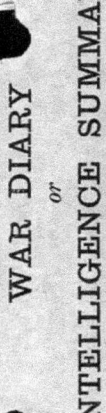

Place	Date	Hour	Summary of Events and Information	Remarks and references to Appendices
BANEUX	17th Sept		Addenda 1 and 2 to Divnl Orders 89 issued (A)	(A) in appendices 7
"	18th Sept		11th Bde Group move to MONDICOURT area	
"	19th		Entrainment of Division in progress	
BANEUX	20th		Entrainment complete. Entraining area de-attached. Div HQ closed at BANEUX (A) and opened at Central Camp TROVEN at same hour. Division came under Command of XIV Corps	(A) See Ap.S.12.
TROVEN (Central Camp)				
TROVEN	21st 22nd 23		Training carried out on the Somme train to Pas division in case / facilities in present area not good.	Tr.ps (b) in appendices 2
"	24th		Div Order 60 issued (b) 4th Div (New Army) will relieve 20th Bde (New Army) on 26th & 27th in right sector of XIV Corps front. G.O.C. 4th Div will assume command at 10am 29th Sept. H.Q. will be established at MEZSM Fm	(b) in appendices 8
"	25th 26th		Training	

Army Form C. 2118.

WAR DIARY
or
INTELLIGENCE SUMMARY.
(Erase heading not required.)

Instructions regarding War Diaries and Intelligence Summaries are contained in F. S. Regs., Part II. and the Staff Manual respectively. Title pages will be prepared in manuscript.

Place	Date	Hour	Summary of Events and Information	Remarks and references to Appendices
PROVEN	Sept 27th		Move of 12th Bde., 406 F.Coy., 234 M.G. Coy. in accordance with Order to complete Div Order No 61 issued (J)	(J) see appendix 9
"	28th		124 Bde relieved 61st Bde (20th Div) in front line (K) Div Order No 62 issued (L) 11th Bde relief 12th Bde night 1/2nd Oct.	(K) see appendix 8 (L) see appendix 10
PROVEN WELSH FM	29th		G.O.C. 4th Division assumed command of Right Sector VIII Corps front at 10 am. Div H.Q. to 2(?)(M) at WELSH FM. for distribution of units see appendix (M) location report attached (*)	(*) see appendix 11
WELSH FM	30th		Durnit night of 29/30 Left Sector Stables and Machine gun posns. area West of LANGEMARK shelled indiscriminately. Boats were dropped during night on Chinen Wood are 2E.17.S.18 Camp. During day enemy shelling of area round DUNSTECOTE.	

WAR DIARY, GENERAL STAFF, 4TH DIVISION.

1st - 30th Sept., 1917.

APPENDICES.

1. Operation Order No. 58.
2. Correspondence showing lines on which training is to be carried out.
3. Diagrams showing formations for attack.
4. Programme of training.
5. Farewell order by Major General HON. W. LAMBTON C.V.O., C.B., C.M.G., D.S.O.
6. Warning order.
7. Div. Order No. 59 with addendas.
8. Div. Order No. 60 with addendas.
* 9. Div. Order No. 61 with Instructions Nos. 1 to 7.
* 10. Div. Order No. 62.
11. List showing positions of Brigades on 29th September.
12. Billeting list showing disposition of Division 21st Sept.
* 13. Preliminary orders for M.G. barrage.
14. Revised App. No. 7 - Defence of Monchy.
   (See Defence Scheme forwarded with War Diary for August).
15. 4th Division Defence Scheme (Provisional).

* These appendices are required in connection with operations and will be forwarded with War Diary for October.

SECRET.   Copy No...21...

4th DIVISION OPERATION ORDER No. 58.

Reference 1/10,000 PLOUVAIN Sheet.   2nd Sept., 1917.
1/100,000 LENS Sheet.

1. The 4th Division (less artillery) will be relieved by the 15th Division (less artillery) in the line during the period 5th to 8th Sept., and come under the orders of the VI Corps from 10 a.m. on latter date.

2. The relief and subsequent moves to the ADINFER Area will be carried out in accordance with attached table.

   Details to be arranged direct between B.G's.C. concerned.

   Completion of reliefs and moves to be reported to Divisional Headquarters.

3. 4th Divisional artillery reliefs will take place during the nights Sept 8/9th - 9/10th and 10/11th.

   Orders regarding reliefs will be issued in due course.

4. D.M.G.O will arrange for the relief of 254th M.G.Company by 225th M.G.Company on 7th and night 7/8th Sept.

5. Field Companies and Pioneer Battalion will be relieved by corresponding troops of 15th Division under arrangements to be made by C.R.E's concerned.

   The two sections of the N.Z.Tunnelling Coy will come under the orders of the 15th Division at the time the command of the sector passes.

6. Separate instructions will be issued for the relief of working parties.

7. Field Ambulances will be relieved under orders of A.D.M.S.

8. Divisional Gas Officer will arrange to hand over to D.G.O., 15th Division all gas appliances by evening 7th Sept.

9. All defence schemes. trench maps, air photos and lists of position calls together with a statement of work in hand and work proposed will be handed over to relieving Brigades.

10. Command of the sector passes to G.O.C 15th Division at 10 a.m. on 8th Sept.

    Command of the artillery will pass to the C.R.A., 15th Division on completion of the artillery reliefs.

11. Divisional Headquarters will close at G.16.b.7.7. at 10 a.m. on Sept 8th and reopen at BASSEUX at the same hour.

12. ACKNOWLEDGE.

A.F.C. Williams
Lt-Colonel,
General Staff, 4th Division.

Issued at 7 p.m.

Copies to :-

No. 1. to 10th Brigade.
    2. 11th Brigade
    3. 12th Brigade.
    4. C.R.A. 4th Divn.
    5. C.R.E., 4th Divn.
    6. A.D.M.S., 4th Divn.
    7. A.P.M., 4th Divn.
    8. Signals 4th Divn.
    9. D.M.G.O., 4th Divn.
   10.)
   11.) 4th Divn "Q".
   12.)
   13. Divn Gas Officer.
   14. Camp Commandant.
   15. 12th Division.
   16. 15th Division.
   17. 17th Division.
   18.)
   19.) XVII Corps.

   20.)
   21.) War Diary.

   22. File.
   23. VI Corps

4th DIVISION.

MOVEMENT TABLE ISSUED WITH 4th DIVISION OPERATION ORDER NO.58.

SERIAL NO.	DATE	UNIT	FROM	TO	ROUTE	REMARKS
1	5th Sept.	11th Inf. Bde.) 11th Inf. Brig.) 526th Fd.Co.R.E.) Group.) 11th Fd.Ambce.	Present Camps.	POMMIER Area.	BLANGY Bridge and any roads South of SCARPE.	Under B.G.C. 11th Inf.Brig. Infantry to be clear of camps by 12 noon but not to start before 11 am
2	6th Sept.	Support and Reserve Battalions 16th Inf.Bde.	Present Camps.	BASSEUX Area.	BLANGY Bridge and any roads South of SCARPE.	On relief by 2 Bns. 45th Inf.Bde. Not to start before 12 noon.
3	Night 6/7 Sept.	10th Inf.Bde. (less 2 Battalions).	ROEUX Sub-sector.	LEWIS Barracks ARRAS.	Any.	On relief by 45th Inf.Bde. (less 2 Battns.) 15th Div.
4	7th Sept.	10th) 10th Inf.Bde. Inf.) (less 2 Battns) Brig.) 9th Fd.Co. R.E. Group.) 10th Fd.Ambce.	ARRAS and present camps.	BASSEUX Area.	ARRAS - DOULLENS and BLANGY Bridge - WAILLY Roads.	Under B.G.C. 10th Inf.Brig.
5	7th Sept.	Support and Reserve battalions 12th Inf.Bde.	Present Camps.	HENDECOURT Area.	BEAURAINS - FICHEUX.	On relief by 2 Bns. 46th Inf.Bde. Not to start before 12 noon.
6	Night 7/8	12th Inf.Brig. (less 2 Battalions).	FEIVES Sub-sector.	LEWIS Barracks ARRAS.	Any.	On relief by 45th Inf.Bde.(less 2 Battns.) 15th Div.

SERIAL NO.	DATE	UNIT	FROM	TO	ROUTE	REMARKS
7	8th Sept.	12th Inf. Brig. Group.) 12th Inf.Bde. (less 2 Battns).) 466th Fd.Co.R.E.) 12th Fd.Ambce.) 21st West Yorks.) 234th M.G.Coy.	ARRAS and present camps.	HENDECOURT Area.	BLANGY Bridge and any roads South of SCARPE.	Under B.G.C. 12th Inf.Bde. To be South of ARRAS-CAMBRAI road by 11 a.m.
8	8th Sept.	Divnl.Headquarters. Divnl. R.E. Hd.Qrs. Ed.Qrs.) 4th Sig.Coy. No.1 Sectn)	Present Camps.	BASSEUX.	BLANGY Bridge and any roads South of SCARPE.	Under Camp Commdt. To be clear of camp by 10.15 a.m

1. All units not mentioned in above table will move under the orders of A.A. & Q.M.G.

2. East of a line drawn from BLANGY to TILLOY all movements by units will be by platoons at 200 yards distance.

3. West of the above line the following distances will be maintained between units on the march :-

    Between Companies.   200 yards.
       "   Battalions.   400 yards.
       "   Transport of   100 yards.
          units.

4th Division No. G.B. 9/51.

10th Infantry Brigade.
11th Infantry Brigade.
12th Infantry Brigade.

1.   The Divisional Commander wishes training during the period that the Division is in the ADINFER Area to be carried out on the lines indicated below :-

The time available for training is short and will probably not exceed a fortnight, consequently the importance of drawing up beforehand carefully prepared programmes so as not to waste time on arrival in the new area must be impressed on Battalion Commanders.

2.   The 1st week from September 9th to September 15th will be devoted to :-

A. The Organization and training of Platoons.
B. Company Training.

The number of days allotted to Platoon and Company training is left to the discretion of Brigade Commanders.

A. Platoon Training will comprise :-

(a) Musketry, to include rapid loading, fire control and Mutual Support.
(b) The attack from a trench line.
(c) The attack over the open.
(d) The attack on a Strong Point, such as a machine gun emplacement or machine gun nest, which may call for independent action by a Platoon Commander.

In conjunction with the above, full use should be made of the rifle to provide fire to cover movement.

Platoons will be organized in accordance with S.S. 143 "Instructions for the Training of Platoons for Offensive action", under their probable Commanders as soon as possible.

An understudy for each platoon and section commander should be trained. His name should be made known to all ranks and he should be given opportunities of commanding.

B. Company Training will be carried out on the same lines, special attention being paid to the following points :-

B. Company Training will be carried out on the same lines, special attention being paid to the following points :-

(a) <u>Mopping-up Parties</u> both for trench, semi-open or open warfare.
In the recent fighting in FLANDERS, it has been found that supports and reserves have frequently suffered severely from machine gun fire owing to organized shell holes and other concealed defences being left uncleared.

(b) <u>The importance of rifle fire and Lewis gun fire should be impressed on all ranks.</u>
The rifle is the principal weapon of Infantry, grenades are merely secondary and used for special occasions.

(c) <u>The use of Machine guns and Stokes Mortars.</u>
A proportion of these should be allotted to Companies when doing tactical exercises.

(d) <u>Frequent gas helmet drill</u>; men should be accustomed to wearing their helmets for lengthy periods and should be practised in musketry, digging and marching with their helmets on.

(e) <u>Intensive digging, consolidation and use of shell holes.</u>

(f) <u>The organization of working and carrying parties</u> should be gone into carefully.
The YUKON Pack has proved of great use in the recent fighting in FLANDERS.
10 men per Infantry Company, machine gun company and trench mortar battery should be trained in the use of the pack and in the method of securing loads on to it.

Programmes of training for the 1st week will be submitted to Divisional Headquarters by 12 noon on 8th Sept.

3. If time permits Battalion training will be carried out.

4. All officers should study the pamphlet S.S. 135 "Instructions for the training of Divisions for offensive action".

Copies of "Notes on recent information regarding German methods of defence" are being issued separately.

5. Whilst the Division is in the training area all reinforcements on arrival will be sent direct to their units.

(Sgd) A.F.C.WILLIAMS, Lt-Colonel,
General Staff, 4th Division,

4th Sept., 1917.

Copy to C.R.E.

App. 3

BATTALION ATTACK
Two Companies Each On Two Platoon Front.

(Diagram showing battalion attack formation)

Skirmishing Line extended to 5 paces or more
75ˣ — 12 to 15 Men (repeated across front)

No 3 Coy — No 2 Platoon / No 1 Platoon (Section Columns)
No 1 Coy — No 2 Platoon / No 1 Platoon (Section Columns)

No 4 Platoon / No 3 Platoon — Section Columns
Moppers Up ← From reserve platoons or companies

No 4 Coy — Platoon or Section Columns
No 2 Coy — Platoon or Section Columns

Attacking Line — 100 yds
Support Line — 100 to 150 yds
Reserve Line — 150 to 200 yds

B/

BATTALION ATTACK
Four Companies Each on one Platoon Front

	No.4 Coy No.1 Platoon	No.3 Coy No.1 Platoon	No.2 Coy No.1 Platoon	No.1 Coy No.1 Platoon
75 yds — 15 Men	Skirmishing line 5 paces extension	Skirmishing line 5 paces extension	Skirmishing line 5 paces extension	Skirmishing line 5 paces extension

Section Columns — Section Columns — Section Columns — Section Columns

No.2 Platoon — No.2 Platoon — No.2 Platoon — No.2 Platoon

Moppers Up — No.3 Platoon

Artillery Formation — No.4 Platoon

Distances:
- 100 yds
- 100 to 150 yds
- 150 to 200 yds
- 150 to 200 yds

App 4

PROGRAMME OF TRAINING - 4th DIVISION. 9th to 15th September.

BRIGADE and LOCATION of BRIGADE.	NATURE OF TRAINING.	REMARKS.

10th Brigade.
BAILLEULMONT,
(W.2.c.5.0.)
 	
11th Brigade.
FOMMIER,
(W.25.c.4.8.)
 	
12th Brigade.
BLAIREVILLE,
(R.34.d.3.3.)
	A. ORGANISATION & TRAINING OF PLATOONS.
	        - 3 days -
	
	B. COMPANY TRAINING.
	        - 3 days -
	
	Also (1) Lectures on Fire Control,
	        Lessons from recent fighting near YPRES, and on above mentioned subjects.
	    (2) Recreational Training and Games.
	    (3) Map Reading and Compass work for officers.
	    (4) Training of certain Specialists.
		A. includes :-
		
		  (a) Musketry, to include rapid loading, fire control and mutual support.
		  (b) The attack from a trench line.
		  (c) The attack over the open.
		  (d) The attack on a Strong Point, such as a Machine Gun Emplacement or Machine Gun Nest, which may call for independent action by a Platoon Commander.
		
		In conjunction with the above, full use should be made of the rifle to provide fire to cover movement.
		
		B. includes :-
		
		  (a) MOPPING UP parties both for trench, semi-open or open warfare.
		  (b) The importance of rifle fire and Lewis Gun fire.
		  (c) The use of Machine Guns and Stokes Mortars.
		  (d) Frequent Gas Helmet Drill.
		  (e) Intensive digging, consolidation and use of shell holes.
		  (f) The organisation of working and carrying parties, including use of YUKON PACK.

App. 5

SPECIAL ORDER

BY

MAJOR GENERAL HON. W. LAMBTON, C.V.O., C.B., C.M.G., D.S.O.
COMMANDING 4TH DIVISION.
****

Having to relinquish the command of the Division owing to an accident, I wish to thank all ranks for their loyal assistance, during the two years I have commanded the Division.

During this time the Division has thoroughly upheld its character for brilliant fighting qualities, and steadiness in defence.

I am confident that ~~whenever~~ whatever tasks it is called on to perform in the future, these same qualities will be present.

I wish them all possible good fortune.

                    Sgd. W. LAMBTON.   Maj.General,
15th September, 1917.   Commanding 4th Division.

SECRET.   Copy No. ......

WARNING ORDER.

Reference - 1/100,000 LENS.   14th September, 1917.

1. The 4th Division (less Artillery) will be prepared to entrain on 19th September on transfer to 5th Army.

2. Entraining stations will be :-

    i.   BEAUMETZ RIVIERE - 12th Inf.Brig.Group.
    ii. SAULTY LARBRET   - 10th Inf.Brig.Group.
    iii. MONDICOURT   - 11th Inf.Brig.Group.

3. 11th Inf.Brig.Group will move to MONDICOURT area on 18th September.

4. Detailed orders for entrainment will be issued by 'Q' 4th Division.

5. ACKNOWLEDGE.

                                           Lieut.Colonel,
                           General Staff, 4th Division.

Issued at 12 noon.

Copy No. 1 to 10th Brigade.
        2 to 11th Brigade.
        3 to 12th Brigade.
        4 to C.R.A.
        5 to C.R.E.
        6 to A.D.M.S.
        7 to A.P.M.
        8 to Signals.
        9)
       10) to 4th Div. Q.
       11)
       12 to VI Corps.
       13 to XIV Corps.
       14)
       15) to War Diary.
       16 to File.

SECRET.   Copy No. 15

4th DIVISION ORDER NO. 59.

Reference - 1/100,000 LENS Sheet 11.   15th September, 1917.

1. 4th Division (less Artillery), accompanied by one Divisional Supply Column, will be transferred from Third Army (VI Corps) to Fifth Army.

2. (a) The Divisional Supply Column and other motor vehicles will move by road under orders to be issued by A.A. & Q.M.G.

    (b) The remaining troops mentioned in Para.1 will move by rail.

    Entrainment will begin at any time after midnight 18th/19th September.

    Entraining stations will be as notified in Para. 2 of Warning Order dated 14th September.

    Orders for entrainment will be issued by 'Q' 4th Division.

3. 11th Inf.Brig.Group will move to area about MONDICOURT shown on attached map* on 18th instant, to be clear of present billeting area by 12 noon.

    *Issued to 11th Inf. Bde. and 'Q' 4th Div. only.

    Any roads may be used for the march.

    Arrival in new area to be reported to Divisional Headquarters.

    Accommodation table* is attached.

4. Rations will be carried for the day following day of detrainment.

    Supply railhead will be notified later.

5. ACKNOWLEDGE.

                                                    Lieut.Colonel,
                                            General Staff, 4th Division.

Issued at 12 noon.

Copy No. 1 to 10th Brigade.
         2 to 11th Brigade.
         3 to 12th Brigade.
         4 to C.R.A.
         5 to C.R.E.
         6 to A.D.M.S.
         7 to A.P.M.
         8 to Signals.
         9)
        10) to 4th Div. Q.
        11)
        12 to VI Corps.
        13 to XIV Corps.
        14)
        15) to War Diary.
        16 to File.

SECRET

ADDENDUM NO. 1 TO 4th DIVISION ORDER NO. 59.

Reference Map Sheet 5A HAZEBROUCK 1/100,000:

1. The Division will detrain at :-
   AUDRUICQ,
   ST. OMER,
   WIZERNES,

and will be billetted in the EPERLECQUES area and administered by the XIX Corps.

Details of billeting areas will be issued later.

2. Groups will march to their billeting areas from the detraining stations under the orders of Group Commanders.

There are no restrictions as to roads or times for march of units from detraining stations.

A distance of 500 yards will be maintained between units.

3. Divisional Supply Column will move by road on 19th instant to WATTEN, reporting arrival to Area Commandant, WATTEN.

4. Divisional Headquarters will be at EPERLECQUES where Headquarters will open at 2 p.m. on the 20th, closing at BASSEUX at the same hour.

               Gwiles. Capt.

              Lieut. Colonel,
17th September, 1917. General Staff, 4th Division.

Copies to all recipients of
4th Division Order No. 59.

S E C R E T.

ADDENDUM NO: 2 to 4th DIVISION ORDER NO: 59.

Reference Maps; Sheet 5A HAZEBROUCK 1/100.000,
BELGIUM & FRANCE, Sheets 27 & 28 1/40,000.

1. ADDENDUM No: 1 to 4th Division Order No: 59 dated 17/9/17 is hereby cancelled.

2. The Division will detrain as follows :-

Formation	Detraining Station	Billeting area
10th Bde Group.	PROVEN	PROVEN Area. @
11th Bde Group.	HOPOUTRE (Sheet 27, L.17.d. central).	PROVEN Area. @
12th Bde Group.	PESELHOEK (Sheet 28, A.1.d.	ST SIXTE Area. @

3. Groups will march to their billeting areas from the detraining stations under the orders of Group Commanders.

   There are no restrictions as to roads or times for march of units from detraining stations.

   A distance of 500 yards will be maintained between units.

4. Divisional Supply Column will move by road on 19th inst to ST SIXTE, to report to S.M.T.O, XIVth Corps.
   Route :- via HAZEBROUCK & STEENVOORDE, but not to enter STEENVOORDE before 5 p.m.

5. Railhead - PROVEN, on and from 20th instant.

6. Divisional Headquarters will be at PROVEN, where Headquarters will open at 2 p.m on the 20th inst, closing at BASSEUX at the same hour.

7. ACKNOWLEDGE.

J.K. McConnel Lieut: Colonel,
Capt for General Staff, 4th Divn.

18th September 1917.

Copies to all recipients of
4th Division Order No: 59.

@ Subject to alteration.

SECRET.   Copy No. ......

WARNING ORDER.

Reference - 1/100,000 LENS.   14th September, 1917.

1. The 4th Division (less Artillery) will be prepared to entrain on 19th September on transfer to 5th Army.

2. Entraining stations will be :-

    i.   BEAUMETZ RIVIERE - 12th Inf.Brig.Group.
    ii. SAULTY LARBRET   - 10th Inf.Brig.Group.
    iii. MONDICOURT   - 11th Inf.Brig.Group.

3. 11th Inf.Brig.Group will move to MONDICOURT area on 18th September.

4. Detailed orders for entrainment will be issued by 'Q' 4th Division.

5. ACKNOWLEDGE.

A.F.C. Williams.
Lieut.Colonel,
General Staff, 4th Division.

Issued at *12 noon*.

Copy No. 1 to 10th Brigade.
        2 to 11th Brigade.
        3 to 12th Brigade.
        4 to C.R.A.
        5 to C.R.E.
        6 to A.D.M.S.
        7 to A.P.M.
        8 to Signals.
        9)
       10) to 4th Div. Q.
       11)
      12 to VI Corps.
      13 to XIV Corps.
      14)
      15) to War Diary.
      16 to File.

SECRET.

app 8

ADDENDUM No. 2 to 4th DIVISION ORDER No. 60.
----

1. The following will be the dispositions of Infantry Brigades on completion of all reliefs :-

   12th Inf. Bde. - Front Line.
       Bde. H.Q. - STRAY FARM C.3.c.2.8.
       "A" Battn.- Front Line, H.Q. U.23.d.7.0.
       "B" " (2 coys. LANGEMARK) H.Q. AU BON GITE
              (2 coys. IRON CROSS)
       "C" " CANAL BANK
       "D" " HULLS FARM B.19.c.

   10th Inf. Bde. - Support Area.
       Bde. H.Q. - FUSILIER HOUSE C.13.c.1.2.
       "A" Battn.- SARAGOSSA CAMP B.24.a.1.5.
       "B" " - WOLFE CAMP B.22.d.9.9.
       "C" " - SOULT CAMP B.22.d.7.6.
       "D" " - LEIPZIG CAMP B.23.c.6.4.

   11th Inf. Bde. - Reserve Area.
       Bde. H.Q. - L.2. Works, B.23.c.5.8.
       "A" Battn.- REDAN CAMP B.22.d.5.7.
       "B" " - ROUSSEL FARM B.13.a.3.6.
       "C" " - WINDMILL CAMP (S.W. of ELVERDINGHE)
       "D" " - CARIBOO A.18.a.

2. On the night 27th/28th September the 12th Infantry Brigade will be disposed as under :-

       Bde. H.Q. - FUSILIER HOUSE C.13.c.1.2.
       "A" Battn.- SARAGOSSA CAMP
       "B" " - WOLFE CAMP
       "C" " - CANAL BANK
       "D" " - HULLS FARM

3. Dispositions of Brigade Transport Lines will be as laid down in para. 4 of 4th Division No. Q.R.1003- Instructions No. 6.

4. TABLE "A" issued with 4th Division Order No. 60 should be amended accordingly.

                                                                [signature] Capt.
                                                                for
                                                             Lieut. Colonel,
26/9/17.   General Staff, 4th Division.

Copies to all recipients of Order No. 60.

SECRET.   Copy No. ....

4th DIVISION ORDER NO. 60.

Reference 1/40,000 Shoots 19, 20,   24th September, 1917.
                27, 28.
Traffic Map.

1. The 4th Division (less Artillery) will relieve the 20th Division (less Artillery) in accordance with the attached Table 'A'.

2. (a) The arrangements for moving the personnel of units by train will be issued separately.

   (b) The transport will march under Brigade arrangements.

   (c) 500 yards will be maintained between every 20 vehicles on the march.

   (d) The roads used must comply with the traffic map which has already been issued.

3. Brigadier Generals Commanding Brigades will assume command of their respective areas on completion of their Brigade reliefs.

4. (a) All details of the Brigade reliefs will be made between the Brigadiers concerned.

   (b) The D.M.G.O. will arrange the relief of the Divisional Machine Gun Company.

   (c) The C.R.E. will arrange direct with the C.R.E. 20th Division to take over all work now in progress and the relief of the Field Companies.

   (d) The A.Ds.M.S. concerned will arrange all details concerning the relief of the Field Ambulances.

5. The move of the Train units and Mobile Veterinary Section will be arranged by the Administrative Branch.

6. The G.O.C. 4th Division will assume command of the Right Sector of the XIVth Corps at 10 a.m. on the 29th instant, at which hour Divisional Headquarters will open at WELSH FM and close at PROVEN.

7. ACKNOWLEDGE.

                                            H. Fanshawe
                                            Lieut. Colonel,
Issued at 1 pm.   General Staff, 4th Division.

TABLE 'A' TO ACCOMPANY 4th DIVISION ORDER NO. 60.

No.	Date.	Unit.	From.	To.	Relieving.	Remarks.
1.	27th Sept.	12th Inf.Bde.	S.1 Area.	Support Area.*	60th Inf.Bde.	Bde.H.Q. FUSILIER HO C.13.c 1.2. ∅ To be arranged by C.R.E.
		406th Field Co.	SALEM Camp X.29.c.	CANAL Bank.	∅	
		234th M.G.Co.	P.5 Area.	Support Area.		
2.	27th/28th	12th M.G.Co.	Support Area.	Front System.	217th M.G.Co.	To be arranged by the D.M.G.Co.
		234th M.G.Co.	"	Barrage Area.	60th M.G.Co.	
3.	28th Sept.	12th Inf.Bde.	Support Area.	Front Line.	61st Inf.Bde.	Bde.H.Q. STRAY FM C.3.c 2.8. 'A' Bn. in front line, H.Q. U.23.d 7.C. 'B' Bn. Support, H.Q. AUBONGITE. 'C' Bn. Reserve, H.Q. ADELPHI C.3.b 11. 'D' Bn. Reserve, H.Q. Bde.BARRIERE HO C.2.b 0.7.
4.	28th Sept.	11th Inf.Bde.	P.1 Area.	Reserve Area.*	59th Inf.Bde.	Bde.H.Q. L 2 Works B.23.c 5.8. ∅ To be arranged by C.R.E.
		526th Field Co.	"	CANAL Bank.	∅	
		21st W.Works. (Pioneers)	P.5 Area.	CANAL Bank	11th D.L.I. (Pioneers)	
5.	29th Sept.	10th Inf.Bde.	P.5 Area.	Support Area.*	61st Inf.Bde.	Bde.H.Q. FUSILIER HO C.13.c 1.2. ∅ To be arranged by C.R.E.
		9th Field Co.	"	B.23.b 6.4.	∅	
		Signal Co. Details.	PROVEN "	WELSH FARM. "	Div.H.Q. "	

NOTE. * For detail of Camps in Support and Reserve Areas see 4th Div. Q.R. 1000/A.

Copy No. 1 to G.O.C.
2 to G.S.O.1.
3 to 10th Brigade.
4 to 11th Brigade.
5 to 12th Brigade.
6 to C.R.A.
7 to C.R.E.
8 to A.D.M.S.
9 to A.P.M.
10 to Signals.
11 to 234th M.G.Co.
12 to D.M.G.O.
13)
14) to 4th Div. Q.
15)
16 to D.A.D.O.S.
17 to 21st W.Yorks (Pioneers.)
18 to 20th Division.
19 to 29th Division.
20 to 51st Division.
21 to Guards Division.
22) to XIVth Corps.
23)
24 to XIVth Corps H.A.
25 to 9th Sqdn.R.F.C.
26) to War Diary.
27)
28 to File.

ADDENDUM TO 4th DIVISION ORDER NO. 60.

The Divisional Boundaries are shown on the combined 1/20,000 map (Sheets 19 S.E., 20 S.W., 27 N.E., 28 S.W.) already issued.

Southern Division Boundary is RED line through DAWSONS Corner (Sheet 28 B.22.c 8.7).
Northern Divisional Boundary is YELLOW line through Sheet 23 B.16.central as far as Sheet 20 U.28.a 0.6, thence along BLUE line.

SECRET.   Copy No. 25

4th DIVISION ORDER NO. 67.

Reference – BROEMBEEK and   27th September, 1917.
LANGEMARCK, 1/10000

App 9

1. (a) It is not certain what troops are holding the line
       immediately opposite to us.
       The 208th Division has been holding the line till the
       23rd instant, but as it has suffered very heavy
       casualties it may have been relieved.
       It seems probable that if it has been relieved the
       new Division is the 40th (Saxon) Division.
       The normal method of holding the line is one battalion
       per regiment in front, the 2nd battalion with two
       companies in the Northern end of POELCAPELLE and two
       companies another 1000 yards N.E. The 3rd battalion
       is in and around WESTROOSEBEEK.

   (b) The 2nd and 5th Armies are continuing the attack on
       'Z' day.

   (c) The objective of the 5th Army is shown by the BLUE line
       on the attached map *.
       This objective will be captured by the 18th and 14th
       Corps, the boundary between the two Corps being the
       line U.24.c 4.0 – V.13.d 5.0.
       The 11th Division will be the left Division of the
       18th Corps.

   (d) The objective of the 14th Corps will be captured by
       the 4th Division on the right and the 29th Division
       on the left, the boundary between the two Divisions
       being the line U.23.central – U.18.b 5.0.

2. (a) The 4th Division will attack at ZERO hour with two
       Brigades in front line and one in Reserve.

           11th Brigade will be on the right.
           10th Brigade will be on the left.
           12th Brigade will be in Reserve.

       The boundary between Brigades will be the line
       U.23.b 8.0 – V.13.c 0.5.

   (b) The general direction of the attack is N.E.

3. (a) All Brigades will be in their final positions by
       ZERO – 2 hours on 'Z' day.

   (b) The position of Brigades at ZERO hour will be :–

       11th Brigade in right front area H.Q. STRAY FM.
                                             O.3.c 2.7.
       10th Brigade in left front area H.Q. ADELPHI
                                             O.3.b 2.1.
       12th Brigade in Support area   H.Q. FUSILIER HO.
                                             O.13.c 1.2.

4. The 11th and 10th Brigades will each detail special parties
whose duties are to keep touch with the 11th and 29th Divisions
respectively. They will report the situation on arrival at
the following points :–

Right Bde. KANGAROO trench.   Left Bde. Road junction.
           Cross roads,   U.18.d 00.55.
           V.19.a 25.20.
           Road V.19.b 1.8.

           * Issued to Brigades only.

5. (a) The attack will be supported by a creeping artillery barrage and by a machine gun barrage, details of which will be issued separately.

(b) The 21st W.Yorks.R. (Pioneers) will place two Lewis gun teams (with guns) at the disposal of each of the attacking Bdes. for anti-aircraft work in the front system. These teams will report to the H.Q. 10th and 11th Inf.Bdes. at 11 a.m. on 29th instant for instructions.

6. The R.E. and Pioneers will work under the orders of the C.R.E. who will receive separate instructions.

7. Prisoners will be sent back to ADELPHI where they will be taken over by an escort to be provided by the 12th Brigade.
   This escort will consist of one officer and 20 men and will be at ADELPHI at ZERO hour on 'Z' day.
   They will take the prisoners back to the Cage at CACTUS PONTOON where they will be handed over to the A.P.M. for disposal.

8. Medical arrangements will be issued separately.

9. Brigades will send in reports at least every half hour after ZERO to Divisional Headquarters whether there is anything to report or not.

10. ZERO hour and 'Z' day will be communicated later also the arrangements for the synchronisation of watches.

11. Reports to WELSH FM.

12. ACKNOWLEDGE.

H. Ranstalle
Lieut.Colonel,
General Staff, 4th Division.

Issued at 12 noon

Copy No. 1 to G.O.C.
2 to G.S.O. 1.
3 to 10th Brigade.
4 to 11th Brigade.
5 to 12th Brigade.
6 to C.R.A.
7 to C.R.E.
8 to Signals.
9 to A.D.M.S.
10 to A.P.M.
11 to 234th M.G.Co.
12 to D.M.G.O.
13 to 21st W.Yorks.R. (Pioneers).
14) to 4th Div.Q.
15)
16)
17 to 9th Sqdn.R.F.C.
18 to 11th Division.
19 to 29th Division.
20 to Guards Division.
21) to XIV Corps.
22)
23 to XIV Corps H.A.
24) to War Diary.
25)
26 to File.

INSTRUCTIONS NO: 1
to
4th DIVISION ORDER NO: 6!

THE ATTACK

1. (a)   The fighting dress of the troops taking part in the attack will be as laid down in S.S.135.
   Every man of the attacking Battalions, except those employed on Battalion, Company and Platoon H.Qrs, will carry a pick or a shovel. The proportion of picks and shovels will be 80% shovels, 20% picks.

   (b)   The provisions of Section XXX on page 58 of S.S.135 are to be strictly complied with.

2. Should any part of the line be checked during the advance, rifles must at once be used, to provide covering fire to the further advance of the troops.

3. Arrangements must be made which will ensure all shell holes and concrete emplacements being mopped up during the advance.

4. Low flying hostile aeroplanes must be dealt with. Some Lewis Guns of the Pioneer Battalion will be placed at the disposal of Brigades for this purpose.

5. On reaching the objectives, patrols or covering parties are not to be pushed out more than 100 yards beyond the final line, so as to allow the protective artillery barrage to be sufficiently close to be effective.

6. The closest liaison with Brigades and Battalions on either flank is to be maintained.

7. All Officers and N.C.Os should endeavour to pick up distant distinct marks beforehand, on which they can maintain their direction.

H. Hardcastle
Lieut.Colonel,
27th September 1917.   General Staff, 4th Division.

Copies to all recipients of
4th Division Order No: 6!

SECRET.

ADDENDUM NO. 1
to
INSTRUCTIONS NO. 1.

1. Each of the attacking Brigades and Battalions will detail by name definite counter-attacking units.

These units will act at once on their own responsibility without waiting for orders.

As they are used they will be replaced so as to have always definite counter-attacking troops ready.

2. Attacking Brigades will arrange for at least one section of Vickers guns to be pushed forward as soon as possible to deal with counter-attacks.

3. The advance of the 11th Brigade will halt on the GREEN dotted line, shown on the map as the 1st Bound, and will continue on to the final objective after a pause of one hour.

4. Reference para. 1 of Instructions No. 1.

Bombs will not be carried by other than bombers.

H. Ramsden
Lieut.Colonel,
28th September, 1917.   General Staff, 4th Division.

Copies to all recipients of
Instructions No. 1.

INSTRUCTIONS NO: 2
to
4th DIVISION ORDER NO: 6

CONSOLIDATION

1. On reaching the objective, units must re-organize at once in depth, and be prepared to meet and crush any counter-attack.

2. To make it as difficult as possible for the enemy to deliver a successful counter-attack, as little movement as possible is to take place when once the leading units have re-organized.

3. When re-organizing, the whole front will be arranged in groups consisting of sections or platoons according to strength, all so placed as to be able to support one another. It is important to place the first groups so as to gain a view into the BROMBEEK with the main line of resistance just behind the crest.

4. Lewis and Vickers Guns must be so arranged that a machine gun screen can be placed along the whole front in case of a counter-attack.

5. The positions for groups and machine guns as mentioned in paras 3 and 4 cannot be definitely fixed from the map; they must be selected on the ground.
The attached Map "A" gives an indication of possible places for these.

6. The C.R.E will arrange in consultation with the Brigades, to mark out with stakes, as soon as possible after the objective has been captured, a route across country from the existing trenchboard tracks to the new front line; one track for each Brigade. Suggested routes are shewn on Map "A" issued with Instructions No: 1.
These tracks will be trenchboarded as soon as possible.

7. In the event of the enemy counter-attacking, troops in rear are to counter-attack again <u>at once</u> before the enemy has time to settle down, if he should have been successful in driving back our most forward troops.

H. Kundake
Lieut. Col.

27th September 1917.   General Staff, 4th Division.

Copies to all recipients of
4th Division Order No: 6.

MAP "A".

1:10,000 M.I.

Scale 1:10,000.

26-8-17   No 2 Advanced Section, A.P. & S.S.

TRACKS — — — — —   LEWIS GUNS ▨▬▨

POSTS ⌒

POINTS OF CONTACT WITH FLANK DIVISIONS ✶   VICKERS GUNS ▨▬▨

Message Pad.

Your Message must be such as will enable the Addressee to know what the Situation is with You and your Neighbours.

NEGATIVE INFORMATION IS ALSO VALUABLE.

Strike out and alter sentences as necessary.

TO..

1. Am advancing to..
2. Am putting out (Have put out) protective parties.
3. Am sending out. Have sent out and am keeping out patrols to keep touch with the enemy.
4. Am (Have) consolidating (ed).
5. Our line now runs..
6. I require (give article or articles and number required) :—

    Send the above to..

7. Troops on my right are (give situation)

8. Troops on my left are (give situation)

9. My strength now is..
10. Am being shelled from..
11. Am held up by M.G., T.M., rifle, artillery fire from..
12. Am now ready to..
13. Enemy line runs..
14. Enemy (strength)........................at........................
    doing..
15. Have captured..
16. Enemy prisoners belong to..
17. Enemy counter-attack forming up at..
18. Other remarks—

Time .... a.m. (p.m.)   Name..
Date..   Rank..
Place...   Platoon.................... Company....................
(Map Ref. or mark on back of map.)   Battalion..

SECRET.

ADDENDUM NO. 1
to
INSTRUCTIONS NO. 2.

1. As will be seen from the new map issued the final objective reaches slightly further North of 19 METRE HILL than it did originally, so as to include the concrete shelter shown at U.18.d 3.8.

This point will probably be a suitable place near which to establish a post.

2. As shown on map 'A' already issued there will be two lines organised for defence :-

    (a) The final objective.

    (b) The line FERDAN HOUSE - BEEK VILLAS (U.24.b 8.7) - RED HOUSE - KANGAROO trench - t'GOED TER VESTEN FARM.

The exact location of these lines and the organisation of the troops holding them depend entirely on the ground and must be decided by those on the spot.

3. A Post is to be established in the neighbourhood of FERDAN HO.

H. Hardcastle
Lieut.Colonel,

28th September, 1917.   General Staff, 4th Division.

Copies to all recipients of
Instructions No. 2.

INSTRUCTIONS NO: 3
to
4th DIVISION ORDER NO: 61.

COMMUNICATIONS.

1. (a)   The importance of keeping everybody informed of what is going on, cannot be too strongly impressed on all. The timely arrival at G.H.Q of some information gained by a platoon during the fight, may influence the whole battle.

   (b)   Units and formations must send forward selected Officers as soon after the capture of the objective as possible, to find out the situation.

2. TELEGRAPH and TELEPHONE.

   A buried cable runs from the Canal Bank to ALOUETTE Farm. The Brigades at STRAY FARM and ADELPHI are on this route. The route is being extended to a Battalion Headquarters at U.29.b.7.9, and thence to WHITE TRENCH. Cables will be laid in WHITE and EAGLE TRENCHES to the Battalions there.

   The Brigade Sections of the Brigades in the line will maintain the buried cable trench forward of ADELPHI. If they require assistance, they will call upon the Divisional linesmen, who will be stationed in a dug-out close to STRAY FARM.

3. VISUAL.

   Lucas Daylight Signalling Lamps will be used for all visual signalling. Flags will be provided at all stations for use in the event of lamps being destroyed.

   A complete chain of visual signalling stations will be established working from front to rear, as follows :-

   (a)   A station will be established at ALOUETTE FARM (Station Call "C"), which will receive from two stations, one at U.23.d.90.35 (Station Call "A"), and the other at U.23.b.8.2 (Station Call "B").

   (b)   ALOUETTE FARM (Station Call "C") will send back messages to STRAY FARM via AU BON GITE (Station Call "D"), INGS (U.28.c.30.13) (Station Call "E"), to STRAY FARM, (Station Call "F").

   (c)   From STRAY FARM to Canal Bank (Station Call "J") and thence by wire to Divisional Headquarters.

   (d)   All stations to be manned by Battalion signallers under Brigade arrangements, with the exception of Canal Bank, STRAY FARM, and half of INGS Station, which will be manned by the Divisional Signal Company.

   (e)   The places selected are easily visible from station to station, and this method of communication should save many runners. Messages sent by visual should be concise and as short as possible. Messages cannot be sent forward by this method, but each message will be acknowledged by the station call of the sending station being flashed back by the receiving station. Messages should be repeated until this acknowledgement is received.

   (f)   Visual is only for use when no cable communication is available.

   (g)   As the troops advance, suitable places will be found by Battalion signallers, to signal back to the two stations at U.23.d.90.35 and U.23.b.8.2.

2.

4. WIRELESS.

Two wireless stations will be established, one near STRAY FARM at C.3.c.40.30 working to CORPS DIRECTING STATION at BOESINGHE, the other at AU BON GITE, also working to CORPS DIRECTING STATION at BOESINGHE.

These two stations also work to one another.

5. POWER BUZZERS AND AMPLIFIERS

A Power Buzzer and Amplifier will be installed at Battalion Headquarters at U.29.b.7.9. which will work to an Amplifier and Power Buzzer at AU BON GITE.

At AU BON GITE, the Trench Wireless Stations will pass messages on to the other T.W set at STRAY FARM or to the CORPS DIRECTING STATION at BOESINGHE.

Two Power Buzzers will be available to be carried forward, should Battalion Headquarters move forward, one by a battalion of each attacking Brigade, and will be set up in any suitable place, and will work back to the Amplifier at U.29.b.7.9 under the orders of the Battalion Commander.

6. PIGEONS.

Eight pairs of birds will be sent up daily to the Brigade in the line for distribution amongst the Battalions.

On "Y" Day, 20 pairs will be sent up - 10 pairs for each attacking Brigade for use on "Z" Day. These birds should be given in charge of the trained pigeon men, who will accompany the Battalion Commanders, who should send them forward at his discretion with Company Commanders. One pair should should remain at Battalion Headquarters throughout "Z" Day.

It must be clearly understood that all birds issued, must be released before one hour before dusk on "Z" Day. Only properly qualified Pigeoneers to be entrusted with the birds, and those men to keep in close touch with the Company or Battalion Commanders.

On "Z" Day, 20 more pairs of birds will be sent up for use on "Z" plus 1 Day.

7. RUNNERS.

A relay system must be arranged in each Brigade in advance of Brigade Headquarters, so that no runner has to traverse more than 1,000 yards in any one direction.

In the event of cable communication breaking down between Brigade Headquarters and the Canal, runners must be sent to FUSILIER HQ (C.13.c.3.1) for despatch to Divisional Headquarters.

8.(a) CONTACT PATROLS.) Details of
  (b) COUNTER-ATTACK AEROPLANES.) these will be
) sent out later.

Lieut: Colonel,

27th September 1917.   General Staff, 4th Division.

Copies to all recipients of
4th Division Order No: 61.

SECRET.

ADDENDUM NO. 1
to
INSTRUCTIONS NO. 3.

CONTACT PATROLS.

No flares will be lit until called for.

As far as possible these flares should be lighted in bunches of three.

RED flares will be used.

Each Brigade and Battalion Headquarters will be marked by ground sheets of authorised shape, with the code letters of the unit laid out with white strips alongside. These letters should be 9 feet in depth.

Signalling to aeroplanes will be done by Panels.

Lieut.Colonel,
30th September, 1917.   General Staff, 4th Division.

Copies to all recipients of
Instructions No. 3.

SECRET.

INSTRUCTIONS NO. 4
to
4th DIVISION ORDER NO. 61.

MACHINE GUNS.

1. The machine guns of the Division will assist the attack by means of barrage fire.

The following will be the distribution of the machine guns, vide map issued :-

'X' Group is cancelled.
'P' Group - one section of 234th M.G.Coy.
'O' Group - one section of 234th M.G.Coy.
'M' Group - two sections of 234th M.G.Coy.
'X^2' Group - two sections of 234th M.G.Coy.

These guns will move from 'P' and 'O' Groups at ZERO plus 25 minutes.

'Y' Group - two sections of 11th M.G.Coy.
'N' Group - two sections 10th M.G.Coy.
'N^2' Group - two sections of 10th M.G.Coy.

These guns move from 'N' Group at ZERO plus 30 minutes.

2. TIMES OF FIRE.

'P' Group - ZERO to ZERO plus 20 minutes.
'O' Group - ZERO to ZERO plus 23 minutes.
'M' Group - ZERO to ZERO plus 20 minutes.
'N' Group - ZERO to ZERO plus 30 minutes.
'Y' Group - ZERO to ZERO plus 10 minutes.

'N^2', 'X^2' and 'Y' Groups open for S.O.S. Signal.

3. RATE OF FIRE.

Groups 'N^2', 'X^2' and 'Y' on S.O.S. Signal, intense fire for 10 minutes; reduced to 25 rounds a minute for a further 10 minutes.

Groups 'P', 'O', 'M', 'N' and 'Y' one belt per gun per minute.

4. Two sections will be at the disposal of each of the attacking Brigades from the beginning and will come under the tactical command of the Brigadiers as under :-
S.O.S. barrage guns -
'X^2' and 'Y' Groups - 11th Inf.Brigade.
'N^2' Group - 10th Inf.Brigade.

Brigadiers will not take these guns off their S.O.S. lines except in case of urgent necessity.

5. 12th M.G.Coy. remains under orders of G.O.C. 12th Bde.

6. Os.C. Groups must arrange to warn all troops approaching the danger area in front of their positions.

7. All guns will be in position by ZERO minus five hours.

Os.C. M.G.Cos. will report to Divisional Headquarters and 10th and 11th Brigades when all guns are in position and ready.

They will notify the above by means of the word 'GOOD'.

H. Hamsdalle
Lieut.Colonel,
29th September, 1917.   General Staff, 4th Division.

Copies to all recipients of
4th Division Order No. 61.

SECRET

INSTRUCTIONS NO. 5
TO
4th DIVISION ORDER NO. 61.

DUMPS AND RATIONS.

1. Dumps will be formed, if time permits, as under :-

   S.A.A. and Bombs.

   Adv. Bde. Right - U.29.b 8.9 (approx.)
   "   "   Left - U.23.d 3.6 ("   )
   Adv. Divisional - THE INGS (U.28.c 6.1).

   R.E. Material and Tools.

   Adv. Bde. Right - U.29.b 1.8 (approx.)
   "   "   Left - U.29.a 6.8 ("   )
   Adv. Divisional - U.28.c 9.6 ("   )

2. The replenishment of all S.A.A. and Bombs will be from rear to front.

   Necessary carrying parties to supply Battalions will be kept near Bde. dumps and a party will be kept at the Adv. Divnl. dump to replenish the Bde. dumps.

   Units and formations will merely send back messages stating requirements.

3. Attacking Brigades will arrange to have up forward with them by ZERO hour two days rations.

H. Kendall
Lieut. Colonel,
27th September, 1917.   General Staff, 4th Division.

Copies to all recipients
of 4th Division Order No. 61.

S E C R E T.

INSTRUCTIONS NO. 6
TO
4th DIVISION ORDER NO. 61.

R.E. and Pioneers.

1. One R.E. officer will be attached to each of the attacking Brigades as liaison officer.

He will report to Brigade Headquarters by noon on the 29th instant.

2. The Field Companies and Pioneers will be employed on the following work under the orders of the C.R.E. :-

(a) Accommodation for one battalion in splinter-proof shelters in CANDLE Trench, CANDLE SUPPORT, CANDLE AVENUE.

(b) Accommodation for one battalion in the area VULCAN CROSSING - GAIETY FM - STRAY FM - CORK HO.

(c) Maintenance of tramline and extension of same via LOUIS FM - RED HOUSE - LEMNOS HO.

(d) Maintenance of trench board tracks and their extension as shown on Map 'A' attached to Instructions No. 2.

(e) Marking with white topped stakes the trenchboard tracks and labelling them with distinctive letters, also the extensions as in (d).

(f) Notice and direction boards and nameboards throughout the area.
In this connection boards to be prepared ready for fixing in -

    KANGAROO Trench.
    RED HO.
    FERDAN HO.
    COPSE - U.24.a 7.5.
    BEEK AVENUE.
    TRAGIQUE FM.
    Concrete house U.18.d 0.2.

H. Karslake.
Lieut. Colonel,
27th September, 1917.   General Staff, 4th Division.

Copies to all recipients of
4th Division Order No. 61.

SECRET.

ADDENDUM NO. 2
to
4th DIVISION ORDER NO. 61.

1. The map issued with 4th Division Order No. 61 should be destroyed and the attached map 'X' substituted.

   Note. The points to notice in the new map are :-

   (a) An intermediate (GREEN DOTTED) line for the 11th Brigade and 11th Division.

   (b) A slight alteration in the final objective North of 19 METRE HILL and the final objective of the 11th Division.

2. A contact patrol will fly over the front at -

   ZERO plus 1 hour and 30 minutes,
   ZERO plus 3 hours,
   ZERO plus 5 hours.

   It will also possibly fly over at other times and will always call on the leading troops to show their position by means of -

   (a) Klaxon Horn,
   (b) A series of White lights.

3. Watches will be synchronized by a Staff Officer from Divisional Headquarters at ADELPHI at -

   2 p.m. and 8 p.m. on 'Y' day.

   The following will attend :-

   1 Officer per Bde.H.Q.
   1 Officer per Battn. of the leading Bdes.
   1 Officer per M.G.Coy.

Lieut.Colonel,
General Staff, 4th Division.

28th September, 1917.

Copies to all recipients of
4th Division Order No. 61.

SECRET.

INSTRUCTIONS NO. 7
to
4th DIVISION ORDER NO. 61.

ARTILLERY.

1. The creeping barrage will begin on the GREEN line shown on the attached tracing* at ZERO.

It will begin to move forward at ZERO plus three minutes and it will move at the following rate :-

First 200 yards at 50 yards in two minutes, thence to GREEN dotted line at 50 yards in three minutes.

At ZERO plus 2 hours and 2 minutes the protective barrage covering the GREEN dotted line/(1st bound) will become intense and at ZERO plus 2 hours and 10 minutes will begin to creep at 50 yards in 4 minutes.

All lifts will be 50 yards at a time.

2. From ZERO to ZERO plus 2 minutes there will be an intense bombardment of KANGAROO trench by Stokes Mortars.

For this purpose the 10th and 11th Inf.Bdes. will each have six Mortars in position with 20 rounds per gun.

30th September, 1917.

Lieut.Colonel,
General Staff, 4th Division.

Copies to all recipients
of 4th Division Order No. 61.
   * Tracing to 10th Brigade.
               11th Brigade.
               12th Brigade.
               C.R.A.
               C.R.E.
               29th Division.
               11th Division.
               XIVth Corps.

Identification Trace for

U

To accompany Instructions Nº 7
to 4th Div. Order Nº 61

23

Barrage line ⎯⎯⎯
Starting line ⎯⎯⎯
Our dispositions
according to R.F.C.
Sept 3rd 1917 ⎯⎯

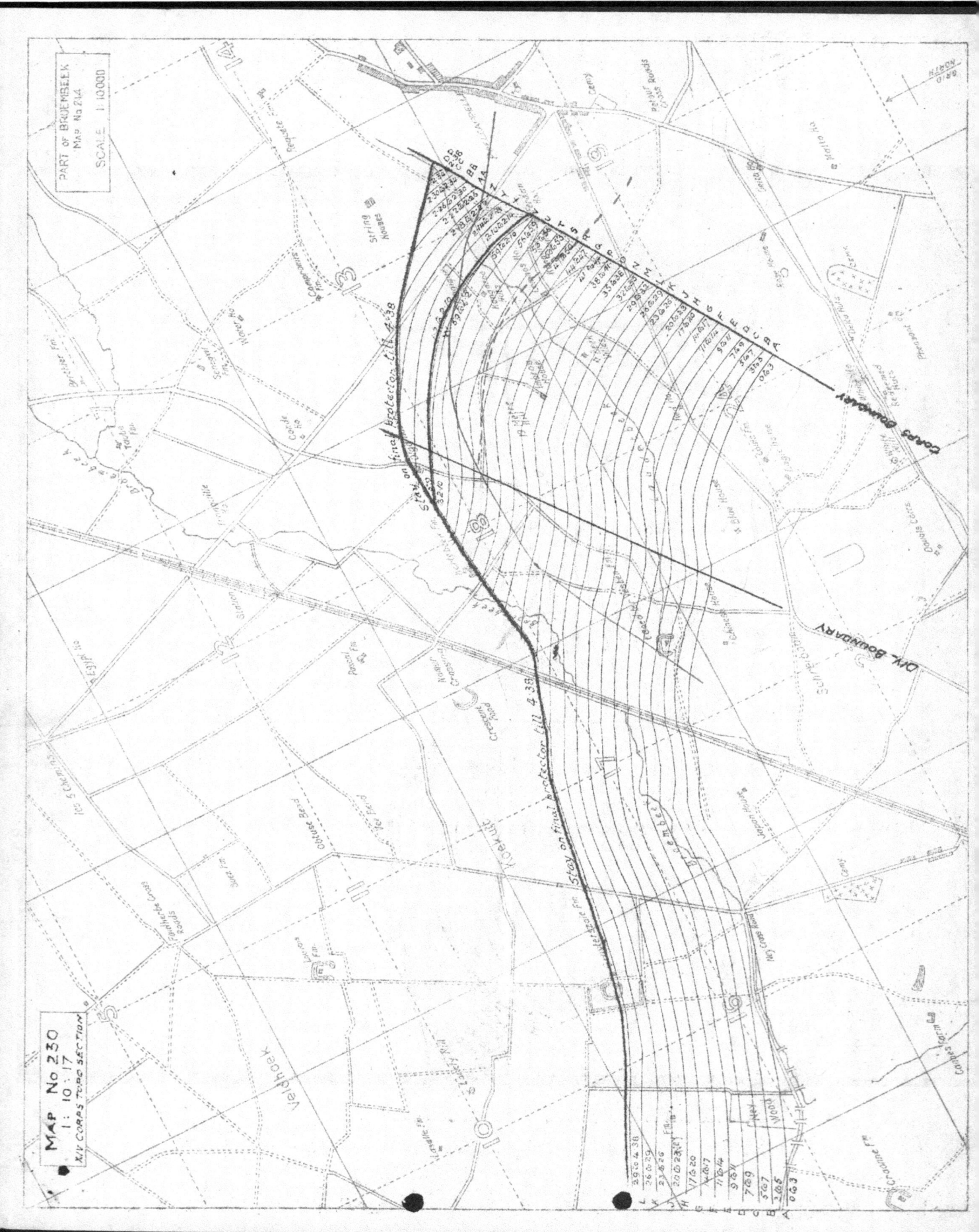

SECRET.

DISTRIBUTION OF TROOPS

(Reference 4th Division Order No. 61).

29th DIVISION 86th Brigade	4th DIVISION 10th Brigade	4th DIVISION 11th Brigade	11th DIVISION 33rd Brigade
(Assaulting Battn)		(1st Objective)	(1st Objective)
1st R. Dublin Fus.	2nd Seaforth Hrs.	1st Hampshire Regt.	1st Somerset L.I.	9th Notts. & Derby Regt.
Blue diamond on back of collar.	Plaid triangle.	Yellow Tiger.	Yellow.	White roman four on green on back of collar.
Red triangle on sleeve.	3/10th Middlesex R.	1st E. Lancs. R.		(2nd Objective)
	Red & Yellow triangle. (Red forward)	Yellow.		6th Border Regt.
	1st R. Warwicks R.	1st Rifle Bde.	Yellow Maltese Cross.	White roman two on green at back of collar.
	Green.			
	The Household Bn.			
	"HOUSEHOLD BATTN".			

NOTE :- Distinctive Badges of 4th Division are in every case on upper part of arm.

4th Division No. G.A. 7/1

Reference Addendum to 4th Division Order No. 60

The Southern boundary crosses CANAL C.19.c.12.92 to C.19.c.20.95.   Accommodation in CANAL Bank in tongue shewn on map already issued has reverted to the Corps on our right.

H. Karslake
Lt-Colonel,
General Staff, 4th Division.

25th September, 1917.

Copies to all recipients
of 4th Division order No 60.

SECRET.   Copy No. ......

4th DIVISION ORDER NO. 62.

28th September, 1917.

1. The 11th Inf.Bde. will relieve the 12th Inf.Bde. on the 1st/2nd October, the relief to be complete by 6 a.m. on October 2nd.

   Bde. H.Q. will be at STRAY FM.

2. One Battalion 10th Inf.Bde. will take over on the same night that part of the front line between U.23.b 8.0 and the left Divisional boundary U.23.b 5.4 including LANGEMARCK.

   This Battalion will be temporarily under the command of the G.O.C. 11th Inf.Bde. and all arrangements for its taking over will be made by the 11th Inf.Bde.

3. On the night 2nd/3rd October the 10th Inf.Bde. will take over the area allotted to them by 4th Division Order No.61 with Bde.H.Q. at ADELPHI.

4. Attached Appendix 'A' gives the dispositions of Bdes. at 6 a.m. on the 2nd October and at 6 a.m. on the 3rd October.

5. Details of reliefs will be arranged between Brigadiers concerned.

6. The G.O.C. 11th Inf.Bde. will take over command from the G.O.C. 12th Inf.Bde. at 10 a.m. on October 2nd.

   The G.O.C. 10th Inf.Bde. will take over command of the left front sector at 10 a.m. on October 3rd.

7. ACKNOWLEDGE.

                                            H. Karslake
                                            Lieut.Colonel,
Issued at 12 noon.   General Staff, 4th Division.

Copy No. 1 to G.O.C.   Copy No.14)
         2 to G.S.O. 1.   15) to 4th Div.Q.
         3 to 10th Brigade.   16)
         4 to 11th Brigade.   17 to 9th Sqdn.R.F.C.
         5 to 12th Brigade.   18 to 11th Division.
         6 to C.R.A.   19 to 20th Division.
         7 to C.R.E.   20 to Guards Division.
         8 to Signals.   21)
         9 to A.D.M.S.   22) to XIV Corps.
        10 to A.P.M.   23 to XIV Corps H.A.
        11 to 234th M.G.Co.   24) to War Diary.
        12 to D.M.G.O.   25)
        13 to 21st W.Yorks.R.(Pioneers). 26 to File.

APPENDIX 'A'
to
4th DIVISION ORDER NO. 62.

DISPOSITIONS 6 a.m. OCTOBER 2nd.

11th Inf.Bde.	H.Q. STRAY FM.
'A' Bn. 11th Bde. Right front line.	H.Q. U.29.b 5.9.
'A' Bn. 10th Bde. Left front line.	H.Q. AU BON GITE. LANGEMARCK and IRON CROSS.
'B' Bn. 11th Bde.	~~CANDLE TRENCH H.Q. JOLIE FM.~~ BRIDGE CAMP
'C' Bn. 11th Bde.	~~CANAL BANK.~~ SARAGOSSA CAMP.
'D' Bn. 11th Bde.	HULLS FM.
12th Inf.Bde.	H.Q. L.2 Works - B.23.c 5.8.
'A' Bn.	REDAN CAMP.
'B' Bn.	ROUSSELL FM.
'C' Bn.	WINDMILL CAMP.
'D' Bn.	CARIBOO.
10th Inf.Bde.	No change except 'A' Bn. to front line.

DISPOSITIONS 6 a.m. OCTOBER 3rd.

11th Inf.Bde.	No change.
12th Inf.Bde.	No change.
10th Inf.Bde.	H.Q. ADELPHI.
'A' Bn.	Left front Bn. including LANGEMARCK.
'B' Bn.	WOLFE CAMP.
'C' Bn.	SOULT CAMP.
'D' Bn.	LEIPSIC CAMP.

- SECRET -

4th Division No: G.A. 3/131

AMENDMENT to APPENDIX "A" - 4th DIVISION ORDER No: 62

Dispositions 6 a.m. October 2nd :-

"B" Battn 11th Inf. Bde ... BRIDGE CAMP.
"C" Battn 12th Inf. Bde ... SARAGOSSA CAMP

per . Lieut: Colonel,
General Staff, 4th Division.

2/10/17.

Copies to all recipients of
4th Division Order No: 62.

4th DIVISION

POSITION OF UNITS - 29th SEPTEMBER 1917

Divisional Headquarters	..... WELSH Fme	(B.14.c.2.1)
10th Inf. Bde H.Qrs	..... FUSILIER HO.	(C.13.c.1.2)
Household Battalion.	..... SOULT CAMP	(B.22.d.9.2)
1st R.War.Regt.	..... WOLFE CAMP	(B.22.d.9.9)
3/10th Middx Regt.	..... LIEPSIG CAMP	(B.23.c.6.4)
2nd Sea.Highrs.	..... SARAGOSSA CAMP	(B.24.a.1.5)
10th M.G.Coy.	.....	(B.23.a.4.2)
10th T.M.Bty.	.....	(B.23.a.4.2)
11th Inf. Bde H.Qrs.	..... L.2.Works.	(B.23.c.5.8)
1st Somerset.L.I.	..... CARIBOO CAMP	(A.18.a)
1st E.Lancs Regt.	..... BRIDGE CAMP	(B.20.b.3.7)
1st Rifle Brigade	..... REDAN CAMP	(B.22.d.5.8)
1st Hamps Regt.	..... ROUSSOL CAMP	(B.13.a.3.6)
11th M.G.Coy.	..... SOLFERINO CAMP	(B.22.b.8.3)
11th T.M.Bty.	..... -ditto-	
12th Inf. Bde H.Qrs .	..... STRAY Fme.	(C.3.c.2.7)
1st King's Own Regt	..... AU BON GITE	
2nd Lancs Fusrs.	..... CANAL BANK	(C.13.c.2.8)
2nd W.Riding Regt	..... U.29.b.68.99	
2nd Essex Regt.	..... HULLS Fme.	(B.18.c)
12th M.G.Coy	..... GEORGE HO.	(U.27.d.80.45)
12th T.M.Bty	..... PERISCOPE HO.	(C.2.d.1.9)

****

SECRET. MAP REFERENCE. (A. BELGIUM Sheet 27 1/40000.
(BELGIUM & FRANCE Sheet 19 S.E.1/20000.

App.B

4th Division No.A.4684/26.

4th. DIVISION BILLETING LIST. To take effect from 21st. instant.

UNIT.	PLACE OR MAP REFERENCE.
Divisional Headquarters.	PROVEN. (Central Camp)
C.R.E.	" " "
4th. Signal Coy. R.E.	" " "
406th.(Renfrew) Field Coy. R.E.	SALEM Camp X.29.c.
526th.(Durham) Field Coy. R.E.	PUTLOWS Camp. P.1 Area Proven.
9th. Field Company R.E.	PATAGONIA Camp. P.5 " "
21st. West Yorks (Pioneers)	PHEASANT Camp. P.5 " "
234th. M.G.Company.	P.5 Area. Un-Named Camp vacated by J.Corps Supply Col.
H.Q. 4th. Divl. Artillery.	Sheet 28 A.15 b.7.6.
H.Q. 10th. Infantry Brigade.	POONA Camp.)
Household Battalion.	PATALIA. ")
1st. R. Warwick Regt.	PALMA ") P.5 Area
2nd. Seaforth Hldrs.	PERSIA ")
3/10th. Middlesex Regt.	PEFA ") PROVEN.
10th. M.G.Company.	PAPAMA ")
10th. T.M.Battery.	PRETORIA ")
11th. Infantry Brigade H.Q.	POURDON Camp.)
1st. Somerset L.I.	PITCHCOTT ")
1st. East Lancs Regt.	POODLE ") P.1 Area.
1st. Hants Regt.	PIDDINGTON ")
1st. Rifle Brigade.	PRATTLE ") PROVEN.
11th. M.G.Company.	PILCH ")
11th. T.M.Battery.	PRESTWOOD ")
12th. Infantry Brigade.H.Q.	SERINGAPATAM Camp X.28.d Central.
1st. Kings Own R.L.R.	SARAWAK Camp.F.5.a.)
2nd. Lancs Fusiliers.	SUTTON Camp.F.10.b.)
2nd. West Riding Regt.	SUEZ Camp.X.29.d.3.2.) S.1 Area
2nd. Essex Regt.	SWINDON " X.29.d.3.7.)
12th. M.G.Company.	SASKATOON Camp.X.29.c.)ST SIXTE
12th. T.M.Battery.	SELKIRK Camp. X.29.a.)
H.Q. 4th. Div. Train.	PROVEN. (Central Camp)
H.Q. Coy. Div. Train.	A.21.b.0.8. Belgium & France Sheet 28 1/40000.
No. 2 Company.	PARDO Camp P.5 Area Proven.
No. 3 Company.	PASTURE Camp.P.1 Area Proven.
No. 4 Company.	SOUTHEND " F.25.A.1.5.St Sixte
10th. Field Ambulance.	PANAMA Camp. P.5 Area Proven.
11th. Field Ambulance.	PRIORY " P.1 " "
12th. Field Ambulance.	SINGAPORE " X.29.c.St Sixte.

P.T.O.

(2)

A.D.M.S.	PROVEN. (Central Camp.)
A.P.M.	" " "
D.A.D.V.S.	" " "
No. 4 Mobile Vet. Section.	PROVEN E.18.b.4.2. P.5. Area.
No. 4 Div. Supply Column.	F.3.b.25.
4th. Div. Gas Officer.	F.3.b.25.
D.A.D.O.S.	PROVEN. E.18.b.4.2.
Ordnance Dump.	" " "
4th. Divl. Emp. Company.	PROVEN. (Central Camp.)
French Mission.	" " "
Senior Chaplain C of E.	" " "
Claims Officer.	" " "
4th. Div. Salvage Officer.	" " "
Railhead for Leave.	POPERINGHE.
Railhead for Reinforcements.	ARNEKE.
Railhead for Supply and Ordnance.	PROVEN.
Corps Depot. } Div. Depot Battalion. }	HERZEELE.
4th. Divisional Band.	PROVEN. (Central Camp)
E.F.C.	PROVEN. } POPERINGHE. } ARNEKE. } WORMHOUDT. }

=

app.13

SECRET.

PRELIMINARY ORDERS FOR MACHINE GUN BARRAGE.

1.   Positions shown on the attached map will be reconnoitred and prepared for firing by 1st October 1917.

2.   4000 rounds per gun S.A.A. will be placed in a suitable position near each position.

27th September 1917.

H. Hansladle
Lieut. Colonel,
General Staff, 4th Division.

Copies to :-

       10th Brigade (2).
       11th Brigade (2).
       12th Brigade (2).
       234th M.G. Coy.

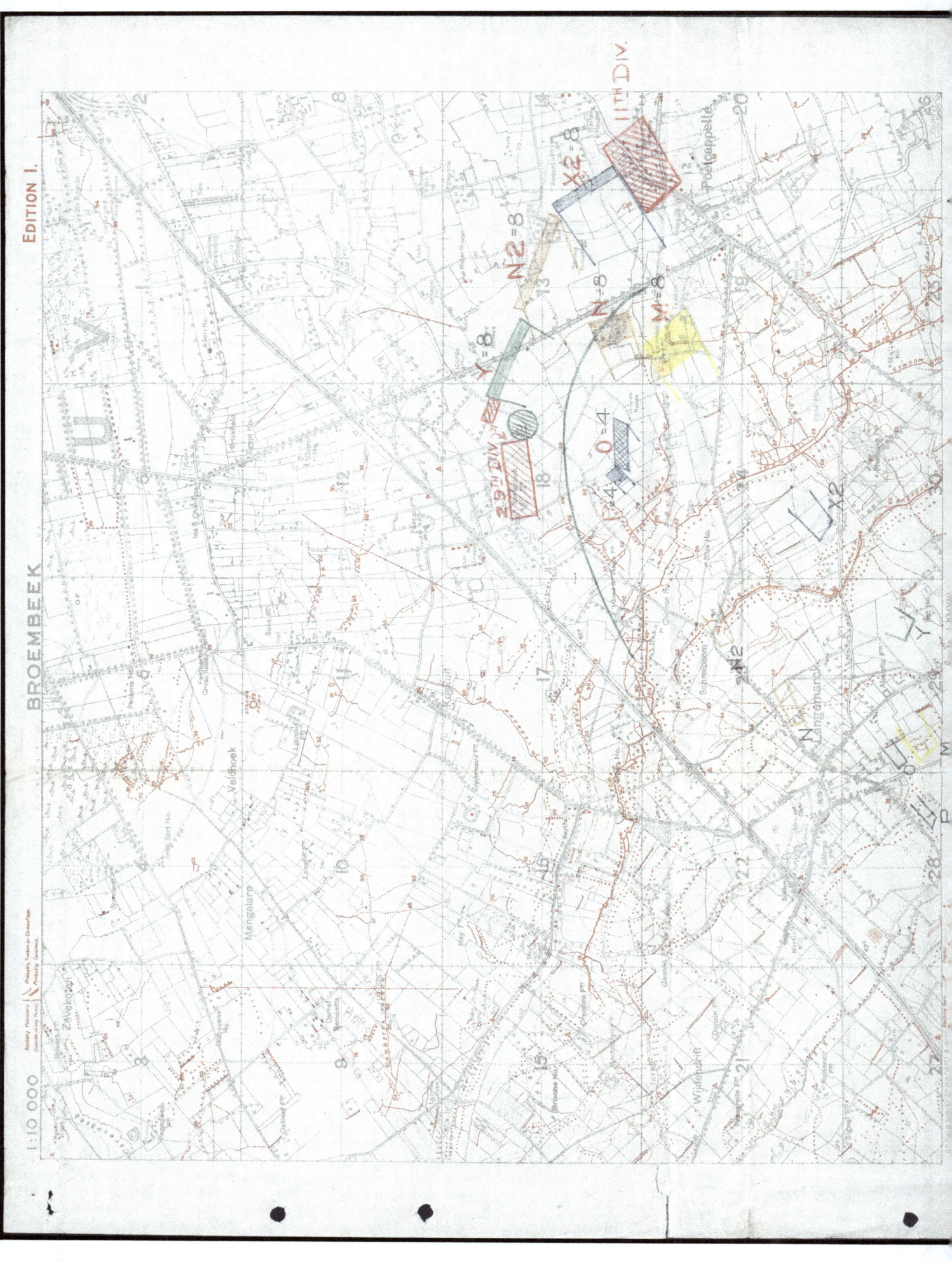

APPENDIX 7.

DEFENCE OF MONCHY.

1. The defences of MONCHY are designed to prevent the enemy from gaining a footing on the high ground in Squares N.6.a & b, O.1, N.12.b & d, and O.7.a & c.

    (a) The immediate defence of the village will be provided by EAST and ORCHARD RESERVE Trenches, and by CIRCLE Trench, garrisoned by the Right Division.

    (b) The defence of the spurs South and North West of the village will be provided for as follows :-

        (i) Right Division. By B. C. D. and F. strong points and by the machine gun nests in SPADE RESERVE at the junction of FORK RESERVE and VINE LANE, in SHOVEL Trench (O.7.d 1.8) and in DRAGOON LANE.
Supporting machine gun nests are situated at N.6.c 9.3 and N.6.a 9.7.

The garrison of (a) and (b) (i) above will consist of 1 battalion.

        (ii) Centre Division. By G. and H. strong points.

These strong points and machine gun nests are to be permanently manned and the troops garrisoning them are not to be employed for local counter-attacks.

2. Owing to the wet nature of the soil between INFANTRY LANE and BIT LANE it is difficult to maintain trenches in a defensible condition in this area. The defence of this portion of the front will therefore be assured by flanking machine gun fire; every machine gun of the Right and Centre Divisions which can fire over this area will have a line of fire marked on its range card to cover some portion of the area. For this purpose machine guns of the Centre Division have been sited and are in position as under :-

    (a) 2 guns in BRIDOON ALLEY traverse the Northern face of the ridge East of MONCHY and enfilade trench O.2/6 in case of necessity.

    (b) 1 gun in CURB SWITCH North (I.31.b 3.6) sweeps the Northern face of the ridge from NO MAN'S LAND to MONCHY.

(c) 1 gun in RIFLE SUPPORT (I.31.b 45,05) sweeps the ridge in NO MAN'S LAND.

(d) 1 gun in G. post brings indirect fire on to the ground between ARROW Trench and DEVIL'S Trench about I.32.c 5,2.

In addition the following switches have been organised to meet the eventuality of a local 'break through':-

<u>Centre Division.</u> (i) BRIDOON ALLEY organised to fire South East in the case of trenches O.2/6, 7 and 8 being lost.

(ii) CURB SWITCH North and South, as a support to BRIDOON ALLEY.

<u>Right Division.</u> A new switch is to be built South of CANISTER AVENUE facing North East from about O.8.b 1,0 to about O.2.c 10,55.

3. The gap between the North end of HOOK Trench and trench O.2/6 will be strongly wired and BRIDOON ALLEY and CANISTER ALLEY will be wired along their Southern and Northern sides respectively.

SECRET.   Copy No. 19

Reference 4th Division DEFENCE SCHEME dated 29/9/17.

Herewith APPENDIX 7 - "DEFENCE OF MONCHY".

Please acknowledge receipt.

                                    A.F.C.Williams
                                              Lieut.Colonel,
5th September, 1917.   General Staff, 4th Division.

Copies to all recipients of
4th Division Defence Scheme.

SECRET.   APPENDIX 7.
-----------   ----------

DEFENCE OF MONCHY.

1. The defences of MONCHY are designed to prevent the enemy from gaining a footing on the high ground in Squares N.6.a and b, O.1, N.12.b and d, and O.7.a and c. The immediate defence of the village will be provided by EAST and ORCHARD RESERVE trenches, and by CIRCLE trench: the defence of the spurs South and North West of the village will be provided by 'B', 'C', 'D', 'F' and 'G' and 'H' strong points and by the machine gun nests in SPADE RESERVE at the junction of FORK RESERVE and VINE LANE, in SHOVEL trench (O.7.d 1.8) and in DRAGOON LANE. Supporting M.G. nests are situated at N.6.c 9.3 and N.6.a 9.7. These strong points and M.G. nests are to be permanently manned.

2. Owing to the wet nature of the soil between INFANTRY LANE and BIT LANE it is impossible to maintain trenches in a defensible condition in this area. The defence of this portion of the front will therefore be assured by flanking machine gun fire; every machine gun of the Right and Centre Divisions which can fire over this area will have a line of fire marked on its range card which will cover some portion of the area.

In addition, the following switches will be organised to meet the eventuality of a local break-through, viz:-

(a) BRIDOON ALLEY organised to fire South East in the case of trenches O.2/6, 7 and 8 being lost.
(b) CURB SWITCH North and South, as a support to BRIDOON ALLEY.
(c) A new switch to be built South of CANISTER AVENUE facing North East, from about O.8.b 1.0 to about O.2.c 10.55.

The gap between the North end of HOOK trench and trench No. O.2/6 will be strongly wired and BRIDOON ALLEY and CANISTER ALLEY will be wired along their Southern and Northern sides respectively.

3. The garrison of the MONCHY defences will consist of 1 battalion found by the Right Division, except that strong points 'G' and 'H' will be garrisoned by the Centre Division. These troops are not to be employed for local counter attacks.

S E C R E T.

Reference 4th Division DEFENCE SCHEME dated 29/8/17.

The attached APPENDIX 7 - DEFENCE OF MONCHY, will be substituted for the one forwarded to you on 5th September which should be destroyed.

Please acknowledge receipt.

A.F.C.Williams.
Lieut.Colonel,

7th September, 1917.   General Staff, 4th Division.

Copies to all recipients of
4th Division DEFENCE SCHEME.

Copy No. 15

"SECRET"   4th Divn No: G.A. 4/20.

App/15

Herewith copy No: _____ of 4th Division

Defence Scheme (Provisional).

Please acknowledge receipt.

H. Ransome
Lieut Colonel,
30th September 1917.   General Staff, 4th. Divn.

Copy No: 1 to 10th Inf.Brigade
         2 to 11th Inf.Brigade
         3 to 12th Inf.Brigade.
         4 to C.R.A, 4th Divn.
         5 to C.R.E, 4th Divn.
         6 to 21st W.Yorks Regt.
         7 to Signals.
         8 to A.D.M.S, 4th Divn.
         9 to 4th Divn "Q"
       10 to D.M.G.O, 4th Divn.
       11 to 11th Divn.
       12 to 29th Divn.
       13 to XIVth Corps.

14 } War Diary
15 }
16   File

S E C R E T.

4th DIVISION DEFENCE SCHEME (Provisional).

1. The Divisional front extends from U.24.d.0.5 - U.23.b.6.6.

2. The defence of the Divisional front will be organised as follows :-

   (a) Front System consisting of :-

   Outpost line
   U.24.c.9.5 - LOUIS FARM (incl.) - BLUE HOUSE - U.23.b.6.5.

   Main line of resistance.
   U.24.c.4.0. - EAGLE Trench.

   (b) LANGEMARCK Defences.
   BIRD HOUSE - U.29.b.5.9 - U.23.c.7.5. - U.23.c.5.5.
   These defences include two groups of concrete houses.

   (c) IRON CROSS Area.
   This consists of a series of concrete houses between the GAIETY Fm. - VULCAN CROSSING Road and the STEENBEEK.

3. (a) Normally the front area will be held by one Brigade distributed in depth :-
   One battalion front system.
   One battalion LANGEMARCK and IRON CROSS Areas.
   One battalion CANDLE Trench (when ready).
   One battalion CANAL BANK.

   (b) The Brigade in the line will have in addition to its own M.G.Company :-
   2 sections of the Supporting Brigade M.G.Coy.
   2 sections of the Divisional M.G.Coy.
   The barrage lines of the latter will be arranged by the Division and will not be altered without reference to the Division. They may be employed for harassing fire by the Brigade in the line but must always maintain 4,000 rds. per gun for S.O.S. purposes..
   When the S.O.S. Signal is sent up they will at once open rapid fire for 10 minutes after which they will slacken the fire.

4. (a) The principles of the defence are the same as usual, i,e.,
   No ground to be given up.
   In the event of any ground being lost it is to be retaken as quickly as possible.

   (b) Every unit and formation will have a unit detailed by name as the "Counter attacking" unit.
   The duty of this unit is to counter attack at once without waiting for orders. Unless this counter attack can be delivered at once before the enemy has time to settle down it must wait for artillery support and will therefore be arranged by the Brigade.
   (c) Whenever a counter attack is made a proportion of Infantry and machine guns must always be left in each defensive system until it can be replaced by units from the rear.

5. With the exception of the machine guns in the front system the following will normally be given barrage lines on which they will open in case of attack :-
   2 sections of the supporting Brigade.
   2 sections of the Divisional Company.

The machine guns of the Brigade in the line will be entirely at the disposal of the Brigadier subject to the co-ordination of the defence on both flanks of the Division which will be arranged by the D.M.G.O.

6. In the event of the S.O.S. Signal being sent up the artillery covering that particular front will at once open its barrage.

The C.R.A. will be responsible for establishing a chain of posts by which the signal can be passed back in foggy weather.

Every effort must be made to locate the point from which the S.O.S. light is fired so that guns will not open fire unnecessarily.

Should the enemy commence a heavy bombardment of our front system the Brigadier in charge of that section of the line will, if he considers it to portend an attack, call upon his artillery Liaison officer, or if he is not present the C.R.A. for counter preparation.

On the other hand the artillery will not hesitate to open this kind of fire on their own, if they consider the situation demands it, reporting at once to the Brigadier in the line for information.

7. In the event of the attack becoming really serious, the supporting Brigade which is in camps immediately West of the Canal, may be ordered forward to :-

(a) Take over the IRON CROSS Defences with one battalion.
(b) Place a second battalion temporarily in CANDLE Trench.
(c) Move up the Brigade via the Water course running N.E. from JOLIE FM (C.9.a.2.8) to regain the high ground East of LANGEMARCK by an attack from the direction of RAT HOUSE.

All Brigade Staff Officers and as many officers of battalion and battalion Scouts and Runners should reconnoitre the area thoroughly so as to know how to get to any part of the area.

8. All working parties East of the STEENBEEK when the attack takes place will come under the orders of the Brigadier holding the line and will be disposed as he wishes.

West of the STEENBEEK working parties will rejoin their own units.

4th Division
War Diaries
General Staff

October 1917

4TH DIV.
G. S.
October, 1917

Army Form C. 2118.

WAR DIARY or INTELLIGENCE SUMMARY.
4th DIVISION
OCTOBER 1917.

(Erase heading not required.)

Place	Date	Hour	Summary of Events and Information	Remarks and references to Appendices
ELVERDINGHE (Welsh Fm)	1st Oct		On the morning of October 1st the 4th Division was disposed as follows:—	
			Distribution of Battalions:—	
			FRONT LINE — 12th Inf Bde — Bde HQ at STRAY FM	1st Kings Own in FRONT LINE (V29d05-V23b75) 2nd Duke of Wellingtons in Support 2nd Lancs Fusiliers in CANAL BANK 2nd Essex Regt in HULL FM
			SUPPORTING Bde — 10th Inf Bde — Bde HQ at FUSILIER HQ (C13c12)	4 Battalions in vicinity of BRIELEN (MALAKOFF FM)
			RESERVE Bde — 11th Inf Bde — Bde HQ at L2 D'Ypres (B23c58)	4 Battalions between BRIELEN and ELVERDINGHE
			Divl. HQ at WELSH FM	
			During the night 1st/2nd the 11th Infantry Highlanders (10 Inf Brigade, temporarily under orders of G at 11th Bde) relieved the 12th Inf Bde in the front line. The Seaforth Highlanders took over the battle front allotted to the 10th Bde to the 11th Brigade. On completion of relief the 12th Inf Bde passed with Divisional Division into Reserve into billets vacated by the 11th Infantry Brigade.	

WAR DIARY
or
INTELLIGENCE SUMMARY.

Army Form C. 2118.

Place	Date	Hour	Summary of Events and Information	Remarks and references to Appendices
-do-	2nd		Notice moving that 2nd and 1st Battln. of 10th Infantry attached too hitherto the front as forward:— 1st Rifle Brigade on the Right; 2nd Seaforths (detached) on the Left. 1st Hampshire Regt— in support along the YPRES–BOESINGHE CANAL. 1st Somerset L.Inf in Reserve in HULL FARM just West of CANAL. 1st E. Lancs Regt in BRIDGE CAMP at ELVERDINGHE. The 10th Infantry Brigade remained in the support area (MALAKOFF) in vicinity of BRIELEN and the CANAL and the 12th Infantry Brigade the Divisional Reserve in place just 11 Bde.	
-do-	3rd		At 10.am the G.O.C 10th Infantry assumed command just left centre of this Divisional front (held by 2nd Seaforths) at their hour to 1st Brigade Headquarters opened at ADELPHI C.3.b.2.1. During the night 3rd/4th all units maintained their ordinary positions. the attack on October 4.	

A 5834 Wt.W4973/M687 750,000 8/16 D.D. & L. Ltd. Forms/C.2118/13

WAR DIARY or INTELLIGENCE SUMMARY

Army Form C. 2118.

Place	Date	Hour	Summary of Events and Information	Remarks and references to Appendices
do	4th		At 6. a.m. the Division was attacked with the 11th Inf Bde on the right, 10th Inf Bde left and 12 Inf Bde in Divisional Reserve in conjunction with the Division on the right & left – (vide G.O.C's Order No. 61) and the attached Appendix (B "Account of operations on Oct 4th-7th 1917" as issued with No. 63). It was during the afternoon of Div order No. 64 (B) however shortly cancelled.	(a) See App 9 Div Order for Oct, 4th (b) See App. 1 (c) See App 2 (d) See App 3
do	5th		Fairly quiet day – nothing of importance occurred – Div. Orders issued 6 & 7 p.m. (B)(C) 11th Inf. Bde extended its	(e) See App 4
do	6th		Left owing the line U23 b 70 – V13 a 00 relieving the 10th Inf. Bde – at the same time the portion of the 10th Inf Bde front north of the new boundary line was taken over by the 12th Div. The 10th Infantry Brigade on relief concentrated in the	(f) See App 5
do	7th		MALAKOFF area with Brigade Headquarters at FUSILIER HQ during the night. The 12th Infantry Brigade relieved the 11th Infantry Brigade, leaving one Battalion, west of the CANAL. 10th Inf Bde then Supporting Bde and 11th Bde Reserve	

WAR DIARY or INTELLIGENCE SUMMARY.

Army Form C. 2118.

Place	Date	Hour	Summary of Events and Information	Remarks and references to Appendices
-do-	8th		During the evening the 10th and 12th Bns moved up to their positions for the attack on the 9th October. - 12th Brigade in front line - 10th Bn in Support - 11th Bn remaining in Divisional Reserve -	
CANAL BANK C.19.a.00	9th		4th Division Advanced HQ moved forward from WELCH FM and was Established on the BOESINGHE - YPRES CANAL BANK (C.19.a.00) by Zero hour - At zero hour 5.20 am, the 9th Division attacked in co-operation with British ions on either flank. The attack was carried out by the 12th Infantry Brigade with the 2nd Essex Regt on the right, 2nd Lancs Fusiliers on the left, the 2nd West Riding in Bde Support and the 1st Kings Own in Reserve. 12 Infantry Brigade HQ were Established in LANGEMARCK - The 10th Rifle Bde in support with 1 Battalion (HOUSEHOLD BATTALION) ready to move forward and come under orders of G.O.C. 12 Bde if required. The 1st Warwicks Regt were concentrated in the vicinity of STRAY FARM with Battalion Headquarters and the 2 remaining Battalions of 14th Brigade remained in their camps west of the CANAL. (For account of operations on OCT 9th vide appendix (a)	See App/B

Army Form C. 2118.

WAR DIARY
or
INTELLIGENCE SUMMARY.
(Erase heading not required.)

Instructions regarding War Diaries and Intelligence Summaries are contained in F.S. Regs., Part II. and the Staff Manual respectively. Title pages will be prepared in manuscript.

Place	Date	Hour	Summary of Events and Information	Remarks and references to Appendices
CANAL BANK C19 a 00	9th	9/am	4th Divn Operation Order No 67 (a) was issued concerning the relief of the 4th Divn. Division by the 38th Division —	(a) See app. 7 (b) See app. 8.
		9.30/am	4th Divn Order No 68 (b) issued —	
— do —	10 hr — 11 hr	}	Nothing of importance occurred.	
— do —	12 hr		At 5.25 am the 4th Division again attacked with the 12th Infantry Bde and 2 Battalions of the 10th Bde attached to 12th Bde — The attack was carried out with the Hawkesbury Battalion on the right and the 1st Warwicks on the left, the 1st King's Own were in the support and the 1st Rifle Brigade in Divisional Reserve. The 2nd Essex Regt and the East Kings Own remained in the and STRAY FARM area. During the day the 11th Brigade moved by rail to the PROVEN area being relieved by the 103rd Brigade —	
— do —	13 hr		102nd Brigade moved by rail to the PROVEN area being relieved by the Order No 69 issued for move of XIV Corps area to XVIII Corps (c) during the night 13/19 hr the 103rd Brigade 34 wagons took over front land from the 12th Infantry Brigade moved back on completion of relief to the STRAY FM — MALAKOFF area.	(c) See app. 9

Army Form C. 2118.

WAR DIARY
or
INTELLIGENCE SUMMARY.
(Erase heading not required.)

Instructions regarding War Diaries and Intelligence Summaries are contained in F.S. Regs., Part II. and the Staff Manual respectively. Title pages will be prepared in manuscript.

Place	Date	Hour	Summary of Events and Information	Remarks and references to Appendices
PROVEN.	14th		By the At 10.am the G.O.C. 34th Division took over command of the Divisional front from G.O.C. 4th Division – 4th Division Headquarters moved to PROVEN – (less Artillery) by lie evening of the 14th the whole of 4th Division (less Artillery and Pioneer Battalion, 21st W. Yorks Regt.) was concentrated in the PROVEN area as under:–	
			Divisional Headquarters PROVEN.	
			10th Infantry Brigade – PROVEN No. 3 area.	
			11th Infantry Brigade – do No. 2 area.	
			12th Infantry Brigade – do No. 4 area.	
do –	15th		4th Division (less Artillery and Pioneer Battalion) moved from XIV = Corps PROVEN area into POPERINGHE (XVIII Corps area) remaining under the XIV Corps for administration – (12th Bde did not move)	(a) See App. 10
POPERINGHE			12th Infantry Brigade Batt'n. & other units by Motor to POPERINGHE & No. 4 area moved from PROVEN to St. JAN TER BIEZEN.	(b) See App. 11
POPERINGHE	16th –			
DUISANS.	17th – 18th – 19th –		On the 17th, 18th and 19th the 4th Division (less Artillery and Pioneer Battalion) moved by rail from POPERINGHE area to DUISANS area and were transferred from XIV to XVII Corps – 4th Division	

A 583+ Wt. W4973/M687 750,000 8/16 D.D. & L. Ltd. Forms/C.2118/13

WAR DIARY or INTELLIGENCE SUMMARY

Army Form C. 2118.

Place	Date	Hour	Summary of Events and Information	Remarks and references to Appendices
			Headquarters were established in DUISANS at 2pm on 17th October – on the same date Brigadier General A.G. PRITCHARD (Commanding 10th Infantry Brigade) assumed temporary command of the 4th Div. in the absence of Maj Genl T.G. Matheson on sick leave – arrived in the DUISANS area disposed as follows:–	
			10th Inf Bde – DUISANS area with Bde HQ in "Y" HUTS.	
			11th Inf Bde – WARLUS area – DAINVILLE	
			12th Inf Bde – HABARCQ area – HABARCQ.	
do	20th 21st		Only 11 rumour during 20th/12 & 21st/12 the 4th Div Right Inf Bde reported (a) Brigades arrived in DUISANS area.	(a) See a/f/12
do	22nd		Moving forward into the line at MONCHY in relief of 12th Div Brig Genl T.M. WADE D.S.O. assumed command 11th Bde vice Brig Gnl R.A. BERNERS D.S.O. 11th Inf Bde Group with 10th and 23rd Lt M.G. Coys and 10th T.M. Batty moved from the WARLUS and DUISANS area into ARRAS area in relief of 35th Inf Bde (12th Div)	
do	23rd		10th Inf Brigade moved from the DUISANS area into ARRAS area – 11th Infantry Brigade moved from ARRAS into the line.	

WAR DIARY or INTELLIGENCE SUMMARY

Army Form C. 2118.

Place	Date	Hour	Summary of Events and Information	Remarks and references to Appendices
-do-	24.		12th Infantry Brigade moved from HABARCQ area to ARRAS area into the line. 10th Infantry Brigade moved from ARRAS area into the line. (2nd Essex Regt. 12th Brigade remained at GOUVES until 27th October) Owing to asphyxiated cases (? mustard) at 10 am G.O.C. 4th Division took over command of the night Divisional Sector (XVII Corps) from G.O.C. 12 Division who this had as on completion of relief the of Division was:-	
ARRAS.	25.		4th Divisional Headquarters – ARRAS. 10th Infantry Brigade – Right front line – HQ at N 9 c 97 } Sheet 51 B. S.W. 11th Infantry Brigade – Left front line – HQ at N 5 a 38 } 12th Infantry Brigade – Divisional Reserve – 1 Battalion in BOIS DES BOEUFS 1 Battalion in ARRAS 1 Battalion in ATHIEUCOURT (1 Battalion temporarily at GOUVE'S) Bde HQ in ARRAS. 2 Coys of 9th Gordon Highlanders (15th Div: Pioneer Battalion) and 1 Company of	

WAR DIARY
or
INTELLIGENCE SUMMARY.
(Erase heading not required.)

Army Form C. 2118.

Place	Date	Hour	Summary of Events and Information	Remarks and references to Appendices
do	—		1/5th Duke of Cornwalls L. Inf. (61st Division Pioneer Battalion) were loaned to the 4th Division from 25th Oct. on the 21 WestYorks (Pioneer) Regt. had remained under XIV Corps when 61st Division. Army men.	
do	26th		Very quiet day - Maj. Genl. SCOTT, Lieut. Col. MOTTE and Captain SCOTT (A.E.F.) American Army arrived for 2 days attachment to 4th Divisional Headquarters.	
do	27th		Quiet day - the 3 attached American Officers visited the trenches.	
do	28th		Maj. Genl. T. G. MATHESON rejoined the Division on his return from sick leave. Brigadier Genl. A. G. PRITCHARD CMG who had been commanding 4th Division in the former absence returned to command 10th Brigade. 12th Infantry Brigade was temporary lent to VI Corps and relieved the 154th Brigade (51st Division) in the line on the immediate right of the 4th Division, in order to facilitate the relief of the 57th Division by the 34th Division.	
do	29th 30th 31st		Quiet days - nothing of particular interest to record.	T B Willington Brigadier General

WAR DIARY, GENERAL STAFF, 4th DIVISION.

1st - 31st OCTOBER, 1917.

APPENDICES.

1. Account of operations on 4th October.
2. Division Order 63.
3. " " 64.
4. " " 65.
5. " " 66.
6. Account of operations on 9th October.
7. Division Order 67.
8. " " 68.
9. " " 69.
10. Warning Order.
11. Division Order 70.
12. " " 71.
13. Moves and dispositions of Brigades on 5th & 6th October.
14. Telephone Conversations Battle 4th October.
15. IN Messages - Battle 4th October. (Book form).
16. OUT " - Battle 4th October. (Book form).
17. Telephone Conversations - Battle 9th October.
18. IN Messages - Battle 9th October. (Book form).
19. OUT " - Battle 9th October. (Book form).
20. IN Messages - Battle 12th October. (Book form).
21. OUT " - Battle 12th October. (Book form).
22. Telephone Conversations - Battle 12th October.
22A. Account of operations 12 October
23. Attachment of American Officers.
24. Telegrams IN and OUT for Battle on 4th October.
25. " " " " " " " 9th October.
26. " " " " " " " 12th October.
27. List Of Position Calls.
28. Congratulatory messages.

Attached-Appendices 9 and 10 to War Diary for September.

29. Summary of operations 9 & 12.

ACCOUNT OF OPERATIONS BY
THE 4th DIVISION N.E. OF YPRES
BETWEEN THE 4th AND 12th OCTOBER, 1917.

At 6 a.m. on 4th October the 4th Division (XIV Corps) attacked in conjunction with the 11th Division (XVIII Corps) on its right and the 29th Division (XIV Corps) on its left.

The attack was carried out by the 11th Infantry Brigade on the right, 10th Infantry Brigade on the left and 12th Infantry Brigade in reserve.

The 11th Infantry Brigade was disposed as follows :-

1st Somerset L.I. Right Assaulting Battalion, and
1st Hampshire Regt Left Assaulting Battalion,
1st East Lancs in support, with instructions to advance close up to the 2 Assaulting Battalions, inorder to avoid the enemy's barrage.
1st Rifle Brigade in Brigade Reserve, about STRAY FARM, with orders to move forward to the INGS, at Zero hour.

The dispositions of the 10th Infantry Brigade on the left were as follows :-

2nd Seaforth Highlanders, Assaulting Battalion.
This Battalion was formed up just East of EAGLE TRENCH.

3/10th Middlesex Regt were in support, and the
1st R. Warwickshire Regt in Brigade Reserve, about LANGEMARCK and AUBONGITE.

The remaining Battalion of the 10th Infantry Brigade, Household Battalion (less 1½ companies) remained West of the YPRES-BOSINGHE CANAL. 1½ Companies of this Battalion was employed as Brigade carrying party.

As regards the right of the attack, the 2 Assaulting Battalions of the 11th Infantry Brigade were reported to have reached their 1st Objective up to time, capturing several prisoners and machine guns. After a pause of 1 hour on the first Objective, the advance was continued. The Brigade reached the line of its final objective and consolidated.

Considerable artillery fire and long range rifle and machine gun fire were encountered during the attack. The 11th Infantry Brigade had subsequently to withdraw slightly in order to conform with the 10th Infantry Brigade on its left.

As regards the left of the attack, the assaulting Battalion of the 10th Infantry Brigade, 2nd Seaforth Highlanders, after crossing the LAUDETBEEK Marsh, which proved a difficult obstacle and caused some loss of direction and alignment, encountered opposition from machine gun fire from its left flank, and suffered considerable losses. The Seaforth Highlanders were reinforced by 1½ Companies of the 3/10th Middlesex Regt and succeeded in reaching their 1st objective.

After a pause of 1 hour on the 1st objective, the advance was continued, but became somewhat disjointed owing to heavy rifle and machine gun fire from the left flank. Never-the-less some men of the Seaforth Highlanders succeeded in reaching and establishing themselves on the far slope of 19 METRE HILL, in touch with the 11th Infantry Brigade on their right.

Later in the day, 19 METRE HILL was heavily countered attacked by the enemy and our advanced troops, in that vicinity, fell back slightly until re-established by a counter movement made by a company of the 1st East Lancs Regt and a company of the 1st R. Warwickshire Regt, acting in close co-operation.

At dusk the situation on the left flank of the 10th Infantry Brigade was obscure, as the Brigade on its left had failed to maintain touch. The gap between the 10th Infantry Brigade and the right Brigade of the 29th Division was filled about nightfall by 2 Companies of the 1st Royal Warwickshire Regt.

On completion of the day's operations our line ran approximately as follows,:from right to left:-

FERDAN HOUSE - KANGAROO HUTS just West of TRAGIQUE FARM - 19 METRE HILL (incl) - Road Junction U.18.c.9.5., in touch with Divisions on either flank.

The attack was resumed at 5.20 a.m. on the 9th October.

On this occasion, the attack of the 4th Division was carried out by the 12th Infantry Brigade, with the 10th Infantry Brigade in support and the 11th Infantry Brigade in Divisional Reserve. The 11th Division attacked on the Right of the 4th Division and the 29th Division on the left.

At Zero hour the 12th Infantry Brigade was disposed as follows :-

    2nd Essex Regt..... Right Assaulting Battalion.
    2nd Lancs Fusrs.... Left Assaulting Battalion.
    2nd W. Riding Regt. In Brigade Support and
    1st K.O.(R.L.) Regt in Brigade Reserve.

At 5.20 a.m. the Infantry attacked behind our Artillery barrage and at 5.24 a.m. the enemy's barrage came down roughly on a line through LOUIS FARM. The enemy's barrage was ragged at first, but shortly increased in intensity.

Our advance continued successfully up to the 1st Objective, which was captured along the whole front. After a pause on the 1st Objective the advance was continued towards the final Objective, but was checked by heavy machine fire from the N.E. end of POELCAPPELLE. This heavy machine gun fire was chiefly due to the fact that the Division attacking on the right of the 4th Division was unable to reach its final objective.

The line held by the 12th Infantry Brigade at dusk ran approximately as follows :-

    V.13.d.4.2. - Just West of STRING HOUSES -
    V.13.central - West of COMPROMIS FARM, in touch
    with the 29th Division in the vicinity of huts
    just East of MILLERS HOUSES.

There was a gap of about 200 yards between the right of the 4th Division and the left of the 11th Division (on their right).

The attack was resumed at 5.25 a.m. on the 12th October.

On this occasion the 18th Division (XVIII Corps) attacked on the right of the 4th Division and 17th Division (XIV Corps) attacked on its left.

The 4th Division attack was carried out a composite Brigade under the orders of the G.O.C. 12th Infantry Brigade composed of the following Regiments :-

    Household Battalion..... Right Assaulting Battalion.
    1st R. Warwick Regt..... Left Assaulting Battalion
    1st K.O.(R.L.) Regt..... In Brigade support and
    1st Rifle Brigade....... In Brigade Reserve.

During this attack the Household Battalion on the right were unable to keep in touch with the left Assaulting Battalion of the 18th Division on their right, as the latter were held up by the enemy defences in POELCAPPELLE, and in particular by resistance from the BREWERY.

The 1st R. Warwickshire Regt on the left experienced little difficulty in their advance, and kept in touch throughout with the Right Assaulting Battalion of the 17th Division on their left, and with the Household Battalion on their right.

In consequence of the opposition encountered by the 18th Division, the advance of the Household Battalion was considerable hampered by fire from POELCAPPELLE, and particularly from HELLES HOUSE.

REQUETE FARM was, however, occupied by this Battalion and a defensive flank facing POELCAPPELLE was formed in conjunction with the 1st K.O.(R.L.) Regt.

The 1st Rifle Brigade had moved all four Companies across the 5 CHEMINS-POELCAPPELLE Road by 9.45 a.m.

At dusk the front line held by the attacking troops of the 4th Division ran approximately as follows from right to left :-

    Just West of REQUETE FARM - EAST of BESACE FARM
    to MEMLING FARM, in touch with the Divisions
    on either flank.

During the operations on the 3 dates referred to above

it is estimated that between 200 and 300 prisoners were captured by the 4th Division, and in addition 4th Machine guns.

The total casualties of the 4th Division during these operations amount to 157 Officers and 3412 O.R.

Appendix 22A

Account of operations 12th October.

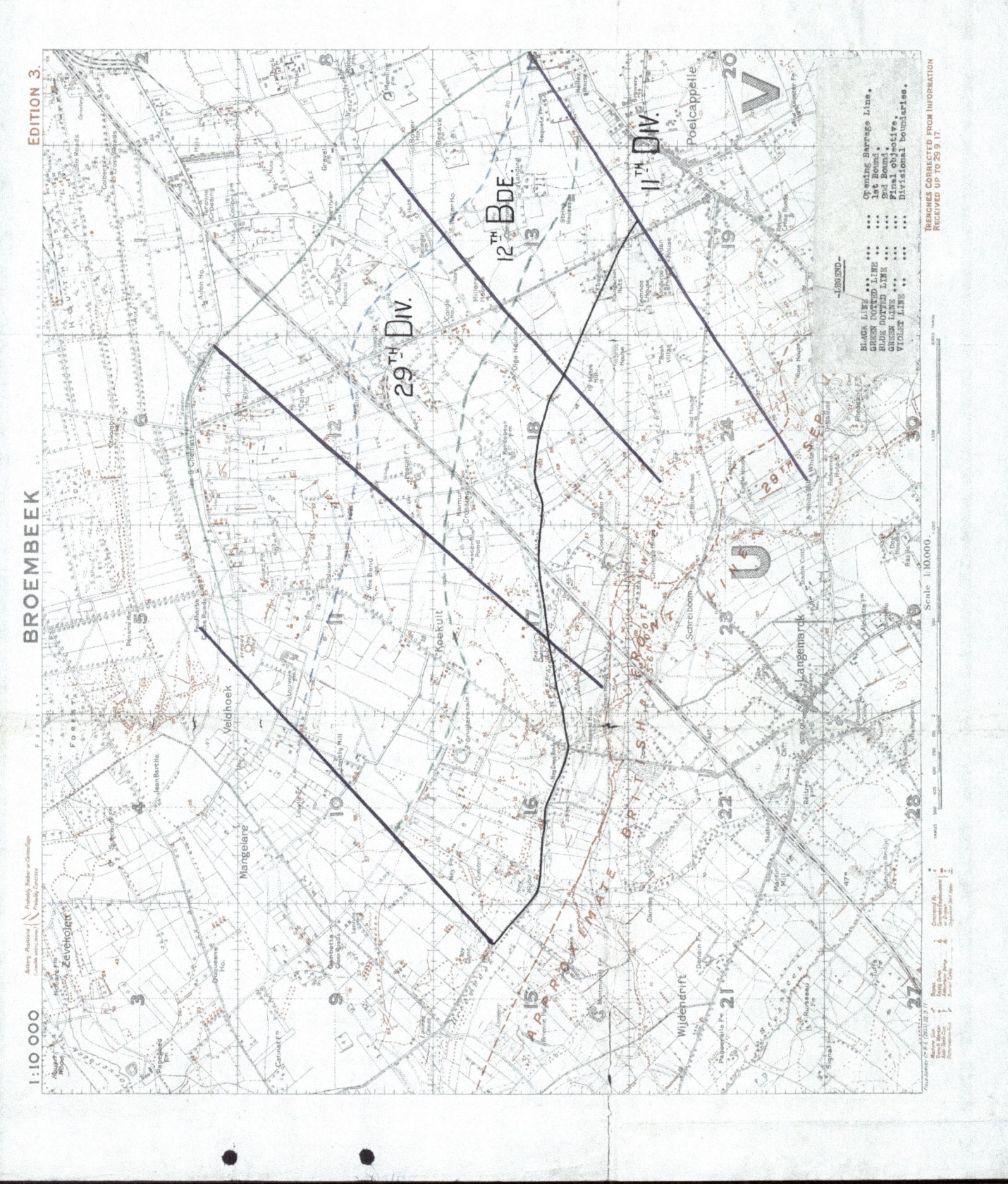

- SECRET -   Copy No: 25

   4th DIVISION ORDER No: 63
   ****

                                                   4th October 1917.

1. (a)   The 11th Infantry Brigade will extend
   its left on the night 5th/6th October as far as
   U.17.d.✕.15, relieving the 10th Infantry Brigade, and
   the 1st R.Dublin Fusiliers of the 29th Division.

   (b)   The 10th Infantry Brigade on relief, will be
   situated as under :-

            H.Qrs   ...   FUSILIER HO.
            "A" Bn   ...   BRIDGE CAMP.
            "B" Bn   ...   HULLS FARM.
            "C" Bn   ...   WOLFE CAMP.
            "D" Bn   ...   SOULT CAMP.

   (c)   The new Divisional boundary will, on
   completion of the relief, be as shown on map issued
   with 4th Divn G.A. 32/17.

2. (a)   On the same night, one section of the 12th
   M.G.Coy, and one section of the 234th M.G.Coy, will
   be placed at the disposal of the G.O.C, 11th Infantry
   Brigade, to relieve two sections of the 11th M.G.Coy.

   (b)   Two sections of the 10th M.G.Coy will be
   withdrawn on this night, leaving two sections under
   the command of the G.O.C, 11th Infantry Brigade.

            The D.M.G.O is placed at the disposal of the
   G.O.C, 11th Infantry Brigade to co-ordinate the
   Machine Gun Defence of the area, and to arrange the
   relief of the machine guns on the night 5th/6th Oct.

3.   The G.O.C, 11th Infantry Brigade will assume
   command of the whole front from V.19.b.2..7 to U.17.d.
   ✕.15 on completion of the reliefs.

4.   A C K N O W L E D G E.

                                          H. Hunstable
                                          Lieut: Colonel,
Issued at 7.30 a.m.   General Staff, 4th Divn.

Copies to :-
         No: 1 to G.O.C.   13 to 21st W.Yorks Rgt
             2 to G.S.O.1.   (Pioneers)
             3 to 10th Brigade.   14) to 4th Divn "Q"
             4 to 11th Brigade.   15) "
             5 to 12th Brigade.   16)
             6 to C.R.A.   17 to 9th Squadron R.F.C.
             7 to C.R.E.   18 to 11th Divn.
             8 to Signals.   19 to 29th Divn.
             9 to A.D.M.S.   20 to Guards Divn.
            10 to A.P.M.   21) to XIVth Corps
            11 to 234th M.G.Coy.   22)
            12 to D.M.G.O.   23 to XIVth Corps H.A.
                        24)
                        25) to War Diary.
                        26 to File.

- SECRET -
****

App. 3

Copy No: 25

4th DIVISION ORDER NO: 64
****

4th Octr 1917.

1. 4th Divn Order No: 63 is cancelled.

2. (a) The 12th Inf. Bde will place one Battalion at the disposal of the 10th Inf. Bde to-morrow, 5th instant.
   This Bn will take over the front now held by the 10th Inf. Bde, and that part of the 29th Divn front as far as U.17.d.20.15.

   (b) The three battalions of the 10th Inf. Bde so relieved will be withdrawn to HULLS FARM, WOLFE and SCULT.

   (c) The new Divisional boundary will, on completion of the relief, be as shown on Map issued with 4th Divn G.A. 22/17.

3. To-morrow night, 5th/6th inst, one section of the 12th M.G.Coy and one section of the 234th M.G.Coy, will be placed at the disposal of the G.O.C. 11th Inf. Bde, to relieve two sections of the 11th M.G.Coy.
   The D.M.G.O will assist the G.O's.C. 10th and 11th Inf. Bdes to arrange the barrages.

4. (a) On the night 7th/8th, the 12th Inf. Bde will relieve the 11th Inf. Bde, which will withdraw to :-

H.Qrs	...	L.2.Works.
"A" Bn	...	SARAGOSSA CAMP
"B" Bn	...	LEIPSIG CAMP
"C" Bn	...	REDAN CAMP
"D" Bn	...	BRIDGE CAMP

   (b) On the night 7th/8th, one Bn will relieve the Bn of the 12th Inf. Bde attached to the 10th Inf. Bde.
   This Bn will move to CANDLE area.

   The situation at 6 a.m on the 8th inst will be :-

   10th Inf. Bde

H.Q.	....	AU BON GITE
"A" Bn	....	)Front system.
"B" Bn	....	)
"C" Bn	....	HULLS FARM.
"D" Bn	....	WOLFE CAMP.

   11th Inf. Bde.

H.Q.	....	L.2.Works.
"A" Bn	....	SARAGOSSA CAMP
"B" Bn	....	LEIPSIG CAMP
"C" Bn	....	REDAN CAMP
"D" Bn	....	BRIDGE CAMP.

   12th Inf. Bde

H.Q.	....	STRAY FARM.
"A" Bn	)	
"B" Bn	)...	Front & support.
"C" Bn	....	CANDLE area.
"D" Bn	....	SCULT CAMP.

P.T.O.

5.   Details of reliefs will be made between Brigadiers concerned.

6.   A C K N O W L E D G E.

                                    [signature]
                                    for
                                    Lieut: Colonel,
Issued at 11.30 p.m.   General Staff, 4th Division.

Copies to :-
         No: 1 to G.O.C.   14)
             2 to G.S.O.1.   15) to 4th Divn "Q"
             3 to 10th Brigade.   16)
             4 to 11th Brigade.   17 to 9th Squad: R.F.C.
             5 to 12th Brigade.   18 to 11th Divn.
             6 to C.R.A.   19 to 29th Divn.
             7 to C.R.E.   20 to Guards Divn.
             8 to Signals.   21) to XIVth Corps.
             9 to A.D.M.S.   22)
            10 to A.P.M.   23 to XIVth Corps H.A.
            11 to 234th M.G.Coy.   24)
            12 to D.M.G.O.   25) to War Diary.
            13 to 21st W.Yorks R.   26) to File.
                 (Pioneers.

SECRET.   Copy No. ....

4th DIVISION ORDER NO. 65.

5th October, 1917.

4th Div. Order 64 is cancelled.

1. (a) The 11th Inf.Bde. will extend its left on the night 6th/7th, to the line U.23.b 7.0 - V.13 a 0.0, relieving the 10th Inf.Bde.

   (b) That portion of the 10th Inf.Bde. from that line to the present boundary will be relieved on the night 6th/7th by the 29th Division.

   (c) The Divisional boundaries will then be as shown on attached map *.

2. The 10th Inf.Bde. on relief will concentrate in the MALAKOFF area, with Headquarters at FUSILIER HQ.

3. On the night 7th/8th the 12th Inf.Bde. will relieve the 11th Inf.Bde., leaving one Bn. West of the Canal.

   The 10th Inf.Bde. will then become the supporting Bde. and the 11th Inf.Bde. the Reserve Bde.

4. The machine guns available for the 11th Inf.Bde. on the night 6th/7th will be :-

   2 sections 11th M.G.Coy.
   2 sections 12th M.G.Coy.
   3 sections 234th M.G.Coy.
   1 section 10th M.G.Coy.

   On the night 7th/8th the two sections of the 11th M.G.Coy. will be withdrawn.

5. All details of reliefs will be made between Brigadiers concerned.

6. ACKNOWLEDGE.

                                                  Lieut.Colonel
Issued at 11.30 p.m.   General Staff, 4th Division

* Issued to Brigades.

Copy No: 1 to G.O.C.
2 to G.S.O.1
3 to 10th Brigade.
4 to 11th Brigade.
5 to 12th Brigade.
6 to C.R.A.
7 to C.R.E.
8 to Signals.
9 to A.D.M.S.
10 to A.P.M.
11 to 234th M.G.Coy.
12 to D.M.G.O.
13 to 21st W.Yorks R.
14)
15) to 4th Divn "Q"
16)
17 to 9th Squadron R.F.C.
18 to 11th Divn.
19 to 29th Divn.
20 to Guards Divn.
21 to 17th Divn.
22)
23) to XIVth Corps.
24) to War Diary.
25)
26 to XIVth Corps H.A.
27 to File.

SECRET.

Copy No. 26

4th DIVISION ORDER NO. 66.

6th October, 1917.

1. (a) The enemy suffered severe losses on the 4th inst.

    (b) The attack is being resumed over a very wide front on Z day.

    (c) The XIV Corps is attacking with 3 Divisions :-

        4th Division on the Right.
        29th Division in the Centre.
        Guards Division on the left.

    (d) The 32nd Infantry Brigade 11th Division is attacking on the right of the 4th Division.

2. The Division will attack with the 12th Infantry Brigade in front line, 10th Infantry Brigade in support and 11th Infantry Brigade in reserve.

3. The attack will be made in three bounds as shown on

Para. 3 (b) The general direction of the advance is N.E.

4. The attack will be assisted by a creeping and also by machine gun barrages, details of which will be communicated later.

5. (a) The Brigades will be formed up ready for the attack at Zero minus two hours as follows :-

    12th Infantry Brigade H.Q. U.29.a.6.7.
        All Battalions East of STEENBEEK.

    10th Infantry Brigade H.Q. STRAY FARM.
        All Battalions East of CANAL, leading Battalions on the GAIETY FARM - IRON CROSS Road.

    12th Infantry Brigade H.Q. L2 Works.
        All Battalions West of CANAL.

At Zero hour the 10th Infantry Brigade will advance to the line FERDAN HOUSE - 19 Metre HILL.

SECRET.

Copy No. 26

4th DIVISION ORDER NO. 66.

6th October, 1917.

1. (a) The enemy suffered severe losses on the 4th inst.

   (b) The attack is being resumed over a very wide front on Z day.

   (c) The XIV Corps is attacking with 3 Divisions :-

       4th Division on the Right.
       29th Division in the Centre.
       Guards Division on the left.

   (d) The 32nd Infantry Brigade 11th Division is attacking on the right of the 4th Division.

2. The Division will attack with the 12th Infantry Brigade in front line, 10th Infantry Brigade in support and 11th Infantry Brigade in reserve.

3. The attack will be made in three bounds as shewn on attached map "A".

   There will be a pause at each bound the duration of which will be communicated later.

4. The attack will be assisted by a creeping and also by machine gun barrages, details of which will be communicated later.

5. (a) The Brigades will be formed up ready for the attack at Zero minus two hours as follows :-

       12th Infantry Brigade H.Q. U.29.a.6.7.
           All Battalions East of STEENBEEK.

       10th Infantry Brigade H.Q. STRAY FARM.
           All Battalions East of CANAL, leading Battalions on the GAIETY FARM - IRON CROSS Road.

       12th Infantry Brigade H.Q. L2 Works.
           All Battalions West of CANAL.

   (b) At Zero hour the 10th Infantry Brigade will advance to the line FERDAN HOUSE - 19 Metre HILL.

10th Brigade Headquarters will move to BIRD HOUSE.

The 11th Infantry Brigade will advance to the area vacated by the 10th Infantry Brigade.

11th Brigade Headquarters will move to STRAY FARM.

6. Reports will be sent in by the two leading Brigades every half hour.

7. Advanced Divisional Headquarters will open at ~~FUSILIER~~ C19 a.0.0 ~~HOUSE~~ (Canal Bank) at Zero hour.

8. ACKNOWLEDGE.

H. Hansdale
Lt-Colonel,
General Staff, 4th Division.

Issued at 11.30 a.m.

Copy to:-
    No. 1 to G.O.C.
        2 to G.S.O.1.
        3 to 10th Brigade.
        4 to 11th Brigade.
        5 to 12th Brigade.
        6 to C.R.A.
        7 to C.R.E.
        8 to Signals.
        9 to A.D.M.S.
       10 to A.P.M.
       11 to 234th M.G.Coy.
       12 to D.M.G.C.
       13 to 21st West Yorks (Pioneers).
       14)
       15) to 4th Div. "Q".
       16)
       17 to 9th Squadron R.F.C.
       18 to 11th Division.
       19 to 29th Division.
       20 to Guards Division.
       21 to 17th Division.
       22) to XIV Corps
       23)
       24 to XIV Corps H.A.
       25) to War Diary.
       26)
       27 to File.

SECRET -

INSTRUCTIONS NO: 1
to
4th DIVISION ORDER NO: 66

1. The two leading Brigades will carry two days rations in addition to the iron rations, and 220 rounds S.A.A per man except rifle grenadiers and bombers.

2. By ZERO hour there will be :-

    1 Power Buzzer and 1 Amplifier at LOUIS FARM.
    1 Power Buzzer at FERDAN HOUSE.

    These two places will then be available for the leading Brigade Commander to move forward to, should he wish to do so.

3. It is hoped that by the morning of the 8th inst, duckboard tracks will be laid up to Road at U.24.b.5.2 (Track "B"), and to IMBROS HOUSE (Track "A").

    These will be continued to REQUETE FARM and COMPROMIS FARM as soon as possible.

4. Brigades must make all arrangements for bringing up supplies and water by pack transport via SCHREIBOOM - POELCAPPELLE -CONDE HOUSE Road.

    This journey will take about 1½ hours from LANGEMARCK.

5. Shelters are being dumped at STRAY FARM to supplement the shelters in CANDLE Trench sufficient for 4 Battalions.

    These will be available on the night 8th/9th October.

H. Kandath
Lieut. Colonel,
General Staff, 4th Division.

6th October, 1917.

Copies to all recipients
of 4th Division Order 66.

SECRET.

INSTRUCTIONS NO. 2
to
4th DIVISION ORDER NO. 66.

1.   The creeping barrage will begin at Zero.

         At Zero plus 4 minutes it will lift 100 yards.

         At Zero plus 10 minutes it will move forward at 100 yards in 6 minutes up to the first bound.

         There will be a pause of 1 hour 12 minutes on arrival at the first bound.

         From the first bound to the second bound the barrage will move at 100 yards in 6 minutes.

         There will be a pause of 1 hour 17 minutes on arrival at the second bound.

         From the second bound to the GREEN Line the barrage will move at 100 yards in 6 minutes.

                                    Lt-Colonel,
7th October, 1917.   General Staff, 4th Division.

Copies to all recipients
of 4th Division Order No. 66.

SECRET.

ADDENDUM NO. 3
to
4th DIVISION ORDER NO. 66.

PRISONERS.

1. Prisoners will be sent back to Brigade Headquarters at U.29.a 6.9 where they will be taken over by an escort, to be provided by the supporting Brigade, and conducted to STRAY FARM.

    At STRAY FARM they will be taken over by an escort, to be provided by the Reserve Brigade, and conducted to the Prisoners Cage at CACTUS PONTOON, where they will be handed over to the A.P.M. 4th Division.

2. The escorts from the Supporting and Reserve Brigades will consist of one Officer and 20 men. They will be at U.29.a 6.9 and STRAY FARM respectively, at ZERO hour on 'Z' day and will carry two days' rations. They will rejoin their units on Z + 1 day at an hour to be notified later.

Spindler Capt.
Lieut.Colonel,
General Staff, 4th Division.

7th October, 1917.

Copies to all recipients
of 4th Division Order No.66.

SECRET.

INSTRUCTIONS NO. 3
to
4th DIVISION ORDER No. 66.

MACHINE GUNS.

1. Certain machine guns of the Division will assist the attack by means of barrage fire.

   The following will be their distribution, vide the attached map :-

   "A" Group - 8 guns of 234th M.G.Coy at about V.19.a.2.3.

   "B" Group - 8 guns of 12th M.G.Coy at about U.15.d.0.0.

   Targets. "A" Group - From V.14.b.4.3. to V.14.a.95.95.
             "B" Group - From V.14.a.6.8. to V.7.d.9.2.

   Times of fire. "A" Group - ZERO to ZERO plus 1.46 minutes.
                   "B" Group - ZERO to ZERO plus 1.46 minutes.
                   After that only in case of S.O.S.

   Rate of fire. Both Groups ZERO to ZERO + 34 minutes, one belt per gun every two minutes.
                  ZERO + 34 minutes to ZERO + 1.46 minutes
                  10 rounds a minute per gun.

   Lifts. "A" Group lifts to 'A' target S.O.S. Line at ZERO + 1.46 min.
           "B" Group lifts to 'B' target S.O.S. Line at ZERO + 1.46 min.
           Both Groups remain on this S.O.S. Line until advance is ordered.

   On S.O.S. Signal. Both Groups intense fire for 10 minutes;
                     reduced to 25 rounds per minute for a further 10 minutes.

2. The 10th and 11th M.G.Coys will remain under the orders of their respective Brigade Commanders.

3. Os.C Groups must arrange to warn all troops approaching the danger area in front of their positions.

4. All guns will be in position by ZERO minus five hours.

   Os.C 12th and 234th M.G.Coys will report to Divisional Headquarters and 12th Infantry Brigade Headquarters, by means of the word "Sound" when all guns are in position and ready.

5. In the event of a move to the PURPLE Line, the signal for which is smoke shells in the Protective Barrage, which becomes intense:-

P.T.O.

"A" Group will move to about V.19.a.1.3.
"B" Group will move to about U.18.c.9.0.

Both Groups will then be prepared, on arrival at the new positions, to open on the new S.O.S Lines "A2" and "B2" when the S.O.S. Signal is given; otherwise they will not fire unless favourable targets present themselves.

Targets:-

"A2" Group V.9.b.80.05 to V.9.b.30.70.
"B2" Group V.3.d.2.1 to V.3.c.6.6.

Rate of fire, as for S.O.S.

6. After the capture of the GREEN Line or before, if the attack is not successful, both these Groups will come under the command of the G.O.C 12th Infantry Brigade.

7. The subsequent relief of the guns of the 234th M.G.Coy will be arranged between the Os.C 234th M.G.Coy and the 12th M.G.Coy.

H. Hardcastle
Lt-Colonel,
General Staff, 4th Division.

7th October, 1917.

Copies to all recipients
of 4th Division Order No. 66.

SECRET.

AMENDMENT NO. 1
to
4th DIVISION ORDER NO. 66.

Delete para 5 and substitute the following :-

5 (a). The 12th Inf.Bde. will be in position at ZERO minus two hours.

The 10th Inf.Bde. will be concentrated in the area IRON CROSS – GAIETY FM. – JOLIE FM. by ZERO hour with Headquarters at STRAY FM.

The 11th Inf.Bde. will be ready to move at very short notice.

(b) At ZERO hour the 12th Inf.Bde. will attack.

Two Bns. of the 10th Inf.Bde. will move forward to the line FERDAN HO – 19 METRE HILL. These two Bns. will come under the command of the G.O.C. 12th Inf.Bde. They will only be used to exploit success to the PURPLE line if there is no Battalion of the 12th Inf.Bde. available to do so when the time comes.

The 11th Inf.Bde. will not move.

H. Karslake
Lieut.Colonel,
General Staff, 4th Division.

6th October, 1917.

Copies to all recipients
of 4th Division Order 66.

- S E C R E T -

REFERENCE AMENDMENT NO: 1 to 4th DIVISION ORDER NO: 66
_____

Para 5 (b) delete, and substitute :-

5. (b) At ZERO Hour, the 12th Inf. Bde will attack.

One Bn of the 10th Inf. Bde will move forward to the line FERDAN HO - 19 METRE HILL.

This Bn will come under the command of the G.O.C, 12th Inf. Bde, but will not be used by him in advance of the line FERDAN HO - 19 METRE HILL, without reference to Divnl H.Q.

The 11th Inf. Bde will not move.

Spindles Capt.
for
Lieut: Colonel,
General Staff, 4th Divn.

8th October 1917.

Copies to all recipients of
4th Division Order No. 66.

SECRET.

ADDENDUM No. 2
to
4th DIVISION ORDER NO. 66.

1. Unless orders are issued to the contrary the advance on Z day will be continued from the GREEN Line to the PURPLE Line at Zero plus 9 hours.

As it may be impossible to convey this order to the troops in the front line, in sufficient time for it to be acted upon, it has been arranged that if the advance is to take place the protective barrage will become intense at Zero plus 9 hours and will contain a proportion of smoke shells.

If the further advance is not to take place no smoke shells will be used.

The advance will be carried out in two bounds :-

<u>1st Bound</u> to PURPLE DOTTED Line with posts at SPIDER CROSS ROADS (V.15.a.0.8) and RUBENS FARM (V.8.c.8.8).

<u>2nd Bound</u> to the PURPLE Line with posts at junction with the XVIII Corps and at BERNADOTTE FARM.

The barrage during this advance will move at a rate of 100 yards in four minutes.

There will be a pause of 45 minutes on the PURPLE dotted line.

2. During this advance some tanks will move from POELCAPPELLE via REQUET FARM - BONER HOUSE - HEMLING FARM - BERNADOTTE FARM.

All ranks should know the signals used by tanks as laid down in "Tank Coloured Disc and Light Code".

Lt.-Colonel,
General Staff, 4th Division.

6th October, 1917.

Copies to all recipients
of 4th Div. Order No. 66.

- S E C R E T -

ADDENDUM NO: 4
to
4th DIVISION ORDER NO: 66

CONTACT AND COUNTER-ATTACK AEROPLANES.

1. A CONTACT aeroplane will fly over the Corps front at -

    ZERO plus 1 hour and 30 minutes.
    ZERO plus 2 hours and 45 minutes.
    ZERO plus 4 hours and 30 minutes.
    12 noon.

    Leading troops will light RED flares, only when demanded by the contact aeroplane sounding its KLAXON Horn or dropping white lights.

    As far as possible flares should be lighted in bunches of three.

    Each Brigade and Battalion Headquarters will be marked by ground sheets of authorized shape, with the code letters of the unit laid out in white strips alongside. These letters should be 9 feet in depth. Signalling to aeroplanes will be done by panels.

2. A COUNTER-ATTACK aeroplane will be up continually during daylight, from ZERO onwards, whose mission will be to detect the approach of enemy counter-attacks.

    Whenever it observes hostile parties of 100 or more moving to counter-attack, it will drop a smoke bomb over that portion of the front to which the enemy is moving. This smoke bomb will burst about 100 feet below the aeroplane, into a white parachute flare, which descends slowly, leaving a long trail of brown smoke behind it.

H. [signature]

Lieut: Colonel,
General Staff, 4th Division.

7th October 1917.

Copies to all recipients of
4th Division Order No. 66.

- S E C R E T -

DISTRIBUTION OF TROOPS

(Reference 4th Division Order No: 66)

29th DIVISION (ELVERDINGHE CHATEAU)	4th DIVISION (C.19.a.0.0)	11th DIVISION (C.1c.c.1.5)
86th Inf. Bde (U.28.b.2.0)	12th Inf. Bde. (U.29.a.6.9)	32nd Inf. Bde. (VARNA FM)
Assaulting battalions	Assaulting Battalions	Assaulting battalions
1st Objective. 1st Lancs Fusrs (U.19.c.4.5) — Back of collar. Red on sleeve.	2nd Lancs Fus (LOUIS FM) 2nd Essex R. (LOUIS FM) — Red.	6th Yorks R. (V.19.a.6.1) — Black roman two on red. Back of collar.
2nd Objective. 2nd Royal Fusrs (U.23.b.6.2) — Back of collar. On sleeve.	2nd Duke of Wellingtons R (To LOUIS FM when vacated by Essex R) — Red. 1st King's Own R. (To LOUIS FM when vacated by Lancs Fus) — Red.	Support. 8th Duke of Wellingtons. (SNIPE FM) — Black roman three on red. In back of collar.

NOTE:- Distinctive badges of 4th Division are in every case on upper part of arm.

Appendix 6

Account of operations 9th October.

SECRET.   4th Division No. G.A. 3/163/1

The attached amendments to TABLE "A" issued with
4th Division No. G.A. 3/163 dated 11/10/17 are forwarded
for your information.

                                              [signature]
                                                  Lt-Colonel,
                                          General Staff, 4th Division.

11/10/17

Copies to all recipients of
4th Division No. G.A.3/163
and Area Commandant CANAL.

SECRET.   Copy No. 25

                    4th DIVISION ORDER NO. 87.   App-7

                                            9th October, 1917.

1.   The 4th Division (less Artillery) will be relieved by the 34th Division in accordance with the attached Table 'A' on the 11th, 12th and 13th instants.

2.   The detailed train arrangements will be issued later by Q.

3.   Details of the Brigade reliefs will be made between the Brigadiers concerned.

     Brigadiers will hand over command of their areas on completion of reliefs.

4.   The A.D.M.S. will arrange the reliefs of the Field Ambulances.

5.   The D.M.G.Os. will arrange the relief of the Machine Gun Companies in the front line.

6.   All movement from and to STRAY FM. area will take place in small parties at intervals of 100 yards.

7.   The G.O.C. 4th Division will hand over command of the area to the G.O.C. 34th Division at 10 a.m. on the 13th instant.

8.   ACKNOWLEDGE.

                                                    Lieut.Colonel,
Issued at 9 p.m.   General Staff, 4th Division.

Copy No. 1 to G.O.C.
         2 to G.S.O.1.
         3 to 10th Brigade.
         4 to 11th Brigade.
         5 to 12th Brigade.
         6 to C.R.A.
         7 to C.R.E.
         8 to A.D.M.S.
         9 to A.P.M.
        10 to Signals.
        11 to 234th M.G.Coy.
        12 to D.M.G.O.
        13)
        14)to 4th Div. Q.
        15)
        16 to 11th Division.
        17 to 29th Division.
        18 to 34th Division.
        19 to Guards Division.
        20)
        21)to XIV Corps.
        22 to XIV Corps H.A.
        23 to 9th Sqdn.R.F.C.

TABLE 'A' to ACCOMPANY 4th DIVISION ORDER NO.67.

DATE	UNIT	FROM	TO	ON RELIEF BY	REMARKS.
11th Oct.	11th Inf.Bde. Fd.Co. R.E.	HALAKOFF area.	PROVEN area.		By train which brings up the 103rd Inf.Bde.
	10th Inf.Bde.	STRAY FM.	HALAKOFF area.	103rd Inf.Bde.	
12th Oct.	10th Inf.Bde. Fd.Co. R.E.	HALAKOFF area.	PROVEN area.	102nd Inf.Bde.	By train which brings up the 102nd Inf.Bde.
12/13th Oct.	12th Inf.Bde.	Front line.	STRAY FM.	103rd Inf.Bde.	
13th Oct.	12th Inf.Bde. Fd.Co. R.E.	STRAY FM.	PROVEN area.	102nd Inf.Bde.	By train from ELVERDINGHE.

Transport will move by road under Brigade arrangements.
Distances of 500 yards to be left between every 20 vehicles during the march.

Units moving back from STRAY FM. will use Track 'A' and CACTUS PONTOON.
Those moving up to STRAY FM. will use Track 'B' and BYRD CAUSEWAY.

S E C R E T.   4th Division No. G.A. 3/163.

Reference 4th Division Order No. 67 dated 9th October, 1917

1. Para 1, line 3 should be amended to read :-
    "On the 12th, 13th and 14th instants".

2. Para 7, line 2 for "On the 13th instant" read :-
    "On the 14th instant".

3. The attached table "A" should be substituted for the table "A" previously issued.

4. ACKNOWLEDGE.

                                                                Capt.
                                                           for
11th October, 1917.   Lt-Colonel,
Issued at......*Camp*   General Staff, 4th Division.

Copies to recipients of 4th
Division Order No. 67 and
17th and 18th Divisions.

TABLE " A " TO ACCOMPANY 4th DIVISION ORDER No.67 dated 9th OCTOBER 1917.

Serial No.	Date	UNIT	FROM	TO	ROUTE	REMARKS
1.	12th Oct.	11th Inf. Bde Group. (less 1 Bn)				Move under orders of B.G.C.,11th Inf. Bde.
		Bde H.Qrs.	L.2.Defences	F R O V E N		
		"A" Bn.	BRIDGE CAMP			
		"C" Bn.	WOLFE CAMP			"B" Bn 11th Bde & 11th M.G.Coy(less 2 Secs) will remain in the Forward area at the disposal of B.G.C, 12th Inf Bde
		"D" Bn.	LEIPSIG CAMP.			
		2 Secs, 11th M.G.O	SOLFERINO CAMP	(F.2)	By rail	
		11th T.M.Bty.	—do—			
		"A" Bn.12th Inf.Bde.	REDAN CAMP	A R E A.		
		526th Field Coy R.E	B.23.b.5.4			
		234th M.G.Coy.	BRIDGE CAMP			
2.	12th Oct.	12th Inf.Bde H.Qrs.	STRAY FARM	L.2.Defences (B.23.o.5.8)	Track "A" —CACTUS —PONTOON (C.7.c.6.5)	
		12th M.G.Coy.	—do— area.	SOLFERINO CAMP		
		12th T.M.Bty.	—do— area.	—do—		
3.	12th Oct.	10 3rd Inf.Bde H.Q.		STRAY FARM (C.3.c.3.8)	BARD'S CAUSEWAY (C.13.o.C.2) thence by track "B" East of the CANAL.	
		"A" Bn.	P R O V E N	STRAY FM AREA		
		"B" Bn.		—do—		
		"C" Bn.	A R E A.	LEIPSIG CAMP		
		"D" Bn.		WOLFE CAMP		
		M.G.Coy.		STRAY FM AREA		
		T.M.Bty.		—do—		

	Date	Unit	From	To	Route	Remarks
4.	13th Oct.	12th Inf. Bde Group. (less 2 Bns) — Bde H.Q., "A" Bn., "B" Bn., 12th M.G.C.(less 1 Sec), 12th T.M.Bty., 9th Field Coy R.E.	L.2 Defences. BRIDGE CAMP SOULT CAMP SOLFERINO CAMP -do- CANAL BANK (G.19.a.c.3)	P R O V E N (P.3) A R E A.	By rail.	Move under orders of B.G.C 12th Inf. Bde. "C" and "D" Bns and 1 Sec, 12th M.G.C will remain in forward area at the disposal of B.G.C, 12th Inf. Bde.
5.	13th Oct.	12nd Inf. Bde H.Q. "A" Bn. "B" Bn. "C" Bn. "D" Bn. M.G.Coy. T.M.Bty.	P R O V E N A R E A.	L.2 Defences. BRIDGE CAMP -do- REDAN CAMP WOLFE CAMP SOLFERINO CAMP -do-		Note :- WOLFE CAMP will not be available until "D" Bn 12rd Inf. do moves forward into the line. (vide Serial No: 7).
6.	13/14th Oct.	12th Inf. Bde Group. Bde H.Q. "B" Bn. "C" Bn. "D" Bn. "C" Bn.12th Bde. "D" Bn.12th Bde. "B" Bn.11th Bde. 12th M.G.Coy. 12th T.M.Bty. 11th M.G.Coy(less 2 Secs) 1 Sec.12th M.G.Coy.	L I N E.	STRAY FARM and MALAKOFF AREA. (Accommodation available :- STRAY FM. AREA - 4 Bns. LEIPSIG CAMP - 2 Bns.)	Track "A" - CACTUS PONTOON (O.7.c.c.5)	Move under orders of B.G.C 12th Inf. Bde.

7.	13/14th Oct.	103rd Inf. Bde H.Q. "A" Bn. "B" Bn. "N" Bn. "D" Bn. M.G.Coy. T.M.Bty.	STRAY FM. STRAY FM AREA -do- LEIPSIG CAMP WOLFE CAMP. STRAY FM AREA -do-	LINE. " " " " "	
8.	14th Oct.	12th Inf. Bde Group. (less 1 Bn). Bde H.Q. "B" Bn. "C" Bn. "D" Bn. "D" Bn.10th Bde. "D" Bn.10th Bde. "B" Bn.11th Bde. 12th F.G.Coy. 12th T.M.Bty. 11th M.G.Coy.(less 2 Secs) 1 Sec.10th M.G.Coy. 406th (Renfrew Fd Coy R.E.	STRAY FARM and MALAKOFF AREA. CANDLE TRENCH. (C.9.a.c.8)	PROVEN (P.4) AREA.	Move under orders of B.G.C, 12th Inf. Bde. Note :- "A" Bn, 12th Bde moves with 11th Bde Group on 12th Oct. By rail.
9.	14th Oct.	102nd Inf. Bde H.Q. Bde H.Q. "A" Bn. "B" Bn. M.G.Coy. T.M.Bty.	L.2 Defences. BRIDGE CAMP. -do- SOLFERINO CAMP -do-	STRAY FM. " area. " area	BARD'S CAUSEWAY -TRACK"B". "C" and "D" Bns remain in REDAN and WOLFE CAMP.

1.	14th Oct.	161st Inf. Bde. (less 2 Bns).	PROVEN AREA.	L.2 Defences. BRIDGE CAMP LEIPSIG CAMP SOLFERINO CAMP.	"A" and "B" Bns are at present in SOULT and SARAGOSSA CAMPS.
		Bde H.Qrs. "C" Bn. "D" Bn. M.G.Coy. T.M.Bty.		-do-	

Transport will move by road under Brigade arrangements. Distances of 500 yards to be left between every 2 vehicles during the march. Units moving back from STRAY FARM will use Track "A" and CACTUS PONTOON. Those moving up to STRAY FARM will use Track "B" and BARD'S CAUSEWAY.

S E C R E T.   4th Division No. G.A. 3/163/1

The attached amendments to TABLE "A" issued with
4th Division No. G.A. 3/163 dated 11/10/17 are forwarded
for your information.

                                                    [signature]
                                                    Lt-Colonel,
                                            General Staff, 4th Division.

11/10/17

Copies to all recipients of
4th Division No. G.A.3/163
and Area Commandant CANAL.

AMENDMENTS TO TABLE "A" ACCOMPANYING 4th DIVISION ORDER NO: 67 dated 9th OCTOBER 1917.

Serial No:-	Date	UNIT	FROM	TO	ROUTE	REMARKS
2	12th Oct.	10th Inf. Bde H.Q.	STRAY FARM	L.2 Defences. (B.23.c.5.8)	Track "A" - CACTUS PONTOON	To be clear by 12 noon.
		10th M.G.Coy. 10th T.M.Bty.	-do- area. -do- area.	SOLFERINO CAMP. -do-	(0.7.c.0.5) -do-	
2 (a)	-do-	"B" & "C" Bns 12th Inf.Bde. (less carrying party)	-do-	LEIPSIG CAMP	-do-	Move under orders of B.G.C.,12th Bde.
3.	12th Oct.	103rd Inf.Bde H.Q.	PROVEN AREA.	STRAY FARM (G.3.c.3.8) STRAY FM AREA	CACTUS PONTOON - TRACK 'A'	One guide per platoon will be provided by 10th Inf.Bde to meet incoming unit at BOESINGHE STATION. Hour of arrival of units of 103rd Inf.Bde will be notified later.
		"A" Bn. "B" Bn. "C" Bn. "D" Bn. M.G.Coy. T.M.Bty. 240th M.G.Coy.		-do- -do- -do- -do- -do- -do-		

Serial No:	Date	UNIT	FROM	TO	ROUTE	REMARKS
5		Delete note in column of remarks.				
6.	13/14 Oct.	12th Inf.Bde Group. Bde H.Q. "D" Bn. "C" Bn.10th Bde. "D" Bn 10th Bde. "B" Bn.11th Bde. 12th M.G.Coy. 12th T.M.Bty. 11th M.G.Coy.(less 2 Sections) 1 Sec.10th M.G.Coy.	LINE	STRAY FARM AREA.	Track "A" -GACTES PONTOON (0.7.0.0.5)	Move under orders of B.G.C, 12th Inf. Bde. on completion of relief by 103rd Inf. Bde. arrangements for relief to be made between Bde Commanders.
7.	13/14 Oct.	103rd Inf. Bde H.Q. "A" Bn. "B" Bn. "C" Bn. "D" Bn. M.G.Coy. T.M.Bty.	STRAY FARM STRAY FM AREA -do- -do- -do- -do- -do-	LINE " " " " "		In relief of 12th Inf. Bde - arrangements for relief to be made between Bde Comdrs.
8.	14th Oct.	102nd Inf.Bde H.Q. "A" Bn. "B" Bn. "C" Bn. "D" Bn. M.G.Coy. T.M.Bty.	L.2 Defences. BRIDGE CAMP REDAN CAMP WOLFE CAMP SOLFERINO CAMP -do-	STRAY FM -do- area -do- " -do- -do- -do- -do-	BARD CAUSEWAY - TRACK "B"	10. DELETE SERIAL No. 10.

"C" Form.
MESSAGES AND SIGNALS.

Army Form C 2123.
(In books of 100.)

No. of Message ....

Prefix	Code	Words	Received From	Sent, or sent out	Office Stamp.
£ s. d.				At m.	RCD 13.X.17 TELEGRAPHS
Charges to collect			By	To	
Service Instructions.				By	

Handed in at .... Office .... m. Received .... m.

TO

*Sender's Number	Day of Month	In reply to Number	A A A

82

..... of NEGUETE FARM ......
MEMLING FARM GRAVEL FARM ....
.... to TURENNE ......
.... to ADEN HORSE ....
FAIDHERBE CROSS ROADS ....
.... yesterday the .... of
MEMLING FARM .... practically
in our hands and ....
of objectives ...... all that
place aaa Prisoners ....
about VIII Central .... Prisoners ......
10 officers 207 OR wounded
2 officers 31 OR wounded
aaa added ....
all ....

FROM
PLACE & TIME: 14th Corps ....

* This line should be erased if not required.

SECRET.

Copy No. 24

App. 8

4th DIVISION ORDER NO. 68.

9th October, 1917.

1. (a) The attack will be resumed at a date which has been communicated to all concerned.

   (b) The XIV Corps is attacking with the 4th Division on the right, 17th Division in the centre and Guards Division on the left.

   (c) The 18th Division is attacking on the right of the 4th Division.

2. The 12th Infantry Brigade will carry out the attack.

   Two battalions of the 10th Infantry Brigade will be attached to the 12th Infantry Brigade for the attack.

3. The objective is the PURPLE Line which has been altered to a line about 200 yards beyond the GREEN Line. The exact line will be notified later.

4. The attack will be assisted by a creeping barrage moving at a rate of 100 yards in 8 minutes.

   The exact line of the initial barrage will be settled after the situation tomorrow has been cleared up.

5. ACKNOWLEDGE.

H. Hanslake
Lt-Colonel,
General Staff, 4th Division.

Issued at 9.30 p.m.

Copy No. 1 to G.O.C.
2 to G.S.O. 1.
3 to 10th Infantry Brigade.
4 to 11th Infantry Brigade.
5 to 12th Infantry Brigade.
6 to C.R.A.
7 to C.R.E.
8 to A.D.M.S.
9 to A.P.M.
10 to Signals.
11 to 234th M.G.Company.
12 to D.M.G.O.
13)
14) to 4th Division "Q".
15)
16 to Guards Division.
17 to 17th Division.
18 to 18th Division.
19) to XIV Corps.
20)
21 to XIV Corps H.A.
22 to 9th Squadron R.F.C.
23) to War Diary.
24)
25 to File.

S E C R E T

ADDENDUM No. 1

to

4th DIVISION ORDER NO. 68.

1. The attack will be made in two bounds :-
    First Bound to the GREEN LINE
    Second Bound to the RED LINE.

2. The following lines will be organised for defence :-
    The RED LINE
    The Line REQUETTE FM - BOWER HOUSE.

3. (a) Posts will be established as follows :-
    REQUETTE FARM
    Junction with 18th Divn. on the RED LINE
    MEMLING FARM.

   (b) The 17th Divn. is establishing a post at GRAVEL FARM.

   The garrisons for these and any other posts which the G.O.C. 12th Infantry Brigade may decide to establish, must be detailed beforehand.

4. The 12th Infantry Brigade will detail special parties to gain touch with,
    18th Divn. at REQUETTE FARM
        On the final objective.
    17th Divn. at WATER HOUSE
        Just W. of BOWER HOUSE
        On the final objective.

5. The artillery barrage will begin to creep at Zero plus eight minutes and will advance at the rate of 100 yards in eight minutes throughout.
    The barrage will begin to creep from the first bound at Zero plus one hour and forty minutes. At this moment a few smoke shell will be fired along the whole Divisional front.

6. (a) A contact aeroplane will fly over at :-
    Zero plus one hour and 15 minutes
    Zero plus three hours and 30 minutes
    12 noon.
    RED flares will be used.

   (b) A counter attack aeroplane will be up continuously during daylight to detect the approach of enemy counter attacks.
    The usual signal will be made if the enemy are seen to be preparing for counter attack.

7. Watches will be checked at 12th Infantry Brigade Hd.Qrs. at 5 p.m. on Z minus one day.

P.T.O.

= 2 =

8.   Prisoners will be sent back to 12th Infantry Brigade Headquarters (U.29.a.4.9.) where they will be taken over by an escort to be provided by the 10th Infantry Brigade. This escort will take them to STRAY FARM and hand them over to an escort to be provided by the 11th Infantry Brigade. Thence they will be taken to CACTUS PONTOON Cage and handed over to the A.P.M.

These escorts to consist in each case of 1 officer and 12 other ranks who are to be at the above mentioned places at Zero hour on Z day.

9.   Reports are to be sent in to Divisional Headquarters every half hour.

10.   Advanced Divisional Headquarters will remain on the CANAL BANK (C.19.a.6.6.).

H. Karslake

10th October 1917.   Lieut. Colonel,
                                      General Staff, 4th Division.
Copies to all recipients of
4th Division Order No. 68.

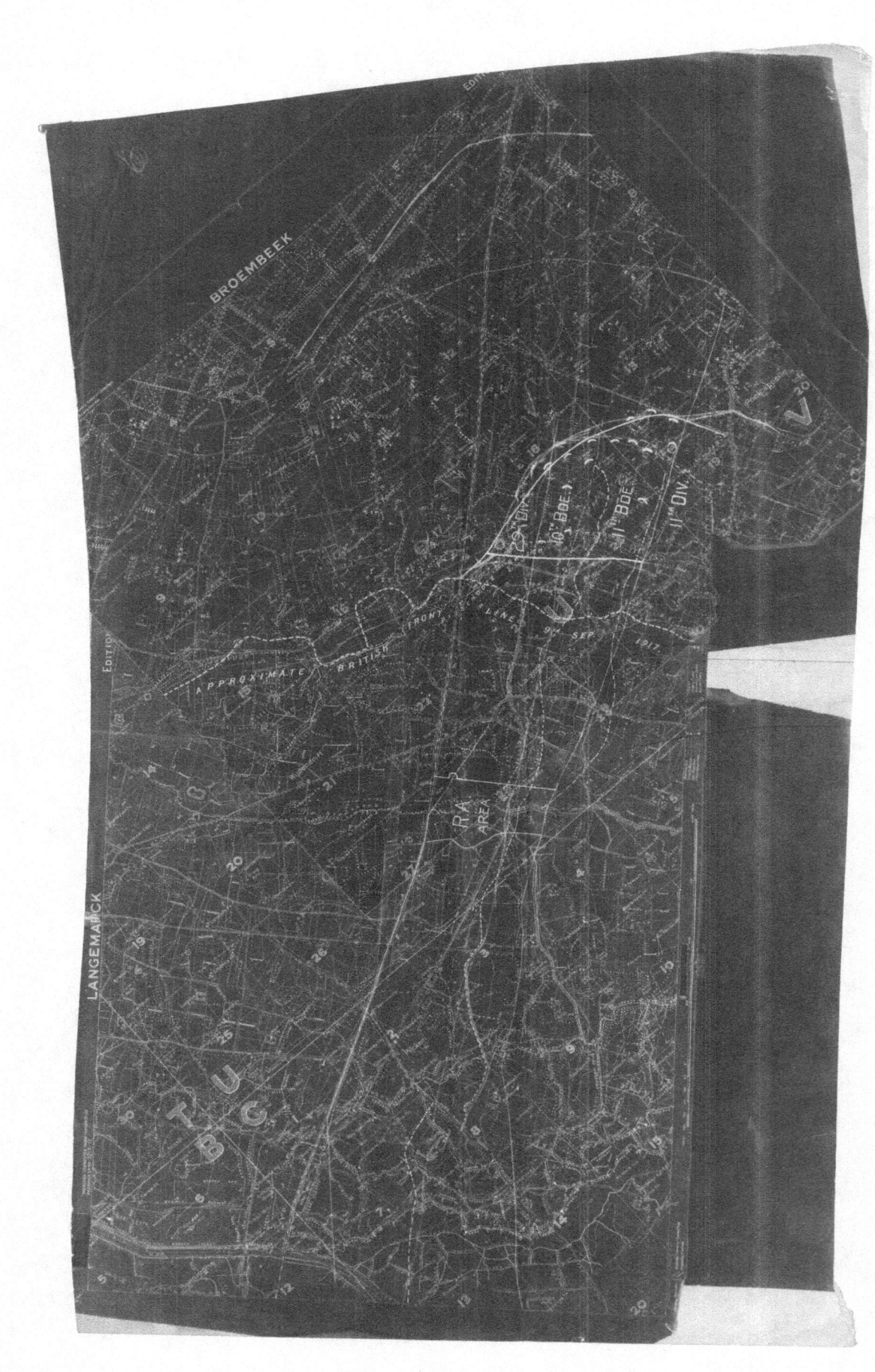

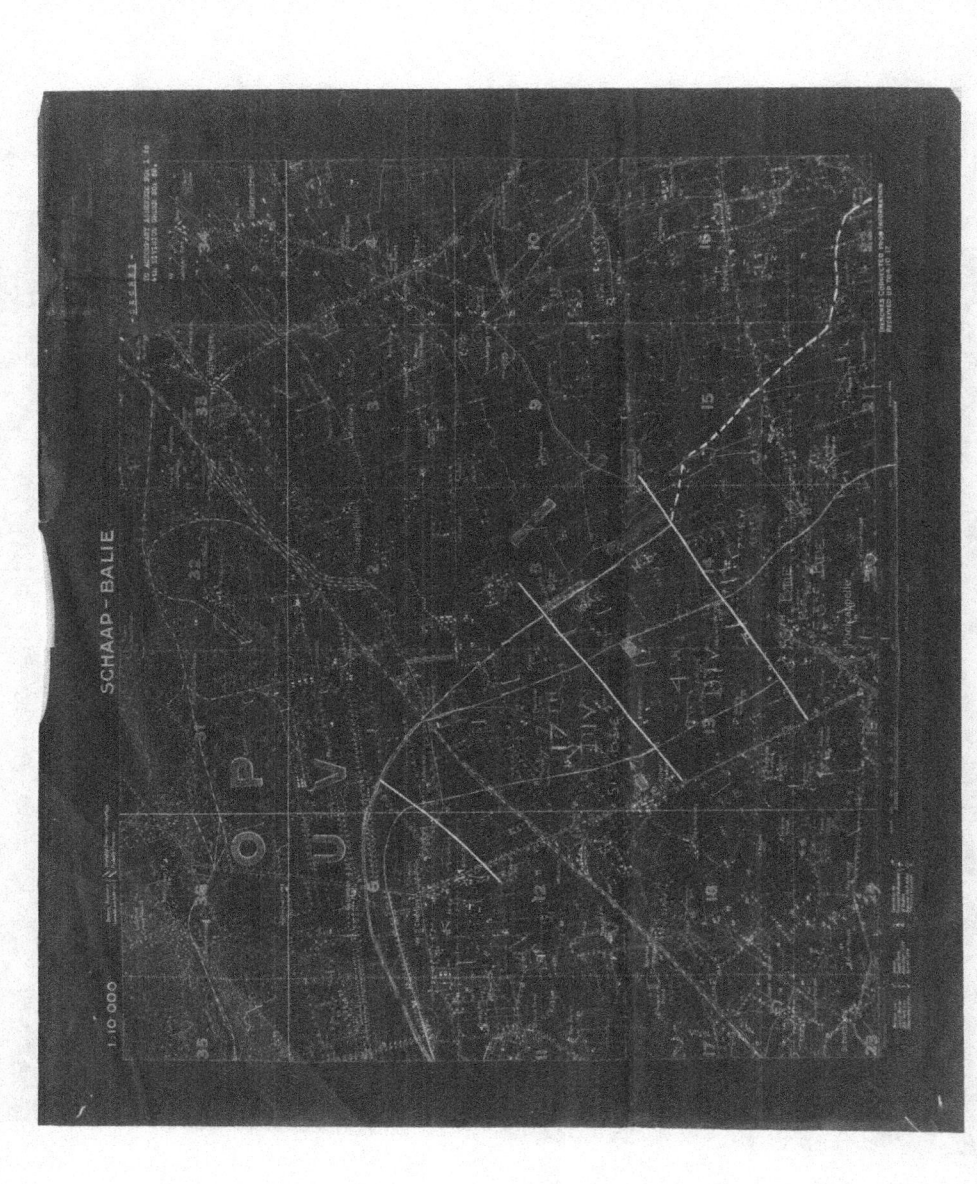

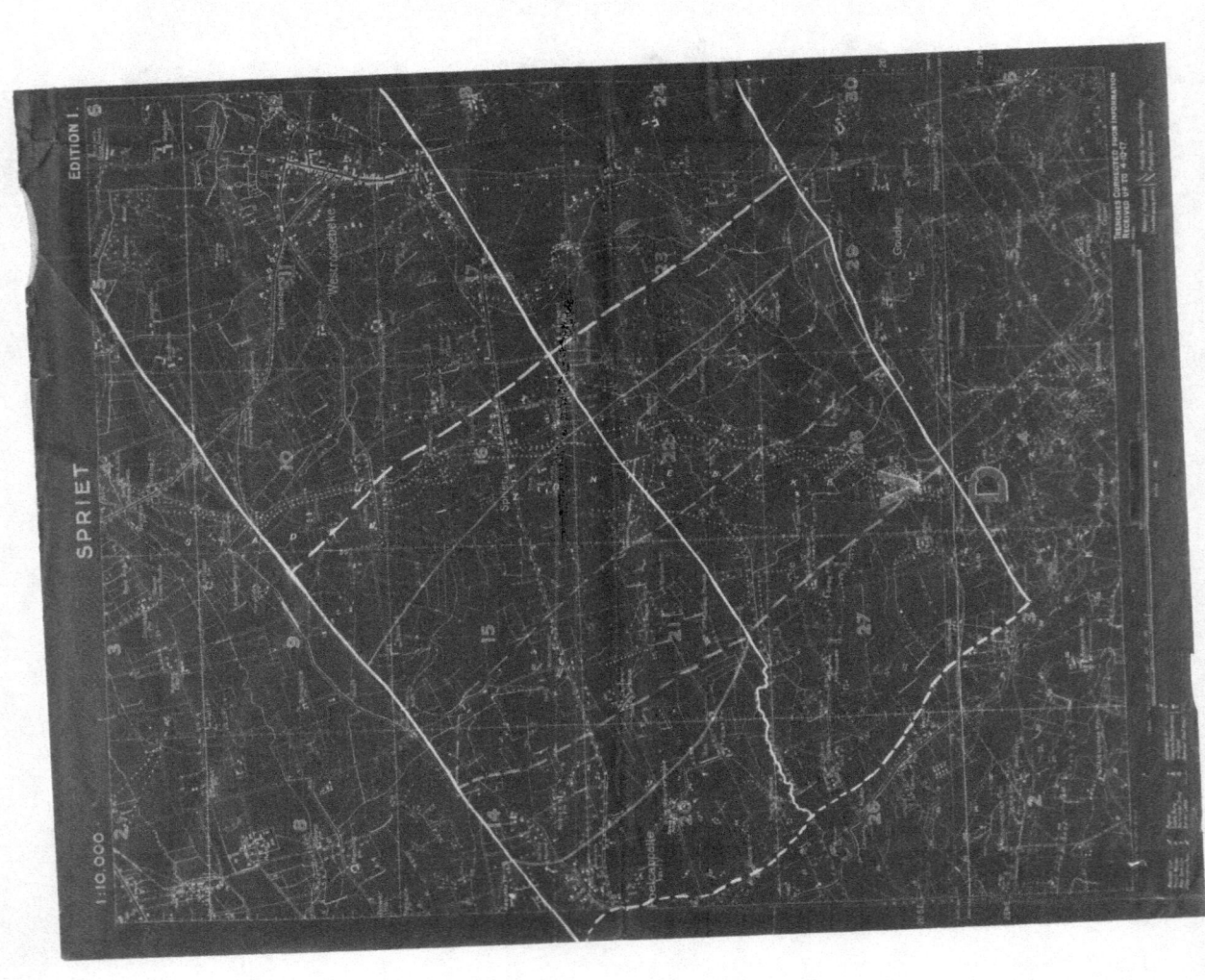

SECRET.   Copy No. 25

4th DIVISION ORDER NO. 69.

App. 9

Reference Map -   13th October, 1917.

HAZEBROUCK 5 A 1/100,000.
Sheets 27 and 28 1/40,000.

1. The 4th Division (less Artillery) will move from the XIV Corps Area, PROVEN 2, 3 and 4 Areas, into the XVIII Corps, POPERINGHE Area, on the 15th and 16th October, in accordance with the attached MARCH TABLE.

2. The composition of Infantry Brigade Groups for the above move will be as follows :-

10th Brigade Group.	11th Brigade Group.	12th Brigade Group.
4 Battalions.	4 Battalions.	4 Battalions.
10th M.G.Coy.	11th M.G.Coy.	12th M.G.Coy.
10th T.M.Bty.	11th T.M.Bty.	12th T.M.Bty.
10th Field Ambce.	11th Field Ambce.	12th Field Ambce.
9th Field Co.R.E.	526th Field Co.R.E.	406th Field Co.R.E.
No.2 Coy Div.Train.	No.3 Coy. Div.Train.	No.4 Coy.Div.Train.
	234th M.G.Coy.	

3. Completion of moves will be reported to Divisional H.Q.

4. 4th Divisional Headquarters will close at PROVEN, North Camp, at 11 a.m. on 15th instant, and will reopen at 6 RUE de POTS, POPERINGHE, at the same hour.

5. The 4th Division (less Artillery) will be transferred to the Third Army by rail on the 17th and 18th October, under orders to be issued later.

6. ACKNOWLEDGE.

H. Harsdale

Lieut.Colonel,
General Staff, 4th Division.

Issued at 12 noon.

Copy No. 1 to G.O.C.
    2 to G.S.O.1.
    3 to 10th Brigade.
    4 to 11th Brigade.
    5 to 12th Brigade.
    6 to C.R.A.
    7 to C.R.E.
    8 to A.D.M.S.
    9 to A.P.M.
    10 to Signals.
    11 to Pioneers.
    12 to 234th M.G.Coy.
    13 to D.A.C.
    14 to Camp Commandant.
    15)
    16) to 4th Div.A.
    17)
    18 to 57th Division.
    19 to Town Major POPERINGHE.
    20 to Area Commdt. St.JAN TER BIEZEN.

Copy No.22) to XIV Corps.
    23)
    24 to XVIII Corps.
    25)
    26) to War Diary.
    27 to File.

MARCH TABLE ISSUED WITH 4th DIVISION ORDER NO.69 dated 13th October.

Serial No	Date	Unit	From	To	Route	Remarks
1.	15th Oct.	10th Bde.Group.	P 4 Area.	School Camp, ST.JAN TER BIEZEN.	Any road S.W. of PROVEN - POPERINGHE Road (excl.)	To be clear of PROVEN area by 12 noon. Advance parties to report to Area Commdt. in ST. JAN TER BIEZEN village.
2.	15th Oct.	11th Bde.Group.	P 2 Area.	POPERINGHE.	Any road N.E. of PROVEN - POPERINGHE road (incl.)	To be clear of PROVEN area by 11 a.m. Advance parties to report to Town Major, POPERINGHE
3.	15th Oct.	Divnl.Hd.Qrs. No.1 Sectn. 4th Signal Coy.R.E.	PROVEN.	POPERINGHE.	Main Road.	Not to start before 11 a.m.
4.	16th Oct.	12th Bde.Group.	P 3 Area.	Road Camp, ST.JAN TER BIEZEN.	Any road.	To be clear of PROVEN area by 12 noon. Advance parties to report to Area Commdt. ST.JAN TER BIEZEN village.

NOTE (a) Units not mentioned above will move under the orders of the A.A. & Q.M.G. 4th Division.

(b) 500 yards interval will be maintained between units.

- S E C R E T -

Copy No: 15

App. 10

4th DIVISION WARNING ORDER

15th Oct. 1917.

1. (a)   The Division will relieve the 12th Division in the MONCHY Sector between the 22nd and 25th October.

   (b)   The 51st Division (VI Corps) will be on the right, and the 15th Division (XVII Corps) on the left.

2.   The dispositions of the 12th Division are as shown on attached Map.

   It is probable that our dispositions will be the same, in which case the

   10th Inf. Bde will be on the right on a one Bn front, and the

   11th Inf. Bde on the left, on a two Bn front.

   The Reserve Brigade is billetted in ARRAS.

3.   A C K N O W L E D G E.

H.H.anstatte
Lieut: Colonel,
General Staff, 4th Divn.

Issued at 11.30 p.m.

Copies to :-
       No: 1 to G.O.C.
            2   G.S.O.1.
            3   10th Bde.
            4   11th Bde.
            5   12th Bde.
            6   C.R.E.
            7   A.D.M.S.
            8   A.P.M.
            9   Signals.
           10   234th M.G.Coy.
           11   D.M.G.O.
           12   4th Divn "Q"
           13   XVIIth Corps.
           14 } War Diary.
           15 }
           16   File.
           17   Divnl Gas Offr

SECRET.   Copy No.......

4th DIVISION ORDER NO. 70.

Reference maps -   15th October, 1917.

HAZEBROUCK 5 A 1/100,000
LENS 11   1/100,000

1. The 4th Division (less Artillery and Pioneer Battalion) will be transferred from XIV Corps to XVII Corps, Third Army, and will move by rail on the 17th, 18th and 19th October.

2. The Divisional Supply Column and other Motor vehicles will move by road on the 17th and 18th October under orders to be issued by 4th Division "Q".

3. Entraining Stations will be HOPOUTRE and PESELHOEK.
   Detraining Stations will be ARRAS and AUBIGNY.
   There will be no restrictions as to routes to entraining Stations, with the exception that POPERINGHE should be avoided, when possible.

4. Train arrangements for the above move will be notified by 4th Division "Q".

5. Completion of moves will be reported to Divisional Headquarters.

6. 4th Divisional Headquarters will close at POPERINGHE at 2 p.m. October 17th and will re-open at DUISANS at the same hour.

7. 4th Divisional Artillery will be transferred to the Third Army at a later date.

8. A C K N O W L E D G E.

Issued at... 4.30 pm   Lt.-Colonel,
                                    General Staff, 4th Division.

P.T.O.

Copies to :-

    No. 1 to G.O.C.
       2 to G.S.O. 1.
       3 to 10th Infantry Brigade.
       4 to 11th Infantry Brigade.
       5 to 12th Infantry Brigade.
       6 to C.R.A.
       7 to C.R.E.
       8 to A.D.M.S.
       9 to A.P.M.
     10 to Signals.
     11 to Pioneers.
     12 to 234th M.G. Company.
     13 to D.M.G.O.
     14 to Camp Commandant.
     15)
     16) to 4th Division "Q".
     17)

     18) to XIV Corps.
     19)

     20) to XVII Corps.
     21)

     22 to XVIII Corps.

     23) to War Diary.
     24)

     25 to File.

SECRET.

4th Division No. G.C. 25/9.

Reference 4th Division Order No. 70.

Brigade Groups on arrival in XVII Corps Area will be located as under :-

    10th Brigade Group

        DUISANS and "Y" Huts.

    11th Brigade Group.

        DAINVILLE - WARLUS - WANQUETIN.

    12th Brigade Group.

        GOUVES - MONTENESCOURT - HABARCQ.

                        Lt-Colonel,
                General Staff, 4th Division.

15th October, 1917.

Copies to all recipients
of 4th Division Order No. 70.

SECRET.

Copy No. 23

App. 12

4th DIVISION ORDER NO. 71

19th October, 1917.

1. The 4th Division (less artillery) will relieve the 12th Division (less artillery) in the Right Sector of the XVII Corps front in accordance with the attached table "A".

2. (a) The field artillery now covering the 12th Division front will come under the orders of the G.O.C 4th Division at 10 a.m. on October 25th.

   (b) At the same time one section N.Z. Tunnelling Company will also come under the orders of the G.O.C 4th Division.

3. The R.E. Companies and Field Ambulances affiliated to the 10th and 11th Infantry Brigades will move with those Brigades, but the details of their reliefs will be arranged by the C.R.E. and A.D.M.S.

   Those of the 12th Infantry Brigade will move separately under the orders of the C.R.E. and A.D.M.S.

4. (a) All details of Brigade reliefs will be arranged between Brigadiers concerned.

   (b) Progress of relief will be reported to Divisional Headquarters.

5. The G.O.C. 4th Division will take over command of the area at 10 a.m. on October 25th, at which hour Divisional Headquarters will open at RUE de LA PAIX, ARRAS and close at DUISANS.

6. A C K N O W L E D G E.

Issued at

Lt-Colonel,
General Staff, 4th Division.

P. T. C.

Copies to:-

No. 1. to G.O.C.
    2. to G.S.O.1.
    3. to 10th Infantry Brigade.
    4. to 11th Infantry Brigade.
    5. to 12th Infantry Brigade.
    6. to C.R.E.
    7. to D.M.G.O.
    8. to 234th M.G. Company.
    9. to A.D.M.S.
  10. to A.P.M.
  11. to D.A.D.V.S.
  12. to D.A.D.O.S.
  13. to 4th Div. Train.
  14. to Signals.
  15. to 4th Division "Q".
  16. to 12th Division.
  17. to C.R.A., 12th Division.
  18.) to XVII Corps.
  19.)
  20 to Camp Commandant.
  21. to 4th Divn. Depot Battalion.
  22.) to War Diary.
  23.)
  24. to File.
  25. to Div. Gas Officer.

TABLE "A"

Serial No:	Date	UNIT	FROM	TO	In relief of	ROUTE
1	22nd Oct.	11th Inf.Bde Group 10th M.G.Coy. 234th M.G.Coy.	WARLUS Area. DUISANS Area.	ARRAS. Bde H.Q. ARRAS. 'A' Bn Brown Line. 'B' Bn BOIS des BOEUFS. 'C' Bn ARRAS 'D' Bn ACHICOURT. Fd Coy R.E. TILLOY. Fd Amb ARRAS. 234th M.G.Coy ARRAS. 10th M.G.Coy.)	35th Inf. Bde Group.	WANQUETIN-WARLUS-DAINVILLE-ARRAS-S.P. Eastern end of DAINVILLE 9 a.m.
2	23rd Oct.	10th M.G.Coy.	ARRAS	Right Front Line.	57th M.G.Coy.	
3	23rd Oct.	10th Inf.Bde Group.	DUISANS Area.	ARRAS Area. H.Q. & 3 Bns ARRAS. 1 Bn ACHICOURT. Fd Coy R.E. TILLOY Fd Amb. ARRAS.		HAUTE AVESNES-ARRAS. 2 Bns to replace 2 Bns of 11th Inf.Bde at ARRAS & ACHICOURT. Not to arrive before 4 p.m. Remainder of Group to start at 9 a.m.
4	23/24th Oct.	11th Inf. Bde	ARRAS Area.	Left front line.	36th Inf. Bde	
5	24th Oct.	2 Secs 11th M.G.Coy 2 Secs 234th M.G.Coy	} ARRAS Area.	Left front line.	36th M.G.Coy. 236th Do.	To be arranged by D.M.G.O.

Serial No:	Date	UNIT	FROM	TO	In relief of	ROUTE
6	24th Oct.	12th Inf. Bde	HABARCQ Area.	ARRAS Area. H.Q & 3 Bns ARRAS 1 Bn ACHICOURT.		WARLUS-DAINVILLE. Not to reach ARRAS before 4 p.m, by which hour 1 Bn 10th Bde in ARRAS and 1 Bn of 10th Inf. Bde in ACHIC-OURT will be clear of these places.
7	24th Oct.	406th Fd Coy R.E	HABARCQ Area.	TILLOY		Under orders of C.R.E.
8	24th Oct.	12th Field Amb.	HABARCQ Area.	WARLUS		Under orders of A.D.M.S
9	24/25th Oct.	10th Inf. Bde	ARRAS Area.	Right front line.	37th Inf.Bde.	3 Bns East of ARRAS 1 Bn in ARRAS.
10	25th Oct.	'A' Bn.12th Inf. Bde.	ARRAS	BOIS des BOEUFS.		For work under the C.R.E.

NOTE :- (a) The troops moving West use the road TILLOY-BEAURAINS-ACHICOURT-BERNEVILLE-WARLUS-VANQUETIN.

(b) Distances of 200 yards will be maintained between Battalions and their 1st Line Transport and between all units when on the march.

APPENDIX 13.

MOVES AND DISPOSITIONS OF BRIGADES ON 5th and 6th OCTOBER.

SECRET.   4th Div. G.A.22/17.

10th Brigade. *
11th Brigade. *
12th Brigade. *
C.R.A.
C.R.E.
Pioneers.
Signals.
4th Div.Q.
D.M.G.O.

App. 13

According to present plans the following moves will take place.

1. On the night 5th/6th October the 11th Inf.Bde. will take over the whole front from V.19.b 2.7 to U.17.d 20.15 and will be so disposed that no troops are North of the left Divisional boundary or West of the GAIETY FM - VULCAN CROSS road.

On the same night one section of the 12th M.G.Coy. and one section of the 234th M.G.Coy. will be placed at the disposal of the 11th Inf.Bde. to relieve two sections of the 11th M.G.Coy.

The 10th M.G.Coy. will withdraw two sections, leaving two sections at the disposal of the 11th Inf.Bde.

The number of Machine Guns allotted to the 11th Inf.Bde. on the 5th/6th will therefore be :-

    10th M.G.Coy.   8
    11th M.G.Coy.   8
    12th M.G.Coy.   8
    234th M.G.Coy. 12

                      36

2. The 10th Inf.Bde. will withdraw to the following camps :-

    H.Q.   FUSILIER HO.
    'A' Bn. ~~CANAL~~ BADGER Camp.
    'B' Bn. HULLS FARM.
    'C' Bn. WOLFE.
    'D' Bn. SOULT.

3. By 6 a.m. on the 6th the 12th Inf.Bde. will be disposed as follows :-

    H.Q.   L 2 Works.
    'A' Bn. CANDLE trench.
    'B' Bn. SARAGOSSA.
    'C' Bn. LEIPSIC.
    'D' Bn. REDAN.

* Map issued to Bdes. only.

4. On the night 7th/8th the 12th Inf.Bde. will take over from the 11th Inf.Bde. the right sector of the Divisional front, the left Battn. of 11th Inf.Bde. remaining under command of 12th Inf.Bde.

H.Q. STRAY FM.

On the night 8th/9th 10th Inf.Bde. takes over left sector of Divisional front.

On this night the 12th M.G.Coy. will relieve the remainder of the 11th M.G.Coy.

Situation at 6 a.m. October 9th.

Right Bde. 12th Inf.Bde. H.Q. STRAY FM.

    'A' Bn. Front line ⎫ East.
    'B' Bn. Support " ⎭
    'C' Bn. CANDLE.
    'D' Bn. CANAL.

All Machine Guns in front system.

Left Bde. 10th Inf.Bde. H.Q. AU BON GITE.

    'A' Bn. ⎫ East of LANGEMARCK.
    'B' Bn. ⎭
    'C' Bn. ⎫ MALAKOFF area.
    'D' Bn. ⎭

5. The objective for the 12th and 10th Inf.Bdes. for the next attack is the GREEN line on attached map, the BLUE line being the starting line.

The probable boundary between Brigades is BROWN and the Divisional boundaries YELLOW.

6. All Brigades should get forward with their detailed arrangements as soon as possible and let their Battalion Commanders know all they can at once.

                                                                     Lieut.Colonel,

2nd September, 1917.   General Staff, 4th Division.

Copies to :-
    11th Divn.
    29th Divn.
    17th Divn.
    XIVth Corps.

-SECRET- 4th Divn No: G.A. 22/17.

Reference 4th Divn G.A. 22/17.

Para 2, line 4, should read -

"A" Battn BRIDGE CAMP.

(signed)
Lieut: Colonel,
General Staff, 4th Division.

2nd October 1917.

Copies to all recipients
of 4th Divn G.A.22/17.

SECRET.   4th Div. G.A.22/17.

In continuation of 4th Div.G.A.22/17.

The dispositions of Brigades on various dates will probably be :-

6 a.m. October 6th.

10th Bde.   H.Q. FUSILIER HO.

'A' Bn.   BRIDGE CAMP.
'B' Bn.   HULLS FARM.
'C' Bn.   WOLFE.
'D' Bn.   SOULT.

11th Bde.   H.Q. STRAY FM.

All battalions East of the GAIETY FM. - VULCAN CROSS road.

12th Bde.   H.Q. L 2 Works.

'A' Bn.   CANDLE area.
'B' Bn.   SARAGOSSA.
'C' Bn.   LEIPSIC.
'D' Bn.   REDAN.

6 a.m. October 8th.

10th Bde.   No change.

11th Bde.   H.Q. L 2 Works.

'A' Bn.   SARAGOSSA.
'B' Bn.   LEIPSIC.
'C' Bn.   REDAN.
'D' Bn.   Left front line.

Note.   During this relief the 11th Inf.Bde. should arrange for battalions coming out of the line to halt in the neighbourhood of STRAY FARM and to have a hot drink there.

12th Bde.   H.Q. STRAY FM.

'A' 'B' 'C' Bns. East of GAIETY FM. - VULCAN CROSS road.
'D' Bn.   CANDLE area.

6 a.m. October 9th.

10th Bde.   H.Q. AU BON GITE.

'A' Bn.)
'B' Bn.)   East of LANGEMARCK.
'C' Bn.   HULLS FM.
'D' Bn.   WOLFE.

11th Bde.	H.Q. L 2 Works.
'A' Bn.	SARAGOSSA.
'B' Bn.	LEIPSIC.
'C' Bn.	REDAN.
'D' Bn.	CANDLE area.
12th Bde.	STRAY FM.

All Bns. east of CANDLE area.

6 a.m. October 10th. ~~October~~.

10th Bde.	H.Q. AU BON GITE.

All Bns. East of CANAL.

12th Bde.	H.Q. U.29.a 6.6.

All Bns. East of CANDLE area.

11th Bde.	H.Q. STRAY FM.
All Bns.	CANDLE area inclusive and West of it.

The actual arrangement of Camps may not suit all Brigades as their occupation will depend on the order in which Battalions are used.

They will however, be approximately as stated above and Brigades will arrange between themselves during reliefs the exact locations of their Battalions.

H. Handalle
Lieut. Colonel,
General Staff, 4th Division.

3rd October, 1917.

Copies to 10th Brigade.
        11th Brigade.
        12th Brigade.
        C.R.A.
        C.R.E.
        Pioneers.
        Signals.
        Q.
        D.M.G.O.

App 14

TELEPHONE CONVERSATIONS.

Battle 4th October 1917.

TELEPHONE CONVERSATIONS.

DATE	TIME	FROM	TO	CONVERSATION.
4/10/17	6.18 am	11th Bde.	4th Div.	Everything started all right. The enemy put down a light barrage before ZERO. Only one casualty whilst troops were assembling.
"	6.30 am	11th Bde.	11th Div	KANGAROO 7 reported captured with little opposition.
"	7 am.	11th Brigade.	4th Div.	Wounded officer had got 500x before he was hit. Advance still going steadily. He saw about 30 prisoners coming back. — Reported by S.L.I.
"	7.10 am	11th Div.	—	Reported having taken 12 prisoners & 371 ZR (normal).
"	7.20	11th Inf Bde.	—	Hants reports at 6.45 am 12 prisoners taken — No definite information — wounded state attack proceeding satisfactorily.
"	7.22.	11. Bde.	—	Hants report at 7.14 am on prisoners: — No written message received from company but amended Report Hants reserve company had reached KANGAROO trench — Further 8 prisoners and 1 light M.G.

TELEPHONE CONVERSATIONS.

DATE	TIME	FROM	TO	CONVERSATION.
4.	7.30.	11 Bde.	—	Somerset L.I. report capture of prisoner 10. Bav. Inf. Regt. (Info. informed.)
4.	7.40.	N.Lanc. I.O.	—	Prisoner of 10th Bav. I.R. and 3/1 I.R. confirmed.
4.	7.45.	11 Bde.	—	Somerset HQ. report German barrage appears to be on KANGAROO Trench (heavy but dispersed.)
4.	7.45.	10 Bde.	—	Wounded highlander reports our people on 19 metre hill (unconfirmed) ✱ Don't inform Corps yet. Spur.
4.	7.45.	11 Bde.	—	Following message received from Hamel's Coy Officer — UNCONFIRMED — "my location uncertain appears to be V19 a 10 85 — all wounded touch but men

TELEPHONE CONVERSATIONS.

DATE	TIME	FROM	TO	CONVERSATION.
4.	8.10.	11 Bde.	—	E Lancs report 8 am 2 front coys in KANGAROO Trench & right about 150 in front of his obj - troops - report from perfects line 7.15 am
4.	8.10 am	10. Bde	—	reports they have reached 1st obj'ective - 2nd obj'ective - Sent up THQ moves to KANGAROO Trench - hourly C.S.M. confirm report that we occupy 15 metre hill.
4.	8.35 am	Capt. G.		11. Bde. F.O.O. reports - "Huns routed 1st obj'ective and consolidating - need further confirmation -

TELEPHONE CONVERSATIONS.

DATE	TIME	FROM	TO	CONVERSATION
4.iii.	9.5am	11 Bde.	—	Following received from 33 Bde by Liaison Officer :- 7.57. Mauberton (34 Bde.) 1st Objective taken.(/1150) 7.48. Enemy bringing up Tanks. 8.16. Wounded Sergeant report Tank at RETOUR CROSS ROADS 8.20 am Liaison Sergeant (Sherwood Foresters) report they have taken 1st Objective.

TELEPHONE CONVERSATIONS.

DATE	TIME	FROM	TO	CONVERSATION
4th	10.9 am	XIV Corps.	—	Left Division XVIII Corps has reached it's final objective. Right Division also reached where reaches final objective. F.O.O. XIV Corps R.A. report has been over between in POELCAPPELLE. S.O.S. reported on own front.
4th	11.15 am	C.R.A.	—	
4th	12.23 pm	B.G.G.S. XIV Corps.	—	B.G.G.S. has been observer of aeroplane who dropped map at 11.35 am. Observer is confident that own troops are east in TRAQ'OUE PM as the foot mark of troops can easily be seen and they do not go as far as TRAQ'OUE PM. General MARKE will arrange provision of tanks to cover advance if needed in advance this afternoon.

TELEPHONE CONVERSATIONS.

DATE	TIME	FROM	TO	CONVERSATION.
4	1.45 p.m.	4 Dn. Arty	G branch	TRAGIQUE Fm. & KANGAROO HUTS are reported by arty. on our right as being held by the enemy.
4	1.47 p.m.	14 Corps.	G.	Result of contact patrol by 9th Squadron R.F.C. summarised as follows:- Our men located between following pts:- U.17.c.8.2.- U.17.d.4.1.- U.17.d.8.2.- U.18.c.2.4. Y along line U.18.c.25.50 - U.18.c.8.8 - U.18.d.3.8 - V.18a.90.55 - V.19a.6.8 - V.19.a.2.5. No sign of any enemy on our immediate front could be seen. De Coeg ter Westen Fm. appears to be unoccupied. Our tracks lead well up to POELCAPPELLE although no men could be seen in the open.

TELEPHONE CONVERSATIONS.

DATE	TIME	FROM	TO	CONVERSATION.
4th	2.10pm	General DAVIS (11th Div)	2nd Div "G"	"Can you confirm capture of TRAGIQUE FM by 11th Bde.? (Capture not confirmed) 11th Divn are continuing their advance to Fork Rds V.20 c 05.75. at 6pm. Further advance at 6.30pm on heavy POELCAPPELLE."
4th	3.40pm	14th Corps "G"	"	The attack by 14 Corps on our right has been countermanded.
4th	3.42pm	2nd Div Arty	"	Report received very heavy bangs put down on our old Front and Support lines.

TELEPHONE CONVERSATIONS.

DATE	TIME	FROM	TO	CONVERSATION
4th	5.19 pm	General Bunnon 11th Bde	4th Div. G.	Stop protective barrage at our pts as have been pound up to 6" fixed objective. We now hold TRABIQUE — TM KANGROO HUTS and road to 1/2 EAST of this place.
4th	6.43 "	4th Div Arty	"	Div Arty report S.O.S. went up in front of our right group about V.20.a. at 6.35 pm
4th	6.54 pm	"	"	Div Arty report S.O.S. went up in front of our left group at 6.45 pm.
4th	8.35 p.m.	29th Div.	"	29th Div. have received telephone message from front line saying that they are in touch with our Regt & that our troops are "in the position we showed Div. them to be"(i.e the GREEN LINE?).

66

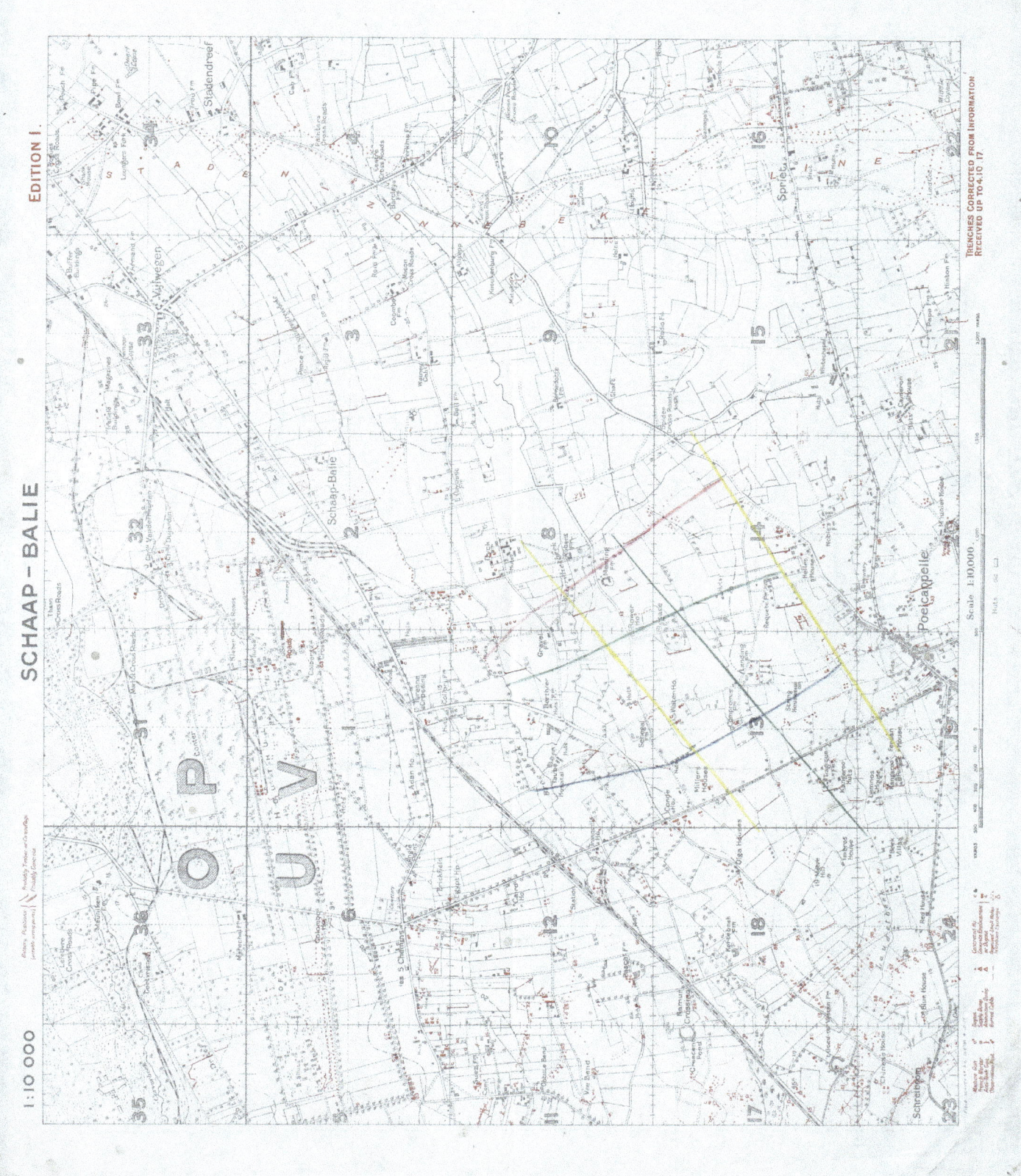

Sequence No.	Time	Type of Message		Contents	Action taken
1.	6.55am	T.	11th Bde. C.1.	KANGAROO Trench captured by S.L.I. at 6.20 am Little Rifle opposition	copy to CRA
2.	6.55	T.	10th Bde. BM569.	Enemy artillery any active for 30 mins. before zero in vicinity LANGEMARK + STEENBEEK. Barrage came down at zero + 3. hot + heavy.	copy to CRA
3.	7.0.	T.	10th Bde. BM 570.	Light barrage continuing. No shelling w. of Things.	copy to CRA
4.	7.5	T.	11th Bde. C.2.	Continuing telephone conversation — Wounded Officer 1 S.L.I. reports advance proceeding well when himself hit 500 x ahead about 30 prisoners seen coming in.	copy to CRA
5.	7.22am	T.	ARTY. R.C.243.	Enemy barrage apparent start at 6.20am was light till 6.15am — visibility poor S.O.S. appears to be Red rocket bursting into two Red followed by a green rocket	—
6.	7.30am	T.	10th Bde. B.M. 571.	Middlesex report 2 prisoners from 351 J.R. passed BON GITE. — requires confirmation	copy to CRA
7.	7.45.	T.	ARTY. F.2.	F.o.o. reports KANGAROO Trench Trench passed 6.30a.m — 100 prisoners passed Red station.	—
8.	7.40.	T.	10th Bde. BM. 572.	17 prisoners 371 J.R. & 10th Bavn.I.R. passed ADELPHI	copy to CRA
9.	8.0.	T.	ARTY. F.G. 246.	7.25am no further news.	—
10.	8.6.	T.	ARTY.	F.o.o reports we are beyond 19 METRE HILL.	—
11.	7.30	T.	11th Bde. C.4.	1/HANTS report 20 prisoners + 1 M.G. brought in on Reserve Coy. reached KANGAROO TRENCH	copy to C.R.A

Sequence No.	Time	Type of Message	Contents	Action taken
12.	7.44 a.m.	T. 11th A.Bde.	C.S. 1/Hants report enemy barrage now on EAGLE Trench - prisoners taken by 1/Hants 1/5/25 Batt. 10 Bav. I.R.	copy to C.R.A.
13.	8.2 a.m.	T. 10th A.Bde.	BM 573. 10th T.M.B. from EAGLE reports attack appears going well - all wounded known in good spirits	copy to C.R.A.
14.	8.5 a.m.	T. 11th Bde.	C.6. Telephone message 1/Hants not yet confirmed states first troops at V.19.a. 10.8.5" in touch with all units - casualties about 10 per coy. - no opposition - conversation on phone difficult.	copy to C.R.A.
15.	8.25 a.m.	T. O/y.	Two Reports - First 7.5 a.m. - Being 4/4 7th weak - mostly single H.2 & 477 Guns - Value 5.gr. - Mg Machine recently E of STEENBEEK - 2nd Mtrgh & WHITE TRENCH.	
16.	8.35 a.m.	Intell. 20 Inf Bde.	At 8.30 a.m. 29 Div. South of Meltzer that Regt. Right Bn. had sent a visual message, part of which only could be (?) - Company & Mtrs objective also clear. It was not known definite. A few missing. Coy having luck along the railway.	
17.	8.25 a.m.	T. Intelligence.	Prisoners of 37th I.R. 10th Bav. I.R. 13th Bav. I.R. Colonist. - 8th Bav. I.R. Not wired 208th Res. four days ago. - ERA of both N & 3 11th Bav. I.R. 13th Bav. 10th Bav. I.R. 871". I.R. 369 I.R. 37th I.S.	
18.	8.40 a.m.	T. 10th Bde.	Following received fm SEAFORTHS - When flare went 1st objective Bn HQrs is advancing to HAMMOND - Time 7.15 am - 2nd in comm. 8/o Middlesex has advanced o/c A Coy - No Coy - No Company has advanced to B+ Area -	
19.	8.55 a.m.	T. O/y.	Enemy holding the light country part of STEENBEEK - POELEN FARM ALOVETTE RIDGE IRAVEMARK CHATEAU - went 1st afternoon - MEEN BEEK batteries having a quiet time - hostility from many shells heavy light aircraft -	

Sequence No.	Time	Type of Message	CONTENTS.	Action taken.
20.	9.8 a.m.	T. 11th Div.	Rpt Bn. tgnt Red Actual line taken. — Cpt Bn. Reserve Red actual line Actual line not confirmed. — Yellow Line Reserve 37th I.R. 10th Bav. I.R. — 1st Bn. 32nd Yäger Regt Inner Barrage — Heavy barrage 6.25 a.m. Au Bon Gite — northwest barrage 6.35 to 7.30 on LANGEMARK Road — 7.35 Enemy shelling old front line	Copy to C.R.A.
21.	9.9 a.m.	T. 11 Bde.	Following message from 2 Lancs Fusrs 8.1A h.: — 2 first companies has advanced to JAMES ROO TRENCH — Yel. Troops on my right are About 150 yds in front of my advanced troops — Pills 8.10 am — Columbia Casualties 100 officers & 50 O.R. —	Copy to C.R.A.
22.	9.14 a.m.	T. 14 Infy.	All information vague but that from Foot and wounded suggest that attack started satisfactorily but that KANGAROO TRENCH has stopped it. First shell report from Foot that 19 Lehr Inftr was repulsed 7.6 am — Also shell fire across Canfilualda	Copy to C.R.A.
23.	9.25 a.m.	T. 10th Bde.	BM.575. 10th M.G.C. report barrage guns gone forward to second position — 1 gun knocked out — Enemy shelling vicinity IRON X & ADELPHI 4.2 & 5.9.	
24.	9.25	T. ARTY.	R.G. 252. 8.50 a.m Fairly heavy shelling (4.2 & 5.9) between RUISSEAU Fm. † MARTINS MILL W. of LANGEMARK — 76 Battys. not being shelled.	
25.	9.27	10th Inf Bde.	BM. 3. Escort missing 12th Bde. not arrived, WARWICKS asked for escort.	
26	9.30	11th Bde.	C.8. /HANTS timed 6.40 report OC Right assaulting company report 6.57 barrage halted — my location uncertain, apparently concrete emplacement V.19.a.10.65 — all units in touch — very mixed — casualties about 10 per coy.	

Serial No.	Time	Type of message	CONTENTS.	Action taken
27.	9.40 a.m.	T. ARTY.	A.F.P.2. - Enemy plane flying low 9.15 a.m firing into our Batteries (5th R.H.A. Bde.)	
28.	9.45 a.m.	T 10th Inf. Bde.	B.M.576. - Nothing further to report.	
29.	9.53 a.m.	T 11th Inf. Bde.	C.9. - Liaison officer with 33rd Bde. reports MANCHESTERS report 1st objective taken 7.51 — 7.48 enemy barraging tracks — 5.16 wounded sergeant reports Tank at RETOUR & Rds. — 8.20 a.m. SHERWOOD FORESTERS taken 1st objective	
30.	10.10 a.m.	T 10th Inf. Bde.	B.M.577. - Prisoners still coming in — Nothing further to report.	
31.	10.12 a.m.	T 11th Inf. Bde.	C.10. - Reserve coy HANTS Report consolidating Line 200 E. of KANGAROO as ordered. — SEAFORTHS have funked on our right — S.L.I. reported at BEER villas — verbal message S.L.I. reports in touch.	
32.	10.35 a.m.	T 4th Div. S.O.	Further information prisoners — 1st Batt. 10th Bav. J.R. relieved 3rd & 8th on night 2/3 — 3rd Batt. had only been in line 2 days after relieving 185 J.R. on night 30 Sept/1 Oct. — An attack had been expected on nights 1st & 2nd knew no attack this morning — an acting officer expects counter-attack by counter-attack Division, but does not know which — Another prisoner had been men of 28 J.R. 16 Div. in a rear area.	

Sequence No.	Time	Type of Message	CONTENTS.	Action taken.
33.	10.40a	T. 9.0. III Div.	Confirms previously discovered order of battle — 3rd R.B." in WESTROOSEBEEK area — 1st Batt. 371.1.R. relieved elements of 2nd Batt. 4 days ago.	
34.	10.40a	T. 11th Bde.	C.12. — From S.L.I. Liaison officer with SHERWOOD FORESTERS reports This R. Coy. have taken objective, no report from left Coy — Tanks seen advancing POELCAPPELLE — S.L.I. officer to be called for to sight, and at V.19.c.10.75".	
35.	10.45	T. 10th Bde.	Asking further to report.	
36.	10.46a	D. L.O. 29th Div.	57th Bde report 10.6 a.m. 1st R.D.F in touch with 2 Sea High." on 19R. held still.	
			33rd Inf. Bde.	
37.	10.45a	T. 11th Bde.	C.14 — L.O. with SHERWOOD FORESTERS reports message picked up by R.F.A from lamp signal runs "Left Battalion taken all objectives — Tanks going out in front of RED LINE.	
38.	10.50.	T. Arty.	Message from F.O. 32 F.A.B sent 7.40 from top of ridge by tank. Recd 9.55 am reports :- Mock Attery secured in front of our attack. Very heavy Artillery on RAIZE HOUSE and EAGLE Trench by S.P. and A.D's — All first objectives taken — Our infantry advancing on POELCAPPELLE and attery towards which having very effective fire behind on tanks having very effective	

Sequence No.	Time	Type of message	CONTENTS.	Action taken.
			Any message read during advance.	
39.	10.60	T. Ary.	Following message from Right Support Coy - "Am on western slope of WALTER FM - Capt. Rood rt. on approaching by going strong refused left flank rear - Thought by L.t. to join up with that from ORCHAZ." Have asked A.ty. to barrage left flank. Have sent forward S.A.A. to this infantry as right going well - seen on southern flank of POELCAPPELLE - No buses ahead right - large numbers of Germans seen to.	
40.	11.15	T. N Div.	Right Bn. opposite GLOSTER FARM. Centre Bn. Reaching CERISIERS - Left Bn. N.W. part of RM. Bn. at BELCAPPELLE CHURCH - Extreme Rd. Short message states left Bn. of left Bn. has not caught whole of Rd. and that part has got on in front - Right opposite GLOSTER - have been fought - No operators at Levy - No barrage very effective - Battle W/y Ruttersh.	
41.	11.15	T. Ary.	Enemy prisoner on exit rt. - the toll of 50 ten ten sen.	
42.	11.16	T. Ary.	Enemy Arty. shelling between MARTIN'S Hill and RUFFRED FARM. Chiefly H.P. Enemy Artillery Nests Also barrage on ALLOETTE RIDGE between ALLOETTE FARM and RAILWAY - STEENBEEK quiet except for an occasional sen. 20 prisoners passed at 9.20. (Right Group)	
43.	11.30	T. 10 Bde.	Following just message picked up at IRON CROSS on a barring of Bn. Hdgrs happens - legues - Enemy shelling TRAITORS FARM. Time 10.35 am. Nothing further to report.	
44.	11.40	T. 3rd Ary.	In continuation 6.th Reid Army be checked at 6. A. M. Report show that return is being satisfactory -	

Sequence No.	Time	Type of Message	CONTENTS.	Action taken.
45.	10.44	T. 1. Bde.	Following from Liason Officer with 83rd Bde – Begun – S80 An STAFFORDS afort first objective taken – in touch with HAMPSHIRES at V.19 D.2.2 and SHERWOOD FORESTERS at V.19 R.8.8. – consolidating Reina Ohio 60.	
46.	10.45	T. to Bde.	Nothing to add.	
47.	11.52	T. ARTY.	R.2.256. Enemy sending up double red rockets about TRANQUILLE Fm.	
48.	12 Noon	T. 11. Bde.	Shall that about 9. A.M. that 6 had reached that consolidating line BEEK NAZAS – RED HOUSE has led him to link up line of NASROS HOUSE – BROWN by man road, making a line 200 yds East of KANGAROO TRENCH – Casualties estimated at 20 per cent. In touch with SOUTH HANTS.	
49.	12.10	T. 11. Bde.	Shall Afoot at 11.10 A.M. moving in Ms. to LOUIS FARM.	
50.	12.10	T. 11. Bde.	O.N.1. shots that SHERWOODS have reached final objective. left with a Road at V.19 B.1.7.	
51.	12.15	T. Arty.	Wounded arriving – the advance fully 1000 yds. Much hung caused by R.62 in shell holes and at back in front of KEN.	
52.	12.20	T. to Bde.	Infantry what to task.	
53.	12.30	T. 11. Bde.	10th Bde. – Tuned 11.Am. shells – Enemy after the shelling TRANQUILLE at 10.25 Am.	
54.	12.35	T. Arty.	Hostile Artillery Inactive	

Sequence No.	Time	Type of message	Contents	Action taken
55.	12:40	D.R. 29th Div.	29th Div. have ath. objective. They have established posts at V.17 d 2.7 - V.17 a.0.5 - V.17 c.4.6. (1st Platoon, 2nd Platoon, 3rd Platoon). Enemy guns holding him from BEAR COPSE. This was at 10.15 A.M.	
56.	12:30	T. to Bde.	Regt. and Cavalry Bgd. of Wiltshires have moved forward to A area - nothing further. Enemy Savage [illeg.] - Ammunition killing of LANGEMARCK and STEENBEEK -	
57.	1:4 P.M.	Telephone 1st Coys.	10th Cole spot. Enemy moving about BREWERY - POELCAPPELLE.	
58.	1:15	T. to Bde.	Working parties to spot. Heavy shelling of Eagle Trench.	
59.	1:20	To 29 Div.	8/R Bn. spot. that they saw the objective except on the right. When situation to take shew - they saw him from from 0.17 c.8.4 to 0.17 a.8.4. Shew is front of 4 block houses at 0.18 a.5 to 0.18 c 96.65 - Shew is a gap between 0.17 a.8.4 & 0.18 c.4.5. Cas. - Shew is being filled. Casualties officer 3 off. two men. About 100 German prisoners & 2 M.G. taken shooting spots. Enemy is light ony -	
60.	1:30	T.O. to Bde.	Patrol of 1st by to Bav. I.R. 11th saw into the right of 2/3 inf. delivery 203 Div. - Prisoners taken on Br. of cars Regt. to line - Othr. of Batt. officers to the North of Point 6th Bav. I.R. 13 Bav. I.R. 10 Bav. I.R. 37th I.R. 369th I.R. 370 R.I.R. - Prisoners of 37th I.R. expect to be relieved by another Div. on night of 5/6 - have heard it is to be 187th but cannot state which.	

Sequence No.	Time	Type of message	CONTENTS.	Action taken.
61.	1.45	T. 11 Bde	0.21. shot fired 12.20 P.h. this line of final objective reached by Right bn. - data that for left command state his line withdrawn thin 100 yds east of FERDAN WOOD owing to casualties from our barrage — this interfere with another effort of place.	
62.	1.45.	L.O. 4th Div T	2 officers sent to O.R. found through stehn. other employed a stretcher bearer. - large number of wounded passed through Mercury Station — Enemy total counted surrounded at 100.	
63.	1.50	Deg Sw.	Hu-tui Ams mines 0.18 a.3.8. 0.18 c.85. 8o. 0.18 a.50.70. 0.18 c.1.3. 0.17 d.7.2. 0.17 d.4.1. 0.17 C.8.1. Posts at 0.17 a.2.6. 0.17 a.0.5. 0.17 c.6.6. fighting too heavy. Posts were counted 100 - large bunch dead and wounded Germans. 2 L.G.; Coy lines.	
64.	2.0 p.m	T. 14 Corps.	G.937. Situation report as above.	
65.	2.5 p.m.	T. 2 on 15th Div	Prisoners of 1st Coy. 10. Bav. J.R., 2nd Coy 371 J.R. 11th Coy 369 J.R. identified.	
66.	2.10 p.m	T. 29th Div	1st K.O.S.B. report 10.15 a.m. all objectives taken N. of Railway — consolidation in progress 1 platoon W.17.d. 20.70. 2 sections U.17.d.0.5. 1 platoon at U.17.c.7.7. — M.Gs. giving trouble from BEAR COPSE.	

Sequence No.	Time	Type of Message	CONTENTS.	Action taken.
67.	2.27pm	T. XIV Corps	B.943. MLn. 6 offset succm - (cancelled later.)	
68.	2.30pm	P. Seaforths	Troops advancing in waves on LEWIS Fm. and enty. hdqrs at once.	
69.	2.35pm	T. 11th Div.	Reports indicate REDLINE captured on divl. front but not officially reported. Patrols at MEUNIER HO. and BEER HOUSES — casualties moderate — one TANK reached GLOSTER Fm. & went on to TERRIER Fm.	
70.	2.40pm	T. 11th Bde.	Brigr. report from front line 2nd S.H.I. A.Coy commander states that he has occupied TRAGIQUE Fm. 10.58 a.m — S.H.I. report being in touch with units on both flanks.	
71.	2.45pm	T. XIV Corps	Bad observation prevents details as to attack being clear — all or practically all objectives have been obtained on 2nd & 1st Army fronts.	
72.	3.10pm	T. 11 Inf Bde.	SoS shown V.13.c. at 12.55 p.m. — 2nd/5th S.H.I. returning from front line reports SEAFORTHS withdrawn from 19 METRE Nhse and Line N.E falling back — counter attack being organised.	

Sequence No.	Time	Type of Message	CONTENTS.	Action taken.
73.	3.25.	5th Army	Our attack offering the heaviest resistance to - Right Coln. that left the whole of final objective behind right the captured. IRON PRINCE FARM. Took wind hill NW of WELLINGTON and attacking Westroy W.V. of D. - Prisoners estimated about 200 - Left Coln. went Australian behind attack at 11.20 am about the line of our objective. O.17.C.91. - O.17.d.4.1 - thence Inf. & U.17.d.4.2. Then to U.18.C.8.8. - U.18.d.3.8. U.18.D.9.6. - U.13.C.4.0. FERAN HOUSE - O19.B.3.25. - Army's right of 1st probable troops have captured final objective line where include POLDER HOEK - REUTEL-NOORD EMMEN - BROODSEINDE - GRAVENSTAFEL Village - ABRAHAM Heights - PIEBROS being W -	
74	3.40	T.4/11th Hants	Report from Units of 10th Bde Informing by last missing to enemy Counter attack now checked on my immediate left - lately of U.24.c.20.99.	
75.	3.50	T. 11 Bde.	P.S.1. 2.55 P.m. Wrote - Thatch gently enforced him - Advance of about 600 yds has been made apparently my left has swung back - my right is in touch with SHERWOODS.	
76.	3.50	T. 10 Bde.	11 Bde wrote as follows:- Sgt.1. who 11 Seaforth falling back of 19 Lakes Hill - North went both flanks enforced and then fallen back to line of BEEK WILLAS - East flank are being organised. East his R.B's have been ordered to counter attack - Wollesen who got to his left flank - Seaforth report that his men are involved in fight on his left flank - Warwick being ordered forward to deliver attack of enemy - details 19 Lakes Hill & south of tramway	

Sequence No.	Time	Type of Message	CONTENTS.	Action taken.
77.	4.5 p.m.	T. 10 Bde.	Counter attack closed on 19 behr Wd - A.B.'s moved up to O area - S/As at IRON CROSS.	
78.	4.5	T. 11th Bde.	Heads Ypert lines a bit by flanks given way far no apparent reason to the lines of LOOS FARM - am holding line of posts BEEK VILLAS - FORT BANN have pushed forward from on Rigual front lines and the rest strong enough to hold it - without supports. As it stands line is absolutely disorganised - would suggest that 12 Bde be sent up at once.	
79.	4.10	T. 11 Div.	O.O. 117 - Entrusting orders of Attack (subsequently Cancelled.)	
80.	4.15	T. 11 Div.	Cancels O.O. 117. Positions being consolidated with a view to further attack in the morning.	
81.	4.20	T. 11 Div.	Situation unchanged. MEUNIER HOUSE reported strongly held by the enemy.	
82.	4.20	T. 10 Bde.	No report of front guard have been received from 6th Bde. Flank (about 2.10 P.M.)	
83.	4.20	T. 11 Bde.	Situation appears to be as follows: - my right in touch with 2nd line of 4th Div about V.19.d 60.15 - by this line there along the LAUDERBEEK - 2 shown line and on by BEEK Village, from Refsesive flank N of HP of HANE - Am by N of BEEK Village Remarks 2 Coms at KAMPAROO have orders R Bi & "KIRK", sight of Hannels who I understand are by retain 19 behr Wd. Have instructed R Bi & Kirk me up at Co. BOX SITE.	

Serial No.	Time	Type of Message	CONTENTS.	Action taken.
84	4.30	I.O.IV Div.	Forward Bn of 10th Bav. I.R. said to have lost 4 Coys in front line - Strength 70 - Further 70 been fir by 3rd to be in rest between of Adinfer - last Coy has Pers Coys to be - Heavy h.G. also suffering the Bn. but further unknown - Four of duty in line 3 days - One of 2nd Coy to Bav. I.R. was captured in POELCAPPELLE - Two heavy h.Gs. in Sw. of POELCAPPELLE are taken to have been stormed and captured by our troops under fire of heavy fire.	
85	4.55	T. 10 B.De.	Nothing to report.	
86.	5.5	T. 10 B.De.	Nothing to report. The Adjoths thirtalion toth in Eagle Lane.	
87	5.20	T. in Note.	Cancelling O. 943.	
88	9.45	T. 10 II Div.	Prisoners 9/10 by 10 Bav. I.R. that 9th and 10th Coys been to POELCAPPELLE to relieve - D.Bn destroying - Prisoners of 2nd + 4th Coys 369 I.R. state Bn sent to reinforce 3 Bn - 7th + 8th Coys of 37 I.R. counter-attacked about 8 A.m. - 8th Coy. withdrawn owing to heavy fire - the barrage - kind of 6th Bav. Div. my had.	
89.	1.30	T. Arty.	3 Y.A.B. 400 north at 145 Ph. enemy attacks to U.18 C+D and a line U.18 C.10.90 to U.18 C.10.90. At 2 P.m. S.O.S sent up about U.18A and V.13.C. The infantry appeared to be retiring from V.13.C. but stopped - At 2.20 p.m. the enemy retire our roofs advanced intermittently - large numbers of enemy cavalries	
90	4.45	T Arty.	400 29th Y.A.B. begins - When the barrage fell this morning many fired S.O.S rocket. area winning STEENBECK LANGEMARCK Thirty Heavy - Pane Au Shelled area winning STEENBECK LANGEMARCK Thirty Heavy - PILCHEM - large numbers of enemy cavalries	

Sequence No.	Time	Type of message	CONTENTS.	Action taken.
	(cont.)			
91.	5.20	T 39 Div	1.0.0. 32 F.A.B. attack at 3.30 large numbers of enemy wounded can be seen retiring - own Casualties after very heavy -	
			All objectives gained in to-day's attack except possibly a extreme right where enemy position identified - Enemy counter attack collecting South of STADEN RLY about 3 P.M. failed to materialize owing to fire of M. Arty - Enemy Arty has quietened down since 5 P.M. - Prisoners estimated 700 + 2 M.G's -	
92.	5.21	T. Arty.	Statement of Guns out of action.	
93.	5.35	11 Bde.	Latest information shows our line running from left to right as follows: - V.18.N.95.45 - TRAGIQUE FARM - V.13.C.8.2. V.13.D.2.0. Right of 2nd Divi just at V.19.A.4.1.	
94.	6.18	XIV Corps	A Contact aeroplane will go out presently as soon as light permits to obtain a situation on Corps front. A photographic machine will be over from daylight till 12 Noon.	
95.	6.15	T. XIV Corps.	Air reconnaissance:- About 800 men to South of fifty lying down at site of road to O.36.D. - 400 P.W. about 150 men in groups of 50 lying down at side of road in P.33 Central.	

Sequence No.	Time	Type of Message	CONTENTS.	Action to.
96.	6.10 p.m.	XIV Corps.	Evening Report :- Seaforths, Hants & S.L.I. Battln. Fusiliers r.K.O.Y.Bi. in order named form right to left attacked this morning - all objective others to bn. Hin. World - At 1 P.M. a counter attack developed against 19 Inche Batt - Situation not clear. Division retired to Munt a Gatasnel has taken place - An effort known. Reports objectives still held. 1 Officer and 86 O.R. announced r 1 officer + 29 O.R wounded have passed through Corps. Cage. 2 M.G.s. captured.	
97.	6.45	T. S.J.I.	Line to follow C18 d 9.6 TRABIQUE FARM ROAD - V13 C.8.2 V.13 d 2.6 - 2nd Lini XEMMOS and FIRDEN HOUSE Also posts at V19 a.4.1 Bn. hy arrived - heavy casualties from our own guns - Post East of TRABIQUE FARM weakly held.	
98.	6.9	T. 11. Div.	Evening Report :- Both Brigades told Red line - 120 prisoners north 37 I.R. and 6th Bav I.R. Forth cage - line to follow.	
99.	7.15	To Bde	Message timed 3.30 P.M. :- The line is to be 19 metre dot - In front of W. Werren and N. of yellow dot on the line a. Keported further that by O C "D" by hillstock. Brigade adds Trench still being taken being fillers to left to left flank.	
100.	7.58	T. ARTY	6.15 p.m. several rockets breaking into two reds one put up about V.13. a 4.0. - Enemy at once put up right barrage that section 51 rout.	

CONTENTS.

Sequence No.	Time	Type of Message	Contents	Action taken
101.	8 p.m.	T. 11 Bde.	1st HANTS ask for 2 or 3 S.Bs. with stretchers to clear brigade area.	
102	8.12	T. 10 Bde	Warwicks have been ordered to take up the situation on 19 Lotts Ave and reestablish a line of posts in touch with 11 B.W. and 8/7th Inf. Bde – Nothing further to report.	
103	8.15	T. Arty.	Warwicks have discovered that the ground in the W.D – Henry Enemy artillery fire on front line. Hottest trenches. Prisoner. 11th missing to.	
104	9.35	T. Arty.	At front – Light activity, little hostility on right.	
105.	9.20 pm	T. 29th Div.	Force reports that FRIEND is in touch with DOZEN and that an approx. on objectives. Slight counter attack this afternoon driven off. Enemy shelling much decreased and everything seems all right. Line reports strong and food.	
106	9.40pm	T Dogger 10 pm	Further from FRIEND light mixed with DOGGER (Seaforth) one officer FRIEND and 2 Seaforths have Rear H.Q. about V.15.c.9.b.	
107.	10.20pm	T. Dozen 10pm	Following received from FORCE (:) report received from FRIEND & tops they are in touch with 10 ABDe and with an officer of Irish light counter attacks. Counter attacks counter attacks this afternoon driven off. Everywhere seems quiet.	

App 16

OUT
MESSAGES
BATTLE 4TH OCTOBER 1917.

Sequence No.	Time	Type of Message	CONTENTS	Action taken
1.	6.30 a.m	T.G.S.99 16 XIV Info.	1st half hourly report — 11th Bde report having started all night.	✓
2.	7.11 a.m	T. G.S.100 16 XIV Info.	2nd half hourly report — 11th Bde. report KANGAROO trench captured — little opposition 6.30 a.m.. Enemy barrage light came down Zero+3. Enemy artillery very active LANGEMARK to STEENBEEK 30 mins before zero — Later report from 11th Bde. advance going well, about 30 prisoners.	✓
3.	—	T. G.S.102 16 XIV Info.	3rd half hourly report — 11th Bde. report attack proceeding satisfactorily at 6.45 am — reserve coy 1st HANTS reported in KANGAROO ave 7.0.0 — Where our barrage good.	✓
4.	—	T. G.S.101 16 XIV Info.	10th Bde. report capture prisoner 10 Bav. I.R. requires confirmation.	✓
5.	7.50 a.m	G.S.103 16 XIV Info.	4th half hourly report — Our troops passed KANGAROO 6.30 a.m. — 17 prisoners (371. I.R. 105. Bav. I.R.) passed ADELPHI — Barrage heavy in KANGAROO Tr. Prisoners belong to 371 I.R. and 2RS Bav. 10 Bav. I.R. confirmed.	✓
6.	8.15	T.G.S. 104 16 XIV Info.	Endeavour discover situation 33rd Inf. Bde. — 11th Div. has no information.	✓
7.	8.20p.	T.G.S. 105 16 XIV Info.	5th half hourly report. F.O.O.a/105 captured (9 metre 14th) aas 11th Bde (unconfirmed) report our troops at V.19.b.10.55. Little opposition as prisoners of 371 I.R. 10 R. Bav. I.R. 125 Bav. I.R. captured aas 6th Bav. Div. relieved 208 6th days ago — also tattle N-S 6th Bav. J.R. 138 Bav. I.R. 10 R. Bav. J.R. 371 2 R. 369 J.R. 370 J.R.	✓
8.	8.37.	T.G.S. 106. 16 XIV Info.		

Sequence No.	Time	Type of Message	CONTENTS.	Action taken.
9.	9 a.m.	G.S.107 to XIV Corps.	6th half-hourly report:- Nothing to report.	
10.	9.35	G.S.108 to XIV Corps.	Following reported by 83rd Bde liaison officer 7.51 a.m. Heavies fire (34th Bde) that first objective 11th Div taken - 8.16 be reported report that at RETOUR CROSS ROADS - 11th Bde open all awake in touch.	
11.	9.45	G.S.110 to all Bdes.	Great or fires are should be sent to ODELPH HOUSE at on - touch of 10th & 11th Bdes will not be used for securing this area. East from ODELPH.	
12.	9.50	G.S.109 to 10th & 11th Bdes	Artillery report our flying aeroplane shooting at batteries NR. STEENBEEK - take steps to prevent.	
13.	10. a.m.	G.S.111 XIV Corps.	7th half hourly report:- Nothing further to report.	
14.	10.35 a.m.	G.S.112 to 10th & 11th Bdes.	Info. reced left div of Corps on our right to have reached final objective - F.O.O. spots Right div. also believed to have reached final objective. Lne seen row held to POELCAPPELLE.	
15.	11.0.0	G.S.113 XIV Corps	8th half hourly report:- Position of 1st Bde 10th Bde I.R. 11th Bde 3rd/10th on Right 9/2nd - 3.73rd Res. in line 2 Btys strong 185 I.R. on Right of 3rd Sept - 10 M.G.. - Attack expected on right 1st & 2nd October. No attack expected this morning. - Reserve Regt nothing of support position in dispositions - Counter attack expects to be made by counter-attack Div. units seen in rear 20th I.R. 15th Bn - the Korp. V/9/10 at V.19 P.10.75 - Tanks seen advancing all POELCAPPELLE.	
16.	12.6 p.m.	C.S.114 to Bde. 4th Div A/M 115 Div	*Very slight opposition has been met during attack this morning and 11th Div will probably push forward this evening to northern end of POELCAPPELLE, about V14.c.54, and be prepared to conform to this movement by establishing outpost line well supported on line	

* URGENT OPERATION

Sequence No.	Time	Type of message	CONTENTS.	Action taken.
16 (cont'd)			(on line) V.14.C.0.5. – STRING/HOUSES – V.13.C.0.6 aaa This forward move will take place at 6.30pm at which hour hostile barrage will become intense and move forward at 100 yds per minute to a line 200x beyond objective as above aaa added DENZIL repto. DUST YOCEAN" (send to 11th Bde URGENT OPERATION)	
17	12.5pm	G.S. 115 XIV Corps all concerned	9th half hourly report Our troops reported to be consolidating line BEER VILLAS – RED HOUSE, no news of IMBROS Hoo, enemy reported shelling TRAGIQUE FM. & KANGAROO HUTS at 11.40 a.m. Div. arty reported S.O.S. on our left front at 11.15 a.m.	
18	12.32pm	G.S. 116. I.O. 4th Div.	Wire no. of prisoners.	
19	12.36pm	G.S. 117. XIV Corps & all concerned	Nothing further to report.	
20	12.40pm	G.S. 118 11th Bde repts 11th Div.	"OCEAN reports their Bgtn on final objective not in touch with your right aaa Report what steps you are taking to gain touch aaa added DENZIL repeated OCEAN".	
21	12.55	A.A. 180 11 Bde.	Two tanks have been ordered forward to TRAFFORD FARM along road from V.19.d.5.1.	
22	12.56	G.S. 189 11 Bde + 11 Bn	According to last report by aeroplane the line runs V.19.B.3.6 – V.19.a.Q.7 – V.19.a.7.7 – V.13.c.4.0 – V.13.c.0.6 – V.13.d.30.88 V.18.d.00.85.	

Sequence No.	Time	Type of Message	CONTENTS.	Action taken.
23.	1.5 p.m.	G.S. 121 to all Bns.	18th Corps c/of front 12.50 p.m. Enemy massing about BREWERY POELCAPPELLE.	
24.	1.19	G.S. 122. 14th Inf.-all continued	Heavy shelling of EAGLE Trench - Nothing further to report -	
25.	1.26	R.I. 123 11th Bn.	Report what relief you have had time for occupation of TRIANGLE FARM.	
26.	2.22 p.m.	G.S. 124 14th Corps etc.	Nothing further to report	
27.	2.38 p.m.	T. G.S. 125 XIV Corps 1.	Prisoners 2nd & 3rd Corps. 13 Bav.I.R. captured IV. of 10 Bav.I.R.	
28.	3.5 p.m.	G.S. 126 XII Corps re.	The Enemy have found to attacked and driven back by whole line roughly to the line of the LAUDER BEEK.	
29.	3.30 p.m.	T. 12 CS Inf. Bde. note. 11.15 " " G.S. 127.	G.S. 127 " Move up one Battalion to CANDLE AREA at once. to come under orders of G.O.C. DENZIL." add. DROP ref. DENZIL	
30.	4.2	T. 113 do. July 1st Div G.S. 128.	G.S. 114 to Churchill.	
31	5 p.m.	G.S. 129 also 14th Corps Report received	Situation still uncertain. No definite information to disposition yet received.	

Sequence No.	Time	Type of Message	CONTENTS.	Action taken.
32	3.5pm	G.S.130 add Dagenet Denije	It is of the utmost importance to maintain our position at TRAGIQUE FM and 19 METRE to protect the flank of OCEAN in POELCAPELLE	
33	5.57pm	G.S.131 add 12○ Bde	Cancel move of battalion as advised G.S.127	
34	6.15pm	G.S.132 add 14th Corps copy all concerned	Overnight Bde is now definitely established on its final Objective. An Officer has visited posts at the following places. U.16.d.9.5.45 - TRAGIQUE FM - V.13.c.5.2 - V.13.d.2.0 - V.19.a.4.1	

App.17

Telephone Conversations

9th October 1917.

TELEPHONE CONVERSATIONS.

DATE	TIME	FROM	TO	CONVERSATION.
9th	6.10 am	G.S.O.1.	12th Bde.	S.S.O.I asked 12th Bde what German barrage was like. Reply :- Ragged - on LOUIS FARM LINE 4 minutes after Zero.
"	6.45 a.m.	12th Bde.	G.S.O.I.	About 30 prisoners coming in — 4/17 15th Regt. 227 Div.
"	7.23 a.m.	12th Bde.	G. Officer	Message received from (Graves?) J.B to say both objectives taken.
"	7.45 a.m.	G.S.O.I.	12th Bde.	There was a slight check on Right at first.
"	8.30 a.m.	"	"	Report states R&S Batt. reached 19 METRE HILL which looked and no stretchers wanted to keep 700x or 600x behind support 13th objective.
"	8.31 a.m.	Div. Arty.	Div G.	F.O.O. reports 12th Bde gained 1st objective easily — going well — prisoners coming in in large numbers — 400 at 1KON X — twice 6.15a.m.
"	8.50 a.m.	B.G.G.S.	G.S.O.I	Div.G. reported that whole situation appeared to be going satisfactorily —

TELEPHONE CONVERSATIONS.

DATE	TIME	FROM	TO	CONVERSATION.
9th	9.37 a.m.	13.C.C.S.	G.S.O.1.	Asked if we had heard anything map - there was about 7.40 a.m. - one aig. it appears to be a BEAD the kind.
"	10.10 a.m.	10th Bde.	G.S.O.1.	10th Bde reports nothing on private track to Cts to keep until a batn. arrives.
"	10.15 am	G.S.O.1.	12 Bde.	(line broken)
"	11.5 am	B.G.G.S.	S.O.I	Last air report shows that no one has yet moved forward from 2nd Objective.
"	11.55 a.m.	12th Bde.	G.S.O.	The B.G.C. has sent out a reconnoissance line dog Pigeon.
"	12.30 pm	G.O.C.17th Bn	G.S.O1	2/7 Essex Rifled Pickd was at Strail all reserve
	12.35 p.m	A.D.M.S.	G.S.O1	2/6, 2nd Aug 4/6 R waiting for about half movement to S.W. direction. 2/0. 46 OR waiting orders. 2/0. 21 OR 7 7 am. up to 11 a.m.

TELEPHONE CONVERSATIONS.

DATE	TIME	FROM	TO	CONVERSATION.
9	1.9 p.m.	B.G.G.S	G.S.O.1	B.G.G.S. rang up to say Corps quite satisfied with line we were on, not to make any further effort to reach GREEN line, but fill up gap between REQUETE Fm. & LANDING Fm.
9	2.59 p.m.	B.G.G.S. 14th Corps	1st Div.	18th Corps are convinced that their line runs just short of Le BRENY, DOELCAPPELLE and that 11th Division is not so far back as they think.

Wk 18

IN
MESSAGES
BATTLE 9ᵗʰ October

Sequence No.	Time	Type of Message	CONTENTS.	Action taken.
1.	6 a.m.	T. 10th Bde.	G.1. Barrage opening ragged — Enemy barrage appeared to come down 2+5. Thin light at first. Heavier on LANGEMARCK.	Copy to C.R.A.
2.	6.20 a.m.	T. 12th Bde.	B.M.C. 79/1. Barrage continues between LANGEMARCK & attacking troops — Deserter 417 Regt. captured — nothing further. (227 Div.)	Copy to C.R.A.
3.	6.40 a.m.	T. 10th Bde.	G.2. Enemy barrage less active.	"
4.	6.48 a.m.	T. 29th Div.	G.M.Q.650 — First objectives reported taken by Right Bde — at least 100 prisoners at 13th J.H.Q., 227th Div. 441 Regt. — Left Bde. reported over BROEMBEKE.	"
5.	6.52 a.m.	T. 12th Bde.	B.M.C. 79/2 — Nothing to report from our front. Barrage continues — 400 prisoners 417 Regt. captured by 82nd Bde (LEFT).	"
6.	7.20 a.m.	T. 12th Bde.	B.M.C. 70/3 — Prisoners from Left Div. still coming in — no news from our front.	"
7.	7.30 a.m.	T. XIV Corps	G. 68. — Situation 7.10 still uncertain — all 3 Divs. report prisoners. French progressing satisfactorily.	"
8.	7.50 a.m.	T. 12th Bde.	B.M.C 70/4 Nothing further to report	"
9.	7.55 a.m.	T. 10th Bde.	G.3. Langemarck barrage slightly uneven — heavy smoke clouds on our Left. Rockets being sent up on Left apparently from behind our line (Indicating in Co 3 or 4 white lights)	

Sequence No.	Time	Type of Message		CONTENTS.	Action taken.
10.	8.0am	T. 10th Bde.	G.4 —	nil. (½ hourly).	Copy to GRA
11.	7.35am	T. S.O. 4 Div.	Prisoners 417 R & 441 J.R. state 227th Div. relieved 8th Bav.Div. last night — 441st J.R. captured near railway — 441st believed to be in their Regt. — location 477th J.R. unknown.		" "
12.	8.20am	T. 12th Bde.	BMC.70/5 — Nothing further to report.		" "
13.	8.0am	T. DARTY	F.O.O. reports still progressing favourably — no unties few — prisoners still coming in.		
14.	8.30am	T. XIV Corps G.69	Contact patrol 6.40am reports first objective gained on entire Corps front — in touch with French on this side.		" "
15.	9.20am	T. S.O. 4 Div.	441 Regt. relieved 13th Bav. I.R. — 417 Regt. had 4 Coys in front line — Coy Trench strength 125 — pow fighting quality — officer deficient did not expect counterattack by 227th Div. but any counterattack troops, units unknown.		Copy Div. Arty
16.	8.35am	T. 10th Inf. Bde.	G.5 — Smoke barrage on left drifting towards own front. Occasional shelling LANGEMARCK Ridge ?		" "
17.	8.50am	T. 12th Bde.	BMC 70/6 — Nothing further to report — Observers report Bdn on left going well.		" "

Sequence No.	Time	Type of message	Contents	Action taken
18.	7.35am (8.35)	F.O.O. ARTY	Second attack progressing favourably – our casualties heavy up to now – Enemy barrage shortened considerably & not very intense – over 100 more prisoners passed by – Fire is burning behind enemy lines	
19.	9.5am	F.O.O. ARTY	Main Cage Prisoners behind the enemy line.	
20.	9.11am	F.O.O. Arty	Intermittent shelling now 5.9 and 4.2 HE, and back areas bombarded at zero plus 16. Zero plus 30 hostile barrage of 4.2 HE on line V21d V21c and LANGEMARCK. 6am 100 prisoners came in and more coming in. 6.45am Infantry still going forward. 6.50am 150 JRK came in.	
21.	9.20am	146 Cpm	Cage on our left have taken prisoners of 135 Regt. 42nd Div from Russia. 42nd Div in process of relieving 1st Div.	
22.	9.16am	I.O. Dukes	Prisoners of 477 I.R. Captured in POELCAPELLE 10th Coy Relieved 10th Bavarian I.R. on night 5/6. Bavarians believed to be in reserve. All 4 Coys of 1st & 2nd & 3rd 477th I.R. in front line. Coy trench strength said to be 130 to 150.	
23.	7.35am	D. Major Campbell / Seaforth Hghrs	39 Div have men of 2/2 objective. 6th BW report 1st objective definitely taken. They say they have never been so many prisoners coming in before. They estimate it at 700, but probably exaggerated.	

Sequence No.	Time	Type of Message	CONTENTS.	Action taken.
24	9.10.	T D/12th Bde	The Honvds Bn is required by 12th Bde to move to area between AU BON GITE and LANGEMARCK. Move to be made by platoons at 5 minutes interval along B.tram deploying in arrival at AU BON GITE. O.C. Honvds Bn to report to 12 Bde as soon as possible. Report arrival to this Office.	Copy to CRA
25.	9.55 am	T 10th Bde	Occasional shelling of LANGEMARCK RIDGE, prisoners still coming in	" "
26.	9.20 am	T 12th Bde	Nothing further from our front. Own arm are moving Bns of 10th Bn forward to AU-BON-GITE	
27.	9.55am	R from Atk	75 and 7 Q report occasional light shelling of positions by 77 mm. Batteries not being satisfactory. Volume of fire. No casualties to equipment. Prisoners from H.41 and H.17 I.R. who only came into line last night.	
28.	9.38 am	R Group	Following from 75. Prisoners are 441 and 447 Regts. Infy report barrage O.K.	
29.	10 am	T 5th Army	Morning report.	Copy to CRA
30	9.35 am	T 14 Corps.	G 73 — Aeroplane patrol reports as follows — 6.30 am to 8.35 am In area - POELCAPPELLE - along road to NAMUR crossing along railway to SCHAAP BAKIE VIJFWEGE and to WEST ROOSEBEKE. No enemy movement or concentration in or behind this area — 7.10 a.m. large fire at DUMP V69 a. 34 — no E.A. seen along front	

Sequence No.	Time	Type of Message	CONTENTS	Action taken
31.	9.30am	T. 12th Bde.	BMG to/r Looking further to report wounded differ in accounts of casualties	Copy to CRA
32.	9.50am / 10.0am	T. 10th Bde.	G.7 — Enemy shelling slightly increased in vicinity of LANGEMARCK CHURCH — Prisoner passed through from 477/R	"
33.	8.25am	T. Div Arty	Progress Report No.1 — Barrage on time — Gops reported in barrage that cannot be located as to whose guns or whose front — certainly not on 17th Div Group front — Ammn. arriving steadily — casualties to personnel slight	"
34.	9.45am	T. Liaison officer with 29th Div.	C/6 — Aeroplane dropped map at 9.30am showing Guards & 29th Div. on 2nd objective except at SENEGAL Fm — Flares shown also at WATER HO. — COMPEONIS Fm — LANDING Fm.	"
35.	9.30am	T. 284 M.G.C.	A battery & one gun knocked out — both officers — shall I have reserve section up — will you wire & communicate Reserve	Passed to DMGO who was ordered to send up one section
36	10.36	T. 10th Bde.	Nil	
37	10.40am	T. R. Gart.	R.G. 333 — Following received 78th Bde — Traffic entitled bad BARD'S CAUSEWAY, much delay	"A" Branch informed

Sequence No.	Time	Type of Message	CONTENTS.	Action taken:
38	10.20am	T. XIV Corps	G.74 — Contact patrol 5.20 a.m shows approx line as follows LANDING Fm — COMPROMIS Fm — WATER Ho — TRANQUILLE Ho — Ry. x? N.W. TRANQUILLE Ho — U12 central — U12a.1.1. — VERE BEND — U11.c.9.7 — U11.A.7.0 — U11a.5.2 — U10.b.4.4	Copy to CRA
39.	10.45am	T. 10 Bde.	BM 62 — Lost platoon H.B? just left assembly area	"
40	10.40	T. Div Arty	Right Group report M.G. fire causing difficulty from NOBLES Farm & HEALS Fm.	—
41	9.30am	T. 11 Div	G.B. 102 — MEUNIER Ho & rear of 1st objective taken, but attack being held up at N.E. Corner POELCAPELLE	Copy to CRA.
42	10.45am	T. XIV Corps	J.G. 256 — Air reconnaissance 9.15 a.m DIXMUDE road running N. & S. through HOULTHULST Forest & WESTROOSEBEKE HOOGKEDE road clear — activity much above normal in HOUTHULST Forest.	Copy to CRA.
43				

Sequence No.	Time	Type of Message	CONTENTS	Action taken
44.	11 am	T. R.A.	nil	Copy CRA
45.	11 am	T. 14th Corps.	Following fm I Army Arm Patrol 10.15 am - area HOUTHULST FOREST - WESTROOSEBEKE - PASSCHENDAELE, all roads clear, flying 1500 ft.	Copy CRA
46.	11.5 am	T. 10th Bde.	P.M.63 — Two allied planes retired + crashed 300× W.81 STRAY Fm ① B 3626 NIEUPORT S.5. & B 36.45 same type ② 2nd Lt. WATES Killed man Second machine unknown. Killed ③ 10.35 a.m by collision — M.G. fire also observed. ④ LANGEMARCK 1/10,000 C 36.15.70 & C.3.6.10.70 ⑤ BoK total wreck.	Repeated Corps. 9 Squadron
47	11.10 am	T. XIV Corps	J.G.258 — Prisoners taken this morning — 31st, 86th, 3.R.18th Div, & 417 J.R. 441 R.J.R(?) 477 J.R. 227th Div in order of Battle N.15 S. as above. Fighting quality, latter Div. poor	
48.	11.35 am	T. 10th Bde	G.10 — Hostile shelling LANGEMARCK Ridge appears to have ceased.	

Sequence No.	Time	Type of Message	CONTENTS.	Action taken.
49	10.55a	T. Liaison off. 29th Div	C.9. — Aeroplane map 10.15am shows Guards & 29th Div. still on second objective — Good many Huns seen in V/8 — This not considered very reliable — map shows flares short of REQUETE farm & at HELLES H.Q.	latter part wired to DOZEN.
50	10.33am	T. 12th Bde.	P.G.1 — Situation 9am. No reports by G.S.O.s line appears to run LANDING Fm. — COMPROMIS Farm — Huts between WATER HOUSE & MILLER HOUSE. No further reports of Right up to date	Copy to C.R.A
51	9am	T. J.O. 11 Div.	J.W.9 — Prisoners of 3rd & 4th Coys 477th I.R. 227th Div. taken in POELCAPPELLE & S. of village respectively — Relieved 189th I.R. early this morning — believed other two Regts. relieved Bavarians — all 4 Coys in line — 68th I.R. believed to be on left.	Copy to C.R.A.
52	11.25am	T. XIV Corps.	I.G.259 — 10.30am small bodies of troops, one behind other, Dike section, moving S.W. on road in V.17.B. — Train moving S.W. from STADEN. P.22.D — 10 motor transport from HOOGLEDE to OOSTNIEUWKERKE moving very fast.	" "

Sequence No.	Time	Type of Message	CONTENTS.	Action taken.
53.	10.33am	P. [?] Essex.	Pigeon message — Situation at present as follows — I have reached line approximately — 75ˣ N.E. POELCAPPELLE - S Chemin Road- Held up at MILLER's HOUSES- cleared up to present — no reports from front companies - Germans massing SENEGAR Fm + WATER Houses - 033 parties Dukes+K.O. near me, but cannot find any touch on my left. Estimated casualties 200	
54.	12.5pm	T. 10ᴬ. Inf Bde G.12	Nothing to report.	
55.	12 noon	T. " " "	G.11. Twice reported seen about E. and HOUTHULST Wood — slight barrage on LANGEMARCK Ridge.	
56.	11.35a	T. 11ᴿ Div	Nothing further to report.	
57.	11.35a	T. 12ᵗʰ Bde	B.M.C. 70/11 — nothing further to report — E.A. still flying low over our troops + firing on them	
58.	11.11am	T. XIV Corps	G.76 — 10 a.m. observer suggests advance not in progress — beyond second objective	

Sequence No.	Time	Type of Message	CONTENTS	Action taken
59	10.2 a.m	T. 12 Bde.	BMC.70/9 — L.F. report at 9.30 situation vague — preliminary attack held up top at MILLERS HOUSE — now cleared, attack appears to be progressing. Estimated casualties 130-150.	Copy CRA.
60	11.30 a.m	Telephone message	G.S.O.3 reports that at 8.50 a.m we were held up at Briggen VILLAS Fm. 29th Div. line V.13.a.6.6. — V.7.c.3.4 — Our line COMPROMIS Fm + LANDING Fm. — hot-air stunt with 29th being actified.	—
61	11.30 a.m	Pigeon mess.	2nd Essex held up by M.G around SPRING Houses from POELCAPPELLE — flanking movement in progress — Batt? HQ FERDAN Ho.	Copy CRA.
62	11.26 a.m	T. Liaison Off. 29th Div.	C/10 — Left Batt? 29th objective proceeding satisfactorily + thought advance on 3rd. Rd gone off all right — E.A. active — hostile shelling heavy but wild — Guards Div. stay air reports shows them on 3rd objective.	Copy CRA.
63	12 noon	T/24 M.C.Coy.	X 293 — Ds relief by 12.15 M.C.C to be carried out today?	Relief ordered.

Message No.	Time	Type of Message	CONTENTS.	Action taken.
64.	12.5p 12.35p	T. 12 Bde	RMC 70/12 } 70/13 } Nothing further to report.	Copies CRA.
65.	12.35p	T. XIV Corps	J.G. 260 — Patrol 10.30 – 11.30 a.m. reports in rear in area STADEN – WEST ROOSEBEKE – WILDEMAN CABARET all clear — no movement seen in HOUTHULST Forest. S.E. Corner — we appear to be shelling heavily there.	Copy CRA.
66.	1.20 p.m.	T. 10½ Bde	G.12. Nothing to report.	Copy CRA
67.	1.5p	T. LO. 29th Div.	C/12. Reporting line by aeroplane map timed 12 noon.	" "
68.	1.5 p.m	T. 12 Bde	2/3 Essex Regt 2 are established their H.Q. at FERDAN HOUSE. Otherwise no fresh Target.	
69.	10 a.m.	Wireless	2/Lancs Fus timed 9.30. Situation at present very good, pushing about to tap at Miller House. There are now cleared and attack appears to be progressing. Batn H.Q. at MILLERS HOUSE Estimate casualties 120 to 150.	
70.	11 a.m.	T 12 Bde	Send up Major Thompson Essex. C.O. Lankone casualty. Estimate casualties of Brigade 600 German aeroplane wounded flying low over our troops and firing at them	
71.	1.45 p.m.	T NME?	When will front from be relieved.	Orders to apply to their Bde.

Serial No.	Time	Type of message	CONTENTS.	Action taken.
72.	2.5pm	11/2 Bde	Shelling further to right	
73.	2.5pm	T. 10 Bde	Enemy artillery fire almost ceased W of LANGEMARCK	
74.	2.45pm	T. 14 Corps	Prisoners of 6th Bav IR 6th Bav Div taken in KOEKUIT Sector	
75.	1.40pm	T. XIV Corps	Aeroplane report shows line now runs BREWERY (POELCAPPELLE) – HELLES HOUSE – V.14.c.4.8. – a gap 15 LANDING Fm – SENEGAL Fm – TAUBE Fm. V.7a.6.0. – Railway at V.7a.6.9. – along final objective. Heavy counterattack in neighbourhood V.7.(c+d) forced that portion of attack to lose its Barrage – Divisions will consolidate ground now held – 4th Div. will close gap between TEQUETE Fm. & LANDING Fm. – Estimated prisoners 600.	Copy to C.R.A.
76.	1.10pm	T. 29 R.Div.	G.1576. Enemy counterattacks our troops on second objective on the right, but were driven off – we are on 2nd objective and in sight – party 60 R.F. hold TAUBE Fm & are in touch with 1st R. Fusr – left, who report Keyhole mentioned not taken. the NEWFOUNDLAND on left, who report Keyhole mentioned not taken. Finl objective – very heavy shelling on front line – Counter attack 200 to 300 Huns at 8.30 a.m. driven off with rifle by R.Fus. front line their barrage – Another counter attack against Right Bde. at 10.40. Driven off. – Prisoners to date 7 officers & 237 or. more coming in.	

Serial No.	Time	Type of Message	Contents	Action taken
77.	1.40pm	T. 11 Div.	G.B. 105. — Situation unchanged.	Copy to CRA
78	1.57pm	T. XIV Corps.	J.G. 264 — 5th Army report — 12.45pm 7 motor transport on LINDEN — STADENDREF road — 12.40pm about one coy moving S. in HOUTHULST Forest along HOUTHULST — POELCAPPELLE Road — 11.45am — 12.45pm Bn resting on side of road XI. Central & a column coming down HOOGAEDE — WESTROOSEBEKE road — a good deal of movement seen.	
79.	2.15pm	T.O. 29th Div.	C.13. — Rt. Bde. 29th report Huns counterattacking	Copy to CRA
80.	2.30pm	T. A.O. 29th Div.	C.14. — Counter attack did not develop.	Copy to CRA.
81.	2.35pm	T. 10th Bde	G.15 — Nil.	" "
82.	2.45pm	T. R.G.A.4	R.G. 330 — Protective barrage R.C. has been placed — V.14.c.70.90 — V.14.A.00.12 — V.13.B.75.67. — One Batt? R.H.A. divown back V 14 C.08.95 — V 13. 13. 90.10, hows on NIKKIP & blocking roads V14a.90.10 & V.14a.10.45.	
83	2.30pm	T. XIV Corps.	J.G. 265 — Roads VYFWEGEN to STADEN & STADEN REEF all clear.	copy to CRA
84	2.55pm	T. XIV Corps.	G. 80 — Contact aeroplane due Corps front 4 p.m.	copy to CRA
85	3.15pm	T. 16th Bde.	G.16 — 2 more prisoners passed through.	" "

Message No.	Time	Type of Message	CONTENTS.	Action taken.
86	2.50 p.m	T. XIV Corps	J.G. 266 — Air reconnaissance 12.15 p.m — 1.30 p.m — no movement on various roads — 4 groups about 20 men each entering WESTROOSEBEKE from 12.40 p.m — 50 men in single file on road from VYWEGEN to SCHAAPBAILLE 12.56 p.m.	Copy to C.R.A
87	3 p.m	T. 29th Div	G 1577 — Reported counterattack by enemy left of Div. line from TURENNE X4 about 2 p.m beaten off	"
88	3.40 p.m	T. XIV Corps	J.G. 267 — Air report 12.30 — 12.45 p.m — Train move rather above normal ROULERS — ROULERS quiet normal.	"
89	12.40 p.m	T. 5th Army.	Continuation morning Report. Line reported as run line — INCH Ho — BERK'S HOUSES — OXFORD HOUSES thence MEUNIER Ho + whole of POELCAPPELLE except BREWERY. Contact patrol 8.20 a.m places our line thro' LANDING FARM — comprises Fm — WATER Ho — TRANQUILLE Ho — U12 Central — V12a.1.1. — U11.c.9.7 — U11.a.7.0 — U11a.5.2 — U10.B.4.7 where we are in touch with French whose line continues thro' U10a.3.4 to line of dugouts at U.B.c.8.3. — Unconfirmed report states that enemy on Righr have taken all objectives.	Copy to C.R.A
90	4.0 p.m	T. Div. Arty.	Intermittent shelling 4.2 + 5.9s on whole area by enemy — his aeroplane numerous very active, flying very low.	

Sequence No.	Time	Type of Message	Contents	Action taken
91.	4.15pm	T. XIV Corps.	5th Army wires:- 1555pm two Bodies troops about 500 in all on DIXMUDE Road P.19(A+c), direction uncertain but probably South — otherwise no road movement in area STADEN — HOOGLEDE — ROULERS — MOORSLEDE.	copy to CRA
92.	4.30pm	T. 10th Dy/Bde. G.17.	E.A. active over Bde H.Q. at great height during last hour.	" "
93.	5.15pm	T. XIV Corps.	G 86 — Divisions will consolidate line shown on map dropped at 4pm and will also gain by patrols tonight all ground possible up to line LANDING FARM — WATER HOUSE — SENEGAL FARM — TAUBE FARM — a strong second line will be made along the road from POEL CAPPELLE to LES 5 CHEMINS — ACK.	Acknowledged
94.	5.20pm	T. XIV Corps.	3.C.269 — Air reconnaissance 9000 ft — 200 Infy marching S. about 1/2 way between CORTEMARCK & STADEN 4.10pm — 5 M.T. moving from THOUROUT to CORTEMARCK 4.20pm — M.T. also moving on road ZARREN to STADEN, number not known — 50 Infy seen at P.25a.5.0.4.47.	copy CRA.
95.	5.20pm	T. 10th Dy/Bde. G.18/S.O.S.	on our left — no signals observed.	

Sequence No.	Time	Type of Message	CONTENTS.	Action taken.
96	5:30p.m.	T. 12th Inf. Bde.	BMC 70/72. Reports from 2/L.F. + 1st K.O. state it is certain that we do not hold LANDING or COMPROMIS Fms. 4p.m.	To CRA.
97	6.15 p.m.	D. Div Arty	G.S. 236 recd.	—
98	6.30 p.m.	T. 14 Corps Arty	R.A. 955 — Instructions to stop counter attacks	—
99	4 p.m.	S.O. 11th Div.	N.C.O. 5th Co. 10th Bav. J.R taken in POEL CAPELLE, left behind to hand over dugout in village to 3rd Boy. 4 77th J.R. aaa Prisoners stated B? moved up from THIELT to WIELDERMAN ESTAMINET E. of WESTROOSEBEKE — passed men of 68th J.R. 40th Div on the way up. No order of battle available.	To CRA.
100	6.30 p.m.	T. 12th Inf Bde	BMC 70/13 — Have sent H.13" back to STRAY Fm.	To CRA.
101	5.45 pm	T. 14th Corps.	Our Right has been driven back from our-3rd Jan's contact aeroplane above line now Farm V13a8.7 V13d36 COMPROMIS Farm V13a8.7 V7c9.0 V7e8.33 V7c3.7 Poilkva at V7a2.b, V7C10 ANGLE Point & CHEMINS U5d6.3 U11b39 U11c75 U5c30.	To CRA
102	7.30 p.m.	T. 12th Inf Bde	BMC 70/14 F.A. Liaison with us has no direct line to this group — This message therefore increase congestion on divisional line — Can be be supplied with a direct line.	To CRA

Serial No.	Time	Type of Message	CONTENTS.	Action taken
103	6 pm	T Duke's	Total estimate casualties from 1st October K.O. 3 Officers 50.O.R. L.F. 6 Officers 200 O.R. Dukes 4 Officers 100 O.R. Essex 6 Officers 150 O.R.	
104.	6.35 pm	T 11 Div	Approx line run V.26.A.25 Beek Houses (unoccupied) Gloster House along to front line to V19.9.95 V20.A.15 V13.d.51. Divn has been ordered to gain touch with flanking division.	
105.	7.52	T 14th Corps	During the day the enemy made several counter-attacks against our right and centre one of these counted not to give ground a status in my Q.57). The remainder were beaten off by rifle and artillery fire. C.B. destroyed 2 howitzers 7 shells 7 uncounted 6 pits hit 15 destroyed 2.0.K 11 explosions 7 fires. Following prisoners have so far passed through Corps Cages unwounded 13 Officers 419 O.R. wounded 41 O.R.	
106		T A.P.M. Duke's	Prisoners of war passed through divisional cage 15.O.R.	

Sequence No.	Time	Type of Message	CONTENTS.	Action taken.
107.	7.45p	T. 11th Div.	Inf. 13. Order battle N. to S. — 68th I.R, 28th I.R, 29th I.R, 16th Division came into line right 7/8th, relieving 187 I.R. 188th I.R., one Battn each regt. in line.	To C.R.A.
108.	7.50p	T. 12th R. Bde.	G.S. 236. received.	—
109	9.57p	T. 12th R.Bde.	G.S 241 Recd.	
110	10 p	T. Div Q.	Q 33. SCHREIBOOM — REDHOUSE — ROEKAPPELLE Rd will be available, as far as E. boundary of C24b., for pack transport on 10th.	
111.	10.18p	T. 11th R.Bde.	G.S. 241 Recd.	

1/9/01

OUT
MESSAGES
BATTLE 9th October

Sequence No.	Time	Type of Message		CONTENTS.	Action taken.
1	5.20am	T	G.S.200 to XIV Corps	Advance Div. HQrs opened at C.19.a.0.0	
2	6.15am	T	G.S.201 to XIV Corps 11 Div. 29 Div.	12th Bde reports 6.10 a.m that enemy barrage opened at zero plus 4 minutes on LOUIS FARM line. It was very ragged. No news of our troops or signs of prisoners at present.	
3	6.55am	T	G.S.202 XIV Corps	Drop reports 6.45am Deserter 4th Regt. 227th Div. captured. About 30 prisoners coming in. Regiment unknown Prisoners between LANGEMARCK and attacking troops.	
4	7.10am	T	G.S.203 12th Bde 29th Bde	First objective reported taken by 12.2nd Bde at about 10 prisoners Left Brigade of 29 Div reported over BROEMBEEK.	
5		T	G.S.204 DUKE A	Col HORSFALL of Dukes will send up major OFFICER to command Bn H.Q. Should report here for information.	
6	7.30am	T	G.S.205 10th Bde 12th Bde	According to air report our troops on first objective at 6.40am along whole front	
7	7.45am	T	G.S.206 14 Corps 11 Div. 29 Div.	12th Bde reports 7.20am Prisoners captured by 29th Div. still coming in. No news from our front. Prisoners state 2/27 Div. relieved 6 Bav Div in the line last night.	
8	8am	T	G.S.207 Dozen Drop	29th Div reports all going well. Guards Div. appear well over BROEMBEEK. Hosp/any German barrage. 1st Lanc Fus reports 200 prisoners taken. 1st Objective definitely taken	

Sequence No.	Time	Type of Message	CONTENTS	Action taken.
9	5.39am	T G S 208 DROP DOZEN DETAIL	Corps report 3rd army on all 1st Objectives	
10.	5.45am	T G S 209 14 Corps 11 Div. 29 Div 111 Bde	Verbal report from F.O.O. timed 6.15am states 12th Bde gained first Objective easily. All going well. Prisoners coming in large numbers.	
11.	9.5 am	T G S 210. 12" Infy Bde.	11th Division report their left checked at BREWERY and HELLES HOUSE NE corner of village V 14 C.5.5. Your right may therefore become a little exposed. Report when and where you move Bn of 10th Bde	
12.	9.10 am	T G S 211 XIV corps 11. Div. 29. Div.	Nothing further from 12th Bde. Observers report 8th Infy Bde seen going forward well	
13.	9.20 am	T G S 212 XIV corps 11 Div 29 Div 11? Bde	F. O. O. reports timed 9.35 a.m second attack progressing favourably enemy barrage shortened considerably but not very intense. Later report timed 9.12 a.m. states many large fires seen behind enemy lines.	
14.	9.42 am	T G S 213 11 ? Bde	Situation from aeroplane at 7.40 a.m. Line runs as follows:- LANDING FM. exclusive - COMPROMIS FM - WATER HOUSE - MILLERS HOUSES - V 7 c 6.0. - V 7 C 2.4 - TRANQUILLE HOUSE thence just west of U 12 central to OBTUSE BEND V 11 d - SOUTH of LOUVOIS FM to just south of VELDHOEK	

Sequence No.	Time	Type of Message	CONTENTS.	Action taken.
15	10.27	G.S.214 90 2 A" 1st Bd	Order 162 received	
16	11 am	T G S 215 12" Bde	Div on right report M.G. fire from NOBLES Farm and HELLES Farm still an obstacle.	
17	11 am	T G.S 216 14th Corps 11 Div 29 Div 11" Bde	No further news from our front. Div on right report M.G. fire from NOBLES Farm and HELLES Farm.	
18	11.25 a.m.	T G.S. 217 XIV Corps No 9 Squadron	Two allied planes attacked and crashed about 300 yards west of STRAY FARM C 3 C sheet 28 (1) B 3626 NIEUPORT SINGLE SEATER B 3645 same type (2) 2/L L.G Watts killed. Second machine (3) 10.35 a.m by collision. M.G. name of pilot unknown. Rest. (4) Vanguard 1/10000 C 3 C 15 7p & C 3 C 10 7 0. fire also observed. (5) BM total wrecks	
19	11.40 a.m	T G S 218 XIV Corps 11 Div 29 Div 103 Bde 11" Bde	Situation at 9 a.m from Att/T Officer near front line. Div appears to run LANDING FM – COMPROMISE FM. Huts between WATER HO & MILLER HOUSES. No further reports of our right up to date. Enemy in front with M.G. Opposition not serious but heavy shelling on leading troops	

Sequence No.	Time	Type of Message	CONTENTS.	Action taken.
20.	11.37 am	T G S 219 12th Bde	Aeroplane map shews place shewd of REQUETE FARM & at HELLES HOUSES	
21.	11.45 am	T G S 220 10 } Bn 12 }	Aeroplane map shewed 10.15 a.m 2 two Guards and 29th Division still on second objective. Report not received very reliable	
22.	12.30 p.m.	T G S 221 12th Bde	Please report as soon as possible when troops intended to proceed to avoid further advance to join objective as S.O.S barrage	
23.	12.35 p.m.	T G S 222 4th Division A	Please send up second in command of 2nd Essex Regt to succeed Lt Col PRATT who has been killed	
24.	12.40 p.m	T G S 223 4th Division A	Estimated casualties of 2nd Essex Regt 130 to 150.	
25	1.15 pm	T G S 224 Dropped 10 } Bde 11 } 12 }	Situation from aeroplane map 12 noon Line runs from from V14c72 through HELLES Farm to V14c27 then gap. Line continues V11 E.E of LANDING Farm through WATERHOUSE – SENEGAL FARM – TAUBE FARM. Line along GREEN LINE on Guards and French front. We also hold line from V13 d73 to V13 d28 including STRING HOUSES.	
26	1.15 pm	T G.S 225 4th Div A 10 } Bde 11 } 12 } 29 Div 11 Div	Dense fog and push beyond line REQUETE Fm – LANDING Fm – WATER HOUSE maintain that line and fill gap reported by air observer between REQUETE and LANDING Fm	

Sequence No.	Time	Type of Message	CONTENTS.	Action taken.
27.	2.20 pm	T. G.S 226 4 Dsn A	Minister casualties of 12th Brigade 600	
28.	2.20 pm	T. G.S 227 to M.G.C	Apply to your Brigade from an under them.	
29.	3.11 pm	T G.S 228 12th Bde	FELIX (29th Div) reports their right Bde being counter attacked. Message timed 2.15 P.M.	
30.	3.15 pm	T G.S 229 12th Bde	Reference G.S 228 enemy counter attack died out dunlops.	
31.	3.20 pm	T G.S 230 R.A 14th Corps	your A.R 196 received.	
32.	3.40 pm	T G.S 231 14 Corps Dept ae Prisoners.	Nothing further to report.	
33.	3.45 pm	T G.S 232 officer 1/c Prisoners Cage.	How many prisoners have passed through your cage.	
34.	4.10 pm	T G.S 233 10th Bde	Detail 2 officers + 100 men to report to representative of 9th Field Co RE. at 6 PM at AU BON GITE to carry trench boards to IMBROS HO. 2 officer 100 men to report to representative of 406 Renfrew at 6 PM at BIRD HO to carry trench boards to FERDAN HOUSE	

Sequence No.	Time	Type of Message	CONTENTS.	Action taken.
35	4.25 pm	T G.S 234 12th Bde	Gun line according to latest air report runs V13 D 6.3 – west of STRING HOUSES V13 d 5.1 – V13 b 0.2 – V13 a 5.9 – HUTS V13a 70.75 V7c 85.00 – V7c 25.30 – V7c 3.8 – V7a 3.2. There is one post at V13 d 60 yds 7.5.	
36		G.S 235 " Bde " " " Midd 234	11" M.G.b will relieve 234" M.G.C on night 10/11. Details of relief will be arranged by O C Companies on completion of relief 11" M.G.b comes under orders Bde c. 12th Bde.	
37	5.53 pm	G S 237 T. XIV Corps.	Your G S 6 received.	
38	6 pm	G S 236 T. DROP. DUST.	Divisions have been ordered to consolidate line as shown on map dropped at 4 pm given to you over the telephone and repeated in wire G.S. 234. They will also join by patrols tonight all ground gained up to line LANDING F.M – WATERHOUSE – SENEGAL F.M TAUBE F.M. During 2nd line will be made along road from POELCAPPELLE to LES. S. CHEMINS	
39	6.4 pm	T G S 238 RA XIV Corps	Instructions in 15 received	

Sequence No.	Time	Type of Message	CONTENTS.	Action taken.
40	6.45 pm	T GS 239 12 Bde CRA	Explanation of map dropped at 4. p.m. 200 men appear in occupation of trench S.W. of COMPROMIS Fm at V 13 a 9.1. Enfd Men Run V 13 d 1.6 - 1.5.- 3.6. South front of STRING HOUSES - V 13 D. 7.2 - V 14 c. 1.1. In front of 4pm there was one isolated yellow flare at V 13 d 65.80 No enemy cards to seen in vicinity of WATER HOUSE - LANDING Fm + REQUETE Fm, or anywhere in V 13 B-	
41	8.15 pm	T GS 240 12 Bde CRA Omeo	Informing unit to [line] of A O d barrage for tonight V 14 c 36 — V 14 a 15 — V 7 d 6 3.	
42	9.30pm	T GS 241 10 Bde 12 Bde	The Household Batt? and 1st Royal Warwicks employed at the disposal of 12 Bde from tomorrow 10inst. inclusive.	
43	10.14 pm	T GS 242 113 Bde	Please report deficiencies of any of S.A.B code	

Sequence No.	Time 10/10/18	Type of message	CONTENTS	Action taken
44.	8.55 am	T G S 243 12" Bde Div Arty	Contact patrols this morning reports our line running as follows: V13 D 20.35 - V13 D 16 - V13 D 09 - V13 a 90.05 V13 a 90.40 - V13 a 90.5 - V13 a 9b 65	
45.	9.5 am	T G S 244 4 Div A	2" Major WATKINS 2 Lanc Fus wounded last night. 12" Bde does not want Cl. GLENN. Send up.	
46.	9.21 am	T G S 245 4 Div A	Capt MARTIN 2 Lanc Fus reported wounded. Please send up Col. GLENN at once	
47.	9.30 am	T G S 246 10/11 R Sc	Escorts for prisoners of war will report their units forthwith	
48.	9.30 am	T G S 247 12 Bde CRA	The attached map shows in BLUE the approximate front line we hold at present and in RED the situation which is to be taken in lieu of the purple line on a date which has been communicated to you. The donnée will be forwarded shortly. Please acknowledge by line	
49.	9.50 am	T G S 248 12 Bde	Signals are laying an artillery telephone line	
50.		G S 249		

App 20

IN
MESSAGES

BATTLE 12TH OCTOBER 1917.

Sequence No.	Time	Type of Message	CONTENTS.	Action taken.
1.	6.30am	T. 12 Bde to Bdo	Nothing to Report yet	
2.	6am	V 12 B/de	Nothing to Report yet	
3.	6.55am	T. 12 Rdg	Verbal message from Household Cav 12 Bde Pink Objective taken. Infantry will advance on Blue. Men of 11th Rd 6-10am Pink Objective probably means COMPROMIS FM LAMDING	
4.	7.5am	T. 17. Div.	No further information.	
5.	7.40 am	T. 11 Rde.	Right Co Commd 1st Household wounded. Reports when hit he was within 50yds of REQUETE FARM nill in touch with 8th Rde and no no seem to have gone through POELCHAPPELLE from where that is much nuffle fire. Enemy reinforced appears not cut. He is rearing his arms and firing. Left Company Household Rd saw Blue Objective 13th Royal Irish Rft. are forming defensive flank towards POELCHAPPELLE	
6.	8am	22 Bde RFA	we hit REQUETE FARM. but the people in our right do not appear to had POELCAPPELLE.	

CONTENTS.

Sequence No.	Time	Type of Message	Contents	Action taken.
7	7.50am	T. D.R.S.	Rugelwink Kent acknowledges units barrage in advance abcie V13 b77 no prisoners 470 YR 66 Coy	
8	8am (approx)	T. D.R.S.	Rifle Bde which is Bde reserve reports Left Co has reached line 200 yds ahead of line WATER HOUSE - LANDING Fm advance progressing normally.	
9	8.20 am	T. D.R.S.	Household Bn report at 7.25 am our left aa. kept Coy 300 yards Least Landing Johnmann Right Coy formed defensive flank towards Bde capture ma M.G. fire from village arr.	
10	8.35 am 9.30 a—	T. 14th Corps.	Pigeon message from Sherwood Foresters 31st Bde Brigan. All going well on our front. Leupal. Fm taken advance proceeding. Very little opposition M.G. fire. Enemy barrage falling on road. CON DE HOWE. very light. Reptl. Plank forg. well. East	
11	7.30am	T. Friday	On farms I can see from my position Kangaroo. Lots our troops are holding Riding Stones Compercio farm. Landing farm. Enemy barrage not as heavy. a fair number of prisoners seen to be coming in.	

Serial No.	Time	Type of Message	CONTENTS.	Action taken.
12.		Report 13Bde.Hors	Following message received by Wireless from adv. Bde H.Q. Thenault 2am ann. "R.W.Kents here own advancing on the left. at 6 am also the troops the Battn of our left and no news from right had Wounded Cpl. from Buffs reports that when he left Buffs were on first objective ann Later report most unreliable	
13.		S.Soot D/B Bde.	R.A. report Right Support Coy. crossed Poll Cappell - Roe 5 Cluring Road 6-30 am and Right front Coy holding line from Landing station 9.13 d.7.5 am. In touch with left front Cnt. but Not in touch on right, but right front support Coy are working round + clearing up Isle houses on outskirts of Poel Cappell ann Tuesd 7.5 am.	
14.	9.30	9.12 R.B.	Following from Howitzers an 9.30 am Report "R.B. Ble. m.f/Guns exploded by Landing from Requestment."	
15.	do		Kna 87 an 40 prisoners. Earned ten. cods. This positeth 2/20 2 aw coy of R.B. under R.D. Concolahi, after depts.	
16.		Des T 11/B Bdo	Warwicks report 1st Objective taken.	

Sequence No.	Time	Type of Message	CONTENTS	Action taken
17.	8.25 a.m	T 17 Bde	K.O.own report times 6.30 a.m. Situation: Warwicks Rear C.B. 2B. continues line. B. about Regcle to Farm Diggins in front Poelcapelle. from Regcle to v.13.d.7.3. in facing Poelcapelle (from Pipin (Senegal Farm).	
18.	8.55 a.m	T. ham Capnee	6.6 a.m. Sherwood Foresters reported by Pipin (Senegal Farm) taken & P.ow cleaning well.	
19.	9.15 a.m	T. Coy A/Diver	Report from wounded & prisoners regiment line was taken without difficulty, little retaliation. Advanced 500 yds at 6-30 a.m. Casualties not heavy.	
20.	8.10 a.m	T. 19 Div own	Report from Ifouta Farm state advanced at 8 first but halt but from SPRIET RIDGE. Another T. msg states Meunier Farm Captured.	
21.	9.20 a.m	17 Div own	Moving Regiments of Roche Preserve Captured.	
22.	10.10 a.m	lunch	Following from A/S 2784/3286 German officer w/pkg states Capt. Paralyzed. also Enemy thought that we was retaliation for the shelling last night, not expecting attack.	
23.	10.30 a.m	17 Bde	Preungins Reports Confirmed by reconnaissance. Enemy is still in Poelcapelle shooting at our night. Jrieden? Views on his way to Division.	

Sequence No.	Time	Type of Message	CONTENTS	Action taken
24	10 am	S.O.O. (RA)	Lt Col. Major reports 3rd Objective reached. Close up to own barrage. A N.C. Officer sent to Consolidating points. Compromis. Reports our troops also held up F.M. Landing Pt. Requete Farm. at Poelcappelle heavy.	
25.		29th Army	Attack started 5.25am on Army front. our Army on Right indefinite news yet. Army on Right report large numbers of far shell that night in forward area.	
26.	9.55 am	18 Divn	Wounded Officer at 6am stated definitely that between Vaarsen our possession. our troops past it.	
27	10.45	Msge Campbell	Began message 5.4.2.MG Lincolns definitely found 1st Objective. 100 prisoners	
28.	11.5.	15 Bde.	S.R. report Lincolns run v.14.a.6.5. Regrets Fm. 2 Platoons holding defensive flank towards Poelcappelle RSA in touch with 50th Bde.	
29.	11.55	15 Bde C9/4/19	S.R. report trust 11.10 am. Left flank definitely established. Objectives Landing Farm. Strong point left flank captured with 20 prisoners.	

Sequence No.	Time	Type of Message	CONTENTS.	Action taken.
30.	11.25	1st Corps.	Army Air report. Heavy movement transport and troops on HOOGLEDE - WESTROO & BEKE Rd. in N.E. Transport going N.E. Troop uncertain.	
31.	12.30	12 Bde	Nothing further to report.	
32	11.26	Anzac Calphin.	Notified 0.SS. report. holt final objective with 2 Coys from V.1.g.5. to travel farm. that Coy's begin in connection with 4 Div that apparently though 1.SC.1.5. but N.D. say they are in front of PIEBR	
33	11.10	1st Corps.	Air report 10.30 a.m. 71 an All Roads West of a line movements Knollhurst Road practically clear.	
34	1.40.	A.D.M.S. M 2603.	Amri 6 a.m - 4.91 + 12.3 02 hours Transpt. Field ambce.	
35	do.	12 Bde Bure 70/pm.	Confirmation overdue message reporting counter attack at	
36	do.	14 Bde	12.40 p.m. 17 am consolidated and held - Line	
37	do.	G172	BESACE FARM - BERTHIER with G.172.	

Sequence No.	Time	Type of Message	CONTENTS.	Action taken.
38.	11.38 pm	T.&S. 310 to 10th 12th & 103 Bde	Principal events to report. Prisoners to be sent to STRAY Fm. When 103 Bde will send them to CACTUS PONTOON.	
39.	11.47 pm	T.&S. 313. 6/14 Corps & 18th Div.	One uplb was mob of Regt. Fm. Will in feller their Eastof Or in town for defensive purposes.	

App 21

OUT
MESSAGES

BATTLE 12ᵀᴴ - OCTOBER 1917.

Sequence No.	Time	Type of Message	CONTENTS.	Action taken.
1.	6 am	T GS 251 XIV Corps. Guard 11th & 15 Div. 9 Sqdn RFC	No information yet received.	
2.	6.35 am	T. G.S. 252 14 Corps, Guards, 11+15 Div. 9th Sqn. RFC/R.A.	No information yet received	
3.	6.30 am	T G.S. 253 All recipients of GS 252	Situation quiet during night, wounded man of Household Bn reports infantry of enemy although whole Brigade will at march opposition at N.E.F. He was wounded 2 a/c going about 400 yds South thistle. No G. fire during advance. Above requires confirmation.	
4.	7.30 am	T GS 254 14 Corps Recipient concerned	Wounded man from Wurmach states when passed the [name] Verbal message from support Company, Household B[?] north of Flystein Kabur, and in touch with [?]	
5.	7.42 am	T GS 255 14th Corps. All concerned.	Report from Household Bn timed 6.40 am Right Coy Command[?] wounded reports [illegible] Whmt[?] who were within 50 yds of REQUETE FM in touch on left with R. Wear Kent 2 m night had lost touch. No one seems to have got through POELCAPPELE from where line is much in O fire. Life support by Helward O Rn reports left Coy reports the objective and are in touch with Warwicks, King's on Right to form a defensive flank towards POELCAPPELLE	
6.		GS 256		

Sequence No.	Time	Type of message	CONTENTS.	Action taken.
7.	8.20am	T.G.S.267 12.50am	Am event of about 15th Div not gaining POELCAPELLE. Corps Commander hopes to be able both to turn it from north. It is therefore most important front to attain attainment of REQUETE FM	
8.	8.33am	T.G.S.286 11 Corps ? all concerned	Our troops reported about V.13.6.7). at 8am. 1st RB in Bob Rosen. report Left. Coy. has reached this 200yds short of HYDRA HOUSE. Landing 7.50am. advance progressing favourably. impression 4/26 I.R.	
9.	8.20am	T.S.287. CRA 16 DIV.	Re Firing POELCAPELLE from N of 1R.	
10.	9am	G.S.288. 1st Bde CRA.	Artillery: Club flares shown as follows:- V.20.c.3.8. - V.20.d.S.7. Iraco Farm. V.20.d.6.5. 10 V.26.b.5.1 and 1 other. marked as Bursts on Allen front at V.14.C.8.6. Our troops in Itella House. Boche in and around Noble Farm. Own 7.46 am.	
11.	9.30am	G.S.290.	Telephone wire up from Club region ??. Gwounded officer states that Brewery in POECCAPELLE on fire about 8am	
12.	9.45 am	G.S.291.	Dozen of seed of S.M. of fuses to DROP	

Sequence No.	Time	Type of message	CONTENTS.	Action taken.
13.	10 am	T Corps M15 Divn CRO.9.Squad. 45.293	Situation 8.20 am about BESACE Fm. DIB. Continues line to about REQUETTE Fm. RB Dub Coy Dituo + one Coy 9th digging in, facing POELCAPPELLE from REQUETTE Fm. to V.13.d.7.3 am. 9 R.W. Kents apparently held up at Pheasant.	
14.	11.10 am	Dn M. 34 Divn 4.5.293	2 leading Battalions of Eloies on arrival in stray farm area today will come under orders of D.T.M.D. until be Battalions available to relieve 168 Battalions	
15.	11.15	Drop Msgs. 45.294.	2 Battns in stray farm area will not leave their camps until relieving Battns of 10 3 Bde arrive.	
16.	11.16	Corps M.17-16 bus Runado RW 9 RW Dragoons 10 R.F.A. M.R.O. 12 F.A.S. 295.	Wounded NCO of M.G. reports 2nd Objective reached. Close up to barrage. A.M.G. Officers reports our troops Consolidating Compromise landing requette farm.	
17.	12 Noon	Corps 18.17 Guards 9 Squad. A.S. 295.	2th reports 10.5 am. 3 Companies on line from V.14.a.68 to Requette Gang. 3 Platoons holding defensive flank towards Poelcappelle. No mockuen [?] taken on left of Divn.	

Sequence No.	Time	Type of Message	CONTENTS.	Action taken.
18.	12.00	To Bde 12.00 N Cdn. LS 297	Ref. Dept. A received with D.O. 17. 18 Bdo will move to P3 aca n? BdO to P4 instead of as stated	
19.	D.11.40	14 Cnfn. 17.18 circulated from adjacent R3C. LS 298.	Following from N.B. times 11.10 a.m. left flank Bn. definitely establishes wyon E. of Canfry Farm with excellent field of fire. Right and Reserve Cons. Strong Point. Q left flank captured with so previous.TG.	
20.	12.25.	Drop 18 Div 14 Cnfn LS 299.	No further effort is to be made to gain further objectives. These have not already been done. All positions gained to be held at all cost.	
21.	1.25h	Cnfn Blank Div. GS 340	Bnds. reports every counts attacks — This 12.50p.	

Sequence No.	Time	Type of message	CONTENTS.	Action taken.
22.	2 pm	Dublin Pioneers CRE in Corps. GS 301	Asking 3rd Div if they can attach 75 Kirchen O if Lewis guns supplied by Pioneers on ante air craft loop R. add 3rd Regt Ghin	
23.	2.31 pm	14 Corps Br. 18 Guards Bde Appears. GS 302.	Officer report our line REQUESTE FM (w.c.) & just loot over it to MEMLING FM. (w.c.) Enemy wandering about Disorganised at N.E. corner of POELCAPPELLE tm WATERVLIETBEEK by REUBEN'S FARM. taken being dealt with by Artillery	
24.	2.40	Dr.Y. W.R. GS 303	Duke's & Essex Bns now move back to LIEPZIG Camp	
25.	2.50 pm	Army HYTHE. 14 Corps. GS 304.	In view of salient in neighbourhood of MEMLING FM. Bde to arrange for supporting Posts to be established in neighbourhood. Power stored to connect with Sinclair Post to HYTHE. About V.I.A Central. Brigade to get in touch in that vicinity.	
26.	3.30 pm	Clair DroR GS 305.6.7	10 CELSIE will take over Command from JOB Drop at noon tomorrow. 13th Inst.	
27.	4.5	14 Corps. GS 309	1st Corps. G.427 received	
28.	4.38 pm	T G.S. 310 10/23 Blue	Escorts for prisoners of war will report their units to Anzues will to be sent to STRAY FARM where they will be taken over by 103rd RTA who will send them main escort to CACTUS PONTOON	
29.	4.40 pm	T G.S. 311 21 W 4 Regt	You may withdraw the 4 Lewis guns detailed in my GA 415 from their positions tonight	

Sequence No.	Time	Type of Message	CONTENTS.	Action taken.
32		Corps Order 3rd Northumb. W. Corps. U/S 3rd	The four Lewis Guns provided by 2nd West York (Garrison) for Anti. Aircraft. guard/OTR. will be relieved tomorrow at 13th and by 18th Northumberland Fus.	
33	5.25	14 Corps G.A 315	Ambrotect.	
30.	5.30 p.m.	T.O.O 312 14 Corps 12 (?) dism guns	Evening situation report. Enemy shelled SCHREIBOOM – POELCAPPELLE road from 4 p.m. to 4.30 p.m. from 10 morn to 1 p.m. and about 150 yards west of COMPROMIS FM. & STRING HOUSES shelled with shrapnel. Hostile snipers rm & heavy attn from vicinity of HELLES Ho throughout the day. Line now approx 150 yds. W. of REQUETE FM. – 100 yds. E of BETACE FM – MEMLING FM 150 yds. W. of REQUETE FM. in touch with 17th Divn on left but not with 18th inclusive. Intimated capture about 80 other ranks. Divn on right.	
31	4.47 p.m.	T.O.O 313 14 Corps 18 Divn	Our rifle to arm West of REQUETE FARM which a letter for defensive purposes than east of in the farm	
34	6 p.m.	Clair Drop DAG/MG. U/S 316.	A Contact Aeroplane will fly over the Corps from an area as located/formed tomorrow morning.	
35.	6.15	17 Divn MC317	G125 was acknowledged by this office G5305.	

Sequence No.	Time	Type of Message	CONTENTS.	Action taken.
36	8.40	T. Clair Bn/r 318	Repeal of Corps Evening Situation	
37	8.45	Bdy CRA CRA A.Ords. G. 319.	Bdy. Repeat Corps Commander wire (Confabulation)	
38	9.35	1st Corps 45 322	Your OO no received.	

App 22

Telephone Conversations
Battle 12th October 1917.

SPECIAL ORDER.

The Army Commander has seen the Divisional Commander today and has asked him to convey to all ranks who took part in the operations yesterday his great appreciation of the manner in which the attack was carried out under such adverse conditions.

The Army Commander fully realizes that the Division had already taken part in two successive fights only a few days previously, in the worst weather conditions possible, which necessarily caused great exhaustion, and having regard to these circumstances he considers that yesterday's performance was marvellous.

Lieut.Colonel,
13th October, 1917.   General Staff, 4th Division.

4th DIVISION SUMMARY OF OPERATIONS.
12th OCTOBER, 1917

On the 4th Divisional front the Household Battalion were the Right Assault Battalion and the 1st R. Warwicks the left. The 1st K.O.(R.L) Regt being in support and the 1st Bn the Rifle Brigade in Reserve.

Zero hour was 5.25 a.m.

The Left Assault Battalion experienced little difficulty in their advance, and kept throughout in touch with the 17th Divisional Troops on their left and the Household Battalion on their right.

The Right Assault Battalion were unable to keep in touch with 18th Divisional Troops on their right, the latter being held up by the enemy defence of POEL-CAPPELLE and in particular by resistance from the BREWERY. In consequence of this the advance of the Right Assault Battalion was considerably hampered by fire from POELCAPPELLE and particularly from HELLES HOUSE. REQUETE FARM was however occupied and a defensive flank towards POELCAPPELLE formed in conjunction with the 1st K.O. (R,L) Regt. The 1st Rifle Brigade moved forward and had all four of their companies over the 5 CHEMINS - POELCAPPELLE Rd. by 9.45 a.m.

The front line held by the attacking troops of the Division was approximately as follows from left to right :-

Reference
WESTROOSEBEKE
Sheet
1/10,000

V.8.d.4.5. (Junction W. of MEMLING FARM), then a little E. of BOWER HOUSE and BESACE FARM to V.14.d.3.8. junction W. of REQUETE FARM, thence S.W.

Prisoners taken approximated to 80 and 4 enemy M.Gs were reported captured by the Household Battalion and used against the enemy.

SECRET.

ADDENDUM No. 1.
to
4th DIVISION ORDER No. 66.

1. The following lines will be organized for defence :-

    The BLUE DOTTED Line
    The GREEN Line.

    In addition, posts will be established in the neighbourhood of -

    REQUETE FARM
    LANDING FARM
    BESACE FARM

    The garrisons of these posts are to be told off in advance.

2. Special parties will be told off by the 12th Inf. Bde. to gain touch with the left Division of the XVIII Corps at -

    V.14.c.1.6.
    REQUETE FARM
    V.14.central,

    and to gain touch with the 29th Division at -

    MILLERS HOUSES
    WATER HO.
    On the final objective about V.7.d.8.5.

3. The protective barrage on the GREEN DOTTED and BLUE DOTTED lines will become intense at three minutes before it begins to creep.

    The final protective barrage will be placed 300 yards beyond the GREEN Line.

4. Four tanks will be operating in the Corps area, but independent of the Infantry arrangements.

    These tanks will move forward from the neighbourhood of POELCAPPELLE at ZERO along the POELCAPPELLE - les 5 CHEMINS road.

    Two of these tanks will, on arrival at CONDE HO, operate towards BERTHIER HO.

    The remaining two, having cleared up the situation in the neighbourhood of TRANQUILLE HO, will cross the railway, and operate towards EGYPTE HO.

5. In case of a complete breakdown of the enemy's opposition, the Division must be prepared to make a further advance to the objective shewn in PURPLE on the attached Map.

6. Watches will be synchronized at Adv. Bde.H.Q. U.29.a.6.7. at 8 p.m. on "Y" Day for the leading Bde. and at FUSILIER HO. for the other two Bdes.

(Sd.) H. KARSLAKE.

6th October 1917.
Copies to all recipients
of 4th Divn. Order No.66.

Lieut.Col.
General Staff, 4th Division.

TELEPHONE CONVERSATIONS.

DATE	TIME	FROM	TO	CONVERSATION
12th	6.35 am	G.S.O.2	BM. 12 Bde.	No conversation — Line broken —
12th	6.40 am	I.O. DROP.	G.S.O.2.	got away all night. 400 x b/you wounded no brisk encounter — m.g. fire — quiet.
12th	6.55 am	B.M. DROP.	G.S.O.3.	Wounded back at hour bared farm. A few dead. Guncrew seen. Total casualty from Support Coy of wounded Bn. Stat. first objective taken and in touch with Warwicks on left.
12	7.2 am	B.M. DROP.	Dm. Co.	Above message received at 12th Bde at 6.55am Wounded man put with mean LANDING F.M.
12	7.30 am	B.M. DROP.	R/phone from Dm. Div. / S.O.3	6.40 am. Right M. Coy Comdr wounded report when left. he was within 50 yds of OFFUETE Fm. there is left or left Alt M. Kin is on right has lost touch and is on toward to keep join through POELCAPELLE. heavy MG fire in village. M.g. fire reported from left. Left Coy have got this of Gebis Support Coy that left in in touch with Warwicks. Typy & form Column North towards POELCAPELLE with O.

TELEPHONE CONVERSATIONS.

DATE	TIME	FROM	TO	CONVERSATION.
12th	7.50 am	Major Stansby 49th Div. R.A.	Y.S.O.3.	Wrote REQUEST F.M. and 7.6 Divens on our right appear held up à POELCAPPELLE Message from Liaison officer 12th Bde.
12th	8.22 am	18th Div.	Y.S.O.3. [Written from A.D.R. n/WH.Q.	R.W. Kent have been expensing on 76 Bde. A/6 am also to north of it. Bn on our left. No news from right. Would M.G. relier on left that Tothery tirselath information received. Informed Capture Carr Osson and said that when to left the Ruths was a then established. T.O.O. what Braun that seems to confirm it report that MEUNIER H. has been taken

TELEPHONE CONVERSATIONS.

DATE	TIME	FROM	TO	CONVERSATION
12/	8.40 am	B.M. 11th Bde.	G.S.O.3	Message from 11th R.B. Right support coy crossed road 6.30 am (R.S.M. Allman) + POELCAPPELLE/Right front coy holding line from Landing Tm - K.13.d.7.2. Nothing with left front coy. No telephone on circuit with left front coy. Spare coys are up. But any aft front coy spare coys are looking round. One coy at outskirts of POELCAPPELLE. Third 7.30 am on outskirts of POELCAPPELLE. 1 R. taken N. of POELCAPPELLE. One prisoner 477. I.R. taken N. of POELCAPPELLE.
12/	9.10 am	B.M. 12. Bde.	G.S.O.2	Enemy resign. 1 combr battn at Aun. Landing Tm + R.7 guite Tm at V13d87 40 prisoners known.
12/	9.20 am	18th Div.	G.S.O.2	Awards officer of 18th Div stating that Brewery in POELCAPPELLE has been captured. Officer saw at about 8 am difficult

441. 227.

TELEPHONE CONVERSATIONS.

DATE	TIME	FROM	TO	CONVERSATION.
12th	10.43 am	BM 4th Div Arty.	GSO 3.	F.O.O. has received information from infantry that half the BREWERY in POELCAPPEL has not been captured. Our troops consolidating line COMPROMIS FM - LANDING FM - REQUETE FM with a defensive flank towards POELCAPPELLE M.G. Fire coming from direction of POELCAPPELLE
12th	11.50 am	GSO1 17 D—	GSO1	Right Bn. Canadn. just entered their at 10.15 a.m. their Bn. was in touch with our left on final objective. Centre Bn. of 17 D— on the platform. Casualties very slight, attained TAURUS FM.
12th	11.35am	GSO1 17 D—	GSO3	10th ? Right Bn. report at 9.45. they had tried to carry GRAVEL FM ad not in touch with 18th to C was in touch with 11 about BOWER Ho.
12th	11.50 am	Gen. de Wind.	GSO 3.	On being heavily shelled from POELCAPELLE. Could some arrangement be made with 18th Div. for artillery to fire on POELCAPPELLE.

TELEPHONE CONVERSATIONS.

DATE	TIME	FROM	TO	CONVERSATION.
12	2.5 pm	G.O.C. 11.Bde	G.S.O.1	Hodges has retired and we are all round REQUESTS PM and TLu ATHEMLING, RUBENS PM and HELLES South road about RUBENS PM. Brooks Reserve should be kept under fire. Brooks is anxious about Bay which must go O.S. 01 T/d B.O.C. 12. Bde at ange 7pm on Support to relieve ATHEMLING 12PM on Support to relieve ATHEMLING 8PM. Line BOWER HO -BERTHIER PM. Reported situation.
	2.10 p.m	G.S.O.1	B.G.G.S.	
	3 p.m	G.O.C. 103: Bde.	G.S.O.1	Upon arriving STRAY PM will put in which unit G.O.C. 12. Bde. is relief. Agree that it better for 12. Bde to keep command till tomorrow.
12"	6.27 pm	B.M. Div Arty	G.S.O. 3	Red & Green attack was delivered from RUBENS PM at 5.10 pm. Artillery fire on S.O.S.

APPENDIX 23

ATTACHMENT OF AMERICAN OFFICERS.

4th Division No. G.D. 156.

10th Infantry Brigade.
11th Infantry Brigade.

1.	At the request of the American Authorities it has been decided that American Officers attached to Army Infantry Schools will visit forward areas on the termination of the present series of Courses.

2.	11 American Officers who are at present attending A Course at the Fourth Army Infantry School will be attached to Brigades in the line, from 3rd to 8th November, as under.

        10th Infantry Brigade.... 4
        11th Infantry Brigade.... 7

3.	These officers should be attached to Battalions in the trenches.

4.	They will travel from FLIXECOURT to ARRAS, by rail, with the officers of this Division who are attending the present Course at the Fourth Army School, which disperses on 3rd November.

5.	The hour of arrival of their train will be notified later.

                      (Sgd) E.G.MILES, Capt.,
                for   Lt-Colonel,
31st October, 1917.   General Staff, 4th Division.
Copy to A/Q.

Third Army G.71/164.

XVII Corps.
----

1. At the request of the American Authorities it has been decided that American Officers attached to Army Inf. Schools will visit forward areas on the termination of the present series of courses.

2. American Officers now at the Infantry Schools of Third, Fourth and Fifth Armies will visit Divisions in the line on the front of Third Army. They will proceed to those Divisions with Students returning from the course at at the School.

3. Where possible it has been arranged for American Officers to be conducted by British Officers who have been attending at the same School of Instruction.

4. The American Officers will leave the bulk of their kits at the Infantry Schools where they have attended courses, during their visit to the forward area, and will return to Infantry Schools on conslusion of their visit in order to collect kits. They will not be accompanied by servants.

5. On conclusion of their visit to forward areas, the American Officers will proceed via the Infantry School concerned to report to H.Q., 1st American Division for duty, the Senior Officer of each party will report to H.Q. A.E.F. en route. The Commandants of the Infantry Schools will provide them with the necessary movement orders.

6. Arrangements for the return of American Officers to the Infantry Schools from Division to which they have been attached will be made between Corps and Schools concerned.

7. Each party of American Officers should be divided into smaller groups of two or three during the visit and be attached to different Brigades. It is not necessary that they should be attached to the particular units who have had officer students at the present course; these Officer students should conduct them to the H.Q. of Divisions to which they will be attached, and they should then be sent on under Divisional arrangements.

8. American Officers will be detailed in parties by the Commandants of the Schools to which they are at present attached.

29th October, 1917.

Sgd. G.THORPE. Lt.Colonel,
for Major General, 3rd Army.

XVII Corps G.43/9.
4th Div. G.D. 166.

4th Division.

The following programme is submitted for Major General SCOTT of the United States Army, his Chief of Staff and A.D.C. attached to the 4th Division, and for the two General Staff Officers of Major General SCOTT's Staff attached to the 61st Division.

TUESDAY 30th October.

Lunch at XVII Corps Headquarters 1.15 p.m.
Visit Intelligence branch General Staff 2 p.m.
Visit 13th Sqdn.R.F.C.   )
        and Topo Section.) 3 p.m.

WEDNESDAY 31st October.

Leave 4th Divisional H.Q. 10 a.m.
Arrive XVII Corps Infantry School 10.20 a.m.
Lunch Corps School.
Meet C.E. XVII Corps 2 p.m.
Visit Dumps, Workshops, etc.

A G.S. officer of the XVII Corps will call at 4th Divisional H.Q. at 9.55 a.m. guide General SCOTT and party.

THURSDAY November 1st.

Visit Corps Heavy Artillery H.Q. 10.30 a.m.
Lunch at Corps Heavy Artillery H.Q.
Visit a Heavy Battery in action in the afternoon.

An Officer of the Corps H.A. will call at 4th Divisional H.Q. at 10.15 a.m. to guide General SCOTT & party.

FRIDAY November 2nd.

Leave 4th Divisional H.Q. 9.30 a.m.
Arrive Corps Musketry & Reinforcement Camp 10 a.m.
Leave Corps Musketry & Reinforcement Camp 11.30 a.m.
Arrive Cavalry Corps Headquarters 1 p.m.
Afternoon under arrangements of the Cavalry Corps.

A G.S. officer of the XVII Corps will call at 4th Divisional H.Q. at 9.25 a.m. to guide General SCOTT's party.

H.Q. XVII Corps.   Sgd. U.T. Brock. Captain,
29/10/17.   for Brig.Gen. Gen. Staff.

XVII Corps G.43/7.
4th Div. G.D. 156.

4th Division.

Major General SCOTT of the United States Army with his Chief of Staff and A.D.C. will be attached to the 4th Division for a period of 12 days from the 26th October.

2. The last two days of the attachment will be devoted to seeing training arrangements in rear of the line.

3. The hour of arrival of the above named General Officer and his Staff will be notified as early as possible.

H.Q. XVII Corps.   Sgd. J.R.E. CHARLES. B.G.
25th October, 1917.   General Staff.

APPENDIX 27.

LIST OF POSITION CALLS.

SECRET.

4th Division No. G.A. 12/35.

    10th Infantry Brigade... 8 copies.
    11th Infantry Brigade... 8 copies.
    12th Infantry Brigade... 8 "
    C.R.E., 4th Divn......... 4 "
    D.M.G.O................. 1 "
    234th M.G.Company........ 1 "
    A.D.M.S................. 4 "
    "Q" 4th Divn............ 2 "
    Gas Officer............. 1 "
    Signals................. 4 "

1.   Attached is a list of "POSITION CALLS", which have been allotted to the right Division area.

2.   All telephone instruments within 3,000 yards of the front line are in the "Danger Zone". Instruments outside the 3,000 yards limit will also be considered in the danger zone, when they are in direct communication with an instrument in the danger zone.

3.   Every Signal Office in, or in direct communication with, the "Danger Zone" has been allotted a "POSITION CALL".
    In each Signal Office a notice board, showing the "POSITION CALL" of the office; has been fixed.

4.   The object of POSITION CALLS is to prevent the enemy obtaining identifications, by means of his listening sets, when reliefs have taken place.
    Thus the POSITION CALL of a Signal Office at a Battalion Headquarters might be KY 6. No matter what Battalion is there, the Battalion to whom the office is allotted will be addressed simply as KY 6, and so no indication will be given to the enemy when Battalions change.

5.   The guiding principles for telephonic and telegraphic communications within the danger zone are as follows :-

    In all messages in the ADDRESS TO and FROM use the POSITION CALL; but in the text of the message use the CODE NAME of the unit concerned.

6.   Application for the allotment of additional POSITION CALLS will be made to O.C., 4th Signal Coy.
    A POSITION CALL when once allotted will not be changed, irrespective of the changes of units or formations.

                                            Lt-Colonel,
22nd October, 1917.   General Staff, 4th Division.

Copies to :-

        XVII Corps.
        15th Division.
        61st Division.
        C.R.A., 12th Division.

- S E C R E T -
****

POSITION CALLS

RIGHT DIVISIONAL SECTOR.

Nature of Signal Office.	Map reference	Position Call
Divisional Headquarters.	G.21.c.3.3	T.F.104
ARTILLERY.		
Divnl Artillery H.Qrs.	G.21.d.05.45	TF 105
H.Q. 62nd Bde R.F.A & Test Pt.	N.9.b.3.0	TB 11.
A/62 H.Qrs	N.4.b.42.23	TO 14
A/62 Section	N.4.d.38.87	TC 16
B/62 Section	N.17.c.51.30	SK 101
B/62 H.Qrs	N.11.c.95.58	TB 18
C/62 H.Qrs	N.5.d.53.36	TO 9.
D/62 H.Qrs	N.4.a.67.56	TC 17
H.Q. 63rd Bde R.F.A.	N.5.a.7.4	TC 11.
A/63	N.11.b.82.95	TB 19
B/63	H.34.d.14.49	TD 16.
C/63	N.4.b.35.56	TO 12.
D/63	N.6.c.11.24	TC 8.
Battery R.F.A	N.4.b.22.72	TB 8.
-do-	N.4.b.4.2	TB 12.
-do-	N.4.b.35.56	TB 16.
H.Q. 48th Bde R.F.A	N.2.d.5.9	TC 22.
A/48	H.34.d.37.80	TD 13
B/48	H.34.c.93.71	TD 11.
C/48	H.34.c.55.95	TD 12
Detachment C/48	H.28.c.75.05	TE 113.
D/48	N.4.b.22.72	TC 34
Detachment 48th A.F.A Battery	H.34.b.00.50	TD 14
Detachment 48th A.F.A.Bde	H.22.d.6.1	TF 15.
O.P, 63rd Arty Bde	N.12.b.9.7	TB 15
O.P.2, 48th Fd Arty Bde	H.36.d.4.4	TD 102
O.P.3, 48th Fd Arty Bde	H.23.d.7.3	TF 16.
O.P, Artillery, SURLEW.	N.24.d.7.9	SF 101
O.P, 48th A.F.A.Bde (HOOK TR)	O.2.d.4.9	TC 46
O.P, MONCHY	O.1.c.7.9	TC 40.
Visual Station, 48th A.F.A.Bde	N.4.b.4.4	TC 35.
D.A.C	G.32.c.6.5	TD 111.
48th A.F.A., D.A.C	G.26.b.1.9	TE 114
48th Bde Exchange	N.4.a.1.4	TC 37
R.A.Y.L.R (Adv. Arty & Divnl Exchange)	N.2.central.	TC 36.
H.Q. Wagon Lines 62nd Bde	M.6.a.7.5	TC 27.
" " " 63rd Bde	M.6.b.45.70	TC 28.
48th A.F.A. Bde Rear H.Q.	G.27.d.central	T.E.109.
A.R.P	G.34.c.3.4	TD 112.

Nature of Signal Office.	Map reference	Position Call

INFANTRY.

Right Bde.(CAMBRAI ROAD Sub-Sector)

Infantry Bde H.Q.	N.9.a.3.4	TB 20.
Gordon Bn H.Q.	O.7.d.4.0	TB 7.
"B" Strong Point Bn H.Q	N.18.b.25.90	TA 202
BROWN Line Bn H.Q	N.10.d.5.7	TB 21.
Saddle Coy H.Q	O.8.c.55.90	TB 2.
Front Line Coy H.Q	O.14.a.12.87	TB 201.
Joy H.Q.	O.8.c.45.20	TB 26.
Coy SPADE Reserve.	O.7.d.60.45	TB 10.
Coy H.Q SPADE Reserve	O.7.d.60.65	TB 27.
Brigade Relay (Les FOSSES FM)	N.12.a.3.3	TB 17.
W.T (FOSSES)	N.11.c.9.4	TB 23.
"C" Strong Point Platoon H.Q.	N.12.d.9.9	TB 14.

Left Bde.(MONCHY Sub-sector)

Inf. Bde H.Q	N.5.a.3.8	TC 10.
Bn H.Q	N.3.b.4.0	TC 21.
PICK Bn H.Q	O.7.b.65.25	TB 4.
SHRAPNEL Bn H.Q.	O.2.c.22.10	TC 26.
CIRCLE Bn H.Q	O.1.c.8.1	TC 41.
FEUCHY CHAPEL QUARRY Bn H.Q.	N.3.b.8.3	TC 20.
PICK Bn Right Coy	O.8.a.7.6	TB 1.
" " Left Coy	O.2.c.90.05	TC 2.
SHRAPNEL Coy H.Q.	O.2.c.3.5	TC 24.
HILL Coy H.Q	O.2.d.1.5	TC 23.
HILL Support Coy H.Q	O.2.d.10.35	TC 43.
EAST Coy H.Q (Front Bn)	O.1.d.65.45	TC 25.
"E" Strong Point Coy H.Q	N.6.d.2.2	TC 7.
"F" " " "	H.36.c.9.0	TD 1.
EAST Coy H.Q (MONCHY Bn)	O.1.d.8.2	TC 3.
CIRCLE Coy H.Q	O.1.c.95.20	TC 4.
NORTH Coy H.Q (QUARRY Bn)	N.4.a.5.5	TC 18.
SOUTH Coy H.Q "	N.4.a.35.35	TC 19.
Coy H.Q (FORK Reserve)	O.7.b.4.7	TB 29.
Prisoners Cage (MAISON ROUGE)	N.3.a.5.7	TC 44.
Brigade Relay Post.	O.7.a.0.6	TB 6.

MACHINE GUNS.

Right Brigade.

M.G.Coy H.Q	N.10.a.8.7	TB 22.
M.G.Coy H.Q (SPADE Res.)	O.7.d.60.45	TB 10.

Left Brigade.

M.G.Coy H.Q	N.4.b.8.4	TC 15.
-:- (CIRCLE TR)	O.1.a.4.4	TC 6.
-:- (VINE AVENUE)	O.7.b.0.8	TB 5.
M.G.Position	O.1.c.65.90	TC 45.
-:-	N.6.b.95.00	TC 47.
Reserve M.G.Coy H.Q	M.10.b.2.2	TB 25.
M.G.Position	N.18.b.9.4	SK 26.
-do-	N.24.d.65.75	SF.18.

Nature of Signal Office.	Map reference	Position Call
TRENCH MORTARS.		
T.M.(KNIFE TRENCH)	O.8.c.5.3	TB 3.
T.M.H.Q	O.8.b.4.6	TB 28.
L.T.M.H.Q	N.5.a.0.8	TC 42.
MISCELLANEOUS.		
A.D.M.S	G.21.d.0.8	TF 109.
Bde Rear H.Q	G.27.d.35.95	TE 105.
Bde Rear H.Q	G.27.b.8.2	TE 106.
Bde Rear H.Q	G.27.b.15.75	TE 107
Divisional Train	G.19.c.5.8	TF 107
Bde Transport	G.28.d.2.3	TE 104.
BOIS des BOEUFS Bn H.Q	H.32.c.7.3	TD 110.
ACHICOURT Bn H.Q	G.32.d.8.5	TD 109
BEAURAINS Bn H.Q	M.10.d.2.7	TB 24.
Reserve Bn H.Q (Right Bde)	G.27.b.4.8	TE 112.
Bn H.Q (Pioneers)	N.1.a.8.9	TC 33.
Field Coy R.E.	N.2.d.5.7	TC 32.
Field Coy R.E	N.2.c.8.3	TC 38.
O.P Infantry (CURLEW)	N.24.d.7.9	SF 101 A.
Visual (PLACE ST CROIX)	G.22.c.95.80	TF 106.
Wireless.	N.6.b.7.3	TC 1.
B.V Divnl Test Point	H.26.d.4.3	TE 101.
T.H " "	H.34.d.4.7	TD 15.
BULLDOG DUMP	G.28.d.5.7	TE 102.
ALADDIN DUMP	G.28.b.85.00	TE 103.

****

Appendix 28

Congratulatory Messages.

G.O.C.

4th Division No. G.S. 81.

```
10th Brigade.      234th M.G.Coy.
11th Brigade.      Div Train.
12th Brigade.      21st West Yorks (Pioneers).
C.R.E.             Div. Gas Officer.
C.R.A.             Signals.
A.D.M.S.           "2".
A.P.M.             Camp Commandant.
D.M.G.O.           Employment Coy.
D.A.D.O.S.         Supply Column.
D.A.D.V.S.
```

The following message has been received from the G.O.C Fifth Army.

> "During the short time you have been under my command you have fought magnificently. You have had to contend not only with a desperate resistance on the part of the enemy but also with rain and mud equally formidable. In spite of this the 4th Division has fought as successfully as it has done gallantly. I send you my best congratulations and my warmest thanks".

GENERAL GOUGH.

H. Ramsden
Lt-Colonel,
General Staff, 4th Division.

18th October, 1917.

TO ALL RANKS OF THE 4th DIVISION.

Nobody will ever forget the part taken by the 4th Division in the Great Battle of FLANDERS 1917.

In eight days you have had three fights in the most trying conditions that any troops have had to endure, and in the words of the Army Commander "the performance was marvellous".

The demands made on the Artillery have surpassed all previous records and the gallantry and determination of the Infantry have been beyond all praise.

Machine Gun Companies and Light Trench Mortar Batteries have materially assisted the Infantry and in spite of heavy losses have shown the finest spirit throughout.

As usual the gallantry of the linesmen and devotion to duty of all members of the Signal Service have been splendid.

But for the unceasing energies of the R.E. and Pioneers the movement across country and the transport of material up to the front would have made the operations impossible.

Last but not least a great debt of gratitude is due to the R.A.M.C. personnel with the attached Infantry stretcher bearers for their never ceasing efforts to bring in the wounded and save them from unnecessary suffering.

Nobody could be more proud than I am of commanding such troops.

I thank and congratulate you all.

T. G. Matheson.

Major General,
13th October, 1917.   Commanding 4th Division.

G.O.C, R.x,

　　Right Artillery

　　　　The G.O.C wishes me to ask if you will be good enough to convey to all ranks of the Horse and Field Artillery who have assisted us during the past 10 days, his own thanks, and those of the whole of the 4th Division.

　　　　Their devotion to duty under the most trying conditions in order to help the gallant Infantry to carry out their tasks, has been magnificient.

　　　　　　　　　　　　　　　　H. Hanslake
　　　　　　　　　　　　　　　　Lieut Colonel,
13th October 1917.　　　　　General Staff, 4th Division.

App 29

4th DIVISION SUMMARY OF OPERATIONS.

5.30 a.m. to 12 noon October 4th, 1917.

Reference attached map.

5.30 a.m. - 6 a.m.	Enemy artillery active around LANGEMARCK and STEENBEEK.
6 a.m.	Attack commenced. 1st Som.L.I. (11th Bde.) on right. 1st Hamps.R. (11th Bde.) in centre. 2nd Seaforths (10th Bde.) on left.
6.3 a.m.	Enemy barrage opened but not heavy.
6.15 a.m.	" " thickened.
6.20 a.m.	KANGAROO TRENCH reported captured with little opposition.
7.5 a.m.	Wounded officer 1st Som.L.I. reported attack appeared to be progressing satisfactorily.
7.15 a.m.	2nd Seaforth Highlanders reported to have reached 1st objective. Report confirmed by wounded Coy.Sergt.Major. 2nd Seaforth Highlanders Headquarters moved forward to KANGAROO TRENCH.
7.40 a.m.	Prisoners of 371st I.R. and 10th Bav.I.R. passed ADELPHI.
7.45 a.m.	An officer of 1st Hamps.Regt. reports his location uncertain but believed to be V.19.a 1.8 and that all units in touch but mixed up. Casualties not heavy.
8 a.m.	1st E.Lanc.Regt. (Support Bn. 11th Bde.) report their 2 leading Coys. arrived in KANGAROO TRENCH.
8.25 a.m.	Div.Intelligence Officer ADELPHI reports prisoners of 371st I.R., 10th Bav.I.R. and 13th Bav.I.R. captured.
8.25 a.m. - 8.55 a.m.	Hostile shelling weak - mostly East of STEENBEEK.
10.12 a.m.	1st Som.L.I. reported at BEEK VILLAS (verbal message). Reserve company 1st Hamps.Regt. consolidating line 200 yards East of KANGAROO TRENCH.
10.50 a.m.	Following intercepted received by Artillery :- "Am on reverse slope of 19 METRE HILL - Capt.WARD, O.C. assaulting Coy. going strong, refused help from me - troubled by machine gun fire from left flank - from O.C. "D" Coy." Artillery report Infantry seen in Southern Farm of POELCAPPELLE.
11.10 a.m.	1st Hamps.Regt. Headquarters reported moving forward to LOUIS FARM.
11.15 a.m.	Report received from 11th Division that their right Bn. reports GLOSTER FARM captured and being consolidated and that their left Brigade report some Infantry at POELCAPELLE CHURCH.

11.30 a.m.	10th Inf.Bde. report having intercepted following lamp message :- "Enemy shelling TRAGIQUE FARM - time 10.25 a.m. - nothing further to report."
11.45 a.m.	Aeroplane map received showing Infantry on line, marked in RED, on attached map.
12 noon.	No further information received.

Major General,
4th October, 1917. Commanding 4th Division.

4th DIVISION SUMMARY OF OPERATIONS.

12 noon to 6 p.m. Oct.4th,1917.

11.53 a.m.	1st Som.L.I. report SHEERWOOD FORESTERS on Right reached final objective, with left resting on road at V.19.b 1.7.
12.30 p.m.	H.Q. and remaining Coy. MIDDLESEX report moving forward to A area. Enemy barrage ceased. Intermittent shelling LANGEMARCK and STEENBEEK.
1 p.m.	EAGLE TRENCH heavily shelled.
1.4 p.m.	18th Corps report by telephone enemy seen massing about POELCAPELLE BREWERY.
1.30 p.m.	Report received from 11th Inf.Bde. that Right Coy. 1st Som. L.I. in report timed 12.20 p.m. had reached their final objective but later withdrew to a line 100 yards East of FERDAN HOUSE owing to casualties from our barrage.
1.45 p.m.	1st Som.L.I report capture of TRAGIQUE FM at 10.58 a.m and Company in touch with units on right and left.
1.45 p.m.	Arty 18th Corps state TRAGIQUE Fm and KANGAROO HUTS reported occupied by the enemy.
2.30 p.m.	11th Inf. Bde report our S.O.S fired at 12.55 p.m. Adjutant 1st Som. L.I returning from front line reported 19 Metre Hill evacuated and line to the N.E retiring. Counter-attack being organized.
2.31 p.m.	Pigeon message received from Seaforths "Huns advancing in mass on LEWIS FARM, send artillery help at once "
3 p.m.	10th Inf. Bde report no definite news of counter-attack on their front, but 3/10th Middlesex apparently involved in the fight. 1st R.Warwicks send up to counter-attack and retake 19 Metre Hill if necessary. Aeroplane observer reports we still hold 19 Metre Hill.
4.42 p.m.	Very heavy barrage reported on our original front and support lines.
5.19 p.m.	11th Inf. Bde report final objective retaken. They now hold TRAGIQUE Fm and KANGAROO Huts and road to East of these places. Situation on 10th Bde front still obscure. A report received from F.O.O states that at 1.45 p.m. enemy attacked in U.18.c and d.At 2 p.m S.O.S went up in U.18.a and V.13.c. Our Infantry appeared to be withdrawing from V.13.c but stopped. At 2.20 p.m our troops advanced and enemy retired.

4th October 1917.

Major General,
Commanding 4th Division.

SUMMARY OF OPERATIONS ON 4th DIVISION FRONT

FROM ZERO HOUR TO 12 NOON 9th OCTOBER, 1917.
===

ZERO hour 5.20 a.m.

12th Infantry Brigade attacked with -

    2nd Essex Regt. on the right,
    2nd Lan.Fus. on the left,
    2nd Duke of Wellington's in support,
    1st King's Own in Reserve.

10th Infantry Brigade in Support.

11th Infantry Brigade in Divisional Reserve.

Enemy barrage opened ZERO plus four approximately on line through LOUIS FARM, ragged at first - intensified later.

No definite information received until 8 a.m. when aeroplane dropped map showing situation at 6.40 a.m. reporting 1st Objective gained on entire Corps front.

8.30 a.m.

Smoke barrage was reported on our left drifting towards our front. In addition to German barrage LANGEMARCK RIDGE shelled intermittently.

9.10 a.m.

G.O.C. ~~12th Infantry Brigade~~ ordered Household Battalion to move forward to area between AU BON GITE and LANGEMARCK and to come under the orders of G.O.C. 12th Infantry Brigade.

10 a.m.

Enemy shelling reported to have increased slightly.

10.33 a.m.

Message received quoting situation at 9 a.m. showing line as follows :-

LANDING FARM - COMPROMIS FARM - Huts between WATER HOUSE and MILLER HOUSES.

10.40 a.m.

Right Group Artillery reported hostile machine gun fire from NOBLES and HELLES FARM.

Prisoners of following Regiments captured on Divisional front :-

        417th I.R.
        441st I.R.

They state 227th Division relieved 6th Bavarian Division on night 8th/9th.

The positions of the leading Infantry as reported by airmen are shown on the attached map as follows :-

    6.40 a.m.   BLUE.
    7.40 a.m.   RED.
   10.15 a.m.   GREEN.

                                              Major General,

9th October, 1917.   Commanding 4th Division.

Copies to XIVth Corps.
          Guards Division.
          11th Division.
          29th Division.

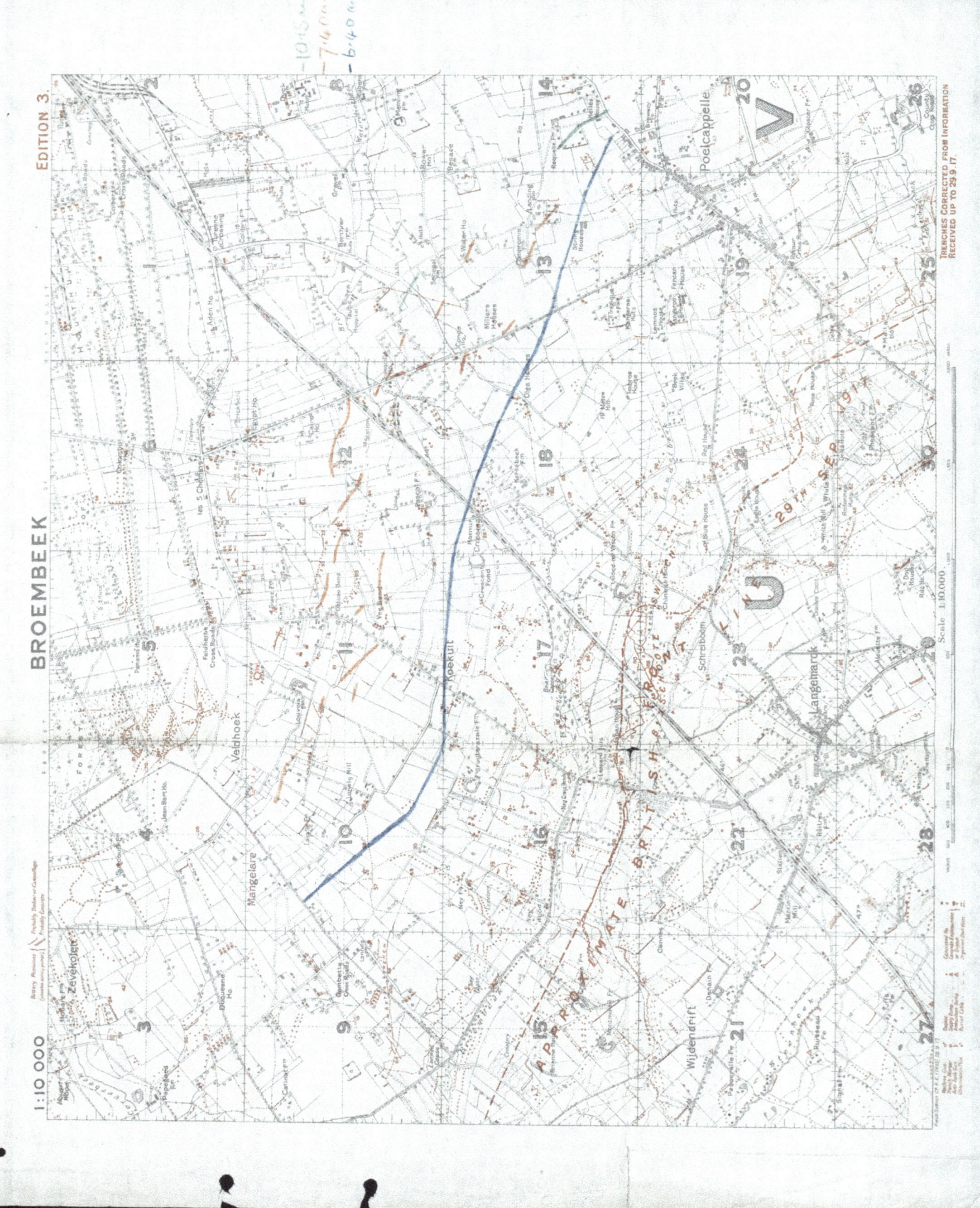

SUMMARY OF OPERATIONS ON 4th DIVISION
FRONT FROM 12 NOON TO 6 p.m. 9th OCTOBER, 1917.

Aeroplane report timed 1.40 p.m. showed line running from BREWERY (POELCAPPELLE) - HELLES HOUSE - V.14.c.4.8., thence a gap to LANDING FARM - SENEGAL FARM.
4th Division ordered to consolidate ground held and to close gap between REQUETE FARM and LANDING FARM.

Enemy artillery fire West of LANGEMARCK almost ceased after 2 p.m.

At 2.15 p.m. Right Brigade of 29th Division reported enemy about to counter attack. This attack failed to develop.

In accordance with XIV Corps order, contact aeroplane flew over our line at 4 p.m. and reported it to run as follows :-
V.13.d.6.3 - West of STRING HOUSES - V.13.b.5,1 -
V.13.b.0.2 - V.13.a.5.9 - Huts (V.13.a.70.75) -
V.7.c.85.00 - V.7.c.25.30 - V.7.c.3.8 - V.7.a.3.2.
One post reported at V.13.d.60.75.

Reports from 2nd Lancs Fusrs and 1st K.O.R.L Regt at 4.30 p.m. stated that it is certain that we do not hold LANDING or COMPROMIS FARMS. This agreed with air report.

In accordance with the instructions received from Corps, 12th Infantry Brigade ordered to join up by patrols to-night all possible ground up to the line LANDING FARM - WATER HOUSE - SENEGAL FARM, and to establish a strong second line along Road from POELCAPPELLE to les 5 CHEMIN.

Subsequent report on aeroplane map dropped at 4 p.m., it appears that 200 men occupy Wood S.W. of COMPROMIS FARM at V.13.a.9.1., line then runs V.13.d.1.8 - 1.5. - 3.6., just short of STRING HOUSES - V.13.d.7.2 - V.14.c.1.1. One isolated yellow flare, possibly German, seen at V.13.d.65.80.
No enemy could be seen in the vicinity of WATER HOUSE - LANDING FARM and REQUETE FARM or anywhere in V.13.b.

Attached map illustrates approximately the line held by leading Brigade at 4 p.m.

Major General,
Commanding 4th Division.

9th October, 1917.

Copies to :-

    XIV Corps.
    Guards Division.
    11th Division.
    29th Division.

BROEMBEEK

1:10,000

EDITION 3

⊕ ISOLATED YELLOW FLARE SEEN AT THIS POINT

TRENCHES CORRECTED FROM INFORMATION
RECEIVED UP TO 29.1.17

4th Division
War Diaries
General Staff

November 1917

4th Division. MGC A20 Army Form C. 2118.

NOVEMBER 1917.   Vol 40

SECRET.
10.
4th Div. A.

Herewith War Diary, General Staff, 4th Division, for month of November, 1917, with Appendices.

[signature]
Lieut.Colonel,
General Staff, 4th Division.

4th December, 1917.

		Remarks and references to Appendices
	retaliation to our T.M. fire — [cut off]	
	[cut off] below normal. [cut off] between 11.45 am & 1 pm.	App 11a
4.	MONCHY. Shelled slightly about 1 pm; a few gas shell fell in vicinity of Left Batn HQ. Enemy during night. Quiet day with exception of hvy 10.5cm shells in neighbourhood of VINE AV about noon. Own 75 using (4) 12 bore relieving 11 bore in Left sector 9 Bn front.	(b) App 11a (c) App 1(b)
5.	Quiet day. Warwick relieving Honeychurch Battn in front line of CAMBRAI Road Sector (10 Bde) Order 76 varied (a) instructions regarding hostile instrumental (b) the enemy 15th DROCOURT – QUEANT line.	(a) App. 1
6.	Hostile artillery active on junction B DALE and CANISTER. 12 M.G.C relieving 11 M.G.C. Order 77 covering wiring raid to be	(b) App. 2
7.		

4 Division. HQ. G.S.   Army Form C. 2118.

INTELLIGENCE SUMMARY.
(Erase heading not required.)

NOVEMBER 1917.

Vol 4.

Place	Date	Hour	Summary of Events and Information	Remarks and references to Appendices
ARRAS.	1.		During the day Intense wire slight retaliation to our T.M. fire. 12th Brigade rejoined division from VI Corps.	
	2.		Quiet day.	
	3.		Quiet day. Enemy artillery activity below normal. Our & 7H sound T(A) Hostile T.M.s active on Left sub-sector between 11.45 am & 1pm.	
	4.		MONCHY shelled slightly about 1pm.	(a) App 1(a)
	5.		A few gas shell fell in vicinity of Left Bde HQ, Legrete during night. Quiet day with exception of a few 10.5cm shells in neighbourhood of VINE AV about noon. Own 75 wired (a) 12 Bde relief " " "A" in" Left sector D Bn front.	(c) App 1 (A)
	6.		Quiet day. Warwick relieve Hampshires Batln in front line of CAMBRAI Road Sector (10 Bde) Own 76 vanish (b) Instructions regarding the intermediate of the enemy is the DROCOURT - QUEANT line.	(b) App 1
	7.		Hostile artillery active on junction of DALE and CANISTER. 12 M.G.C. relieves 11. M.G.C. Own 77 casualties. Raid to be	(b) App 2

Army Form C. 2118.

WAR DIARY
or
INTELLIGENCE SUMMARY.
(Erase heading not required.)

Instructions regarding War Diaries and Intelligence Summaries are contained in F. S. Regs., Part II. and the Staff Manual respectively. Title pages will be prepared in manuscript.

Place	Date	Hour	Summary of Events and Information	Remarks and references to Appendices
	8.		Carried out by 10 Bde.	
	9.		Quiet day. 2/5 W. Yorks Pioneers relieved Regimental Division.	
			12 Bde relieved 11 Bde in MONCHY Sector.	
	10.		Quiet day.	
	11.		Quiet day.	
	12.		Quiet day. MONCHY lightly shelled about 1.40 p.m.	
			Hostile light T.M. active opposite 10 Bde.	
	13.		Quiet day. Lancs Fus relieved Kings Own in MONCHY Sector (left subsector). Dukes relieved Essex in Right subsector.	
	14.		During the night - Enemy fired some lachrymatory T.M. Bombs on post kus and C Strong Point. Our artillery and T.M. active during morning	

WAR DIARY
or
INTELLIGENCE SUMMARY.

Army Form C. 2118.

Place	Date	Hour	Summary of Events and Information	Remarks and references to Appendices
	15.		MONCHY lightly shelled - by enemy about 3 p.m. Otherwise quiet.	
	16.		Raid by Lancs. Fus. on O.26.0550 did not succeed in reaching enemy line. See report at app.(h)	(c) 3
	17.		Hornchurch Bullies moved from BROWN LINE to BOIS des BOEUFS. Quiet day. Patrol of Essex Regt. (12 Bde) which went out during night to examine wire did not return. Order 78 issued (a) re Bombardment of enemy's trenches E of MONCHY.	(a) App. 4
	18.		Raid by Kings Own Regt. (12 Bde)(b) Enemy shelled support line and West end of MONCHY in reply to our bombardment and discharge of smoke.	(b) App. 5

Army Form C. 2118.

WAR DIARY
or
INTELLIGENCE SUMMARY.
(Erase heading not required.)

Place	Date	Hour	Summary of Events and Information	Remarks and references to Appendices
	19.		Quiet day - Order 79 issued - (a) at 6.20 am Warwickshires (10 Bde) (b) minded enemy Trenches.	(a) app. 6 (b) app. 7
	20.			
	21.		Quiet day.	
	22.		Quiet day. Warwickshires relieved Honourable Artillery in front line. 9 Rifle Bde in centre Lanc. Fus. relieved Kings Own on L & left subsection. MONCHY Sector Duke Wellingtons relieved Essex in Right subsection.	
	23.		Hostile Trench mortars and artillery more active. Brig. Genl. de Wiart V.C. DSO. cmdg. 12 Inf Bde wounded.	
	24.		Light shelling of M 4. 46. during the evening. 2/Lieut. H.V. Skells killed in ARRAS in the afternoon.	

Army Form C. 2118.

WAR DIARY
or
INTELLIGENCE SUMMARY.
(Erase heading not required.)

Instructions regarding War Diaries and Intelligence Summaries are contained in F. S. Regs., Part II. and the Staff Manual respectively. Title pages will be prepared in manuscript.

Place	Date	Hour	Summary of Events and Information	Remarks and references to Appendices
ARRAS	Nov 25.		11th Bde relieved 12th Bde in the left sector of Div front in accordance with Order. 79. For distribution see Appendix. (a)	(a) App. 8
"	26.		Quiet day. Following reliefs took place in the right sector (10th B Bde) Seaforths relieved Warwicks in front line, Warwicks went to B.O.W. and ROEUX (Reserve) Middlesex relieved H.B.'s in support, H.B.'s moved to ARRAS.	
	27		Intermittent shelling of support & reserve lines in the CAMBRAI Road sector during the day. MONCHY + CIRCLE Trench also shelled about midday. Heavy minenwerfer fire on VITIS AVENUE + SHRAPNEL Trench. Order 80 issued by (b) On 29th inst. 10th Bde will relieve the left battalion. This order was afterwards cancelled. Order 81 issued (c) The following reliefs will be carried out.	(b) App. 9 (c) app. 10
	27/28th Nov.		10th Bde will relieve Northumbs and will relieve right Bn of 11th Bde.
	28th Nov.		10th Bn will open out in left as far as CASE ALLEY (020.4.6:6:5) inclusive.	
	28/29th Nov.		11th R.I.+ will extend its left to SCABBARD Trench inclusive. Relieving the 46th Bde 15th Div. For new boundaries to be attacked see Order No 81.	

Army Form C. 2118.

WAR DIARY
or
INTELLIGENCE SUMMARY.
(Erase heading not required.)

Instructions regarding War Diaries and Intelligence Summaries are contained in F. S. Regs., Part II. and the Staff Manual respectively. Title pages will be prepared in manuscript.

Place	Date	Hour	Summary of Events and Information	Remarks and references to Appendices
ARRAS	Nov 28th		Quiet day. Order Received (a) At 2000 hours (7pm) on December 1st a gas bombardment with 4" Stokes Mortars will be carried out on enemy's front line R. by No 1 Special Coy R.E. Order 83 issued (b) 12th Bde will relieve 10th Bde in the Right Sub-sector of the Divid Front, on 2nd & 3rd December. Movements in accordance with Order 81 completed.	(a) App 11 (b) App. 12
	29th		Enemy put down light barrage on left front & reserve lines of Right Sub. Enemy artillery very active on left Sub-front. Monchy shelled at 1 p.m. Movements in accordance with Order 81 completed. (c) ARRAS shelled intermittently all day. For dispositions see otherwise. with a H.V. gun.	(c) App. 13
	30th		Mid-day relieved Seaforths in front line Right sector (10th Bde). Seaforths moved to Les Fosses Fm. Hostile shelling occasionally above normal. Monchy Docourt heavily shelled with 5.9's 4.2'' ARRAS again shelled with a 24 cm Hi-V. gun.	

WAR DIARY, GENERAL STAFF, 4th DIVISION.

1st - 30th November, 1917.

APPENDICES.

1. Order 76.
2. (a). Order 74.
1 (b). Order 75.
2. Order 77.
3. Report on Raid by 2nd Lan.Fus.(12th Brigade) 15/16 Nov.
4. Order 78.
5. Report on Raid by 1st King's Own (12th Brigade) 17/18 November.
6. Order 79.
7. Report on Raid by 1st R.War.R. (10th Brigade) 19/20 Nov.
8. Distribution of units after relief of 12th Brigade by 11th Brigade in Left Sector of Divnl.front.
9. Order 80.
10. Order 81.
11. Order 82.
12. Order 83.
13. Distribution of units.

- SECRET -   Copy No 26

4th DIVISION ORDER NO: 74

Ref. LENS Sheet 11
1/100,000.

3rd Nov. 1917

1. The 4th Divisional Artillery, and one Ammunition Sub-park marches on November 8th, from VILLERS CHATEL to Wagon Lines in ARRAS.

   Route :- AUBIGNY STATION - ST POL-ARRAS Road.
   Hour of start :- 9 a.m.

2. The 4th Divisional Artillery will relieve the 12th Divisional Artillery on the nights 9th/10th and 10th/11th November.

   Details of relief will be arranged between the G.Os.C, 4th and 12th Divisional Artilleries.

3. The G.O.C, 4th Divisional Artillery will take over command from the G.O.C, 12th Divisional Artillery at 9 a.m on November 11th.

4. ACKNOWLEDGE.

H. Hardcastle
Lieut: Colonel,
General Staff, 4th Division.

Issued at 10 a.m.

Copy No:			
1	to G.O.C.	13	to D.A.D.V.S.
2	G.S.O.1.	14	4th Div Train.
3	10th Inf. Bde.	15	Signals.
4	11th Inf. Bde.	16	4th Div "Q"
5	12th Inf. Bde.	17)	XVIIth Corps.
6	C.R.A, 4th Div.	18)	
7	C.R.A, 12th Div.	19	15th Divn.
8	C.R.E.	20	34th Divn.
9	A.D.M.S.	21	Camp Commandant.
10	A.P.M.	22	4th Div. Depot Bn.
11	D.M.G.O	23	4th Div Gas Offr.
12	234th M.G.Coy.	24	D.A.D.O.S.
		25	File.
		26)	War Diary.
		27	

- SECRET -

App. 1(b.)

Copy No: 19

4th DIVISION ORDER NO: 75

5th November 1917.

1. The 12th Infantry Brigade will relieve the 11th Infantry Brigade in the Left Sector of the Divisional front, the relief to be complete by 6 a.m on Friday, 9th instant.

2. The Machine Guns of the 11th M.G.Coy will be relieved by those of the 12th M.G.Coy before the relief of the Battalions in the front line begins.

All other details of relief will be made between Brigadiers concerned.

3. The 11th Infantry Brigade will take over all working parties and guards now being found by the 12th Infantry Brigade, reliefs being arranged so as not to break the continuity of work.

4. A C K N O W L E D G E.

H. Wanstable
Lieut: Colonel,
General Staff, 4th Division.

Issued at 6 a.m.

Copy No: 1 to G.O.C   11 to A.P.M.
        2   G.S.O.1.   12   234th M.G.Coy.
        3   10th Inf. Bde.   13) XVIIth Corps.
        4   11th Inf. Bde.   14)
        5   12th Inf. Bde.   15   15th Divn.
        6   C.R.A.   16   34th Divn.
        7   C.R.E.   17   D.M.G.O.
        8   A.D.M.S.   18   File.
        9   4th Div "Q"   19)
       10   Signals.   20) War Diary.

SECRET.

App.1.
Copy No. ......

4th DIVISION ORDER NO. 76.

6th November, 1917.

1. (a) The enemy may withdraw to the DROCOURT – QUEANT line or to some Intermediate position.

   (b) It is important to gain early information of this withdrawal so as not to allow it to take place unmolested.
   To gain this information the closest touch must be maintained with the enemy by means of observers by day, patrols at night and by raids.

   (c) Any information gained by patrols and any information gained in any other way which may give any indication of a withdrawal by the enemy must be sent in to Divisional Headquarters at once.

2. (a) ~~The boundaries between the two Brigades during the advance will be O.8.b 1.0 – O.9.central – O.5.central – O.31.central.~~   See attached *

   (b) The Divisional boundaries are shown on attached map.

3. The advance will be carried out in bounds, the troops being securely established at the end of each bound before the advance to the next bound is made.
   Successive bounds are shown on attached map in GREEN, BLUE, BROWN and YELLOW, with an intermediate bound RED.

4. (a) Should the troops in the front line become aware of the fact that the enemy has withdrawn, the Commanders on the spot will, without waiting for orders, send forward patrols as far as the RED line shown on attached map.

   (b) These patrols are to be strongly supported but on no account is our present front system to be given up as the main line of resistance until our advanced troops are firmly established on the BLUE line.

   (c) Any move initiated as above is to be reported at once to flank Brigades and Divisional Headquarters.

   (d) Each successive bound will be carried out in a similar manner but with the exception of the first bound will not be put into execution without orders from Divisional Headquarters. The issue of these orders will be dependent on the moves of the Artillery for which separate instructions will be issued.

   (e) Brigades will pay particular attention to maintaining touch with Brigades on their flanks reporting that this has been done on each objective.

5. (a) As soon as the movement from our present front system begins, the Vickers Guns belonging to the leading Brigades West of the present Support Line may be moved as required by the Brigadier to whom they belong.
   Those in and East of the Support Line will remain in their present position until the BLUE line has been occupied. They can then be moved as required by Brigadiers.
   The Machine Guns of the 234th M.G.Coy. will be concentrated in SPADE RESERVE ready to move as ordered by Divisional Headquarters.

(b) Two of the Field Companies R.E. will work under the C.R.E. in accordance with separate instructions.

One Field Company, to be detailed by the C.R.E., will be placed at the disposal of the C.E. XVII Corps, for work on roads.

(c) The Pioneer Battalion (less two Companies) will work under the C.R.E. in accordance with separate instructions.

Two Companies will be placed at the disposal of the C.E. XVII Corps for work on roads.

(d) The Infantry attached to the Tunnelling Company will rejoin their units.

6. As soon as the GREEN line has been occupied H.Q. will move as under :-

Divisional H.Q. (advanced) to LES FOSSES FARM.
Right Brigade to CRATER SUBWAY.
Left Brigade to PICK CAVE. *See attached ✕*

7. The A.D.M.S. will arrange for pushing forward the necessary dressing stations as the advance progresses.

8. The move of the Reserve Brigade and 1st Line Transport will be ordered by Divisional Headquarters as soon as the situation in front demands it. Their first bound will probably be :-

Reserve Brigade - BROWN LINE and BOIS des BOEUFS.
1st Line Transport - FEUCHY CHAPEL cross roads.

9. The move of all other units not mentioned above will be ordered as required by Divisional Headquarters.

10. ACKNOWLEDGE.

See attached ✕

Issued at 1 p.m.

H. Hanslade
Lieut.Colonel,
General Staff, 4th Division.

Copy No. 1 to G.O.C.
2 to G.S.O.1.
3 to 10th Brigade.
4 to 11th Brigade.
5 to 12th Brigade.
6 to C.R.A.
7 to C.R.E.
8 to A.D.M.S.
9 to A.P.M.
10 to Signals.
11 to Q.
12 to 234th M.G.Coy.
13 to D.M.G.O.
14 to 21st West Yorks. Pioneers.
15)
16) to XVII Corps.
17 to 15th Division.
18 to 34th Division.
19 to C.E. XVII Corps.
20)
21) to War Diary.
22 to File.

SECRET.

AMENDMENT NO.1
to
4th DIVISION ORDER NO.76.

1. Para. 2 (a) delete and substitute -

    The boundary between the two Brigades during the advance will be as shown on attached map.
    This provides for responsibility of various tactical features to be allotted as follows :-

    BOIS du SART to Left Brigade.
    ARTILLERY HILL to Right Brigade.
    KASHMIR WOOD and watercourse South of it
    to Left Brigade.

2. Para. 6 delete and substitute -

    (a) As soon as the GREEN LINE has been occupied, H.Q. will move as under :-
    Right Brigade to CRATER SUBWAY.
    Left Brigade to I.31.c 5.1.

    (b) Advanced Divisional Headquarters will, if necessary, move to the present Right Brigade Headquarters at N.9.c 9.7.

3. Para. 8 delete and substitute -

    The move of the Reserve Brigade and 1st Line Transport will be ordered by Divisional Headquarters as soon as the situation in front demands it. Their first bound will probably be -

    Reserve Brigade   BROWN LINE.
                         BOIS des BOEUFS.
                         WILDERNESS CAMP
                         TILLOY . CAMP.

    Brigade H.Q.   FEUCHY CHAPEL Cross Roads.

    1st Line Transport   FEUCHY CHAPEL Cross Roads.

4. ACKNOWLEDGE.

H. Hursdale
Lieut.Colonel,
General Staff, 4th Division.

3rd December, 1917.

Copies to all recipients of
4th Division Order No. 76.

S E C R E T.

INSTRUCTIONS No. 1
to
4th DIVISION ORDER No. 76.

R.E.

1. In the event of a withdrawal by the enemy, the C.R.E. will arrange for the following reconnaissances to be sent out at once, to report on :-

    (a) Any sources of water supply.

    (b) "Booby" traps left by the enemy.

    (c) Likely places for Battalion and Brigade H.Qrs., and the necessary labour and material required to put them in a good state.

    (d) Roads.

2. The following roads will be made fit at once for pack transport and subsequently for horse transport:-

    (a) Main CAMBRAI Road as far as O.14.a.0.7., and thence via STIRRUP Lane to BOIRY NOTRE DAME.

    (b) Feuchy CHAPEL Cross-roads - Monchy - Road junction O.2.c.8.4. - INFANTRY Lane - BOIRY NOTRE DAME.

3. Picks and shovels may be required to be sent up in considerable numbers. Arrangements must be made for carrying this out with pack as well as horse transport.

4. ACKNOWLEDGE.

H. Karslake
Lt-Colonel,
General Staff. 4th Division.

12th November, 1917.

Copies to all recipients
of 4th Division Order No. 76.

SECRET.

ADDENDUM NO. 1
to
INSTRUCTIONS NO. 1
to
4th DIVISION ORDER NO. 76.

R.E.

1. Trenchboard tracks will be laid and named as under :-

GORDON AVENUE: CAVALRY FARM - Junction of GORDON AVENUE with front line - BEETLE TRENCH thence general direction N.E.

Boards to be taken out of GORDON AVENUE at once and laid above ground.

PICK AVENUE: DRAGOON LANE - along PICK AVENUE - N. edge of BOIS DU VERT - QUARRY O.4.central.

Boards to be taken out of PICK AVENUE at once and laid on top.

CANISTER AVENUE: from MONCHY - along N. side of CANISTER - FOX Trench - S. edge of BOIS DU SART.

Boards to be taken out of CANISTER and VINE AVENUE at once for this track.

2. The responsibility for laying these tracks will be :-

GORDON AVENUE .... Right Brigade.

PICK AVENUE   )
CANISTER AVENUE   ) ...... Left Brigade.

3. C.R.E. will prepare notice boards and white stakes for these tracks and have them ready at CAVALRY FARM, PICK CAVE and CIRCLE Trench respectively.

H. Acknowledge.

H. Kendalle
Lieut.Colonel,
General Staff, 4th Division.

23rd November, 1917.

Copies to all recipients of
4th Division Order No. 76.

SECRET.

INSTRUCTIONS NO. 2
to
4th DIVISION ORDER NO. 76.

SIGNAL COMMUNICATIONS.

1. In the event of the enemy withdrawing D3 Telephones will be taken into use.
   Any circuits which are not metallic to start with must be made so as soon as possible.

2. Brigades must select beforehand, from the map, places at which they can establish forward Stations.
   These Brigade forward stations must be equipped with the following means of communication :-

   Telephone
   Fullerphone
   Runners.
   Visual.
   Pigeon.

   and in the case of the left Brigade, Amplifier and Wireless Set.
   The Left Brigade might with advantage select the QUARRY O.4.c.9.9.
   (a) To this point will be sent, as soon as the BLUE Line is reached, the Amplifier and Wireless Set now at les FOSSES Farm, N.11.b.9.5.
   (The preliminary moves of the Amplifier and Wireless Set will be as follows :-
   From les FOSSES Farm to PICK CAVE O.7.b.7.3.. as soon as
   the RED Line is reached.
   Thence to HILL SUPPORT O.2.d.1.5 as soon as the GREEN
   Line is reached)..
   (b) Three Telephone routes will be laid forward to this point, O.4.c.9.9., as soon as possible.

3. A Divisional Visual Station will be established in the first instance at N.12.b.9.5. and later another at the Southern end of BOIS du VERT. This Station can work to Stations at BOIRY-NOTRE-DAME and ARTILLERY HILL
   Brigades must arrange for Visual Stations within their own Brigades.

4. The following Codes will be used :-

   (a) STATION CODE CALLS (4th Division No. G.A. 19/26) will be taken into use as soon as an advance is made from our original front line.

   (b) B.A.B. CODE will not be used in advance of our present front line, and no B.A.B. Code books will be taken forward in the event of an advance.

   (c) PLAYFAIR CIPHER will be used for messages in cipher between Brigade and Divisional Headquarters.
   All messages in Playfair cipher will begin and end with the letter "K".

P.T.O.

The keyword issued to Brigades under 4th Division No G.A. 19/37 will be used.

(d) **WIRELESS STATION CALLS**. The calls already allotted to Wireless Sets and Power Buzzers will not be affected by the restrictions contained in sub-para (a) above.

(e) **FIELD CIPHER** will be used by all Wireless Sets. The daily Code word as already issued to Divisional Signal company will be used.
Power Buzzer messages may be sent in clear provided that they do not contain any information which would be of value to the enemy.

A C K N O W L E D G E.

Capt for,
Lt-Colonel,
General Staff, 4th Division.

18th November, 1917.

Copies to all recipients of
4th Division Order No. 76.

SECRET.

INSTRUCTIONS NO. 3
to
4th DIVISION ORDER NO. 76.

PRISONERS OF WAR.

1. In the event of an advance prisoners of War will be sent to the Divisional Collecting Station at LES FOSSES FARM, where they will be handed over to the A.P.M.

The A.P.M. will be responsible for the escort of prisoners from the Divisional Collecting Station to the XVII Corps Cage, which will be at the PRISON, ARRAS.

(Para. XIII of 4th Division Q.R. 1014/1 dated 18th November, 1917, will be amended accordingly).

2. Brigades will immediately telegraph to Advanced Divnl. Headquarters the number of the Regiment to which prisoners belong, and place of capture.

Care must be taken to distinguish between active and Reserve Regiments.

3. Brigades will make arrangements for all suspected enemy Headquarters within their areas, to be searched for documents and maps.

All documents and maps so found will be forwarded to the Divisional Collecting Station as quickly as possible, with a written statement as to where they were found.

4. ACKNOWLEDGE.

[signature]

Captai

18th November, 1917.   for Lieut.Col. Gen.Staff, 4th Di

Copies to all recipients of
4th Division Order No. 76.

SECRET.

INSTRUCTIONS NO. 4
to
4th DIVISION ORDER No. 76.

ARTILLERY.

1. As soon as it is known that the enemy is withdrawing, the gun limbers and wagons of those batteries which are first to advance, will be moved up to positions in Squares H.33 or N.3.

2. On receipt of information that the Infantry have reached and are established on the GREEN LINE, the batteries now in rear of ORANGE HILL will move forward by batteries to positions in O.7 and O.13.

3. Subsequent moves of the Artillery will depend on circumstances, but in any case after the move mentioned in para. 2, it will not be necessary to move any guns for the support up to and protection of the Infantry on the BROWN LINE.

4. The C.R.A. will arrange for reconnaissances to be carried out well in advance so as to enable any moves that may be required to take place at short notice.

5. Artillery Brigade Commanders will move their H.Q. with those of the Infantry Brigadiers with whom they are working.

6. The C.R.A. will provide mule draught for two 6" Howitzers of the 328th Siege Battery so that they can move to a position about N.5.d when the advance from the GREEN LINE begins.
   This Battery (328th Siege Battery) is being placed at the disposal of the G.O.C. 4th Division for these operations.

7. Any local Artillery support, including the 6" Howitzers, will be arranged between the Infantry Brigadiers and their affiliated Artillery Brigade Commanders.

8. The only road possible for the Artillery during the early stages of the withdrawal will be -

   Main CAMBRAI road - STIRRUP LANE.

9. ACKNOWLEDGE.

H. Karslake
Lieut.Colonel,
General Staff, 4th Division.

20th November, 1917.

Copies to all recipients of
4th Division Order No. 76.

-SECRET-   4th Division No: G.A.3/205

      Please substitute attached Map for that issued with
4th Division Order No: 76.
     A C K N O W L E D G E.

                                                        Lieut Colonel,
1st December 1917.   General Staff, 4th Division.

Copies to all recipients
of 4th Divn Order No: 76.

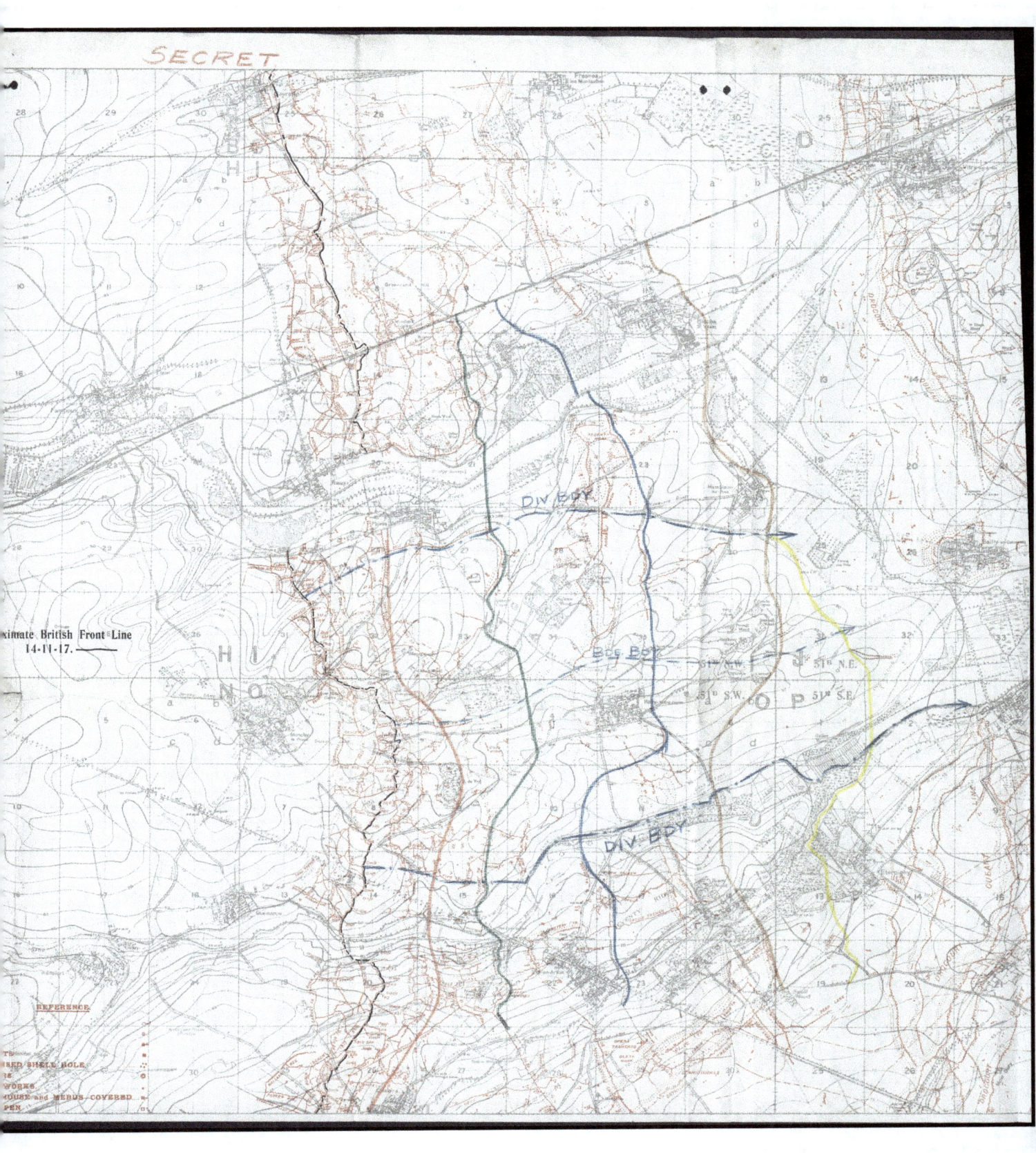

SECRET.   Copy No. 15

4th DIVISION ORDER NO. 77.

Reference attached Map.   7th November, 1917.

1. (a) A raid will be carried out by the 10th Infantry Brigade on a date and at an hour to be notified later.

   (b) The area to be raided is shown BLUE on attached Map.

2. The object of the raid is :-

   (a) To obtain identifications.
   (b) To kill Germans.
   (c) To capture or destroy material.

3. The raid will be assisted by all available Artillery, Trench Mortars and Machine Guns, and dummies.

   Details of these will be issued in the form of instructions but they will be practically as shown on the attached Map.

4. ACKNOWLEDGE.

                                                    Lieut.Colonel,
Issued at 1 pm   General Staff, 4th Division.

Copy No. 1 to G.O.C.
        2 to G.S.O.1.
        3 to 10th Brigade.
        4 to 11th Brigade.
        5 to 12th Brigade.
        6 to C.R.A.
        7 to .R.E.
        8 to A.D.M.S.
        9 to
       10 to 15th Division.
       11 to 34th Division.
       12 to 13 Squadron R.F.C.
       13 to XVII Corps.
       14 to XVII Corps H.A.
       15) to War Diary.
       16)
       17 to File.

LEGEND.

Area to be raided.

18 pdr. Creeping barrage.

3" Stokes.

6" Newtons.

9.45" Heavy.

4.5" and 6" Hows.

Machine Guns.

60 pdr. Shrapnel.

Dummies.

Smoke (18 pdr).

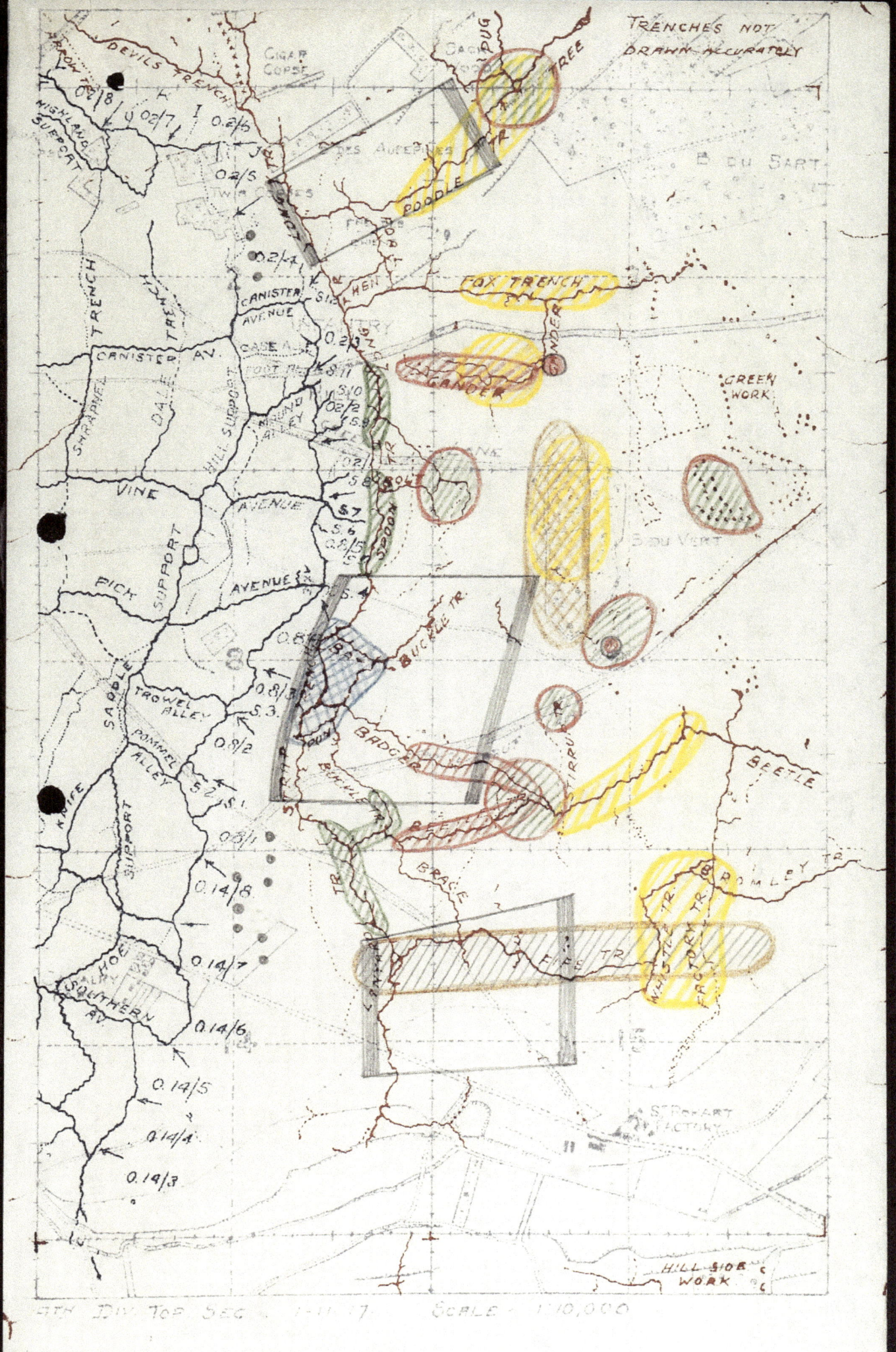

S E C R E T.   Copy No. ..17..

Reference 4th Division Order No. 77 (para. 1 (a))
dated 7th November, 1917.

ZERO hour will be 6.20 AM on 20TH November, 1917.
This information will not be communicated by
telephone or telegraph.

ACKNOWLEDGE.

                                                       [signature] Captain.
                                                      for Lieut.Colonel,

19th November, 1917.   General Staff, 4th Division.

Copies to all recipients of
4th Division Order No. 77.

S E C R E T.

INSTRUCTIONS NO. 1
to
4th DIVISION ORDER NO. 77.

TRENCH MORTARS.

1. Instructions No. 1 issued on November 7th are cancelled.

2. Trench Mortars will assist the raid to be carried out by the 10th Infantry Brigade as under :-

Mortars	Group	No. of guns	to be found by.
3" Stokes	A	6	10th Brigade.
	B	6	11th Brigade.
	C)	6	12th Brigade.
	D)		
	E	6	15th Division.
6" Newtons	F	1	
	G	1	
	H	1	
	K	1	
	L	4	

9.45" Heavy. M N as shown on attached map.

3. Targets for each group are shown on attached map.

4. All Mortars will open fire at ZERO and will maintain the following rates of fire :-

ZERO to ZERO plus 18 mins.   3" Stokes   8 r.p.g.p.m.
                             6" Newtons   3   -do-
                             9.45" Heavy.   rapid.

ZERO plus 18 mins to   3" Stokes   4 r.p.g.p.m.
ZERO plus 25 mins   6" Newtons   2 r.p.g.p.m.
                             9.45" Heavy   rapid.

ZERO plus 25 mins.   All Mortars cease fire.

5. All Mortars to be in position with all ammunition and carefully registered on their own targets by 3 p.m. on the 19th instant.

6. The D.T.M.O. will report to 10th Infantry Brigade Headquarters and Div. Headquarters by 6 p.m. on the 19th inst., that all Mortars are ready, using the word "DONE"

7. To cut the wire and not draw unnecessary attention to the impending raid the D.T.M.O. will arrange the the following bombardments:-

(a) On the 12th instant at 6.30 a.m. a concentrated Trench Mortar bombardment will be carried out on LANYARD Trench from BEETLE Trench Southwards, the bombardment to last 20 minutes.

(b) On the 15th instant at 6.45 a.m. a concentrated Trench Mortar bombardment will be carried out on FOAL Trench, the bombardment to last 20 minutes.

P.T.O.

(c) On the 19th instant at 7 a.m. a concentrated bombardment by Trench Mortars on the wire between PUN and BAT Trenches.
Instantaneous fuzes to be used so that the wire will be completely destroyed; bombardment to last 20 minutes.

8. The G.O.C. 10th Infantry Brigade must report by 3 p.m. on the 19th instant if he is satisfied that the wire is sufficiently cut. If he is not, another bombardment will take place at 7 a.m. on the 20th instant, but this should not be done if it possible to avoid it.

9. All Mortars no longer required will be withdrawn under Brigade arrangements during the night 20/21st instant.

10. ACKNOWLEDGE.

[signature]
Lt-Colonel,
General Staff, 4th Division.

13th November, 1917.

Copies to all recipients of
4th Division Order No. 77.

SECRET.

INSTRUCTIONS NO. 2
to
4th DIVISION ORDER NO 77.

MACHINE GUNS.

1. Machine guns will assist the raid to be carried out by the 10th Infantry Brigade as under :-

No gun is to fire over the heads of the raiding party.

Group	No. of guns	to be found by.
I	4	34th Division.
II	3	10th M.G.Company.
III	4	-do-
IV	4	-do-
V	6	12th M.G.Company.
VI	6	-do-
VII	6	234th M.G.Company.
VIII	6	-do-
	39 guns	

2. The targets for each group are shown on attached map.

3. All machine guns will open fire at ZERO hour and will maintain the following rates :-

ZERO to ZERO plus 7 mins. - one belt per gun per two mins.

ZERO plus 7 mins to ZERO plus 12 mins. - one belt per gun per four mins.

ZERO plus 12 mins to ZERO plus 25 mins. - one belt per gun per three mins.

ZERO plus 25 mins - all guns cease fire.

4.(a) All guns will be in position and ready with water, ammunition etc., by 3 p.m. on the 19th instant.

(b) The D.M.G.C. will report to the 10th Infantry Brigade H.Q. and Div H.Q. at 6 p.m. on the 19th instant that all guns are ready.
The word "GOOD" will be used to convey this information.

5. The ammunition in the battle emplacements required for S.O.S. purposes is to be maintained over and above that to be used for this operation.

6. All guns not required for defensive purposes will be withdrawn under Brigade arrangements at any time after 12 noon on the 20th instant.

7. ACKNOWLEDGE

H.Barnstable
Lt-Colonel,
General Staff, 4th Divn.

12th November, 1917

Copies to 10th Brigade   D.M.G.C.
            11th Brigade.   D.T.M.C.
            12th Brigade   15th Division.
            O.R.A.   34th Division

S E C R E T -   INSTRUCTIONS NO: 3
                          to

               4th DIVISION ORDER NO: 77
                    -------ooOoo-------

                     ARTILLERY.

1.   Instructions No. 3 issued on November 7th are cancelled.

2.   The raid by the 10th Infantry Brigade will be assisted by all available artillery as under :-

        The actual attack, and the northern attack by dummies, will be assisted by a creeping barrage of 50% H.E and 50% Shrapnel.

        All creeping barrages will begin at ZERO, just in front of the enemy front line.

        At ZERO plus 1½ minutes, the barrage will begin to move at the rate of 100 yards in two minutes.
        The barrage will halt when the BOX, as shown on attached map has been completed.

        At ZERO plus 25 minutes, all guns will cease fire.

3.   Rates of fire for 18-pdrs in the creeping barrage -

        ZERO to ZERO plus 12 minutes ...... 4 rounds p.g.p.m.

        ZERO plus 12 mins to ZERO plus
               18 minutes   3   "   "

        ZERO plus 18 mins to ZERO plus
               25 minutes   2   "   "

        Rates of fire for 4.5" Hows -

        ZERO to ZERO plus 25 minutes ...... 3 rounds p.g.p.m.

        Rates of fire for 6" Hows -

        ZERO to ZERO plus 18 minutes 3   "   "

        ZERO plus 18 mins to ZERO plus
               25 minutes   1   "   "

4.   Prior to, and after the raid, the normal S.O.S lines will be adhered to in case of hostile attack.

5.   A C K N O W L E D G E.

                                            H. Ranstall
                                            Lieut: Colonel,
13th November 1917.   General Staff, 4th Division.

Copies to all recipients of
4th Division Order No. 77.

Cancelled — See attached A

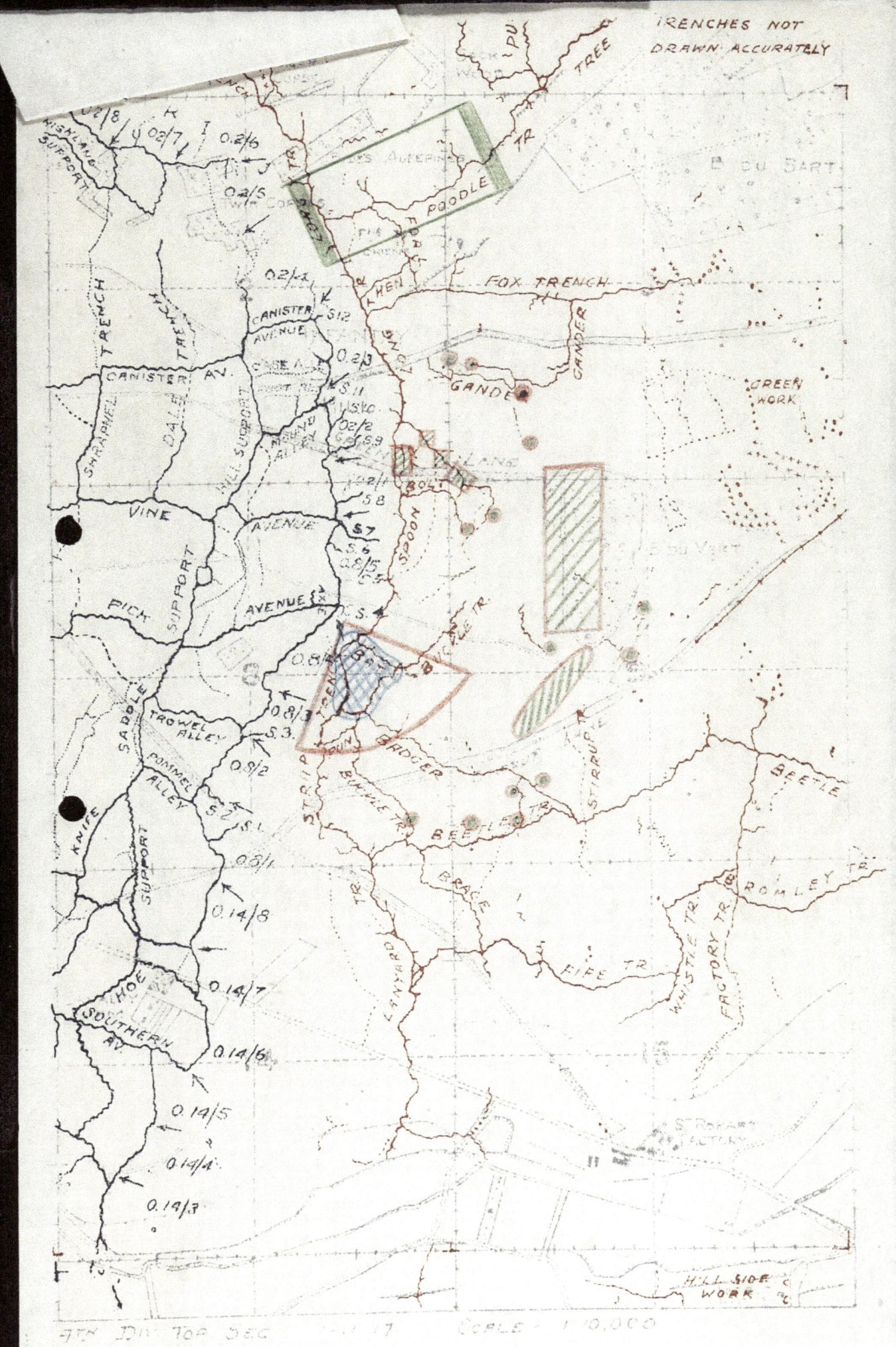

S E C R E T.

AMENDMENT No. 1
to
INSTRUCTIONS No. 3
to
4th DIVISION ORDER NO. 77.

ARTILLERY.

Para 2 line 7 - "At ZERO plus one minute", will be amended to read "At ZERO plus 1½ minutes".

Capt for,
Lt-Colonel,
General Staff, 4th Division.

19th November, 1917.

Copies to all recipients of
4th Division Order No. 77.

SECRET.   4th Div. G.A. 79/32

Reference Instructions No. 3 to 4th Division Order No. 7

Delete para. 3 and substitute –

Rates of fire for 18 pdrs. in the creeping barrage :-

ZERO to ZERO plus 5 mins.	4 rds. p.g.p.m.
ZERO plus 5 mins. to ZERO plus 12 mins.	3 rds. "
ZERO plus 12 mins. to ZERO plus 17 mins.	4 rds. "
ZERO plus 17 mins. to ZERO plus 25 mins.	2 rds. "

Rates of fire for 4.5" Hows.

ZERO to ZERO plus 25 mins.	3 rds. p.g.p.m.

Rates of fire for 6" Hows.

ZERO to ZERO plus 12 mins.	2 rds. p.g.p.m.
ZERO plus 12 mins. to ZERO plus 18 mins.	1 rd. "

H. Hanslash
Lieut. Colonel,
General Staff, 4th Division.

16th November, 1917.

Copies to all recipients of
4th Division Order No. 77.

SECRET.

INSTRUCTIONS NO. 4
to
4th DIVISION ORDER NO. 77.

DUMMIES.

1. In order to prolong the front of attack during the raid by the 10th Infantry Brigade and to draw fire off the point to be raided, two attacks will be made by dummies.

One attack just North of the CAMBRAI road consisting of 5 groups of 2 dummies each.

One attack North of CANISTER AVENUE consisting of two groups of 8 dummies each.

2. The dummies will be raised directly the barrage begins and will be kept up till ZERO plus 7 minutes when they will be lowered.

3. The dummies will be placed in position during the night preceding the raid and will be taken in during the night after the raid.

The whole of the work connected with the dummies will be supervised by Major CHURCHILL (attached Div.H.Q.) who will arrange direct with the 10th and 12th Inf.Bdes. for training the necessary personnel who will work the dummies.

4. ACKNOWLEDGE.

[signature]

Lieut.Colonel,

7th November, 1917.   General Staff, 4th Division.

Copies to all recipients of
4th Division Order No. 77.

SECRET.

4th Division No. G.A. 79/22

10th Inf. Brigade (5)
12th Inf. Brigade (5)

With reference to 4th Division Order No: 77, Instructions No: 4, will you please arrange for a copy of the following instructions to be given to each of the Officers in command of, and with the parties operating the Dummies.

1. Dummies will be placed in position by 12 midnight, 19/20th November, as follows :-

    <u>A Position</u>. 16 Dummies between O.2.d.15.95 and O.2.b.13.08.

    These Dummies will be operated by the party of 1st King's Own Rgt under Lieut: HALLETT.

    <u>B Position</u>. 40 Dummies between O.14.a.78.60 and O.14.a.85.90

    These Dummies will be operated by party of the Household Battalion under Lieut: BLACKBURN.

2. Dummies for use in A Position will be taken up on the night of the 18/19th November, and stored in DALE TRENCH at O.2.c.65.70 till the night of the 19/20th.

    Dummies for use in B Position will be stored at CRATER SUBWAY, O.7.d.3.0, till the night 19/20th November.

3. The Dummies will be raised directly the barrage begins, and will be kept up till ZERO plus 7 minutes, when they will be lowered.

4. The Dummies will be taken in by their respective parties on the night of the 20/21st and will be brought back, those from A position to FEUCHY CHAPEL Cross roads, and stored under cover; those from B position to LES FOSSES FM, and stored under cover.

A.P. Churchill Major
for Lieut: Colonel,
General Staff, 4th Division

18th November 1917.

SECRET.

INSTRUCTIONS NO. 5
to
4th DIVISION ORDER NO. 77.

SMOKE.

1.   Should the wind be favourable smoke will be liberated by means of 'P' bombs along the whole Divisional front, with the following exceptions :-

    (a) No smoke bombs will be thrown out between POMMEL ALLEY and PICK AVENUE.

    (b) If the wind is favourable generally but it is South of West no smoke bombs will be thrown out between GORDON AVENUE and POMMEL ALLEY.

    (c) If the wind is favourable generally but the wind is North of West no smoke bombs will be thrown out between PICK AVENUE and GREEN LANE.

2.   The signal for throwing out the smoke bombs will be the beginning of the Artillery barrage.

    The smoke will be maintained for 20 minutes.

3.   The 10th and 12th Inf.Bdes. will arrange for the throwing out of these smoke bombs within their own areas allowing 20 'P' bombs for every hundred yards of front.

13th November, 1917.   Sgd. H. Karslake. Lt.Colonel,
                                        General Staff, 4th Division.

S E C R E T.   4th Div. G.R. 93.

            Reference Instructions No. 5 to 4th Division
        Order No. 77.

            Para. 2 - for 30 minutes read 20 minutes.

                                        H. Hunlatle
                                        Lieut. Colonel,
    14th November, 1917.   General Staff, 4th Division.

    Copies to all recipients of
    4th Division Order No. 77.

-SECRET-

INSTRUCTIONS FOR DISCHARGE OF SMOKE

In connection with the Raid to be carried out by 10th Infantry Brigade on 20th November 1917, in accordance with 4th Division Order No. 77 etc.

-------oOoOoOo-------

1. UNITS DETAILED TO THROW.

The Divisional Gas Officer will be responsible for discharge of Smoke along the Divisional front at ZERO Hour on the 20th instant. He will have at his disposal for this purpose, the following Infantry personnel, divided into sections, as under :-

    1 Officer)
    2 N.C.Os.)
    13 Men.   )
) of the Household Battalion.
    1 Officer.)
    2 N.C.Os.)
    13 Men.   )

    1 Officer)
    2 N.C.Os.) of 1st King's Own. Rgt.
    1 Officer.)
    2 N.C.Os.)

    1 Officer.)
    2 N.C.Os.)
    15 Men.   ) of 2nd Essex Rgt.
    1 Officer.)
    2 N.C.Os.)
    15 Men.   )

2. FRONTAGE OF DISCHARGE.

Should the wind be favourable, smoke will be liberated along the whole Divisional front on the 20th instant, with the following exceptions :-

    (a) No Smoke (no matter the direction of the wind) will be discharged between POMMEL ALLEY and PICK AVENUE.

    (b) If the wind is favourable generally, but it is South of West, no smoke will be liberated between GORDON AVENUE and POMMEL ALLEY.

    (c) If the wind is favourable generally, but it is North of West, no smoke will be liberated between PICK AVENUE and GREEN LANE.

    (d) The positions of the "Dummies" between O.2.d.1.9 - O.2.b.1.0, and between O.14.a.7.6 - O.14.a.8.9 must not be screened by smoke.

3. DISPOSITION OF THROWERS.

One man will be placed every 20 yards along the front line trench, between the Right boundary of the Division, and POMMEL ALLEY except due West of "Dummies" in O.14.a, and between PICK AVENUE and CANISTER AVENUE.

                                                       F. T.

4. DUTIES OF SECTION OFFICERS.

The Officers i/c Sections (referred to in para.1) will be responsible for the correct placing of the throwers. They will satisfy themselves that each N.C.O and man of their section knows his throwing position, and is fully conversant with his duties. They will each establish a Section Control Post in the front line, which will be their H.Qrs. They will also see that each position is provided with the number of "P" Bombs etc as mentioned below.

5. NUMBER OF "P" BOMBS, ETC, PER MAN

Each man will have at his position, 12 "P" Bombs already detonated,& 25 Smoke Candles, 3 hours before ZERO. He will also possess a brassard 'Fort Fires', for the purpose of lighting damp smoke candles, will be provided.(at the rate of 2 per thrower).

6. METHOD OF THROWING.

In order to obtain a dense cloud immediately, each man will throw 2 "P" Bombs in quick succession. The remaining "P" Bombs and smoke candles will then be thrown as per time table below. This will maintain a cloud for 20 minutes.

Time	Item	Time	Item
At ZERO	2 "P" Bombs.	ZERO + $9\frac{1}{2}$ mins	1 S.Candle.
+ $\frac{1}{2}$ min	1 S.Candle.	+ 10 "	1 "P" Bomb
+ 1 min	1 "P" Bomb.	+ $10\frac{1}{2}$ "	1 S.Candle.
+ $1\frac{1}{2}$ "	1 S.Candle.	+ 11 "	1 "
+ 2 "	1 "P" Bomb.	+ $11\frac{1}{2}$ "	1 "
+ $2\frac{1}{2}$ "	1 S.Candle.	+ 12 "	1 "
+ 3 "	1 "P" Bomb.	+ $12\frac{1}{2}$ "	1 "
+ $3\frac{1}{2}$ "	1 S.Candle.	+ 13 "	1 "
+ 4 "	1 "P" Bomb.	+ $13\frac{1}{2}$ "	1 "
+ $4\frac{1}{2}$ "	1 S.Candle.	+ 14 "	1 "
+ 5 "	1 "P" Bomb.	+ $14\frac{1}{2}$ "	1 "
+ $5\frac{1}{2}$ "	1 S.Candle.	+ 15 "	1 "
+ 6 "	1 "P" Bomb.	+ $15\frac{1}{2}$ "	1 "
+ $6\frac{1}{2}$ "	1 S.Candle.	+ 16 "	1 "
+ 7 "	1 "P" Bomb.	+ $16\frac{1}{2}$ "	1 "
+ $7\frac{1}{2}$ "	1 S.Candle.	+ 17 "	1 "
+ 8 "	1 "P" Bomb.	+ $17\frac{1}{2}$ "	1 "
+ $8\frac{1}{2}$ "	1 S.Candle.	+ 18 "	1 "
+ 9 "	1 "P" Bomb.		

7. SIGNAL FOR DISCHARGE.

The discharge will take place at ZERO Hour (during the early morning) on the 20th instant. The signal for discharge will be the opening of Artillery barrage. Officers and N.C.O's should satisfy themselves that this is clearly understood by the men. ZERO hour will be notified later.

8. ISSUE OF "P" BOMBS, ETC.

Brigades will be responsible that units are issued with the requisite number of smoke producers as mentioned in the above allotment (paras 5 and 9).

9. LOCAL RESERVE OF "P" BOMBS, ETC.

At each Section Control Post, there will be a small reserve of 24 "P" Bombs and 50 S.Candles. These are to replace any useless Smoke producers that may be discovered prior to ZERO Hour.

10. **POSITION OF GAS OFFICER.**

The Gas Officer will be at PICK CAVE. Officers i/c Sections referred to in para. 1 will report to him at 4 a.m on 20th instant, when watches will be synchronised. They will also arrange for an Orderly to report to Gas Officer at 5.30 a.m with a report "ALL READY".

11. **TELEPHONES.**

G.O.C, 12th Inf. Bde will arrange for a telephone to be at PICK CAVE from 3 a.m onwards in communication with 12th Inf. Bde H.Qrs. This telephone will only be used by the Divnl Gas Officer.

12. **WIND OBSERVATION.**

N.C.Os of Sections will make frequent observations on the direction of wind. They will report the result of their observations to their Section Officers, who will, if he deems the wind unfavourable, report that fact to and the direction of the wind, to the Gas Officer.

13. **WARNING OF DANGEROUS WINDS.**

A wind report will be sent out from Divisional H.Qrs to the following, by Priority wire, at about ZERO minus 3 hours.

    10th Inf. Brigade.
    12th Inf. Brigade.
    C.R.A.
    Div Gas Officer.

In this message, the following code words will be used :-

" SMOKE will be discharged ...."JOPPA "
" SMOKE will NOT be discharged ...."JOPPA OFF "

Should the wind turn unfavourable after the word "JOPPA" has been sent out, the Divisional Gas Officer may cancel the discharge. Should he do so, he will immediately notify all concerned.

Similarly, should the wind turn unfavourable within a few minutes of ZERO, the Section Officers referred to in para. 1 will use their discretion as to whether they discharge all or part of their smoke.

14. **DIVNL GAS N.C.Os.**

Divnl Gas N.C.Os attached to Right and Left Bdes will report to Gas Officer at PICK CAVE at 4 a.m on 20th instant.

Lieut: Colonel,
General Staff, 4th Division.

19th November 1917.

App. 3

4th Div. G.A. 79/23.

XVII Corps.

Reference XVII Corps No. G.34/31 dated 26/10/17

REPORT ON RAID CARRIED OUT BY 12th INF. BDE. ON NIGHT 15th/16th NOVEMBER.

(a) 2nd Lieut. WALDEN, 2nd Lan.Fus.
(b) 1 Officer and 20 other ranks, 2nd Lan.Fus.
(c) LONG TRENCH between O.2.b.4.5. - O.2.b.5.0.
(d)(e) At ZERO hour, 2 a.m. as the raiding party was getting out of their starting trench one of our 3" STOKES mortar bombs fell amongst them and disorganised them. They advanced as quickly as they could after this but were not able to make up lost time. Just as they reached the enemy's trench (at ZERO plus 10 mins.) the signal for the party to return was given on a bugle. The party had to return as according to the programme our Artillery barrage was coming back on to the portion of trench to be raided at ZERO plus 15 mins.
The misdirection of the STOKES Mortar bomb cannot be accounted for.
(f) NIL.
(g) 1 Officer missing believed killed and 1 o.r. missing.
(h) The time allowed to carry out the raid (10 mins.) does
(i) not appear to have been sufficient. From earlier reconnaissances the ground in NO MANS LAND appeared to have been in better condition than it really was.

(sgd) T. G. MATHESON.

Major General,
Commanding 4th Division.

18th November 1917.

SECRET.   Copy No. ..18..

4th DIVISION ORDER NO. 78.

17th November, 1917.

1. There will be a bombardment of the enemy's trenches East of MONCHY on 18th November, in accordance with the attached Table.

2. ZERO hour will be 3 p.m.

3. Smoke will be discharged along the whole Divisional front from ZERO to ZERO plus 10 minutes, in accordance with 4th Div. G.A. 1/143 dated 14th November, 1917.

4. G.Os.C. 10th and 12th Inf.Brigades will arrange for all available 3" STOKES Mortars to bombard the enemy's front trenches from ZERO to ZERO plus 10 minutes.

5. Separate instructions will be issued for the co-operation of Machine Guns.

6. ACKNOWLEDGE.

Issued at 2.30 p.m.   Captain,
                                          for Lt.Col. Gen.Staff, 4th Div.

x Issued to 10th, 12th Inf.Bdes. C.R.A., C.R.E., D.G.O.

Copy No. 1 to G.O.C.
         2 to G.S.O.1.
         3 to 10th Brigade.
         4 to 11th Brigade.
         5 to 12th Brigade.
         6 to C.R.A.
         7 to C.R.E.
         8 to A.D.M.S.
         9 to A.P.M.
        10 to Signals.
        11 to 234th M.G.Coy.
        12 to D.M.G.O.
        13 to 21st West Yorks.(Pioneers).
        14 to 15th Division.
        15 to 34th Division.
        16) to XVII Corps.
        17)
        18) to War Diary.
        19)
        20 to Div.Gas Officer.
        21 to File.
        22 to Q

TO ACCOMPANY 4th DIVISION ORDER NO. 76

TABLE OF TASKS FOR FONCHY SECTOR BOMBARDMENT.

UNIT	NATURE OF GUNS	TASKS.	AMMUNITION.	RATES OF FIRE	REMARKS
4th Div.Arty.	18 pdrs.	(i) Enfilade FOX TRENCH O.2.d 60.82 to O.3.c 60.90. (ii) Enfilade HEN O.2.d 55.90 to O.2.b 84.12. (iii) Enfilade POODLE TRENCH O.2.b 38.30 to I.33.c 55.10.	Rds. 18 pdrs. 1100 4.5" Hows. 200 6" Stokes. 150.	18 pdrs. 3 rds.p.g.p.m. 4.5" Hows. 2 rds.p.g.p.m.	
	4.5" Hows. & 6" Stokes Mortars.	Bombard LONG TRENCH O.2.d 68.60 to O.2.b 35.35.			
15th Div.Arty.	18 pdrs.	(i) Bombard DEVILS TRENCH O.2.b 30.75 to I.32.c 82.10. (ii) Bombard Trench I.32.d 25.55 to I.32.d 40.78. Bombard LONG TRENCH O.2.b 35.35 to O.2.b 30.75.	18 pdrs. 400 4.5" Hows. 80		
	4.5" Hows.				
Corps H.A.	6" Hows. (5 Btys.)	(i) Bombard FOAL O.2.d 82.95 to O.2.b 59.52. (ii) Bombard TREE TRENCH I.33.c 70.28 to I.33.c 78.60. (iii) Bombard T.M. Empl. I.33.c 12.41. (iv) Bombard Trench I.33.c 19.60 to I.32.d 85.75. (v) Bombard I.32.d 10.60 to I.32.d 00.50 and I.32.d (5.3) to I.32.d 25.55.	6" Hows. 200	6" Hows. 1 rd.p.g.p.m.	
	6" Hows.) 1 Bty.) 8" How.) 9.2" Hows.)	C.B. work as required.	as required.		

MACHINE GUN TABLE OF TASKS FOR MONCHY SECTOR BOMBARDMENT IN CO-OPERATION WITH ARTILLERY.

Date	Unit	No: of Guns.	Tasks	Time	Remarks
November 18th	10th M.G.Coy	2	POODLE TRENCH from O.3.a.2.6 to I.33.c.c.5.	3 p.m to 3.10 p.m.	One belt every four minutes from Zero - Zero plus 10 mins.
18th	11th M.G.Coy	2	TREE TRENCH in I.33.c.	—do—	—do—
18th	234th M.G.Coy	1	FOX TRENCH in C.3.c HAVERSACK LANE in I.33.c.	—do—	—do—

[signature]
for Lieut: Colonel,
General Staff, 4th Division.

17th November 1917.

CONFIDENTIAL

App. 5

4th Division No. G.D. 79/22

XVII Corps.

Reference XVII Corps No. G. 34/31 dated 26th October, 1917.

The following report on raid carried out by the 12th Infantry Brigade during the night of 17/18th November is forwarded for your information :-

(a) Lieut. WHITE, 1st Kings Own (R.L.) Regt was in charge of the raiding party.

(b) Raiding party consisted of 2 Officers and 25 O.R. of 1st Kings Own (R.L.) Regt.
   This party was divided into :-

   "A" or Right Party, strength 1 Officer and 8 O.R.
   "B" or Left Party, strength 1 Sgt and 8 O.R.
   "C" or Covering Party, strength 1 Officer and 8 O.R.

(c) The Objective was LONG Trench in square O.2.d., in the neighbourhood of its junction with HEN Trench.
   Object of Raid :-

   (i) To capture prisoners.
   (ii) Obtain identification.
   (iii) Kill Germans.

(d) "A" PARTY under Lieut WHITE on reaching the German trench, worked up it in a Northerly direction for about 30 yards when they found 2 Germans in a shelter. They took them prisoner, and as the left party did not appear to be advancing towards them, they withdrew.
   Lieut WHITE had one prisoner and two of his party had the other. The latter were missing until 2 a.m. on the 18th instant, when one of the two came in wounded. He reported that a bomb had fallen among them, had killed the German prisoner and wounded the other man and himself.

   "B" PARTY under a Sergt reached a point within 10 yards of LONG Trench when a hostile Machine Gun opened fire. A bomb was thrown by one of the party and two Germans jumped up. These were both shot.
   The Sergt having been delayed by Machine Gun fire, considered the time allowed was up, so he brought his party back.

   "C" PARTY "The covering party" split in half during the advance. The left portion returned to our lines when "A" Party under Lieut WHITE withdrew. The right portion, however would appear to have lost its way, and is still missing.
   Careful search has been made over the ground, both after the raid and on the night 18/19th, but no trace has been found of the missing men.

(e) & (f). One prisoner of the 179th I.R., 24th Division was brought back to our lines.

(g)   Lieut HART and 6 O.R. missing.

(h)   From all accounts the artillery and Trench Mortar barrage was excellent.

(i)   In order to assist the raiders in returning to our lines it is considered advisable to light some pre-arranged signal „ a lamp or flare, at some distance behind our trenches, to ensure their returning in the right direction.

19th November, 1917.

Major General,
Commanding 4th Division.

SECRET.   Copy No. 19

4th DIVISION ORDER NO. 79.

19th November, 1917.

1. The 11th Infantry Brigade will relieve the 12th Infantry Brigade in the Left Sector of the Divisional front, the relief to be completed by 6 a.m. on the 25th instant.

2. The Machine Guns of the 12th Infantry Brigade will be relieved by those of the 11th Infantry Brigade before the reliefs of the front line Battalions take place.

All other details of relief will be made between the Brigadiers concerned.

3. All working parties and guards now found by the 11th Infantry Brigade will be taken over by the 12th Infantry Brigade.

The arrangements for these reliefs must be such as not to cause any interruption in the work.

4. The G.O.C. 11th Infantry Brigade will take over command from the G.O.C. 12th Infantry Brigade on completion of the relief.

5. ACKNOWLEDGE.

Issued at 8 p.m.

Lieut.Colonel,
General Staff, 4th Division.

Copy No. 1 to G.O.C.
2 to G.S.O.1.
3 to 10th Brigade.
4 to 11th Brigade.
5 to 12th Brigade.
6 to C.R.A.
7 to C.R.E.
8 to A.D.M.S.
9 to Q.
10 to Signals.
11 to A.P.M.
12 to 234th M.G.Coy.
13 to D.M.G.O.
14 to 21st West Yorks (Pioneers).
15) to XVII Corps.
16)
17 to 15th Division.
18 to 34th Division.
19) to War Diary.
20)
21 to File.

CONFIDENTIAL

4th Division No.G.D.79/22/1

app. 7.

XVII Corps.

Reference XVII Corps No.G.34/31 dated 26th October 1917.

The following report on raid carried out by the 10th Infantry Brigade on the morning of the 20th November, is forwarded for your information :-

(a) Captain C.C.OAKEY, 1st Royal Warwickshire Regt was in charge of the raiding party.

(b) The raiding party consisted of 4 Officers and 153 O.R. of the 1st Royal Warwickshire Regt, and was organised as follows :-

    (i) 3 Officers and 10 Assaulting Groups. Each Group consisted of 1 N.C.O. and 8 men, total 3 Officers and 90 O.R.
    (ii) 7 protective Groups. Each Group consisted of 1 N.C.O. and 6 men. Nos.1 and 7 were Lewis Gun detachments and Nos.2 to 6 Bombing Groups, total 49 O.R.
    (iii) O.C., raid 2 stretcher bearers and 6 runners, total 1 Officer and 14 O.R.

(c) The area to be raided was the German front and support line in O.8.b.& d., Bounded on the north by BAT trench and on the South by BADGER trench.

(d) At ZERO hour (6.20 a.m.) our barrage opened on the German wire in front of the area to be raided, and the raiding party advanced from our lines. The barrage remained stationary for 1½ minutes, it then moved forward at the rate of 50 yards per minute. Raiding party had no difficulty in finding the gaps in the German wire, as our trench mortars had carried out their task of cutting the wire in a most efficient manner. The raiding party found the German trenches very badly damaged by our bombardment, and encountered very little opposition. 3 Germans were killed in the sap at O.8.b.5.1. Another 3 were killed in the sap at O.8.b.5.0. A machine gun was also captured and brought back to our lines. There was a little sniping from the enemy in BAT trench, also some bombing, but they were driven back by our bombers and riflemen. 4 dead Germans were found in this trench. Dug-outs were found at following places :-

    A two entrance dug out about 20 yards North of the junction of BADGER and STRAP trenches. One entrance had been completely blown in, and the other partially damaged. Grenades were thrown down the latter entrance, but it is not certain whether this dug out was occupied. The bodies of two dead Germans were found outside it. About 5 to 8 Germans were seen running down BADGER trench. They were fired at and 5 were killed.
    Another two entrance dug-out was discovered about 20 yards North East of the junction of BAT and STRAP trenches. One entrance had been blown in and the other partially damaged. Grenades and P. bombs were thrown down the latter entrance and shouts were heard.
    Another entrance to a dug out was found in BAT trench about 10 yards from its junction with BUCKLE trench, with another entrance in BUCKLE trench. Two Stokes bombs were thrown down each of these entrances both of which had been hit by our shells. BUCKLE trench was empty and no dead Germans were seen.

(e) & (f) The result of the raid may be summed up as follows :-

    The enemy's trenches in area raided were all badly damaged

by our bombardment, several dug outs were blown in and about 20 Germans were killed by the raiders. In addition one machine gun was captured.

(g) Our casualties were one Officer wounded, 8 O.R. wounded (one still at duty) and 4 O.R. missing.

(h) GENERAL

During the raid there was a certain amount of sniping from about O.9.c.1.6. A few Germans could be seen running about while others were using their rifles. Raiders fired on them from BUCKLE Trench and claim to have hit 3.

A machine gun was firing from about O.8.d.8.6. There was some trip wire between the German front and support line.

On the whole the raiding party met with very little opposition. It would appear that the enemy holds his line lightly by day, bringing up men at night to strengthen it. The small parties which were seen retiring may have been leaving the front line after "Stand to".

The trenches were very shallow, most places only about 4 feet deep, without fire steps, and only the support line was revetted, and that only in one place.

Unfortunately no Germans were brought in, as those encountered at close quarters were obstinate, and had to be killed.

The dead Germans were examined but had no shoulder straps on their uniform. However an identification of the 139 I.R. was obtained from a document found on a dead body.

Directly the raiding party returned to our lines, the enemy attempted to follow them across "NO MANS LAND" in considerable strength estimated at about 60. Fire was opened on them with all available Lewis Guns, and they were driven back to their own trenches.

Dummy figures were employed at some distance on the flanks of the raid, and drew considerable artillery fire. The discharge of smoke in connection with the raid was most satisfactory.

The enemy's barrage was put down quickly and fell behind our front line and on our support line.

          (sgd) T.G.MATHESON.

             Major General,
         Commanding 4th Division.

21st November 1917.

app 8.

Distribution of units.
after relief of 12 Bde by 11 Bde.

App. 8

- SECRET -   - 4th DIVISION -

DISPOSITION AND MOVEMENT REPORT

Situation at 12 noon, 28th Nov. 1917

Serial No:	UNIT	Present position.	Moves tomorrow	Remarks
1.	4th Divnl. H.Qrs.	G.21.c.3.5 N.9.c.9.7		
2.	10th.Inf. Bde H.Qrs.	N.9.c.9.7		
3.	Household Battalion.	N.12.a.0.4	G.27.b.4.8	
4.	1st R.Warwick Rgt.	O.7.d.4.0	H.32.c.5.5	
5.	2nd Seaforth Highrs.	H.32.c.5.5	O.7.d.4.0	
6.	3/10th Middlesex Rgt	G.27.b.4.8	N.12.a.0.4	
7.	10th M.G.Coy.	N.10.d.1.8		
8.	10th T.M.Bty.	N.8.d.6.7		
9.	11th Inf. Bde H.Qrs	N.5.a.3.8		
10.	1st Somerset. L.I.	O.2.c.22.10		
11.	1st East Lancs Rgt.	O.7.b.65.25		
12.	1st Hampshire Rgt.	N.3.b.8.3		
13.	1st Rifle Brigade.	O.1.c.8.1		
14.	11th M.G.Coy.	N.4.b.85.40		
15.	11th T.M.Bty.	N.5.a.0.9		
16.	12th Inf. Bde H.Qrs	G.27.d.35.95		
17.	1st King's Own Rgt.	G.32.d.8.5		
18.	2nd Lancs Fusrs.	G.27.a.7.8		
19.	2nd W.Riding Rgt.	G.27.b.0.8		
20.	2nd Essex Rgt.	G.27.b.8.1		
21.	12th M.G.Coy.	G.28.a.10.28		
22.	12th T.M.Bty.	G.27.d.90.98		
23.	21st W.Yorks Rgt.	N.1.a.0.9		
24.	9th Field Coy R.E.	N.12.a.3.2		
25.	526th -do-	N.2.d.5.7		
26.	408th -do-	N.2.d.4.6		
27.	10th Field Amb.	G.21.c.3.4		
28.	11th -do-	H.31.c.6.5		
29.	12th -do-	K.36.d.5.1		
30.	29th Bde R.F.A.	N.9.b.3.0		
31.	32nd -do-	N.5.a.7.4		
32.	4th Divnl. Amm Col.	G.32.c.7.6		
33.	4th Divnl. Train.	ACHICOURT		
34.	234th M.G.Coy.	G.27.b.8.6		

J.H. Fraser. Capt.
for
Major General,
Commanding 4th Division.

SECRET.   Copy No.......

4th DIVISION ORDER NO.80

27th November, 1917.

1. On the 29th instant the 10th Infantry Brigade will extend its left to Sap 4 inclusive.

2. The Boundary between the two Brigades will then run immediately North of PICK EVENUE to the CAMBRAI Road and thence as at present.

3. The accommodation in PICK CAVE will remain as at present with the left Brigade.

4. Details of the adjustment will be made between the Brigadiers concerned.

5. Completion to be reported to Divisional Headquarters.

6. ACKNOWLEDGE.

H. Havelock
Lt-Colonel,
General Staff, 4th Division.

Issued at.. 10 am

Copies to :-
```
        No. 1 to G.O.C.
            2    G.S.O. I.
            3    10th Infantry Brigade.
            4    11th Infantry Brigade.
            5    12th Infantry Brigade.
            6    C.R.A.
            7    C.R.E.
            8    21st West Yorks (Pioneers).
            9    234th M.G.Company.
           10    A.D.M.S.
           11    Signals.
           12    4th Divn. "Q".
           13)
           14)   War Diary.
           15    File.
```

SECRET.   Copy No. 20

4th DIVISION ORDER NO. 81.

27th November, 1917.

1. The following reliefs will be carried out :-

   (a) <u>27th/28th.</u>   10th Inf.Bde. will extend Northwards and
                           will relieve the right Battalion of the
                           11th Inf.Bde. which will move to Camp at
                           BOIS DES BOEUFS.

   (b) <u>28th.</u>   10th Inf.Bde. will again extend its left as
                           far as CASE ALLEY (0.2.d 45,65) inclusive.

   (c) <u>28th.</u>   One Battalion 11th Inf.Bde. to WILDERNESS
                           CAMP
                           One Battalion 10th Inf.Bde. from ARRAS to
                           BOIS DES BOEUFS.

   (d) <u>28th/29th.</u>   11th Inf.Bde. will extend its left to
                           SCABBARD Trench exclusive relieving the 44th
                           Inf.Bde. of the 15th Division.

2. On completion of the above reliefs the Division will be disposed as follows :-

   <u>Right front Brigade</u> - 2 Bns. front line.
                                 1 Bn. Support.
                                 1 Bn. BOIS DES BOEUFS.

   <u>Left front Brigade</u>   - 2 Bns. front line.
                                 1 Bn. Support.
                                 1 Bn. WILDERNESS CAMP.

   <u>Reserve Brigade</u>   - ARRAS.

   Brigades will forward to Divisional H.Q. not later than the 30th instant, a Map showing their dispositions by Companies showing all H.Q.

3. The Boundary between Brigades will be -

   0.2.d 45.65 - CANISTER (inclusive to Left Brigade) - CIRCLE Trench (inclusive to Left Brigade) - DEAD HORSE CORNER - thence due West.

   The Boundary between the 4th and 15th Divisions will be SCABBARD Trench (inclusive to 15th Division) - junction of RIFLE Trench and BAYONET Trench (I.25.a 0.1) - H.30.d 35.00 - H.36.a 15.60 - thence due West.

4. All details of reliefs will be made between Brigadiers concerned.
   Each Brigadier will assume Command of his new area on completion of relief.

Brig.General MacNaughton, C.M.G., D.S.O., C.R.A. 15th Division will assume command of the Field Artillery covering the Right Division of the XVII Corps at 10 a.m. on the 29th instant.

6. Readjustment of the R.E. and Pioneer dispositions and of the Medical arrangements will be made between the C.R.Es. and A.Ds.M.S. concerned.

7. The G.O.C. 4th Division will assume Command of the new front on the completion of the relief of the 44th Inf.Bde. by the 11th Inf.Bde.

8. ACKNOWLEDGE.

H. Kamslake

Issued at 4 p.m.

Lieut.Colonel,
General Staff, 4th Division.

Copy No. 1 to G.O.C.
        2 to G.S.O.1.
        3 to 10th Brigade.
        4 to 11th Brigade.
        5 to 12th Brigade.
        6 to C.R.A.
        7 to C.R.E.
        8 to A.D.M.S.
        9 to A.P.M.
       10 to Pioneers.
       11 to D.A.O.C.
       12 to 204th M.G.Coy.
       13 to Signals.
       14 to A.
       15 to Div.Gas Officer.
       16 to 15th Division.
       17 to 34th Division.
       18)
       19) to XVII Corps.

       20)
       21) to War Diary.

       22 to File.

       23 to XVII Corps H.A.
       24 to 13th Sqdn. R.F.C.

SECRET.

ADDENDUM NO. 1
to
4th DIVISION ORDER NO 81.

1. (a) 10th Infantry Brigade will take over Vickers Gun positions from 11th Inf.Bde. as under :-

   S.2   S.3   S.4.

   (b) 234th M.G.Coy. will take over Vickers Gun positions from 11th Inf.Bde. as under :-

   R.10   R.10 a.

   (c) 234th M.G.Coy. will take over Vickers Gun positions from 10th Inf.Bde. as under :-

   I.1   I.2.

2. Vickers Guns will then be found by Companies as under :-

   <u>10th M.G.Coy.</u>   S.1   S.2   S.3   S.4
                          R.1   R.2   R.3   R.4

   <u>11th M.G.Coy.</u>   R.5   R.6   R.8   R.9
                          and those now found by 44th Inf.Bde.

   <u>234th M.G.Coy.</u> I.1   I.2   I.3   I.4
                          R.7   R.10 R.10 a R.11

3. The Vickers Guns at present at I.5 I.6 I.7 I.8 will be replaced by Lewis Guns of the Battalions occupying those posts.

4. The changes of Vickers Guns as ordered in para. 1 will take place under arrangements to be made between Brigadiers and D.M.G.O. but to be completed by the morning of December 1st, 1917.

5. ACKNOWLEDGE.

H. Karslake
Lieut.Colonel,
General Staff, 4th Division.

27th November, 1917.

Copies to all recipients of
4th Division Order No. 81.

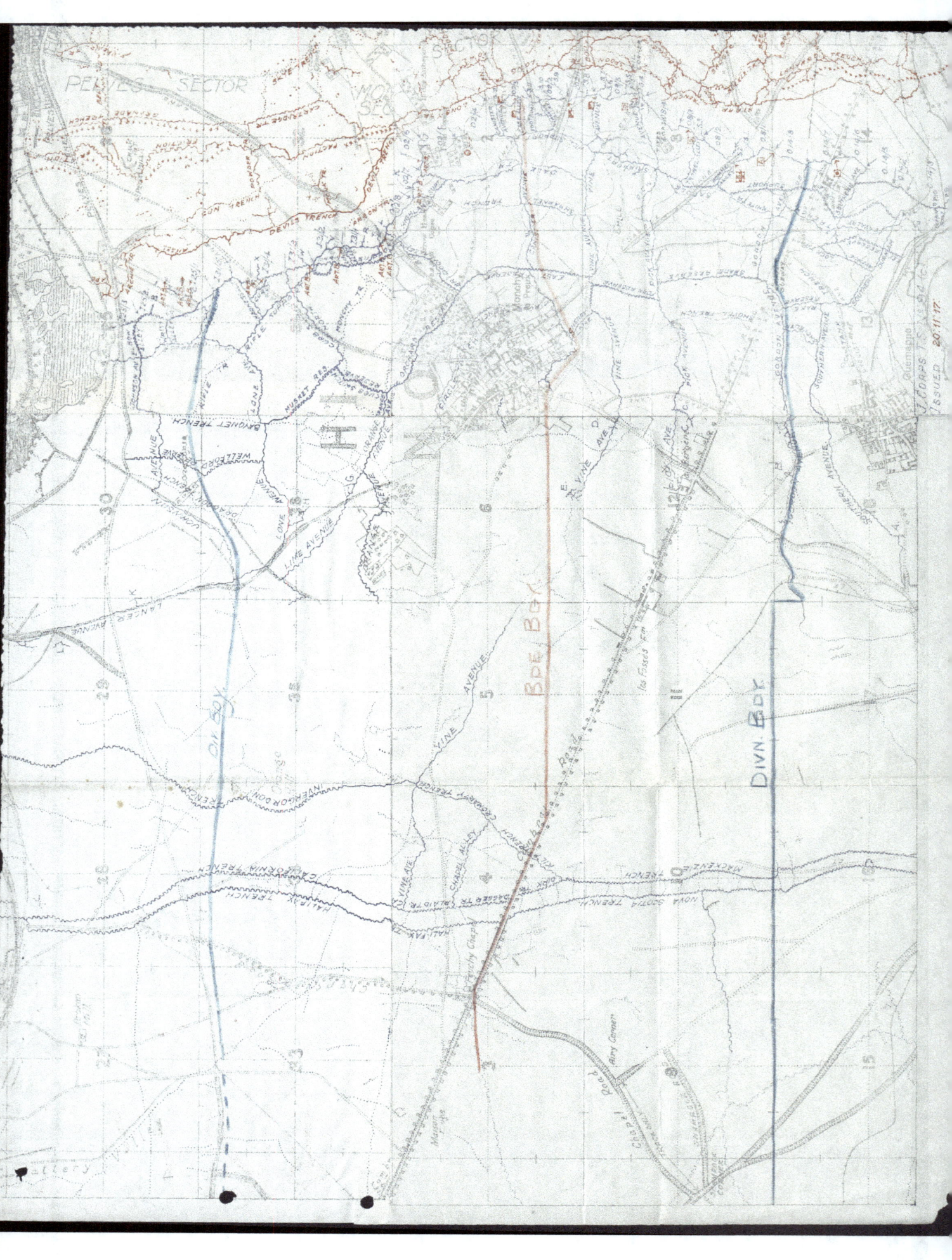

SECRET.

Copy No. 22

4th DIVISION ORDER NO. 82.

28th November, 1917.

1. At ZERO hour on December 1st, 1917, provided the wind is suitable, a Gas bombardment with Stokes Mortars will be carried out on the enemy's front trenches by No. 1 Special Co.R.E.

2. The Mortars will be in four sections, the positions of which, and their targets, are shown on attached Map.

3. (a) The programme for the Stokes Mortars will be :-

   ZERO minus 30 seconds - all Mortars fire five rounds of THERMIT.
   ZERO - all Mortars fire rapid up to 13 rounds of C.G. per Mortar.
   ZERO plus 1½ minutes to ZERO plus 13½ minutes - firing will be intermittent, N.C. and P.S. being used.
   ZERO plus 13½ minutes to ZERO plus 15 minutes - burst of rapid fire with C.G.

   (b) The wind required is between N.N.W. through West to S.W.

4. (a) As a precautionary measure all trenches in the areas shaded BLACK on the attached Map must be evacuated between ZERO and ZERO plus 20 minutes, except the dugouts in the Support Line. All ammunition left in the Saps must be protected. All men in trenches in the intervening spaces in front of the Mortars will wear their Respirators from ZERO minus 5 minutes till ZERO plus 20 minutes.

   (b) No Saps will be re-occupied until an Officer or N.C.O. of the Special Co. has reported them as safe.
   The 10th and 11th Infantry Brigades will arrange direct with the O.C. No. 1 Special Co. R.E. for an Infantry Officer to inspect the Saps with the Officer or N.C.O. of the Special Co.

5. At ZERO all available Artillery and Machine Guns will open fire on all Communication Trenches and roads East of the Western edge of the BOIS DU VERT. Harassing fire will then be kept up for the remainder of the night. The D.M.G.O. will arrange targets with the C.R.A.

6. The O.C. No. 1 Special Co. R.E. will be responsible that the Gas is not projected if the wind is dangerous.
   He will report to Brigades and Divisional Headquarters at once if the operation cannot take place. In the event of the operation not taking place the word "WRONG" will be sent to both Divisional Headquarters and Brigade Headquarters who will at once inform the Artillery Groups.
   He will be at Battalion Headquarters, PICK CAVE, at 5 pm December 1st.

7. Patrols will be sent out at 4 a.m. December 2nd to gain touch with the enemy; by this hour there will be no danger from the Gas but possibly in places a slight Lachrymatory effect may be produced which is quite harmless.

8. ZERO hour will be 7 p.m.

9. An Officer of the Divisional Staff will be at Battalion Headquarters, PICK CAVE, at 3 p.m. December 1st to synchronise watches; the following will attend :-
    1 Officer per Battalion in the front line.
    1 Officer per Machine Gun Company.
    1 Officer per section of No. 1 Special Co. R.E.
    1 Officer per Trench Mortar Battery.

This same officer will be at LES FOSSES FARM at 4 p.m. to synchronise watches; the following will attend :-
    1 Officer per Infantry Brigade Headquarters.
    1 Officer per Artillery Brigade Headquarters.
    1 Officer per R.F.A. Battery.

10. ACKNOWLEDGE.

H. Harsdale
Lieut.Colonel,
General Staff, 4th Division.

Issued at 5 p.m.

Copy No. 1 to G.O.C.
    2 to G.S.O.1.
    3 to 10th Brigade.
    4 to 11th Brigade.
    5 12th Brigade
    6 to C.R.A.
    7 to C.R.E.
    8 to A.D.M.S.
    9 to A.P.M.
    10 to Signals.
    11 to 254th M.G.Coy.
    12 to D.E.G.O.
    13 to Pioneers.
    14 to Div. Gas Officer.
    15 to Q.
    16 to 15th Division.
    17 to 34th Division.
    18 to O.C. No. 1 Special Coy. R.E.
    19)
    20) to XVII Corps.

    21 to XVII Corps H.A.
    22)
    23) to War Diary.

    24 to File.

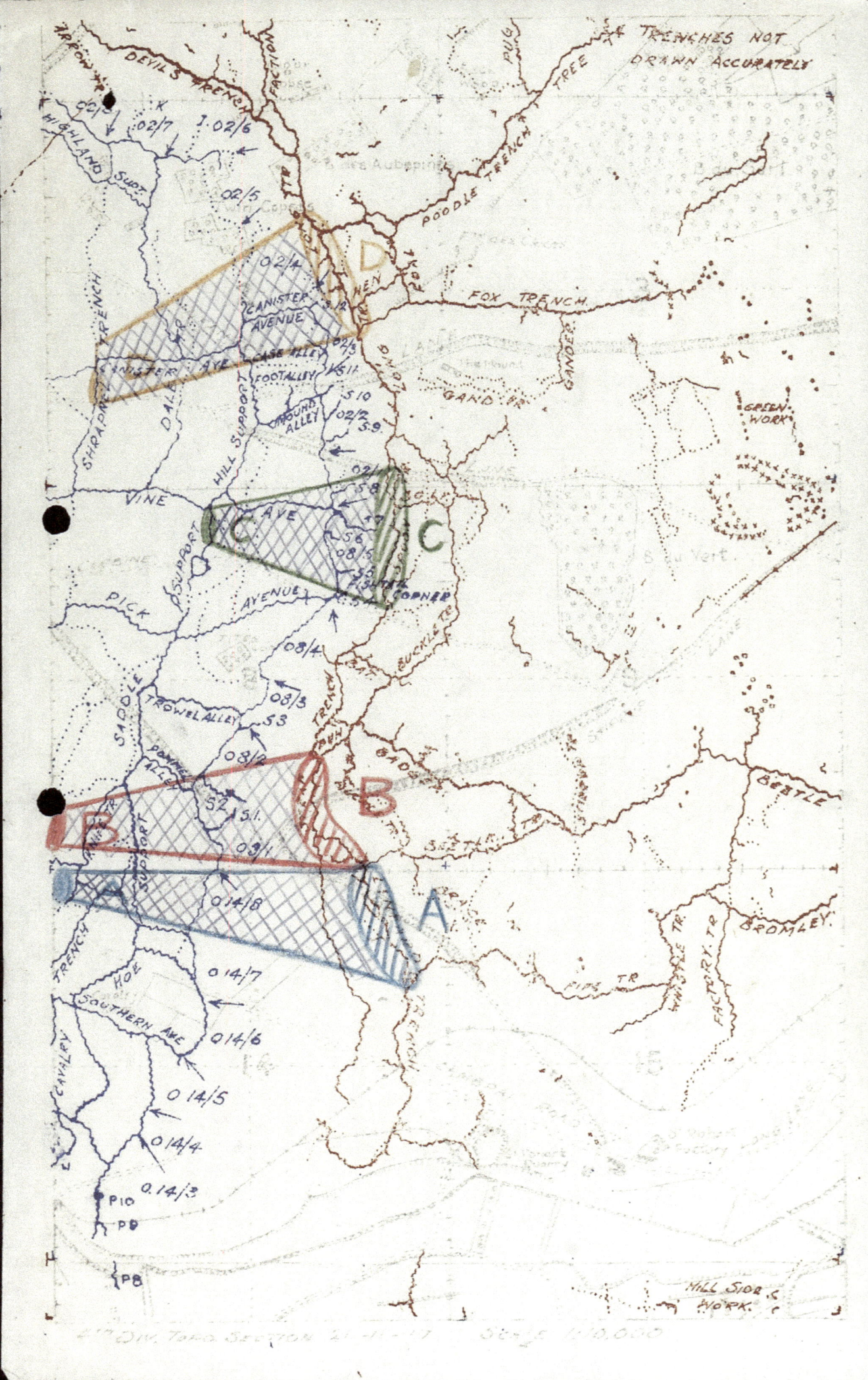

SECRET.

ADDENDUM NO. 1
to
4th DIVISION ORDER NO. 82.

Machine Gun co-operation with artillery will be as under :-

1. Right Bde.   3 guns FIFE Trench from O.15.a.60.40 to
                             O.15.b.35.40.
    254th M.G.Coy   3 guns BEETLE Trench from O.9.c.55.28 to
                             O.9.d.35.55.
    Right Bde.   1 gun STIRRUP Lane from O.9.c.55.75 to
                             O.9.c.90.85.
    254th M.G.Coy.   2 guns STIRRUP Lane from O.9.c.90.85 to
                             O.9.b.50.40.
    Left Bde.   3 guns INFANTRY Lane from O.3.c.60.70 to
                             O.3.d.50.75.
    Left Bde   3 guns FOX Trench from O.3.c.60.90 to
                             O.3.d.50.95.

2. Time of fire :-

    ZERO to ZERO plus 16 minutes

        6 bursts of 45 rounds each
            at the following times :-
        ZERO plus 4 minutes.
        ZERO plus 8 minutes.
        ZERO plus 10 minutes.
        ZERO plus 14 minutes.
        ZERO plus 16 minutes.

3. Harassing fire will be carried out during the night as already arranged after ZERO hour.

4. ACKNOWLEDGE.

                                        H. Kanedall
                                        Lt-Colonel,
30th November, 1917.   General Staff, 4th Division.

Copies to all recipients of
4th Division Order No. 82.

SECRET.   Copy No. ...19...

4th DIVISION ORDER NO. 83.

28th November, 191

1.   (a) The 12th Infantry Brigade will relieve the 10th
         Infantry Brigade in the Right Sector of the
         Divisional front on the 2nd and 3rd December.

     (b) The relief of the Infantry to be completed by
         6 a.m. on December 3rd.

     (c) The Machine Guns will be relieved after the
         relief of the Infantry has been completed.

2.   All working parties and guards now found by the
12th Infantry Brigade will be taken over by the 10th
Infantry Brigade.

3.   The G.O.C. 12th Infantry Brigade will assume Command
of the Sector on completion of the relief of the Infantry.

4.   ACKNOWLEDGE.

                                              Lieut.Colonel,
Issued at 5 p.m.   General Staff, 4th Division.

Copy No. 1 to G.O.C.
         2 to G.S.O.1.
         3 to 10th Brigade.
         4 to 11th Brigade.
         5 to 12th Brigade.
         6 to C.R.A.
         7 to A.D.M.S.
         8 to A.P.M.
         9 to Signals.
        10 to Q.
        11 to Pioneers.
        12 to 25th M.G.Coy.
        13 to D.A.G.O.
        14 to Div.Gas Officer.
        15 to 15th Division.
        16 to 24th Division.
        17)
        18) to XVII Corps.
        19)
        20) to War Diary.
        21 to File.

App.13

- SECRET -   - 4th DIVISION -

DISPOSITION AND MOVEMENT REPORT

Situation at 12 noon 29th Nov 1917.

Serial No.	UNIT	Present position	Moves tomorrow	Remarks
1	4th Divn H.Qrs	G.21.c.3.5		
2	10th In. Bde H.Qrs	N.9.c.9.7		
3	Household Battalion	H.32.c.5.6		
4	1st R.Warwick Rgt	O.7.b.65.25		
5	2nd Seaforth Highrs	O.7.d.3.0		
6	5/10th Middlesex Rgt	N.12.a.0.4		
7	10th M.G.Coy	N.10.d.1.8		
8	10th T.M.Bty.	N.8.d.6.7		
9	11th Inf. Bde H.Qrs	N.5.a.3.8		
10	1st Somerset L.I	O.1.c.7.1		
11	1st East Lancs Rgt	H.31.a		
12	1st Hampshire Rgt	H.36.b.5.4		
13	1st Rifle Brigade	I.31.c.3.1		
14	11th M.G.Coy	N.4.b.85.40		
15	11th T.M.Bty	N.5.a.0.9		
16	12th Inf. Bde H.Qrs	G.27.d.35.95		
17	1st King's Own Rgt	G.32.d.8.5		
18	2nd Lancs Fusrs	G.27.a.7.8		
19	2nd W.Riding Rgt	G.27.b.0.8		
20	2nd Essex Rgt	G.27.b.6.1		
21	12th M.G.Coy	G.28.a.10.28		
22	12th T.M.Bty.	G.27.d.90.98		
23	21st W.Yorks Rgt	N.1.a.0.9		
24	9th Field Coy R.E	N.12.a.3.2		
25	526th -:-	N.2.d.5.7		
26	406th -:-	N.12.a.1.4		
27	10th Field Amb.	G.21.c.3.4		
28	11th -:-	H.31.c.6.5		
29	12th -:-	K.36.d.5.1		
30	29th Bde R.F.A	N.9.b.3.0		
31	32nd -:-	N.5.a.7.4		
32	4th Div Ammn Col.	G.32.c.7.6		
33	4th Divnl Train.	ACHICOURT		
34	2/4th M.G.Coy	G.27.b.8.6		

Major General,
Commanding 4th Division.

4th Division
War Diaries
General Staff

December 1917

Army Form C. 2118.

WAR DIARY
or
INTELLIGENCE SUMMARY.
(Erase heading not required.)

Summary of Events and Information	Remarks and references to Appendices

Quiet day. Western edge of N.6. Ranenaped with 10.5"cm + few shell. Gas bombs + shrapnel carefully proper(?) by Hog Sound (?) Bn but enemy hindered according to programme. Enemy opened a heavy barrage on Front + Support lines almost immediately

N.34.d. shelled constantly throughout the morning. Shews recently fell on N. edge of MONCHY.

Very little hostile artillery activity. Enemy aircraft active very scarce. Valley. One H.V. shell fell in ARRAS. Following reliefs took place:-
Right Sector 11th Bde relieved 10th Bde. 10th Bde moved to ARRAS.
Left Sector Somerset L.I. relieved 16 R.T.R. a 8th Bn to Sector. R.B. moved to Wilderness Camp. East Lancs. relieved Rampo Bgt in left subsector troops coming to MONCHY Defences. No supporting troops to Spandeler's in the Bays line for R.E. a companies at 16th Bn and MG RAL. (Others heavy men in bivouacs).

G. Quiet day.
Hostile artillery inactive enemy TMs fired a few rounds on Mulhan Support + Chin Support.
A. Quiet day. H.M. Salient was much used by the division on our left.

WAR DIARY
or
INTELLIGENCE SUMMARY.

(Erase heading not required.)

Army Form C. 2118.

Instructions regarding War Diaries and Intelligence Summaries are contained in F. S. Regs., Part II. and the Staff Manual respectively. Title pages will be prepared in manuscript.

Place	Date	Hour	Summary of Events and Information	Remarks and references to Appendices
Arras	7		Monday shelled intermittently with S.O.S. Throughout morning. Arras shelled with H.V. gun during the morning. Following relief complete. Right Sector: Lancashire Fusiliers relieved Kings Own to right Subsector – Kings Own to Brown Line. Duke of Wellington's relieved Essex in Left Subsector – Essex to Bois des Boeufs. Left Sector: R.B.s relieved Som. L.I. in right Subsector. Som L.I. to Wilderness Camp. Staffs relieved East Lancs in Left Subsector. East Lancs to Monchy Avenue.	(a) app. 2
	8		A few gas shells and light Trench Mortars near Tank Copses during the night. Enemy Artillery active on Essex Avenue in am 4360+d Order 54 issued (a) 9/10 Brigade relieved 11th Bde in Left Sector in 10/11th without incident.	(b) app. 3
	9		About 30 gas shells fell in Bois S.J. Artillery Mortars during the morning over estaminet. The Division came to in a state of readiness in case of enemy attack from 10th m.n.	(c) app. 4
	10		A quiet day – Occasional Trench Mortar fire on Chain Support Active own Squadrons 012 ad 0.8 Order 56 issued Bde relieved Bns from Bois des Boeufs and Wilderness Camps not more to act remain in the Brown line on	
	11		12ʰ December. Enemy Nothing less active than usual – Slight Retaliation in reply to on T.M. fire. Orders 57 issued (a) 3rd A.F.A. Bde into Corps into action on right. 14/12. Discuherical Corps under orders of C.R.A. 4ᵗʰ Div. Relief by 11ᵗʰ Bde by 10ᵗʰ Bde in Left Sector completed in accordance with Bde Order 54 for disposition see Appendix (a).	(a) app. 5 (b) app. 6
	12		Quiet day. No unusual activity shown by enemy.	
	13		Shrapnel Traced slightly shelled during morning. Enemy Trench Mortars active on our Front line O.B/3.	

WAR DIARY
or
INTELLIGENCE SUMMARY.
(Erase heading not required.)

Army Form C. 2118.

Place	Date	Hour	Summary of Events and Information	Remarks and references to Appendices
Arras	14		Hostile Artillery active on Reserve Line and Front Area — Mostly heavy stuff during afternoon.	
"	15		Orchard Reserve heavily shelled during the morning — A raid was carried out by 2nd Essex (12th Bde) with the object of capturing prisoners. Enemy wires was fair back on Buckle Trench when entered and searched. No enemy could be found in the area raided. (a) 11th Bde came relieve 12th Bde in Right Section on 15/9/17 (b) 11th Bde HQ issued 88 'O'ma at.	App 7 App 8
"	16		Quiet day — Order on.	
"	17		Hostile Trench Mortars active — Enemy Artillery inactive — Order S.9 issued (b)	
"	18		Hostile Artillery Slightly 15 cm and 10 cm howitzers active on Right Brigade Front especially on Front Trench and area between "Tommel" and "Foote". None not badly damaged.	App 9
"	19		Quiet day. Relief of 12th Brigade by 11th Brigade in Right Sector completed in accordance with Order 68. For Disposition see Appendix (a)	
"	20		Very Quiet day — Slight Trench Mortar Activity on Junction of Pick Ave and Front Line C.	
"	21		A few hostile Trench Mortars on our Front Line C, apparently in retaliation for our T.M. fire. On all nights a raid by party 9th O. German against the Household Battalion was repulsed leaving one dead German in our hands. Our casualties were 1 Officer Killed 11 OR? wounded — (b)	App D

Army Form C. 2118.

WAR DIARY
or
INTELLIGENCE SUMMARY.
(Erase heading not required.)

Place	Date	Hour	Summary of Events and Information	Remarks and references to Appendices
ARRAS	22/12	-	Quiet day	
"	23/12	"	Intermittent shelling in vicinity of KNIFE and LADLE Trench. O.S.C. A few slight stabs fell on our front-line trenches about midday. Orders A.A. Issued (a) 12 Para went return 10 A.M. in left Sector of front front on 26/27 Dec. Report on enemy raid on Y Sap (held by 1st R. Berwicks) (b) Scheme of relief complete. MONCHY Section. Searchlights returned staffs in right out sector. Apps. to outpost. "" "" "" "" middleness no left out sector. middleness to reserve. CAMBRAI Rd Section. R. Bns. returned Somersets in right out sector. G.H.I. to outpost. "" "" "" "" "" in left- "" "" changes to reserve. Hamps R.	(a) See app. 11 (b) See app. 12
"	24/12	-	Hostile artillery inactive. Enemy T.M. activity considerably below normal.	
"	25/12	-	Quiet day	
"	26/12	-	Slight hostile T.M. activity in S.39 & and at about midday and about N.3 central obtained with 8" obella at the vicinity of 1 or 2 a minute. Enemy aircraft active over our lines.	

WAR DIARY
or
INTELLIGENCE SUMMARY.
(Erase heading not required.)

Army Form C. 2118.

Place	Date	Hour	Summary of Events and Information	Remarks and references to Appendices
ARRAS	27/12	—	"Quiet" Heavy enemy Tm. bombardment of water tanks at 21.S.9 & 8.H where unavailable damage was done. Relief of 10th Hants. bn. 12 A.M. to handover with in day 8.0 invisible 23/12/17. Two machine guns aff [S]. In the Right Section Lyttonian vehicles were carried out. Forwards returns Rts. in Right e of centre. Etc. were to span Lanes & support "Front Lines", Noncombat R., two left a subsection. Somp.R. to form back Reserve	App. 13.
	28/12	"	Quiet - Clear. Our E.A. Guns fired 15 shooting near an spare Im. the two remnants being captured.	
	29/12	"	A larger Tm. shell with 4.2's during the morning & also a few shells near MONCHY, otherwise very quiet day.	
	30/12	"	Intermittent shelling of MONCHY, hostile artillery otherwise quiet. Stretch minimum of no active against our front & support lines in O.3. Hellmann b. move took place. 4th bn. from ARRAS to Wilderness Camp. 2nd bn. from After the Corner to ARRAS. 5th bn. Moves from the Corner to ARRAS. 6th bn. Moves from Wilderness Camp to ARRAS. Australians from ARRAS to Paris des Grands.	

WAR DIARY
or
INTELLIGENCE SUMMARY.

Army Form C. 2118.

(Erase heading not required.)

Place	Date	Hour	Summary of Events and Information	Remarks and references to Appendices
ARRAS	2/6/18	—	Reliefs of troops in Eastern Rd Sector completed. 11-Bde. R.130. relieved Canadians in Right outpost; 2h.l. 18 men sent home to outpost. 21st under R " 2nd " " left - " " " MENCHY Section. 12 Bde. 1am. 5ro. relieved Range Arm in Right outposts; R.O. to outpost. Dustns " relief in Left " " " " " ready to receive.	
"	3/6/12	"	About 12 men every ford a number of 4.20 an SADDLE support; FORM RENIRE, and PICA Avenue, otherwise quiet; any 11 fale in Right Sector on Order 91 under (a) 10 fale with relieve 3/4 Dan 1B1S.	App 14

SECRET

FILE No. **G.12.**

Sub-Nos. 180-

SUBJECT. Minor Operations.

Sub-head. Attempted Enemy Raid on 4 Divn. on 21 Decr, 1917.

XVII Corps.

Referred to	Date.	Referred to	Date.

S E C R E T.   Third Army No. G.12/180.
XVII Corps No. G.28/14.
4th Division No. G.D.79/34.

XVII Corps.

The following is an account of the attempted German Raid on the evening of 21st December :-

At 5.15 p.m. the enemy put down a heavy Trench Mortar and Artillery barrage on our front and support lines for about 50 yards North and South of Sap 12. At the same time hostile machine guns firing from the North swept the Sap.

At 5.20 p.m. the machine gun fire ceased and an enemy party of some 30 strong rushed Sap 12 on both sides.

Lewis guns in CANISTER AVENUE just West of the entrance to the Sap and the Lewis gun in SHELL crater a little further North opened fire.

The Lewis gun section of the 1st East Lancashire Regt. also opened fire from about O.2.d.5.7.

Some 4 or 5 Germans succeeded in entering the Sap and ceased hold of a man of the Household Battalion. The rest of the garrison of the Sap, led by Cpl.DAVIS, Household Battalion, immediately attacked the enemy with the bayonet. All the Germans with the exception of one who was killed managed to escape through a gap where the Sap had been blown in. On their return some of the raiders were dispersed by their own Minenwerfer falling amongst them.

As soon as the German barrage opened at 5.15 p.m. our artillery opened fire on their S.O.S. lines without waiting for the signal.

The enemy barrage died down at about 5.45 p.m. and our artillery also ceased firing.

As a result of the raid one dead German belonging to the 6th Company, 179 I.R., 24th Division (SAXON), remained in our hands and many are believed to have been wounded. None of our men are missing.

Our front line was effectually blocked by large craters on both sides of raided area. Our support line was badly damaged.

Our casualties are - 1 Officer, 2/Lt.BIRD killed, and two N.C.Os. and 4 men wounded, all of the Household Battalion. These casualties were all caused by the hostile barrage.

I consider that great credit is due to the artillery for their prompt action and to all ranks of the Company of the Household Battalion concerned, for the manner in which they dealt with the situation.

23rd December, 1917.
(Sgd). T.G.MATHESON. Major-General.
Commanding 4th Division.

2.

Third Army.

Forwarded for information and return please.

25/12/17.
(Sgd) J.R.C.CHARLES. B.G.
for G.O.C., XVII Corps.

3.

XVII Corps.

Returned as requested.

Third Army.
27/12/17.
(Sgd). Louis Vaughan. M.G. G.S.

WAR DIARY, GENERAL STAFF, 4th DIVISION.

1st - 31st DECEMBER.
1917.

APPENDICES.

1. Dispositions 3rd December.
2. Order 81.
3. Order 85.
4. Order 86.
5. Order 87.
6. Dispositions 11th December.
7. Order 88.
8. Order 89.
9. Dispositions 19th December.
10. Report on attempted enemy raid against Household Battalion (10th Brigade) evening 21st December.
11. Order 90.
12. Report on enemy raid on Y Sap (held by 1st R.Warwicks) 23rd December.
13. Dispositions 27th December.
14. Order 91.
15. 4th Division Defence Scheme

Appendix 1

- SECRET - - 4th DIVISION -

DISPOSITION AND MOVEMENT REPORT

Situation at 12 noon 3rd December/17

Serial No.	UNIT	Present position	Moves tomorrow	Remarks
1	4th Divn H.Qrs.	G.21.c.3.5		
2	10th Inf. Bde H.Qrs	G.27.d.9.8		
3	Household Battalion	G.27.b.0.3		
4	1st R.Warwick Rgt	G.27.b.8.1		
5	2nd Seaforth Highrs	G.27.a.7.8		
6	3/10th Middlesex Rgt	G.21.c.2.0		
7	10th L.G.Coy	G.28.a.10.25		
8	10th T.M.Bty	G.27.d.90.98		
9	11th Inf. Bde H.Qrs	N.5.a.3.8		
10	1st Somerset L.I	I.31.c.5.1		
11	1st East Lancs Rgt	H.36.b.5.4		
12	1st Hampshire Rgt	C.b.c.7.1		
13	1st Rifle Brigade	H.31.a		
14	11th L.G.Coy	N.4.b.65.40		
15	11th T.M.Bty.	N.5.a.0.9		
16	12th Inf. Bde H.Qrs	N.9.c.9.7		
17	1st King's Own Rgt	O.7.d.4.0		
18	2nd Lancs Fusrs	N.12.a.0.4		
19	2nd W.Riding Rgt	H.32.c.6.4		
20	2nd Essex Rgt.	O.7.b.65.20		
21	12th L.G.Coy	N.10.d.1.		
22	12th T.M.Bty.	N.c.d.6.7		
23	2nd W.Yorks Rgt.	N.1.a.0.9		
24	9th Field Coy R.E	N.12.a.5.2		
25	526th -:-	N.2.d.5.7		
26	405th -:-	N.12.a.1.4		
27	10th Field Amb.	G.21.c.3.		
28	11th -:-	H.31.c.6.5		
29	12th -:-	K.36.d.5.1		
30	29th Bde R.F.A	N.9.b.3.0		
31	32nd -:-	N.5.a.7.4		
32	4th Div Amm Col.	G.32.c.7.6		
33	4th Div Train.	ACHICOURT		
34	25th L.G.Coy	G.27.b.6.6		

Major General,
Commanding 4th Division.

Appendix 2.
21

SECRET.   Copy No. ......

4th DIVISION ORDER NO. 84.

8th December, 1917.

1. The 10th Infantry Brigade will relieve the 11th Infantry Brigade in the Left Sector of the Divisional front on the 10th and 11th insts.

The Infantry relief to be complete by 6 a.m. on the 11th instant.

The relief of the Machine Guns will take place after the completion of the Infantry relief.

2. The G.O.C. 10th Infantry Brigade will assume Command of the Left Sector on completion of the Infantry relief.

3. The 11th Infantry Brigade will take over all working parties and guards now found by the 10th Infantry Brigade, arranging so as not to break the continuity of work.

4. ACKNOWLEDGE.

Lieut.Colonel,
General Staff, 4th Division.

Issued at 4 p.m.

Copy No. 1 to G.O.C.
2 to G.S.O.1.
3 to 10th Brigade.
4 to 11th Brigade.
5 to 12th Brigade.
6 to C.R.A.
7 to C.R.E.
8 to A.D.M.S.
9 to A.P.M.
10 to Q.
11 to 234th M.G.Coy.
12 to D.M.G.O.
13 to Pioneers.
14 to Div.Gas Officer.
15 to Signals.
16 to 15th Division.
17 to 34th Division.
18 to Guards Division.
19) to XVII Corps.
20)
21) to War Diary.
22)
23 to File.

Appendix 3

Copy No. 21

SECRET.

4th DIVISION ORDER NO. 85.

9th December, 1917.

1. (a) The enemy has apparently made up his mind to retake the HINDENBURG LINE during the next few days.
   (b) This effort may be made in several places and by surprise.

2. The Division will be in a state of readiness daily from tomorrow the 10th instant inclusive and the following procedure will be adopted :-
   (a) The following machine gun emplacements will be permanently manned :-

   By the Right Brigade- S1, S3, S5, S6.
   By the Left Brigade - S8, S9, S12, S13.

   (b) The Reserve Battalions of the two front Brigades will move into battle positions in the CORPS Line in their own areas by 7 a.m. daily.
   The Battalion from BOIS DES BOEUFS will be clear of FEUCHY CHAPEL cross roads by 6 a.m. and the WILDERNESS Battalion will not reach that point before 6 a.m.

   (c) The Reserve Brigade will from 6.30 a.m. daily be ready to move at half-an-hour's notice.

   (d) All dug-outs will be cleared at "Stand to" in the morning and the troops kept in a state of readiness till DISMISS is sent out by the Division.

   (e) The Artillery will "Stand to" from 6.30 a.m. till 8.30 a.m. daily.

   (f) All working parties will rejoin their units by 6.30 a.m. daily and no fresh working parties will be sent out before DISMISS is ordered.

3. As soon as DISMISS is sent out from Divisional Headquarters everything will again become normal except as in para. 2 (a) above.

4. Brigades in the front line and Divisional Artillery will report to Divisional Headquarters daily at 8 a.m. if all is quiet or otherwise on their front.

5. ACKNOWLEDGE.

Lieut.Colonel,
General Staff, 4th Division.

Issued at 11.45 p.m.

Copy No. 1 to G.O.C.
2 to G.S.O.1.
3 to 10th Brigade.
4 to 11th Brigade.
5 to 12th Brigade.
6 to C.R.A.
7 to C.R.E.
8 to A.D.M.S.
9 to A.P.M.
10 to Signals.
11 to 234th M.G.Coy.
12 to D.M.G.O.

Copy No. 13 to Pioneers.
14 to Q.
15 to Div.Gas Officer.
16 to 15th Division.
17 to 34th Division.
18 to Guards Division.
19)
20) to XVII Corps.
21)
22) to War Diary.
23 to File.

Appendix H.

Copy No. 21

- SECRET -

4th DIVISION ORDER NO 86

10th December 1917

1. On the 12th instant, the Battalions now in BOIS des BOEUFS and WILDERNESS CAMPS will move to, and remain in, the BROWN LINE.

2. Consequent on this move, para 2 (b) of 4th Division Order No. 85 will be amended to read -

   The Reserve Battalions of the two front Brigades will 'stand to' every morning at 7 a.m, until Brigades report all quiet, when they can be dismissed.

3. A C K N O W L E D G E.

Lieut Col.
General Staff, 4th Division.

Issued at 7 p.m.

Copy No. 1 to G.O.C
2 to G.S.O. I.
3 to 10th Inf. Bde.
4 to 11th Inf. Bde.
5 to 12th Inf. Bde
6 to C.R.A.
7 to C.R.E.
8 to A.D.M.S.
9 to A.P.M.
10 to Signals.
11 to 234th M.G.Coy.
12 to D..G.O.

No. 13 to Pioneers.
14 to "Q"
15 to Div Gas Offr.
16 to 15th Division.
17 to 34th Division.
18 to Guards Division.
19) to XVIIth Corps.
20)
21) to War Diary.
22)
23 to File.

Appendix 5

Copy No 21

- SECRET -

4th DIVISION ORDER NO 87

11th December 1917

1. The 315th Brigade R.F.A is going into action on the night 11th/12th inst into positions as follows :-

   Bde H.Qrs ...... N.2.b.3.

   "A" Battery H.34.d.4.8

   "B" Battery .... (H.34.c.5.9
                    (H.34.c.9.6

   "D" Battery .... (H.34.b.5.55   4 Hows
                    (N.4.b.2.7   2 Hows

   "C" Battery .... (H.28.d.75.05   2 Guns
                    (H.22.d.65.25   4 Guns

   Wagon lines at RONVILLE about G.34.

   Bde H.Qrs, 'A', 'B' and 'D' Batteries will come under the orders of the G.O.C, 4th Divisional Artillery on the 11th inst.

2. Registrations of the above Batteries will be carried out on the 12th instant.

3. B/71 now attached to the 4th Division will cease to be so attached at 12 noon on the 13th inst, and will revert to the 15th Division.

4. A C K N O W L E D G E.

Lieut Colonel,
General Staff, 4th Division.

Issued at 12 noon.

Copy No 1 to G.O.C
        2 to G.S.O.I
        3 to 10th Bde.
        4 to 11th Bde.
        5 to 12th Bde.
        6 to C.R.A.
        7 to C.R.E.
        8 to A.D.M.S.
        9 to A.P.M.
        10 to Signals.
        11 to 234th M.G.Coy.
        12 to D.V.G.C.

No 13 to Pioneers
   14 to "Q"
   15 to Div Gas Offr.
   16 to 15th Division.
   17 to 34th Division.
   18 to Guards Division.
   19) to XVIIth Corps.
   20)
   21) to War Diary.
   22)
   23 to File.

Appendix 6

- S E C R E T - — 4th DIVISION —

DISPOSITION AND MOVEMENT REPORT

Situation at 12 noon, 11th Dec.1917

Serial No.	UNIT	Present position	Moves tomorrow	Remarks
1	4th Divn H.Qrs.	G.21.c.3.5		
2	10th Inf. Bde H.Qrs	N.5.a.3.8		
3	Household Battalion.	I.31.c.5.1		
4	1st R.Warwick Rgt.	H.31.a.		
5	2nd Seaforth Highrs.	O.1.c.7.1		
6	3/10th Middlesex Rgt	H.36.b.5.4		
7	10th M.G.Coy.	N.4.b.85.40		
8	10th T.M.Bty.	N.5.a.c.9		
9	11th Inf. Bde H.Qrs	G.27.d.35.95		
10	1st Somerset L.I.	G.27.b.8.1		
11	1st East Lancs Rgt.	G.32.d.8.5		
12	1st Hampshire Rgt.	G.21.c.2.8		
13	1st Rifle Brigade.	G.27.b.7.8		
14	11th M.G.Coy.	G.28.a.10.28		
15	11th T.M.Bty.	G.27.d.90.98		
16	12th Inf. Bde H.Qrs	N.9.c.9.7		
17	1st King's Own Rgt.	O.7.d.4.0		
18	2nd Lancs Fusrs.	H.32.c.6.4		
19	2nd W.Riding Rgt.	N.12.a.c.4		
20	2nd Essex Rgt.	O.7.b.65.25		
21	12th M.G.Coy.	N.10.d.1.8		
22	12th T.M.Bty.	N.8.d.6.7		
23	21st W.Yorks Rgt.	N.1.a.c.9		
24	9th Field Coy R.E.	N.12.a.3.2		
25	526th -do-	H.35.b.95.10		
26	406th -do-	N.12.a.1.4		
27	10th Field Amb.	G.21.c.3.4		
28	11th -do-	H.31.a.6.5		
29	12th -do-	K.36.d.5.1		
30	29th Bde R.F.A.	N.9.b.3.0		
31	32nd -do-	N.5.a.7.4		
32	4th Div Ammn Col.	G.32.c.7.6		
33	4th Div Train.	ACHICOURT		
34	234th M.G.Coy.	G.27.b.6.6		

Major General,
Commanding 4th Division.

S E C R E T.   Copy No. ......

Appendix 7

4th DIVISION ORDER NO. 88.

16th December, 1917.

1.   The 11th Infantry Brigade will relieve 12th Infantry Brigade in the Right Sector of the Divisional front on the 18th and 19th instants.
   The Infantry relief will be completed by 6 a.m. on the 19th instant.
   The Machine Guns will be relieved after the relief of the Infantry has been completed.

2.   The G.O.C. 11th Infantry Brigade will take over Command from the G.O.C. 12th Infantry Brigade on completion of the Infantry relief.

3.   The 12th Infantry Brigade will take over all guards and working parties now found by the 11th Infantry Brigade.

4.   Acknowledge.

Lieut.Colonel,
General Staff, 4th Division.

Issued at 6 a.m.

Copy No. 1 to G.O.C.
        2 to G.S.O.1.
        3 to 10th Brigade.
        4 to 11th Brigade.
        5 to 12th Brigade.
        6 to C.R.A.
        7 to C.R.E.
        8 to A.D.M.S.
        9 to A.P.M.
       10 to Signals.
       11 to 234th M.G.Coy.
       12 to Pioneers.
       13 to Div.Gas Officer.
       14 to Q.
       15 to 15th Division.
       16 to 34th Division.
       17 to Guards Division.
       18) to XVII Corps.
       19)
       20) to War Diary.
       21)
       22 to File.

SECRET.

Appendix 8.

Copy No. 21

4th DIVISION ORDER NO. 89.

17th December, 1917.

1. On December 18th the Reserve Battalions of the Right and Left Brigades in the line will return from their battle positions in the Corps Line to BOIS DES BOEUFS and WILDERNESS Camps respectively.

2. From December 19th inclusive the Reserve Battalions of the two front Brigades will from 6.30 a.m. daily, till their Brigades report all quiet, be ready to move at half-an-hours notice to their battle positions in the Corps Line.

3. 4th Division Order No. 85 dated 9th December, para. 2 (b), will be amended accordingly.

4. ACKNOWLEDGE.

H. Karslake
Lieut.Colonel,
General Staff, 4th Division.

Issued at 5 p.m.

Copies to all recipients of
4th Division Order No. 85.

Appendix 9

- SECRET -   - 4th DIVISION -

DISPOSITION AND MOVEMENT REPORT

Situation at 12 noon, 19th Dec. 1917

Serial No.	UNIT	Present position	Moves tomorrow	Remarks
1	4th Divn H.Qrs.	G.21.c.3.5		
2	10th Inf. Bde H.Qrs.	N.5.a.3.9		
3	Household Battalion.	I.31.c.3.1		
4	1st R.Warwick Rgt.	O.1.c.7.1		
5	2nd Seaforth Highrs.	H.31.a		
6	3/10th Middlesex Rgt.	H.36.b.5.4		
7	10th M.G.Coy.	N.4.b.85.40		
8	10th T.M.Bty.	N.5.a.6.9		
9	11th Inf. Bde H.Qrs.	N.9.c.9.7		
10	1st Somerset L.I.	O.7.d.4.6		
11	1st East Lancs Rgt.	O.7.b.65.25		
12	1st Hampshire Rgt.	H.32.c.8.4		
13	1st Rifle Brigade.	N.12.a.6.4		
14	11th M.G.Coy.	N.10.d.1.8		
15	11th T.M.Bty.	N.8.d.6.7		
16	12th Inf. Bde H.Qrs.	G.27.d.35.95		
17	1st King's Own Rgt.	G.27.b.7.8		
18	2nd Lancs Fusrs.	N.27.b.8.1		
19	2nd W.Riding Rgt.	G.27.b.6.8		
20	2nd Essex Rgt.	G.21.c.3.6		
21	12th M.G.Coy.	G.28.a.10.28		
22	12th T.M.Bty.	G.27.d.90.98		
23	21st W.Yorks Rgt.	N.1.a.6.9		
24	9th Field Coy R.E.	N.12.a.3.2		
25	526th -do-	H.36.b.95.10		
26	406th -do-	N.12.a.1.4		
27	10th Field Amb.	G.21.c.3.3		
28	11th -do-	H.31.c.6.5		
29	12th -do-	K.36.d.5.1		
30	29th Bde R.F.A.	N.9.b.3.6		
31	32nd -do-	N.5.a.7.4		
32	315th -do-	N.2.b.3.6		
33	4th Div Ammn Col.	G.32.c.7.6		
34	4th Divnl Train.	ACHICOURT		
35	234th M.G.Coy	G.27.b.6.6		

Major General,

4th Division No. G.D. 79/34.

XVII Corps.

The following is an account of the attempted German Raid on the evening of 21st December :-

At 5.15 p.m. the enemy put down a heavy Trench Mortar and Artillery barrage on our front and support lines for about 50 yards North and South of Sap 12. At the same time hostile machine guns firing from the North swept the Sap.

At 5.20 p.m. the machine gun fire ceased and an enemy party of some 30 strong rushed Sap 12 on both sides.

Lewis guns in CANISTER AVENUE just West of the entrance to the Sap and the Lewis gun in SHELL Crater a little further North opened fire.

The Lewis gun Section of the 1st East Lancashire Regt. also opened fire from about O.2.d.5.7.

Some 4 or 5 Germans succeeded in entering the Sap and seized hold of a man of the Household Battalion. The rest of the garrison of the Sap, led by Cpl. DAVIS, Household Battalion, immediately attacked the enemy with the bayonet. All the Germans with the exception of one who was killed managed to escape through a gap where the Sap had been blown in. On their return some of the raiders were dispersed by their own Minenwerfer falling amongst them.

As soon as the German barrage opened at 5.15 p.m. our Artillery opened fire on their S.O.S. lines without waiting for the signal.

The enemy barrage died down at about 5.45 p.m. and our artillery also ceased firing.

As a result of the raid one dead German belonging to the 6th Company, 179 I.R., 24th Division (SAXON), remained in our hands and many are believed to have been wounded. None of our men are missing.

Our front line was effectually blocked by large craters on both sides of raided area. Our support line was badly damaged.

Our casualties are - 1 Officer, 2/Lt BIRD killed, and two N.C.Os and 4 men wounded, all of the Household Battalion. These casualties were all caused by the hostile barrage.

I consider that great credit is due to the Artillery for their prompt action and to all ranks of the Company of the Household Battalion concerned, for the manner in which they dealt with the situation.

23rd December, 1917.

Sgd/ T.G. Matheson,
Major General,
Commanding 4th Division.

Appendix 11.

SECRET.   Copy No. 20

4th DIVISION ORDER NO. 90

23rd December, 1917.

1.   The 12th Infantry Brigade will relieve the 10th Infantry Brigade in the Left Sector of the Divisional front on the 26th and 27th instants.
   The Infantry relief will be completed by 6 a.m. on the 27th instant.
   The machine guns will be relieved after the relief of the Infantry has been completed.

2.   The G.O.C., 12th Infantry Brigade will take over command from the G.O.C., 10th Infantry Brigade on completion of the Infantry relief.

3.   The 10th Infantry Brigade will take over all guards and working parties now found by the 12th Infantry Brigade.

4.   On 26th December the Reserve Battalions of the Right and Left Brigades in the line will move into the BROWN Line.
   From this date the Reserve Brigade will be disposed as under :-

   Bde H.Q. .... ARRAS.
   1 Battn .... BOIS des BOEUFS CAMP.
   1 Battn .... WILDERNESS CAMP.
   2 Battns .... ARRAS
   M.G.Coy .... ARRAS
   T.M. Bty .... ARRAS.

5.   Completion of the above moves and reliefs will be reported to Divisional Headquarters.

6.   ACKNOWLEDGE.

                                    Captain,
Issued at 12 Noon.   General Staff, 4th Division.

Copies to :-

      No. 1 to G.O.C.
          2   G.S.O.1.
          3   10th Brigade.
          4   11th Brigade.
          5   12th Brigade.
          6   C.R.A.
          7   C.R.E.
          8   A.D.M.S.
          9   A.P.M.
         10   Signals.
         11   234th M.G.Coy.
         12   Pioneers.
         13   Div. Gas Officer.
         14   'Q'.
         15   15th Division.
         16   34th Division.
         17   Guards Division.
         18)   XVII Corps.
         19)
         20)   War Diary.
         21)

Appendix 12

REPORT ON ENEMY RAID ON 'Y' SAP HELD BY 1st R. WARWICKS. REGT. 23/12/17-

At 6.18 p.m. enemy opened slow fire with heavy trench mortars which soon increased to drum fire, all calibre guns howitzers and trench mortars being used.
The barrage was heaviest on SCABBARD ALLEY and SUPPORT, BAYONET Trench, WELFORD Reserve and North end of MUSKET were lightly barraged with 5.9". Enemy machine guns opened heavy fire on our front line on both flanks of 'Y' Sap, WELFORD RESERVE was also searched.
   At about 6.23 p.m. 2 enemy parties each estimated to be 20 strong approached the sap, one from a N.Easterly direction, the other from the East.
   The Northern party was seen first. It was driven off by Lewis Guns and rifle fire. In the meantime the second party approaching from the East succeeded in entering the head of the sap and apparently overpowered the post there, for all are missing. The Lewis Gun team further down the sap was still busy with the Northern party and did not realise till too late what had happened. On going up the sap the N.C.O. found it empty; it was immediately occupied.
   A listening post went out at 5.45 p.m. to a position about midway between "X" and "Y" Sap. They were driven in when the barrage started and one man is missing.
   No unusual movement was observed, but what they took to be a working party was heard in a N.E.direction. This was possibly the enemy raiding party.
   After the firing ceased about 7.15 p.m. an officers patrol endeavoured to search "No Mans Land" for killed or wounded, but owing to the moon and prevalence of gas from T.M. shells were unable to get far beyond our wire; this patrol was slightly gassed. Another patrol went out at 4 a.m. but found no signs of wounded or dead. The gas was still hanging about in the shell holes.
   Our artillery barrage was put down very quickly but its effect could not be observed.
   The front line is badly blown in in places from the barrage.
   Half an hour after the bombardment ceased the enemy fired about 20 - 30 trench mortar gas shells in the vicinity of front line, CURB SWITCH N and SCABBARD.
   No Lewis guns are missing.
         Casualties :-

                    Killed 4
                    Wounded 9
                     Shell shock 2
                    Gassed .... 8 slightly
                    Missing 9

- S E C R E T -   - 4th DIVISION -

DISPOSITION AND MOVEMENT REPORT

Situation at 12 noon 29th Dec.1917.

Serial No.	UNIT	Present Position	Moves tomorrow	Remarks
1	4th Divnl H.Qrs.	G.21.c.3.5		
2	1oth Inf. Bde H.Qrs.	G.27.d.35.95		
3	Household Battalion.	G.27.b.6.1		
4	1st R.Warwick Rgt.	H.32.c.6.4		
5	2nd Seaforth Highrs.	H.31.a		
6	3/1oth Middlesex Rgt.	G.27.b.6.6		
7	1oth M.G.Coy.	G.22.a.10.90		
8	1oth T.M.Bty.	G.27.d.90.91		
9	11th Inf. Bde H.Qrs.	N.9.c.9.7		
10	1st Somerset L.I.	O.7.d.4.6		
11	1st East Lancs Rgt.	O.7.b.65.95		
12	1st Hampshire Rgt.	N.12.a.0.4		
13	1st Rifle Brigade.	N.10.d.5.7		
14	11th M.G.Coy.	N.10.d.1.9		
15	11th T.M.Bty.	N.9.d.6.7		
16	12th Inf. Bde H.Qrs.	N.5.a.3.6		
17	1st King's Own Rgt.	I.31.c.7.1		
18	2nd Lancs Fusrs.	O.1.c.7.1		
19	2nd W.Riding Rgt.	N.3.b.8.5		
20	2nd Essex Rgt.	H.36.b.5.4		
21	12th M.G.Coy.	N.4.b.95.40		
22	12th T.M.Bty.	N.5.a.6.9		
23	21st W.Yorks Rgt.	N.1.a.6.9		
24	9th Field Coy R.E.	N.10.a.3.9		
25	500th -do-	H.36.b.95.10		
26	46oth -do-	N.12.a.1.4		
27	1oth Field Amb.	G.21.c.3.3		
28	11th -do-	H.31.c.6.5		
29	12th -do-	K.36.d.5.1		
30	29th Bde R.F.A.	N.9.b.3.6		
31	32nd -do-	I.5.a.7.4		
32	315th -do-	N.9.b.3.6		
33	4th Div Ammn Col.	G.29.c.7.8		
34	4th Divnl Train.	ACHICOURT		
35	254th M.G.Coy.	G.27.b.6.6		

Major General,
Commanding 4th Division.

- SECRET -   Copy No. 20

4th DIVISION ORDER No 91

31st December 1917.

1. The 10th Infantry Brigade will relieve the 11th Infantry Brigade in the Right Sector of the Divisional front on the 3rd and 4th January 1917.

   The Infantry relief will be completed by 6 a.m on the 4th January.

   The Machine Guns will be relieved after the relief of the Infantry has been completed.

2. The G.O.C, 10th Infantry Brigade will take over command from the G.O.C, 11th Infantry Brigade on completion of the Infantry relief.

3. The 11th Infantry Brigade will take over all Guards and Working parties now found by the 10th Infantry Brigade.

4. Completion of the above reliefs will be reported to Divisional Headquarters.

5. A C K N O W L E D G E.

                                                    Major
                                        General Staff, 4th Division.

Issued at 12 noon.

Copies to :-
   No. 1 to G.O.C.
       2 to G.S.O.1.
       3 to 10th Brigade.
       4 to 11th Brigade.
       5 to 12th Brigade.
       6 to C.R.A.
       7 to C.R.E.
       8 to A.D.M.S.
       9 to A.P.M.
      10 to Signals.
      11 to 234th M.G.Coy.
      12 to Pioneers.
      13 to Div Gas Officer.
      14 to "Q"
      15 to 34th Divn.
      16 to 15th Divn.
      17 to Guards Divn.
      18) to XVIIth Corps.
      19)
      20) to War Diary.
      21)
      22 to File.

SECRET.

Copy No. 17

appendix A

4th DIVISION DEFENCE ORDERS.

6th December, 1917.

1. 4th Division Defence Orders dated October 28th are cancelled.

2. (a) No ground is to be given up.
   Should the enemy enter any portion of our defensive system he is to be ejected at once by the troops on the spot.
   No troops are to withdraw from any trench.
   Should local counter-attacks fail, the Brigade concerned will not make further counter-attacks until all preparations for a further attack including the co-operation of the Artillery, have been made.

   (b) The Battalion detailed by the Left Brigade for the defence of MONCHY is not to be used for local counter-attacks.

3. (a) The Field Company R.E. and Pioneers billetted in the HAPPY VALLEY will, in case of attack, come under the orders of the G.O.C. Left Brigade.
   They will not be used East of the Intermediate Line.
   The two Field Companies R.E. billetted about LES FOSSES FARM will, in case of attack, come under the orders of the G.O.C. Right Brigade.
   They will not be used East of the Intermediate Line.

   (b) All working parties in or East of the Reserve Line will in case of attack, come under the orders of the Infantry Brigadier in whose area they are working.
   All other working parties will rejoin their own units.

4. (a) In case of attack, the Reserve Sections of the Right and Left Brigade Machine Gun Companies will occupy the positions S 3, S 4, S 5, S 7 and S 8, S 10, S 12, S 13 respectively.
   These will be reinforced by the 234th Machine Gun Company which will take over positions S 2, S 6, S 9 and S 11.
   The remaining Sections of the 234th Machine Gun Company will remain in ARRAS.

   (b) Each Brigade in the line will have at least one Company of Infantry in the CORPS LINE, until such times as they can be relieved by the Reserve Brigade.

5. On the receipt of the orders "Stand by", the Reserve Brigade will make all preparations to move at short notice to the CORPS LINE.

6. Divisional Headquarters will remain in their present position.

7. ACKNOWLEDGE.

H. Ransome
Lieut. Colonel,
General Staff, 4th Division.

Issued at 11 p.m.

Copy No. 1 to G.O.C.
2 to G.S.O.1.
3 to 10th Brigade.
4 to 11th Brigade.
5 to 12th Brigade.
6 to C.R.A.
7 to C.R.E.
8 to A.D.M.S.

Copy No. 10 to Signals.
11 to 234th M.G.Coy.
12 to D.A.G.O.
13 to Q.
14 to 15th Division.
15 to 34th Division.
16 to XVII Corps.
17) to War Diary.
18)
19 to File.

4th Division No. G.A 4/38

AMENDMENT NO 1
to

4th DIVISION DEFENCE ORDERS
-------ooOoo-------

Para 2 (b) delete and substitute -

(b) The battalions detailed by the Left Brigade for the defence of LONCHY may be used for local counter-attack, except the garrisons of Posts F, G and H.

Add sub-para (c) and (d) :-

(c) The garrisons of Posts B, C, D and E are not to be used for local counter-attacks.

(d) All posts in the Intermediate Line, and all Machine Gun posts, east of the Corps Line, are to be permanently manned.

Para 4 (a), line 3, the positions should read -

S1, S3, S5, S6 and S8, S9, S12 and S13.

In line 6, they should read -

S2, S4, S7, S11.

A C K N O W L E D G E.

H. Hardacre
Lieut Colonel,
General Staff, 4th Division.

11th December 1917.

Copies to all recipients of
4th Division Defence Orders.

SECRET. APPENDIX 'B'.

4th DIVISION DEFENCE SCHEME.

MACHINE GUNS.

1. The defence of the area is assisted by 40 machine guns which are permanently in position.
    Of these 32 are in and East of the Intermediate Line and 8 are in the Corps Line.
    The position of the guns is shown on Map F.

2. The remaining machine guns of the Division i.e. 8 of the Divisional Company and 16 of the Company of the Brigade in Reserve are kept in Reserve.

3. Each gun East of the Corps Line has an S.O.S. Line and a Battle Zone.
    These are shown on Map F.

4. In case of attack all guns at once open fire on their S.O.S. Lines until such time as they see the enemy advancing over our front line when they at once engage any target which presents itself in their own zone

5. All guns are mounted and are kept ready to open fire on their S.O.S. lines from sunset to one hour after sunrise.

6. At each emplacement water, oil and S.A.A. are kept in the following quantities :-

    S.A.A.   10000 rounds per gun.
    Oil.   According to supply.
    Water.   2 petrol tins.

7. The rate and duration of fire in case of S.O.S. is as follows :-

    rapid for the first five minutes,
    after that reduce to 1 belt per two minutes.

    If while firing on the S.O.S. lines, the enemy is seen approaching in the zone of the gun, the fire will at once be directed on to them.

8. ACKNOWLEDGE.

H. Hundaske
Lieut.Colonel,
17th December, 1917.   General Staff, 4th Division.

Copies to all recipients of
4th Division Defence Scheme.

SECRET.   Copy No. 20

4th Div. G.A.4/40.

4th DIVISION DEFENCE SCHEME.

th December, 1917.

1.   The present front line is practically the line reached during the Battle of ARRAS.
    The enemy made a great effort to prevent us capturing the high ground VIS-EN-ARTOIS - BOIS DU VERT - GREENLAND HILL, this being essential to him to enable the QUEANT - DROCOURT Line to be constructed and also as a thrust here threatened his salient further South.   His dispositions are shown on attached Map 'B'.
    He has always shown considerable anxiety lest we should make an effort to secure the high ground which he is now defending and has made several local attacks to improve his position.

2.   For many months the enemy has been purely on the defensive on this front but he may at any time assume the offensive either on a small scale to draw troops from elsewhere, or on a large scale to break through on a front of some 20 to 30 miles.

3.   As far as the Divisional front is concerned the following features might form objectives for the enemy and are shown on Map 'C':-
    (a) The Spur running South from TWIN COPSE.
        His line might run as follows :-
            Junction of BIT LANE with front line - DALE Trench - SADDLE SUPPORT - CAVALRY FM.
    (b) The Spur North and South of and including MONCHY.
        His line might run as follows :-
            LA BERGERE FM - INTERMEDIATE LINE as far as H Post and thence Northwards along the Spur to the SCARPE.
    (c) ORANGE HILL and the high ground North and South of it along which runs the CORPS Line.

4.   Objectives (a) and (b) could be undertaken without necessitating the move forward of the enemy's Artillery.
    Objective (c) would involve the move of his Artillery.

5.   In the present state of the ground the enemy might employ Tanks, but it is not likely until the ground becomes considerably more solid by frost or a spell of dry weather.

6.   It is not essential that the enemy's attack should be prepared by a bombardment.
    It has been shown that surprise can be effected and the attack be successful without any preliminary bombardment.

7.   To meet this situation the area is divided up into the following defensive systems which are shown on Map 'A' :-

    1. Front line system consisting of
            Front line,
            Support line,
            Reserve line.
    2. Intermediate Line consisting of a continuous belt of wire and a series of Posts.
    3. Corps Line consisting of a continuous trench protected by a belt of wire.

8.   The Divisional front is held by two Brigades with one Brigade in Reserve.   The Boundaries between Brigades and the Divisions on either flank are shown on Map 'A', also the dispositions of the Battalions by Companies.
    The Left Brigade in the line has one Battalion detailed for the defence of MONCHY.

The Garrisons of the various Posts in the Intermediate Line are not to be used for local counter-attacks.
For Defence Orders see Appendix 'A'. (Already issued)
The details of the Artillery, trench mortar and Machine Gun defence of the area are dealt with in the various Appendices.

9. In considering the employment of the Brigade and Divisional Reserves, the various objectives which the enemy is likely to capture must be the basis for their employment.

<u>1st Objective</u>. Our Support Line as far North as BIT LANE.

When the enemy is in possession of this line any attack we make will have to cross at least 500 yards of ground open to view to the enemy.
This front is however divided into two by the rising ground just North of PICK AVENUE.
In view of the shortage of Artillery, it would be best therefore to attack with the left on PICK AVENUE and recapture the Spur between the CAMBRAI Road and PICK AVENUE.
This would be carried out by the Reserve Bn. of the Right Brigade which would be dribbled up from the Corps Line to SPADE RESERVE.
The attack could not take place for at least three hours and would be assisted by the Artillery and Machine Guns of the Division on our right.
If this attack is successful, the Reserve Bn. of the Left Brigade would attack North of PICK AVENUE two hours after the first attack (see Map 'D').

<u>2nd Objective</u>. MONCHY and the high ground N. and S. of it.

Having gained this the enemy will have put out of action at least three of our Batteries so that the Artillery available for the counter-attack will be very feeble. It is quite impossible therefore to think of counter-attacking along the whole front.

There are then three alternatives :-

(a) Attack North of MONCHY.
(b) Attack between MONCHY and the COJEUL.
(c) Attack between the CAMBRAI Road and the COJEUL.

In case (a) it would be very difficult to get troops across the HAPPY VALLEY in daylight.
(b) The advance would be very open and difficult in daylight.
(c) The counter-attacking troops could dribble round the COJEUL and along the CAMBRAI Road and form up for attack under cover of all the guns available.
If this attack was carried out at once it would probably be successful. If however it is delayed it would be better to carry out a night advance and attack between VINE AVENUE and the river in the early morning with the Reserve Battalions of the front Brigades. Subsequently the Reserve Bde. would attack on the left of this and include MONCHY. (see Map 'E').

10. In all these attacks the main consideration is time.
The distance of the Reserve Battalions of the front Brigades from the Reserve Line is about 2 miles.
It would take them at least 2 hours to be assembled and ready to attack from the Reserve Line against enemy 1st Objective.

If the enemy objective was the 2nd Objective the distance they would have to go is only 1½ miles and they could attack in 1½ hours.

The Reserve Brigade in ARRAS is about 5 miles from the BROWN Line. It would take two hours at least to reach that line; it could therefore attack four hours after the enemy had captured his 2nd Objective.

11. In all these counter-attacks the Artillery will be augmented by machine guns.

Against the 1st Objective, besides those in position already, the 8 guns in the Corps Line would be used, the 8 guns of the Divisional Company being left in the Corps Line.

The Machine Gun Company of the Reserve Brigade would also be moved up, but it would probably not be in time to participate in the attacks on the enemy 1st Objective or in the attack South of the CAMBRAI Road against his 2nd Objective.

12. In order to carry out the counter-attack on the enemy's 1st Objective the whole operation as outlined above would be carried out on the orders of the G.O.C. Right Brigade who would have the Reserve Battalion of the Left Brigade placed at his disposal.

Similarly the counter-attack against the enemy's 2nd Objective would be carried out on the orders of the G.O.C. Right Brigade who would have besides his own Reserve Battalion the Reserve Battalion of the Left Brigade and the Reserve Machine Gun Sections of both the front Brigades.

The attack by the Reserve Brigade would be under the orders of the G.O.C. Reserve Brigade who would have his H.Q. at N.10. d 5.7

13. Although the plans outlined above may have to be modified, they form the basis on which G.Os.C. Brigades and the C.R.A. can work out plans.

14. Should the enemy succeed in capturing the Corps Line a line will be taken up along the high ground running North and South through TILLOY.

15. ACKNOWLEDGE.

H. Kumdale
Lieut.Colonel,
General Staff, 4th Division.

Issued at 3 pm

Copy No. 1 to G.O.C.
2 to G.S.O.1.
3 to 10th Brigade.
4 to 11th Brigade.
5 to 12th Brigade.
6 to C.R.A.
7 to C.R.E.
8 to A.D.M.S.
9 to A.P.M.
10 to Signals.
11 to Q.
12 to 234th M.G.Coy.
13 to Pioneers.
14 to 15th Division.
15 to 34th Division.
16 to Guards Division.
17 to XVII Corps.
18 to XVII Corps H.A.
19 to 13th Sqdn. R.F.C.
20) to War Diary.
21)
22 to File.

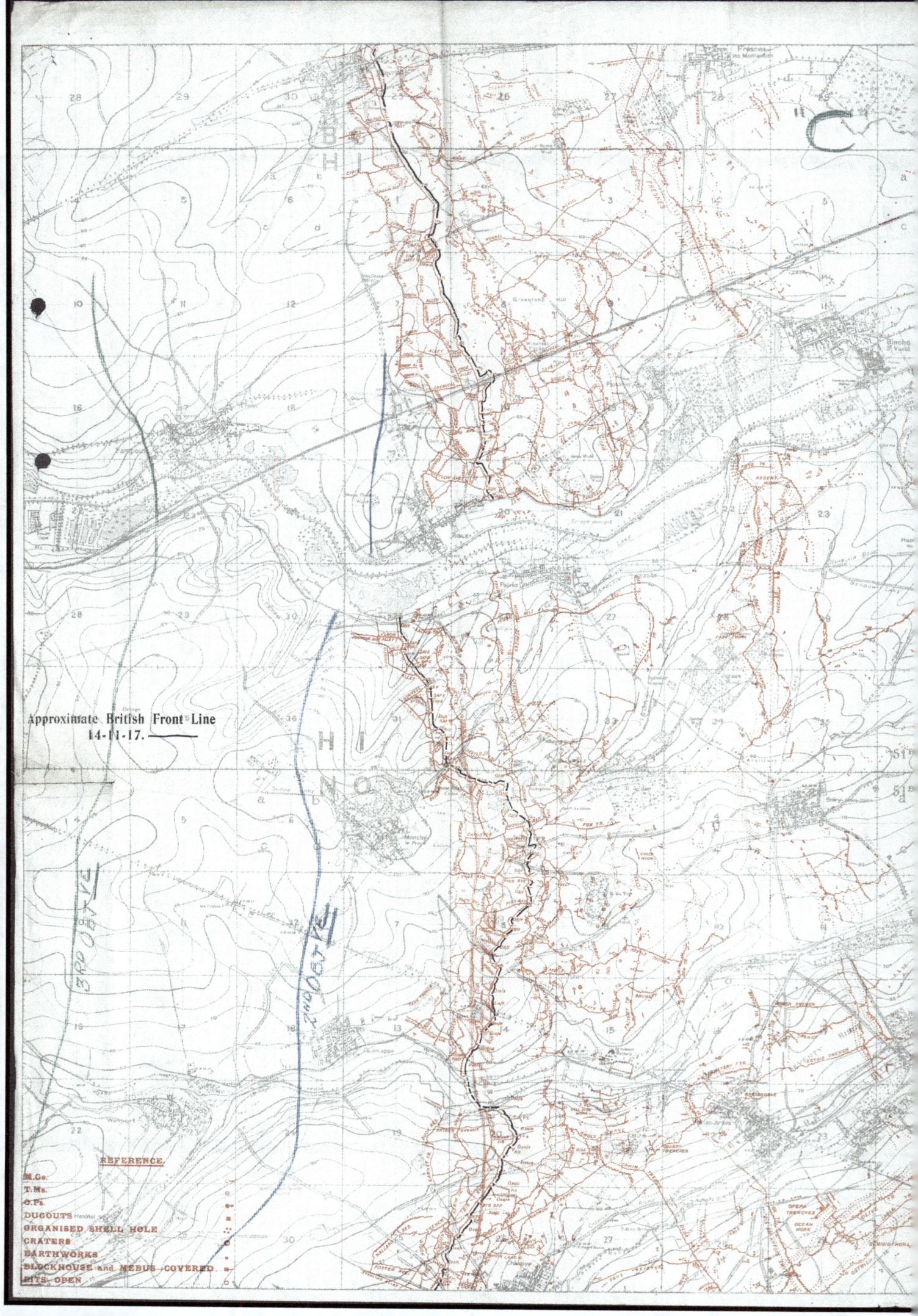

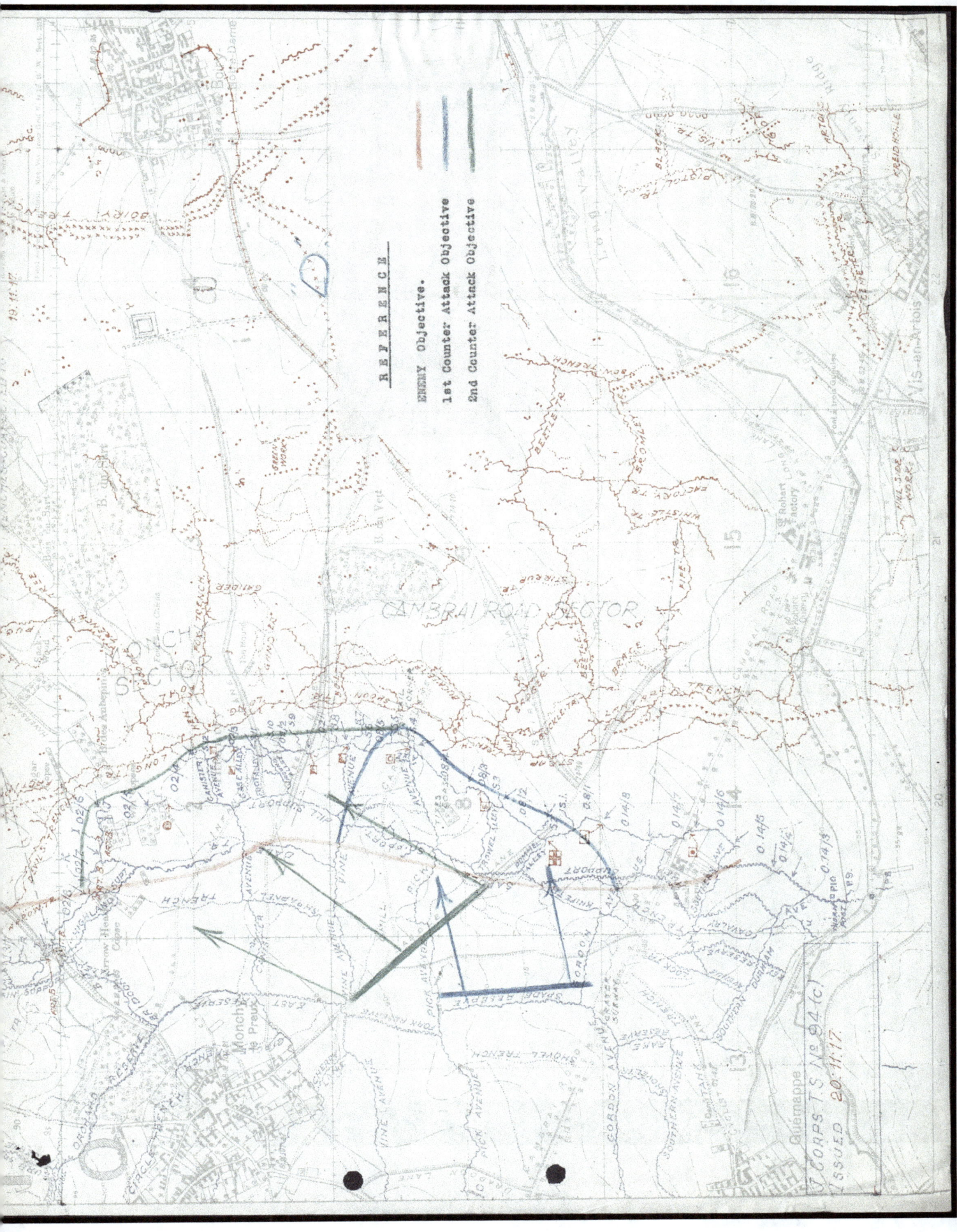

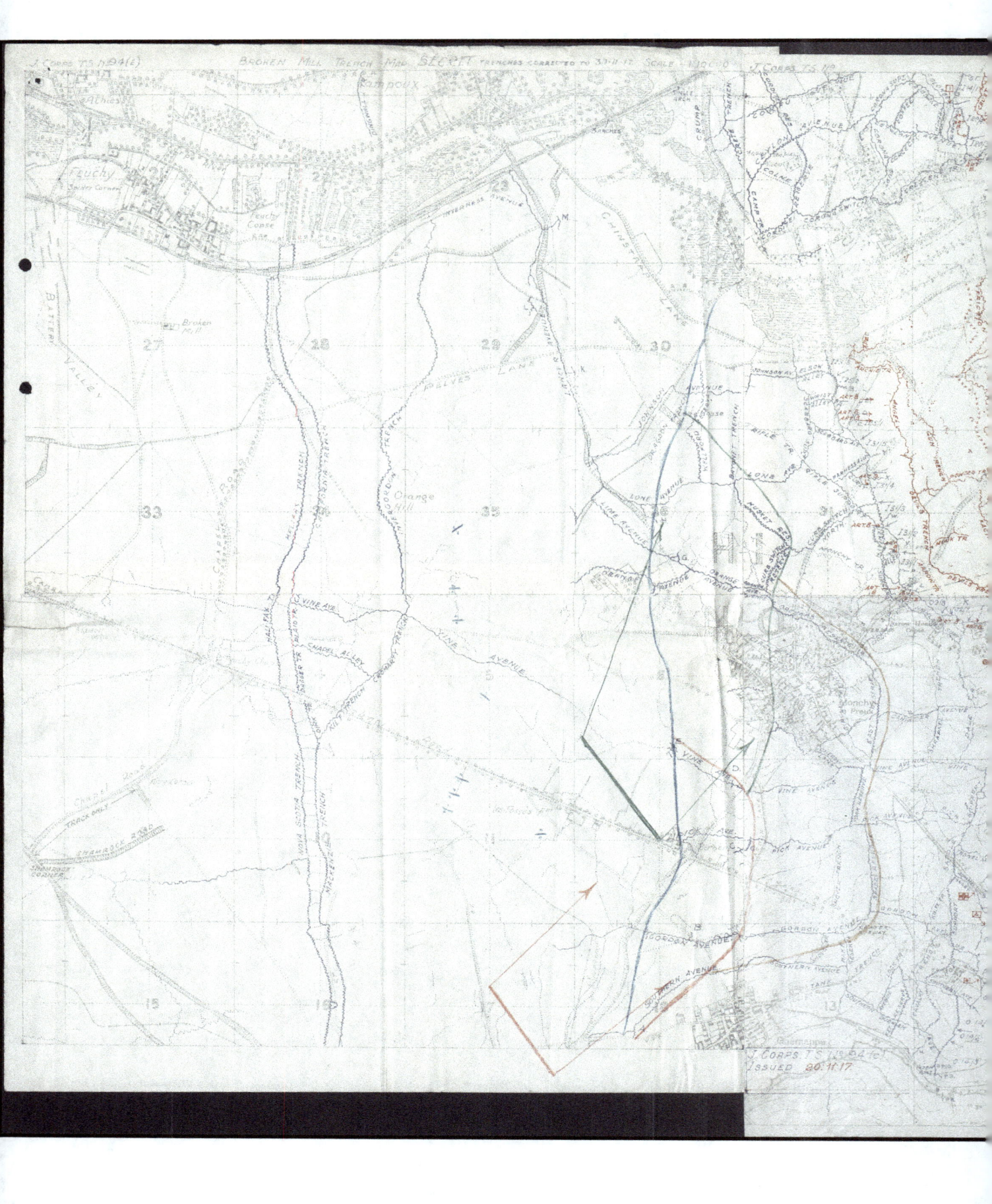

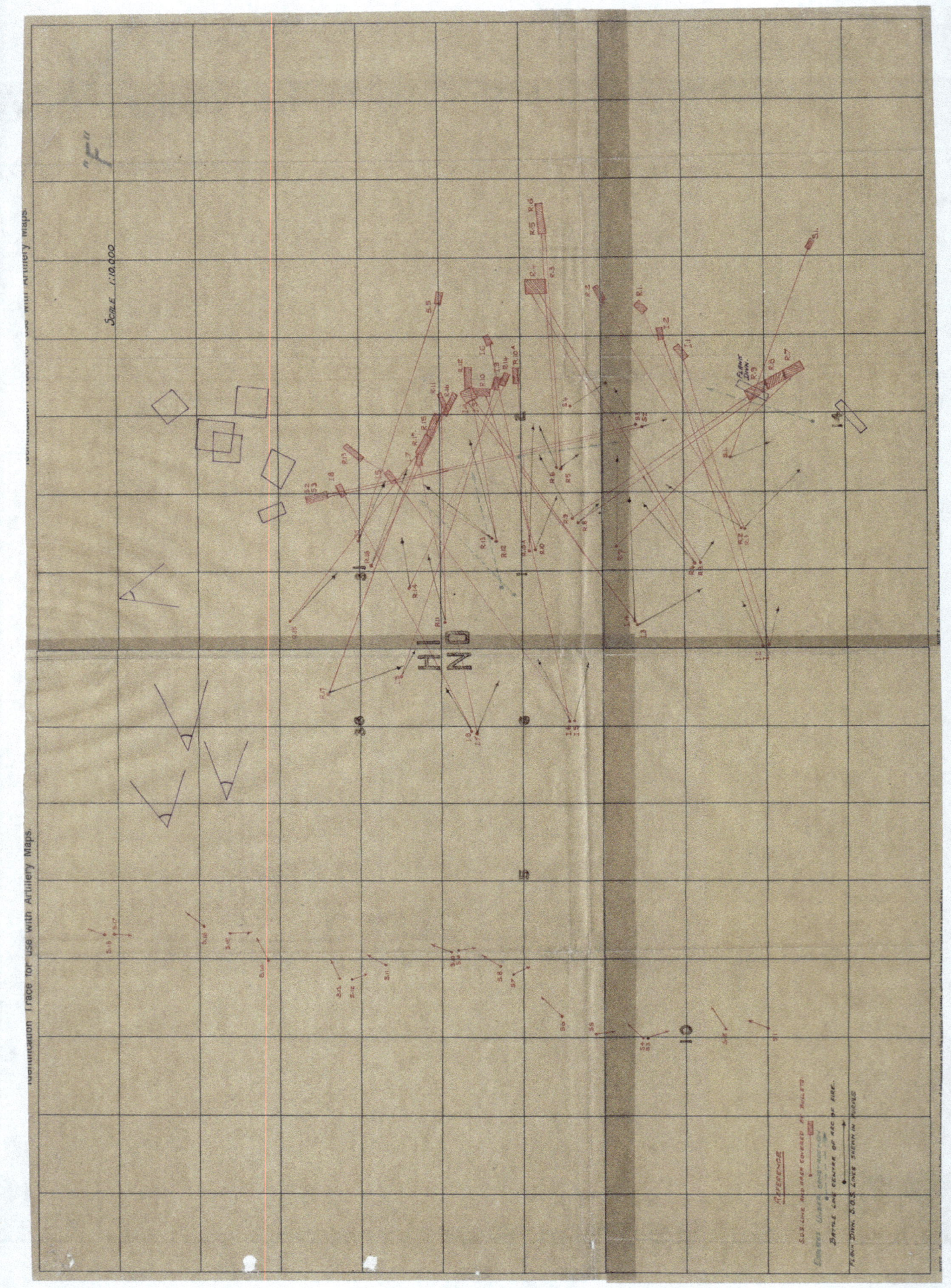

SECRET.   APPENDIX 'O'.

4th DIVISION DEFENCE SCHEME.

ARTILLERY.

1. The Field Artillery at present available for the protection of the Division consists of
   - 29th Brigade, R.F.A.
   - 32nd Brigade, R.F.A.
   - 315th A.F.A. Bde. (less one 18 pdr.Battery).

2. This artillery is divided into two groups.-

   The Right Group covering the Right Section consisting of the 29th Brigade, R.F.A.

   The Left Group covering the Left Section consisting of the 32nd Brigade, R.F.A. and the 315th A.F.A. Brigade (less one 18 pdr.Battery).

3. The positions of all batteries, Brigade H.Q., O.Ps. and S.O.S. lines are shown on Map 'G'.

4. The H.Q. of each artillery Brigade is close to the Infantry Bde. H.Q. with which it is working so that no artillery liaison officer lives at the Infantry Bde. H.Q.
   There is however an artillery liaison officer at the H.Q. of each Battalion in the front line.

5. In the event of the enemy bombarding our trenches and it appears to the Infantry Brigadier that it is the prelude to an attack, he will ask the Artillery Group Commander to begin counter-preparation at once.
   This does not preclude battery or Artillery Brigade Commanders from beginning this counter-preparation without waiting for the request of the Infantry Brigadier should they consider it advisable.

6. In the event of the S.O.S. signal (2 RED and 2 WHITE) being fired all batteries open at once on their S.O.S. lines.
   All O.Ps. have a supply of S.O.S. rifle grenades so that they can pass on the signal to the Batteries if necessary.

7. The S.O.S. lines of the Siege Artillery are shown on Map 'G'.

8. Owing to the shortage of artillery it is not possible to put an effective barrage down along the whole of the Divisional front.
   The fire is therefore concentrated on the most important portions of the front and can be switched right or left according to requirements.
   This scheme applies equally to the Siege and Field Artillery.
   The various barrages for attacks on the different portions of the Divisional front are shown on the attached Map 'G'.

9. In the event of the enemy making a successful attack the positions of batteries and O.Ps. for the protection of the Intermediate and Corps Lines are shown on the attached Map 'G'.

10. ACKNOWLEDGE.

                                                    Lieut.Colonel,
18th December, 1917.   General Staff, 4th Division.

Copies to all recipients of
4th Division Defence Scheme.

SECRET.   APPENDIX 'D'.

4th DIVISION DEFENCE SCHEME.

TRENCH MORTARS.

1. In each Brigade Section of the line there is a group of Trench Mortars.
    These groups are :-

Group	Commanded by	Consisting of
Southern	Captain DEMPSTER. H.Q. FORK RESERVE.	6 - 6" Newton Trench Mortars. 2 - 9.45" Heavy T.Ms. 6 - 3" Stokes.
Northern	2nd Lieut.R.W.H.DAVIS. H.Q. CHAIN SUPPORT. (I.31.d)	5 - 6" Newton Trench Mortars. 1 2" Medium T.M. 5 3" Stokes.

2. The position of these mortars and their S.O.S. lines are shown on Map 'G'.

3. The following ammunition is maintained at the gun pits for each mortar :-

    9.45" Heavy T.M.   20 rounds per gun.
    6"   Newton T.M.   120 "   "   "   (20 fused).
    3"   Stoke T.M.   200 "   "   "

4. At least 50% of the personnel for each mortar lives close to it so as to be ready in case of attack or in case of anything being required by the Infantry.

5. ACKNOWLEDGE.

                                              H. Vansittart
                                              Lieut.Colonel,
                                              General Staff, 4th Division.

18th December, 1917.

Copies to all recipients of
4th Division Defence Scheme.

SECRET.   Copy No. 2.

AMENDMENT NO. 1 TO APPENDIX 'D'
to
4th DIVISION DEFENCE SCHEME DATED 18th DECR, 1917.

1. 'SOUTHERN GROUP'. Please substitute 5 for 6. 3" Stokes Mortars

2. Attached tracing* shows positions and S.O.S. lines of 3" Stokes Mortars of Southern Group.
   This amends Map 'C' of Divisional Defence Scheme.

                                                H Hallett
                                                      Major,
28th December, 1917.   General Staff, 4th Division.

Copies to all recipients
of 4th Division Defence Scheme.

   * Issued to :-
                        10th Infantry Brigade.
                        11th Infantry Brigade.
                        12th Infantry Brigade.
                        C.R.A.
                        34th Division.
                        XVII Corps.

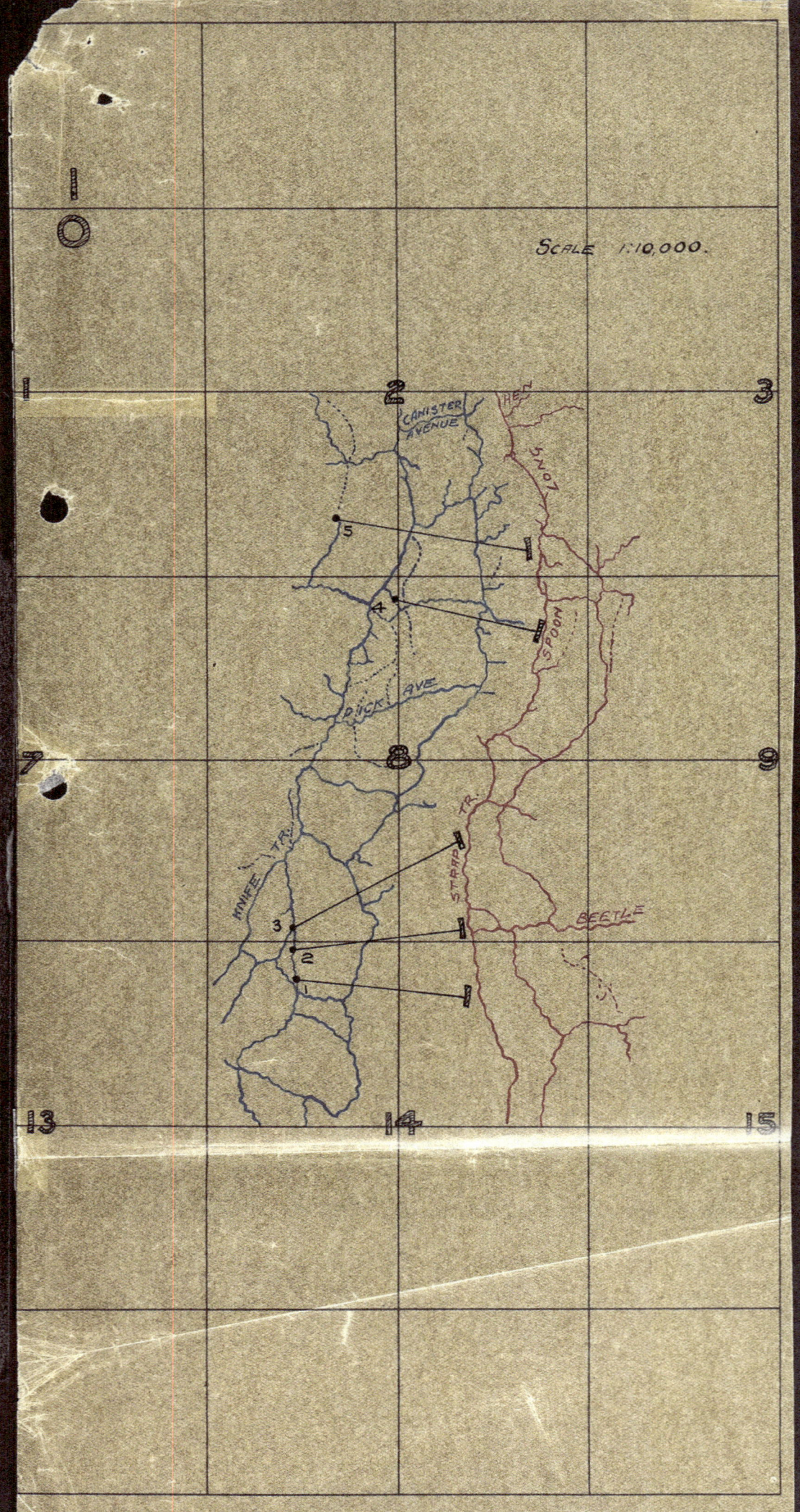

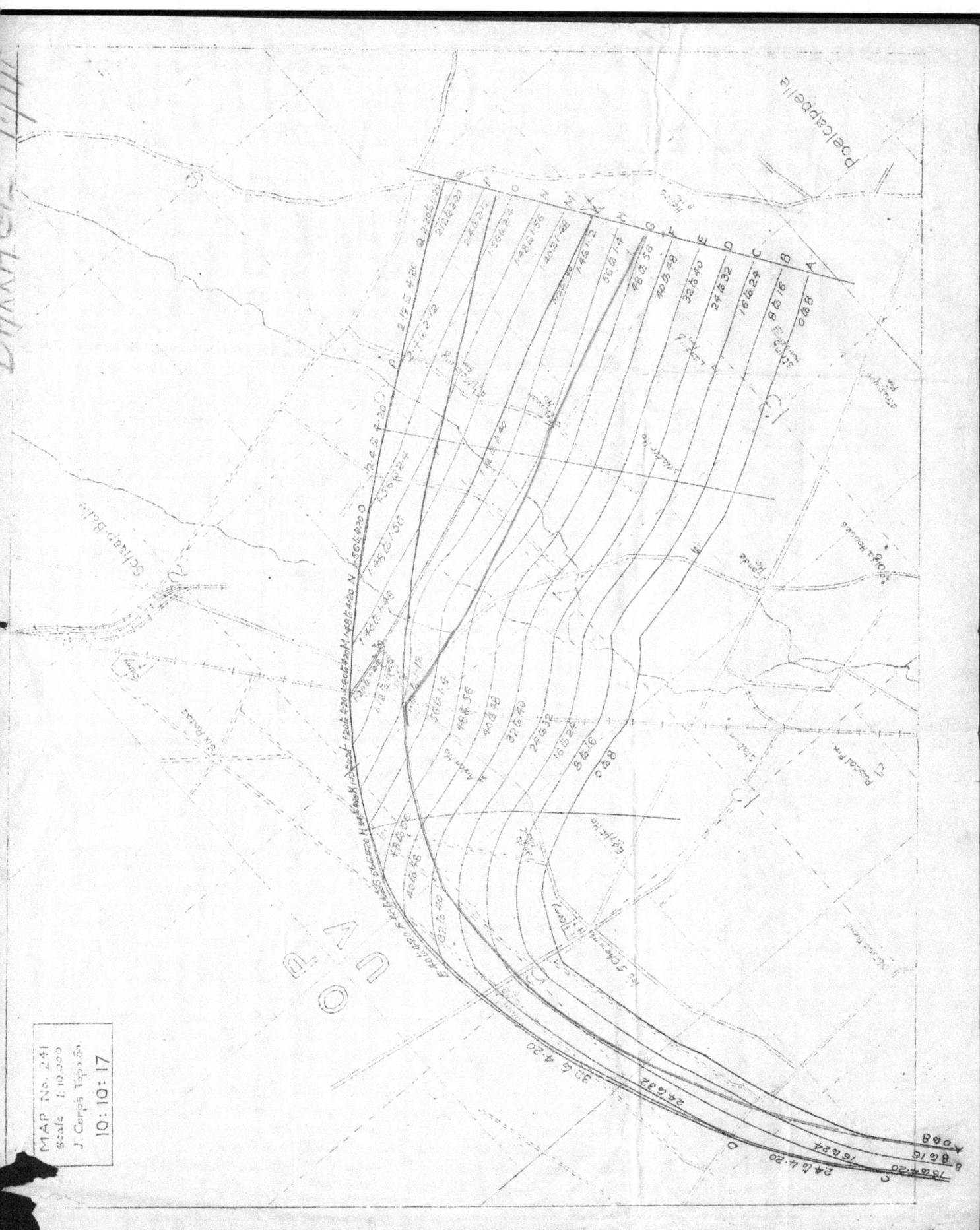

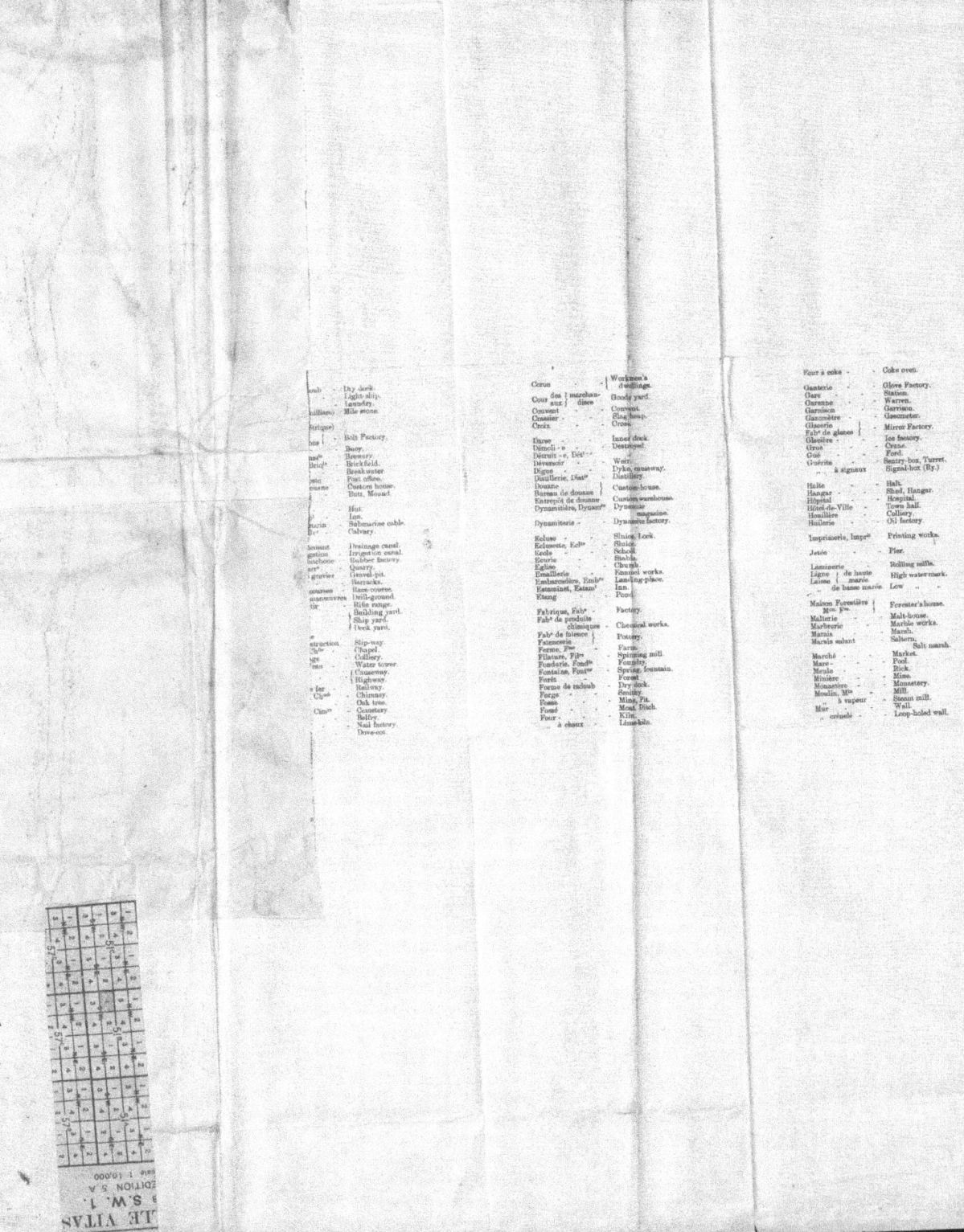

Four à coke	Coke oven.
Ganterie	Glove Factory.
Gare	Station.
Garenne	Warren.
Garnison	Garrison.
Gazomètre	Gasometer.
Glacerie, Fab^{ue} de glaces	Mirror Factory.
Glacière	Ice factory.
Grue	Crane.
Gué	Ford.
Guérite	Sentry-box, Turret.
,, à signaux	Signal-box (Ry.)
Halte	Halt.
Hangar	Shed, Hangar.
Hôpital	Hospital.
Hôtel-de-Ville	Town hall.
Houillère	Colliery.
Huilerie	Oil factory.
Imprimerie, Impr^{ie}	Printing works.
Jetée	Pier.
Laminerie	Rolling mills.
Ligne de haute	
Laisse } marée	High water mark.
,, de basse marée	Low ,,
Maison Forestière, M^{on} F^{re}	Forester's house.
Malterie	Malt-house.
Marbrerie	Marble works.
Marais	Marsh.
Marais salant	Saltern. Salt marsh.
Marché	Market.
Mare	Pool.
Meule	Rick.
Minière	Mine.
Monastère	Monastery.
Moulin, M^{in}	Mill.
,, à vapeur	Steam mill.
Mur	Wall.
,, crénelé	Loop-holed wall.

Nacelle	Ferry.
Orme	Elm.
Orphelinat	Orphanage.
Oseraie	Osier-beds.
Ouvrage	Fort.
Ouvrages hydrauliques	Water works.
Papeterie	Paper-mill.
Parc	Park, yard.
,, aérostatique	Aviation ground.
,, à charbon	Coal yard.
,, à pétrole	Petrol store.
Passage à niveau P.N.	Level-crossing.
Passerelle, Pas^{lle}	Foot-bridge.
Pépinière	Nursery-garden.
Peuplier	Poplar tree.
Phare	Light-house.
Pilier, Pil^r	Post.
Plaine d'exercice	Drill ground.
Pompe	Pump.
Ponceau	Culvert.
Pont	Bridge.
,, levis	Drawbridge.
Poste de garde-côte	Coast-guard station.
Station ,,	
Poteau F^{on}	Post.
Poterie	Pottery.
Poudrière, Poud^{re}	Powder magazine.
Magasin à poudre	
Prise d'eau	Water supply.
Puits	Pit-head, Shaft, Well.
,, artésien	Artesian well.
,, d'airage	
,, ventilateur	Ventilating shaft.
,, de sondage	Boring.
Quai	Quay, Platform.
,, aux bestiaux	Cattle platform.
,, aux marchandises	Goods platform.
Raccordement	Junction.
Raffinerie	Refinery.
,, de sucre	Sugar refinery
Râperie	Beet-root factory.

Remblai	Embankment.
Remise des Machines	Engine-shed.
,, aux ,,	
Réservoir, Rés^r	Reservoir.
Route cavalière	Bridle road.
Rubanerie	Ribbon Factory.
Ruine	
Ruines	Ruin.
En ruine	
Ruiné - e	
Sablière	Sand-pit.
Sablonnière, Sablon^{re}	
Sapin	Fir tree.
Saule	Willow tree.
Saunerie	Salt-works.
Scierie, Sc^{ie}	Sawmill.
Sondage	Boring.
Source	Spring.
Sucrerie, Suc^{ie}	Sugar factory.
Tannerie	Tannery.
Tir à la cible	Rifle range.
Tissage	Weaving mill.
Tôlerie	Rolling mill
Tombeau	Tomb.
Tour	Tower.
Tourbière	Peatbog, Peat-bed.
Tourelle	Small tower.
Tuilerie	Tile works.
Usine à gaz	Gas works.
,, électrique	Electricity works.
,, d'électricité	
,, métallurgique	Metal works.
,, à agglomérés	Briquette factory.
Verrerie, Verr^{ie}	Glass works.
Viaduc	Viaduct
Vivier	Fish Pond.
Voie de chargement	
,, déchargement	
,, d'évitement	Siding.
,, formation	
,, manœuvre	
Zinguerie	Zinc works.

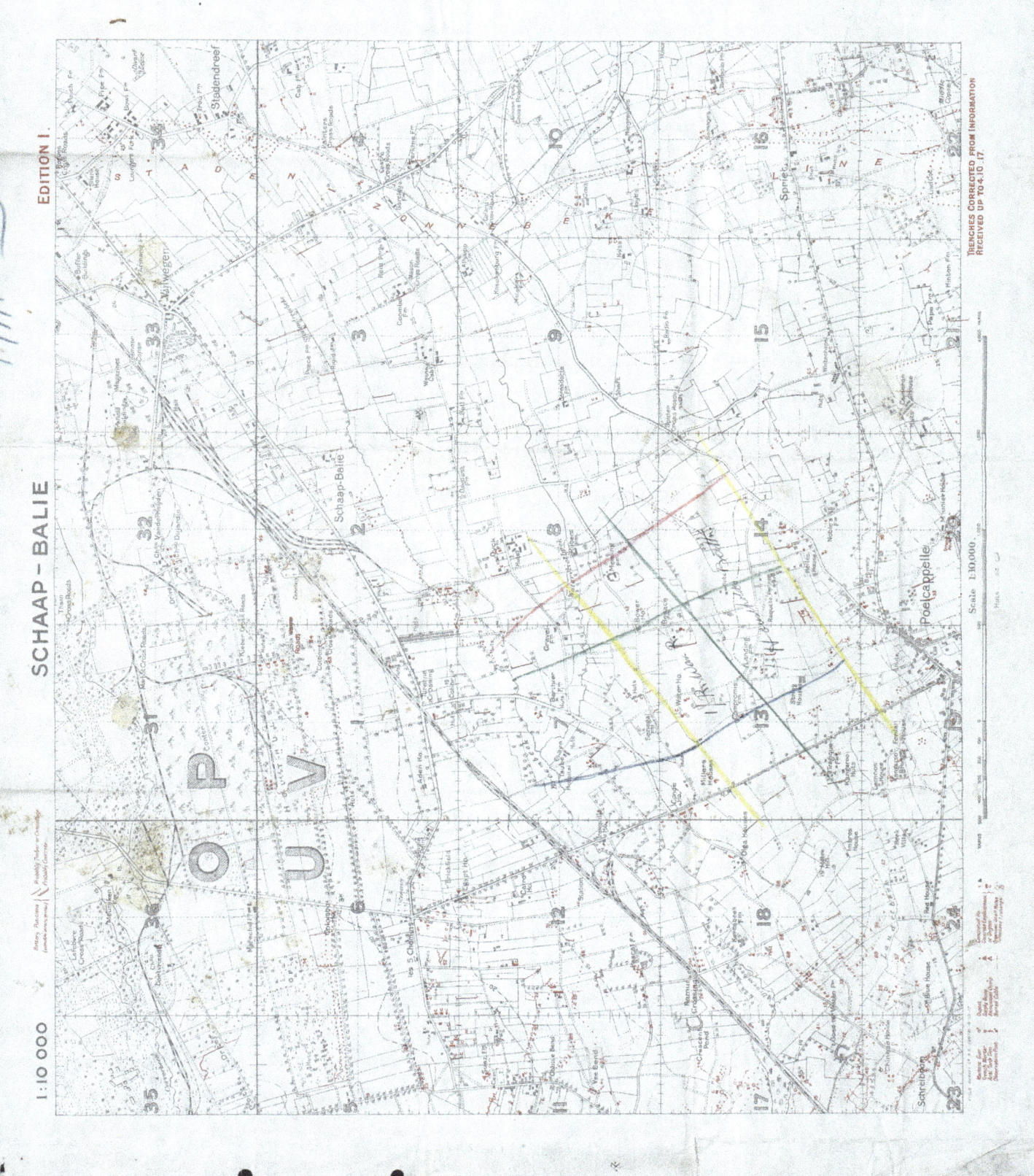

BROEMBEEK

1:10,000 — Edition 2

Scale 1:10,000

TRENCHES CORRECT'D FROM INFORMATION
RECEIVED UP TO 8.9.17